12.50

06

TO THE HALLS OF
THE MONTEZUMAS

The Soldier in Mexico

TO THE HALLS OF THE MONTEZUMAS

*The Mexican War in
the American Imagination*

Robert W. Johannsen

New York   Oxford
OXFORD UNIVERSITY PRESS
1985

OXFORD UNIVERSITY PRESS
Oxford   London   New York   Toronto
Delhi   Bombay   Calcutta   Madraś   Karachi
Kuala Lumpur   Singapore   Hong Kong   Tokyo
Nairobi   Dar es Salaam   Cape Town
Melbourne   Auckland

and associated companies in
Beirut   Berlin   Ibadan   Mexico City   Nicosia

Copyright © 1985 by Oxford University Press, Inc.

Published by Oxford University Press, Inc., 200 Madison Avenue
New York, New York 10016

All rights reserved. No part of this publication may be reproduced,
stored in a retrieval system, or transmitted, in any form or by any means,
electronic, mechanical, photocopying, recording, or otherwise, without
the prior permission of Oxford University Press.

Library of Congress Cataloging in Publication Data

Johannsen, Robert Walter, 1925–
    To the halls of the Montezumas.

    Includes index.
    1. United States—History—War with Mexico, 1845–
1848.   2. United States—History—War with Mexico,
1845–1848—Influence.   3. United States—History—
War with Mexico, 1845–1848—Literature and the war.
4. United States—History—War with Mexico, 1845–1848—
Art and the war.   I. Title.
E404.J64   1985   973.6'2   84-20696
ISBN 0-19-503518-6

Printing (last digit)   9 8 7 6 5 4 3 2 1

Printed in the United States of America

For Lois

Preface

"It is hard to write the history of an exciting event . . . [long] after it has transpired," observed a writer in the *American Review* in June 1848, "for while the *statistics* may be correct, the *spirit* is wanting." Those who believe that "the *facts* of history are given when every statement is made out with accuracy," the writer continued, are in error, for the "greatest fact of all is the feeling which originated the movement, and the enthusiasm which bore it onward."[1]

It is this "spirit" or "feeling" that shaped popular attitudes toward the Mexican War which I have tried to capture in the following pages. This is not a history of the war nor does it offer an analysis of the war's causes; no effort is made to assign responsibility for its outbreak. My purpose has been modest: simply to suggest some of the ways in which Americans perceived the war and how these perceptions revealed some of the characteristics of mid-19th-century American thought and culture. In carrying out this purpose, I have tried to keep before me the reminder of some midcentury Americans that history must address "the sensibility and imagination, as well as the understanding," that (in the words of George Lippard) history should "speak to the heart."[2]

The Mexican War, the nation's first foreign war, was an event of major importance in the young life of the United States. Indeed, there were those who insisted that the war would stand as one of the significant episodes in world history. The United States at midcentury was a nation still in search of itself and the war became an exercise in self-identity. It was a major crisis faced by the American people during a period of dramatic social and economic change. Older values of patriotism and civic virtue seemed threatened by newer concerns for commercial, industrial, and material advancement. Furthermore, the romanticism that had molded the American imagination during the early 19th century seemed to be on the wane; a golden age of heroism and chivalry (to paraphrase one of the period's spokesmen) was giving way before a brazen age of commerce. Midcentury America was charged with tensions and anxieties, with uncertainty over the true nature and purpose of the republic, the preservation of the country's revolutionary idealism, and the role of the individual in a rapidly changing social environment. For a time and for some people, the war with Mexico offered reassurance by lending new meaning to patriotism, providing a new arena for heroism, and reasserting anew the popular assumptions of America's romantic era. The war, it was thought, held an even broader importance, for it strengthened republicanism, demonstrating to a doubting world that republics held the capacity to wage successful foreign wars, and legitimized long-held convictions of mission and destiny. "Our country," declared the journal of the Whig party, "has entered on a new epoch in its history."[3]

At the same time, midcentury Americans were reaching out beyond their borders. Technological improvements in transportation and communication were eroding the nation's geographic and cultural isolation. The expansion of commerce, an increase in travel (especially to Europe and the Levant), and a heightened interest in exploration were carrying Americans to the far corners of the globe. A publication explosion placed the works of European writers and thinkers within the reach of virtually every American. The Mexican War played an important part in the breakdown of American parochialism. It marked America's first intimate exposure to a life and culture that differed significantly from anything in the American experience. The war was a "window" through which Americans could see and appreciate a strange and exotic land of alien manners, customs, and attitudes. America, some were convinced, would never again be the same.

It is in these contexts that I have sought to place the Mexican War, in the hope that the meaning of the war and of the times in which it took place might be better understood. By focusing on the perceptions of the war (which like all perceptions may or may not correspond to reality), I have tried to answer the question: What did the Mexican War mean to Americans in the mid-19th century? In the answer lies the very nature and character of midcentury America itself.

In addressing that question, I have deliberately avoided the conventional (and frequently overworked) political utterances of the time—for example, Congressional debates, campaign rhetoric, and party statements—not because such statements cannot offer clues to an understanding of midcentury America but rather because of a suspicion that politics can and often do obscure popular attitudes. Instead, I have concentrated on the books and periodicals that issued from the nation's presses, were widely available to the population, and almost as widely read. While I do not contend that these sources by themselves capture that elusive concept "public opinion," I do feel that they offer reliable clues to the nature of popular perception. "The people of the United States are emphatically a reading people," wrote Emerson Davis in his summation of American development during the first fifty years of the 19th century. "One may judge, therefore, of the taste of the people, by looking at the character of the books and periodicals that are published from month to month."[4]

In the interest of brevity and precision, the characteristically long and delightfully descriptive 19th-century book titles have been condensed. Northern Mexico's most important city and the site of one of the war's critical battles has been spelled the way it was in the mid-19th century, Monterey, rather than the way it is spelled now, Monterrey. In the case of Matamoros, for which the contemporary spelling varied, the modern version has been used.

To the outstanding collection of the University of Illinois Library (especially in early and mid-19th-century books, periodicals, and pamphlets), I owe an enduring debt of gratitude. Its rich holdings enabled me to complete virtually all my research and to write the drafts of the manuscript amid the familiar surroundings of my own campus. Members of the University Library staff were unhesitating in their efforts to facilitate my use of the collection and to provide me with work space within easy reach of my materials. For those publications which the Library could not provide (even the best of libraries does not have everything), I am indebted to the courteous efficiency of the interlibrary loan staff of the Lincoln Trails Library System. The Graduate Research Board of the Graduate College of the University of Illinois generously provided support to the project in its last stages, including the typing of the final manuscript. Sheldon Meyer of Oxford University Press, as usual, has been a constant source of encouragement and advice; Oxford's Leona Capeless made important suggestions for the improvement of the manuscript. My deepest gratitude is extended once again to my wife Lois for understanding what I was trying to do, for her gentle admonitions, and for her patient and sympathetic support.

Urbana, Illinois   R.W. J.
May 1984

Contents

TO THE HALLS OF
THE MONTEZUMAS

Washington, July 4, 1848

President James K. Polk began his schedule early when he received more than 200 Sunday school children in the White House. Afterward, with members of his cabinet, he rode to the City Hall, took his place at the head of a long and colorful procession, and paraded through the streets to a grassy knoll on the banks of the Potomac where the cornerstone of the Washington Monument was to be dedicated.

Robert Mills's design for the monument—"a grand circular colonnaded building" from which would rise a 600-foot "obelisk shaft"—had been approved years before, but it was not until the end of 1847 that sufficient funds were collected to begin the work. The cornerstone, an immense block of marble that had been quarried near Baltimore and carried to Washington by train, was pulled through the streets in a stone-wagon by an enthusiastic group of citizens, escorted by a detachment of Marines and the Marine Band. An American flag flew from the wagon and a live eagle perched on the stone.[1]

For days the call had gone out to the people to take part in the grand parade. The monument, declared a Washington editor, "shall be the work of the Nation." As enduring as the Pyramids and symbolic of American democracy, it would not be erected "by the labor of slaves, under the lash of absolute monarchs," but by "freemen, in grateful honor of the Father of his country." Let the people come, "from their mountain homes, from the Atlantic Coast, and from the broad prairies of the West, and with pious zeal aid in laying the first stone in this sacred edifice." If the people did not come from as far afield as the editor hoped, they did pour into the capital from the surrounding countryside. The city had not been so thronged since the inauguration of William Henry Harrison in 1841.[2]

Since dawn, the atmosphere had been punctuated by pealing church bells and the sounds of firecrackers, pistol shots, rolling drums, and blaring bugles. "Every thing seemed alive" as elements of the proces-

3

sion gathered on the military mustering ground opposite the City Hall. Soldiers led by brightly plumed officers on curvetting horses formed their lines. Cavalry, infantry, and Marine detachments, some recently returned from the battlefields of Mexico, were joined by militia units, each with its own band. At their head rode Major General John A. Quitman, one of the army's highest ranking volunteer officers, veteran of Vera Cruz and Cerro Gordo and reputed to have been the first American officer to enter Mexico City; and Lieutenant Colonel Charles A. May, the ostentatious hero of Resaca de la Palma. Falling in behind the soldiers were fire companies from Washington and Baltimore, their polished engines "glittering and glancing with brass and varnish."

Senators and Congressmen, foreign diplomats, delegations from the states and members of fraternal organizations took their places in line. Temperance enthusiasts—the Freemen's Vigilant Total Abstinence Society, the Sons of Temperance, and the Junior Brothers of Temperance—pulled a wagon bearing a large cask of water inscribed "Fountain of Health." Members of benevolent societies, literary associations, and young men's organizations, Sunday School students with their "shining morning faces," and private citizens joined the march. A sensation was created by a group of Cherokee, Chickasaw, Choctaw, and Creek Indians who had traveled to the capital for the occasion, some of the older Indians wearing medals bearing George Washington's likeness which they had received more than fifty years before.

As the procession began, with brightly colored flags and pennants, gay costumes, and martial music, people gathered along the streets. Marching eight abreast, the paraders took almost an hour to pass "at a steady marching pace, any given point." As they approached their destination, the marchers passed under a "triumphant" arch, each side of which bore the names of fifteen states, with the word "Independence" emblazoned on the keystone. Meanwhile crowds converged on the mall west of the Capitol. Refreshment booths and fireworks stands had been set up on the lawn, groups of "ladies and gentlemen, citizens and soldiers" strolled about in the bright sunlight, and some spread elaborate picnics on the grass.

The parade terminated at the monument site, where seats had been erected for the special guests. Seated near the President were the aged Dolley Madison, 91-year-old Elizabeth Schuyler Hamilton, the widow of Alexander Hamilton, and George Washington Parke Custis, whose father had been the first President's stepson. Nearby stood a second arch covered with colored cotton and bearing on its top an American eagle, the same bird it was said that had surmounted the welcome arch for Lafayette more than twenty years earlier.[3]

The ceremonies began with a lengthy prayer by the Grand Chaplain of the Masonic Lodge. Robert C. Winthrop, distinguished Congressman from Massachusetts and Speaker of the House of Representatives, then rose to deliver the dedication oration. The occasion, he noted, was indeed an auspicious one for the United States, marking "the precise epoch at which we have arrived in the world's history, and in our own history." A war against a foreign foe had just been won, and he paid tribute to the "veterans of the line and volunteers," fresh from their triumphs on Mexican fields, their swords now wreathed in myrtle. Second, he pointed to the revolutions at that moment convulsing Europe, popular uprisings in which "the influence of our own institutions" and the "results of our own example" could be seen. The "great American-built locomotive, 'Liberty' " (symbol of the nation's new industrial age), was racing along the "track of human freedom," proclaiming the doctrines of the American Revolution. "The whole civilized world resounds with American opinions and American principles."

The age was not only America's, it was also Washington's. "In the whole history of the world," Winthrop asserted, "it may be doubted whether any man can be found, who has exerted a more controlling influence over men and over events than George Washington." He urged his countrymen to heed the example of the nation's founder and to dedicate themselves anew to his principles. "Let the column which we are about to construct be at once a pledge and an emblem of perpetual Union!" Let America fulfill the mission left to it by Washington and the Revolutionary Fathers, Winthrop exclaimed, let it "stand before the world in all its original strength and beauty, securing peace, order, equality, and freedom to all within its boundaries, and shedding light and hope and joy upon the pathway of human liberty throughout the world."[4]

Following these words, the Grand Master of the Masonic Lodge in the District of Columbia, wearing an apron and using a trowel once owned by Washington, consecrated the cornerstone in the "usual masonic ceremony." Various items were deposited in the stone, and a hymn was sung. The capstone was lowered, the stone was sealed, and the brethren clapped their hands "three times three." Robert Treat Paine sang a patriotic song, and a benediction closed the ceremony.

The troops re-formed their lines, the units of the parade fell in behind and all marched to the White House, where President Polk, on horseback, reviewed the soldiers. Later that evening, the parlors of the Presidential mansion were opened to the public, the Marine Band played on the south lawn, and the sky was lit by a spectacular display of fireworks.[5]

Polk had no sooner returned from the ceremony when an army surgeon, weary and disheveled, appeared at the White House with dispatches from Mexico. In his pouch was the treaty of peace between the United States and Mexico, bearing the long-awaited ratification by the Mexican Congress. Polk conferred immediately with Secretary of State James Buchanan, summoned his private secretary, and drafted a proclamation. Later that night, amidst the festivities in the White House, he placed his signature on the document officially ending the war with Mexico. "I desired to sign it," he wrote in his diary, "on the anniversary of Independence."[6]

By the end of the day, the dedication of the Washington Monument had become even more symbolic than anyone had expected. "This great anniversary," declared one citizen, "has never come in, with more of enjoyment to be thankful for, and more of promise to cheer and encourage us." The terms of the Treaty of Guadalupe Hidalgo, as amended by the United States Senate, had been known for some time. Ratification by Mexico, anxiously awaited as the Mexican Congress sought a quorum of its members, did not alter the provisions. The Rio Grande was recognized as the boundary of Texas, and New Mexico and California—over half a million square miles of territory—were ceded to the United States. On its part, the United States assumed the unpaid claims of American citizens against the Mexican government and agreed to pay Mexico the sum of $15,000,000.

Never before had American independence been "more joyfully commemorated." The brilliant success of "our brave and magnanimous army in Mexico" recalled the struggles of the Revolution, and the leader of that Revolution now stood forth as the "founder of an empire" which would soon eclipse anything that the "world has heretofore produced."[7]

CHAPTER 1

America's First Foreign War

Early in February 1846, Zachary Taylor, commanding a force of fewer than 4000 men camped at the mouth of the Nueces River near Corpus Christi, Texas, received orders from the War Department to prepare for the 150-mile march to the Rio Grande. The so-called Army of Observation (or Army of Occupation as it was later called), comprising half the total strength of the United States army and the largest body of troops assembled since the War of 1812, had been in camp for almost seven months, and the men rejoiced that the tedium of camp life was about to end. The prospect of action after the long period of idleness was exhilarating.

As Taylor's men broke camp and began their march, fears for their safety were felt throughout the country. Relations with Mexico, already bad, had been aggravated by the annexation of Texas early in 1845 and by Texas's admission to the Union in December. Mexico responded swiftly, refusing to recognize the annexation and breaking off diplomatic relations with Washington. Its threats against Texas and an increasingly bellicose stance against the United States, matched by American insistence on the Rio Grande as the country's new southern boundary, carried the two nations to the brink of war. Older, unresolved issues, such as the unpaid claims owed by Mexico to the United States, were given new emphasis and added fuel to the fire. As the Mexican position moved closer to the belief that war was the only solution, so also did opinion in the United States, encouraged by an outburst of expansionist sentiment. With the failure of John Slidell's peace-making mission to Mexico City and the downfall of the moderate Mexican government in a *coup* led by the military leader General Paredes, hostilities between the United States and Mexico appeared to be the only remaining option.

Reports that the Mexican army on the south bank of the Rio Grande had received reinforcements heightened the fears for Taylor's force.

7

The Americans reached the river opposite the Mexican city of Matamoros by the end of March, but their position was precarious. "The danger of our little army is confessed," declared one Washington newspaper. Taylor's position was "almost a forlorn hope." News was expected daily that the army had been overwhelmed by Mexico's larger and more experienced force, and anger was directed toward President Polk for having placed an undermanned army in such an exposed and dangerous position. Fragmentary reports of the murder of several soldiers by guerrillas increased the anxiety and the suspense.

The decision for war was finally and reluctantly taken by President Polk and his cabinet. Slidell arrived in Washington on May 8 and reported the failure of his mission, reason enough for a state of war; the next day word was received of the ambush of an American unit north of the Rio Grande in which several lives were lost. Hostilities, Taylor stated in his dispatch, had commenced. Whatever doubts still remained were now removed. On May 11 Polk sent his war message to Congress, and two days later both houses approved a war bill by overwhelming majorities.

Congress's action unleashed enthusiastic public demonstrations throughout the country. Twenty thousand Philadelphians gathered to voice their support for the war, and in New York even more thronged a mass meeting to cheer the patriotic oratory of the city's leading citizens. It was a spectacle that "made the heart of every true American swell with patriotic joy." In Richmond an immense crowd gathered at the city hall and martial music was heard in the streets, and in Louisville all was "life and bustle" following the arrival of the war news. The *New York Herald* predicted that the war would "lay the foundation of a new age, a new destiny, affecting both this continent and the old continent of Europe."[1]

Unknown to the people in the United States, the two armies on the Rio Grande had already met in combat. Taylor's makeshift fort opposite Matamoros had been placed under bombardment, and Mexican forces crossed the river in strength. Two battles were fought on successive days, May 8 and 9, the first on the plain of Palo Alto and the second at a palm-filled ravine known as Resaca de la Palma. Although outnumbered, Taylor's army forced the withdrawal of the Mexicans from the field, and after their defeat on the 9th the Mexican soldiers fled in panic across the Rio Grande, many of them drowning in their flight. Following a half-hearted effort to negotiate with the Americans, the Mexican General Arista ordered the evacuation of Matamoros, and on May 18 Taylor's troops occupied the Mexican town.

News of the American victories at Palo Alto and Resaca de la Palma did not reach Washington until May 23. Even then the reports were fragmentary and incomplete. Less than a week before, the *Union* had announced in bold headlines that Matamoros had been destroyed and 700 Mexicans killed. It proved to be a false report. When the first news

Map of the battlegrounds. From Edward D. Mansfield, *The Mexican War* (1849).

of the battles was received, the press was understandably cautious. Taylor's position on the Rio Grande was known to be precarious, the Mexican force that faced him superior in numbers. Rumors of Taylor's fate had circulated, emphasizing the dangers that faced the small American army. Public alarm mounted until the people half-expected to hear that some terrible disaster had befallen their soldiers. When the first reports of the victories were received, the *Union* warned that they might well be exaggerated.

The suspense ended quickly. Official dispatches from Taylor confirming his success were received by the government on May 25, and the capital immediately assumed an air of celebration. The moral effect of the triumph upon the country, declared the Democratic paper, would be irresistible. "It secures us a short war." Not to be outdone, the Whig *National Intelligencer,* which only a week before had insisted that the war "will be unpopular," now predicted that partisan differences would be erased. Taylor's victories should produce the "most ardent and gratifying emotions in the bosom of every American." "No matter *now* how it came," declared another Whig paper; war was a reality and Whigs would join with Democrats in its support.[2]

Ten days before, the first call for volunteers had been issued by Secretary of War William L. Marcy. Fifty thousand volunteers to serve for twelve months or the duration of the war had been authorized by the initial war legislation, the number to be apportioned among the states. Twenty thousand men drawn from those states in the South and West closest to the battle front were to be pressed into immediate service; 25,000 more from the East and Northeast were to be enrolled for service at a later time. Recruitment, administered by state authorities, was just getting under way when news of Taylor's victories flashed across the country.

The news was received with relief mixed with surprise, relief that Taylor's army was safe, and surprise that it had defeated the Mexican force so handily in not one but two sharp engagements. The impact on volunteering was immediate. Concern that it would be difficult to raise a volunteer force after so long a period of peace quickly evaporated. The victories seemed to promise a short war, so there was an enthusiastic scramble to become involved before it was too late. A wave of excitement for "military adventures" spread from town to town; public demonstrations, bonfires, and illuminations heightened a war spirit. From his home in Lansingburgh, New York, Herman Melville observed that "people here are all in a state of delirium . . . A military ardor pervades all ranks . . . Nothing is talked of but the 'Halls of the Montezumas.' " In New York City, placards suddenly appeared on the streets bearing such slogans as "Ho, for the Halls of the Montezumas" and "Mexico or Death." Editor Park Benjamin issued his own poetic appeal:

> Arm! Arm! your country bids you arm!
> Fling out your banner free—

> Let drum and trumpet sound alarm,
> O'er mountain, plain and sea.

A great war meeting gathered in Lowell, Massachusetts, the largest assemblage ever for that city, to cheer the gallantry of Taylor's army and to respond to the governor's call for volunteers. A letter from Daniel Webster's son Fletcher was read urging support for the government, and two independent military companies announced their readiness to march to the Rio Grande. In Baltimore, volunteers came in so fast that the city's quota was filled in less than thirty-six hours.[3]

In the West, the scene recalled the romance of Sir Walter Scott's accounts of border warfare. The government's summons, declared one orator, passed through the countryside "like the fiery cross of Clan Alpin through the hills of Scotland," rousing the people "to emulate the deeds of their ancestors." Every town and village, wrote a Tennessee volunteer, was inflamed by the "shrill fife and spirit-stirring drum," as men poured in from the mountains, plains, and valleys to offer their services. Thirty thousand Tennesseeans responded to the call for 3000 soldiers and the selection had to be made by drawing lots, leaving many young men disgruntled and frustrated. In Cincinnati, 12,000 people gathered on the river front to celebrate the news of Taylor's victories with gun salutes, parades, and harangues. Ohio's quota was filled within two weeks, and Illinois, where towns blazed with excitement, provided enough men for fourteen regiments when only four were called.[4]

A war mood that approached hysteria was expressed in a myriad of ways in the few weeks following the news of the battles. The nation's leading engraving firm immediately put on sale a series of four pictures portraying, among other things, the battle of Palo Alto and the bombardment of Matamoros (which never happened), while publishers rushed into print with books on Mexican geography and infantry movements and exercises. Anything that "tends to throw light on Mexico or her history" was in sudden demand. A new edition of "Tanner's Travelling Map of Mexico," providing a table of distances and a map of all roads leading to the Mexican capital, was advertised. New York's theatres vied with one another in their support of the war. At the Greenwich, actress Caroline Chapman interrupted her role with a "patriotic poetical address" on the Mexican War; the Chatham advertised a "grand national drama" entitled "The March of Freedom," featuring General Taylor and the Goddess of Liberty; and the popular Bowery (the "People's Theatre") presented "The Campaign on the Rio Grande," a "rich treat" for all who wished to experience "the thrilling scenes at the seat of war." In Philadelphia, a drama depicting the falsely reported destruction of Matamoros was written, rehearsed, and acted within five hours of the receipt of the news. Merchants advertised the sale of Palo Alto hats and Palo Alto root beer, while Palo Alto houses, Resaca le la Palma saloons, and Taylor taverns sprang up almost overnight. The popular singing group the Alleghanians included "The Soldier's Farewell" on their concert program ("The drum resounds, to arms! to arms!") and graduating students at Yale College delivered orations on "The Importance of a National Military Institution" and "The Energy of Republics in War" at their commencement exercises.[5]

Little thought was given to the needs of the war, the sacrifices that would be required, or the manner in which it would be conducted. All such serious considerations were drowned out in the excitement. The victories at Palo Alto and Resaca de la Palma seemed to forecast a short war in any case. It was apparent that Mexico's soldiery, even though outnumbering the American, was no match for the troops of the republic; certainly it was not the superior force many had been led to believe it was. Mexican overtures to negotiate an end to the conflict were expected momentarily. Obviously, one Whig paper suggested, the administration had summoned many more volunteers than would be needed. The President, the editor charged mischievously, really intended to send the troops against Great Britain in a war over Oregon and merely used the Mexican crisis to mask his intentions. It was not long before the people came to realize, in the sobering light of reality, that their war would be neither short nor easy.[6]

The War with Mexico, as Americans were so fond of pointing out, was unique in the nation's experience. It was America's first foreign war (the War of 1812, a second war for independence against the erstwhile mother country, did not qualify) and the first American war to be fought almost entirely in a strange and distant land. Mexico's tropical climate, its wild and barren topography and exotic vegetation and wildlife, the unfamiliar ways of its people, the differences in language, customs, and heritage all gave the war a romantic appeal that had never before been experienced. For the first time, Americans were exposed to an alien land, to a culture not their own, and the effect was broadening, educational and even startling. The Mexican War was a window through which Americans were able to view another land, another people, and thus overcome a limiting parochialism.

Looking back on the war, a writer in the *Southern Quarterly Review* reviewed those factors that separated the conflict from all that had gone before: a greater and more sustained enthusiasm among the people, fewer errors by those who directed the campaigns, the remarkable success of the military forces, and the greater skill on the battlefield. All these added up to an "increased confidence" in the strength of the republic. Although brief (less than two years), the war bore fruits "more real and tangible" than those of any episode since the achievement of independence. The war, in fact, carried the United States into the modern world. "It is one thing," the writer suggested, "for a people to show themselves equal to the defence of their homes and firesides; but the greatest test of the powers and resources of a nation will be found . . . in its capacity for foreign warfare."[7]

The achievement was deemed the more remarkable because the country was unprepared to fight a war on the scale demanded by the conflict with Mexico. The United States army in the mid-1840s was small and inexperienced. The Seminole War, a costly inconclusive campaign against Indians in Florida, had ended in 1842 but it hardly provided guidance to the military planners in 1846. When war came, the country was compelled for the first time in its history to raise large numbers of troops in a short time, to train, equip, and move them to distant points with as little delay as possible. The vast area covered by the military operations, from the Rio Grande and Mexico's eastern shore to California, the inhospitable nature of the terrain, and the long distances over which men and supplies had to be moved, severely strained a government that was ill-suited to meet the problems.

Military officers lacked both experience and training for a rapid mobilization of men and resources. Knowledge of Mexico was sketchy and the means for gathering intelligence were crude, if they existed at all. Ordnance, including artillery pieces and shells, arms and ammunition, had to be produced on an unprecedented scale with little advance notice or preparation. Quartermaster stores—uniforms, wagons, horses, mules, camp equipage, foodstuffs, in short everything necessary to the support of an army in the field—had to be provided with a minimum of delay. Because the war involved the country's first overseas military campaigns, ships had to be built, purchased, or chartered in sufficient number to carry men and supplies to distant ports. The need to coordinate naval and land operations and to direct the movement of troops deep in enemy territory placed a premium on military skill and ingenuity. As more and more Mexican territory came under occupation, a potentially hostile population had to be governed; without the guidance of precedent, military governments were established and officers assigned to the direction of civil affairs.

On the whole, the government proved equal to the task. The War Department bureaus performed well in carrying out their assigned functions, although the Department's organization proved inadequate to a close direction of the actual campaigns. A large burden of responsibility, with a wide area of discretion, was left to the commanders in the field. The recruitment of troops, a task which the government shared with the states, was carried out with amazing swiftness.[8]

The supply system also worked well, considering the lack of advance planning, shortages of money, wasted time, extravagance, and some profiteering. The procurement of wagons, horses, and other essentials was speeded by the use of the newly invented telegraph. Contracts were issued for the construction of additional wagons in Cincinnati,

Philadelphia, Newark, and Boston. For the first time the government
assumed total responsibility for clothing the army. Volunteers were at
first required to provide their own clothing, but in January 1848 Congress authorized the department to supply uniforms to the volunteers
as well (actually, clothing had been issued to volunteers in limited quantities earlier). The Schuylkill Arsenal in Philadelphia, where the clothing was produced, contracted with textile mills throughout the East for
the purchase of cloth and increased the number of tailors and seam-
stresses employed by the Arsenal from four hundred to about four
thousand. Shoes (as many as 12,000 pairs a month by the war's end)
and tents were also produced at Schuylkill. In order to relieve the
pressure on the Arsenal, the procurement of knapsacks, canteens, iron
camp kettles, and mess pans was assigned to quartermasters in Pittsburgh and Cincinnati.[9]

The urgent need for arms and ammunition taxed the capacities of
the national armories and arsenals. At the St. Louis Arsenal, 200 young
boys were employed to fill cartridges, or "Mexican Pills." Historian
William H. Prescott visited the Albany Arsenal in the summer of 1846
to witness the manufacture of arms, saw 100,000 weapons stacked
around the walls "shining like the pipes of an organ" and was reminded of Longfellow's familiar poem "The Arsenal at Springfield."
Similar activities were being carried out in more than twenty other
government arsenals. Private contractors, such as E. I. duPont and
Samuel Colt, manufactured artillery pieces and vast quantities of shells
(in the bombardment of Vera Cruz alone almost half a million pounds
of iron were hurled at the enemy). Nearly all the furnaces in the country willing to accept contracts were pressed into service. The speed with
which ordnance was produced and shipped to the army surprised even
those who were in charge. Within a four-month period, for example,
forty-nine 10-inch mortars and 50,000 shells were ordered, manufactured, transported to Atlantic ports, and carried to Vera Cruz—an
achievement, in the words of one officer, that spoke "volumes of the
mechanical resources of the American republic for war."[10]

Transportation was the most crucial, and potentially the weakest, link
in the supply chain. Because the fighting was far distant from the
points of manufacture, special problems arose, not the least of which
was the creation of an adequate fleet of vessels to carry the material to
the war zones. Sea-going steamers, sailing vessels, and shallow-draft
river steamboats were chartered, purchased, and constructed, but
never in sufficient numbers to meet the need. The obstinacy of shipowners and the exorbitant prices they charged the government, the
demand for ships to carry grain to Europe, even the rise in the price of
cotton that diverted ships to the European trade, all made the task of
the Quartermaster Corps difficult and frustrating. The initial shortage
of transport vessels caused long delays in supplying General Taylor's
army on the Rio Grande, and at least one critic argued that had needed

equipment been more promptly provided to Taylor "he would have captured the entire Mexican force opposed to him, and brought the war to a speedy close." Many of the ships that were pressed into service proved to be unseaworthy or ill-suited to navigation along the Mexican coast or on the Rio Grande, so many of the supplies, including horses and mules, were lost along the way. War matériel accumulated in New Orleans, clogging the levee while awaiting shipment to Mexico in vessels often unsuited to the task—evidence, complained *Niles' Register,* that by late 1846 the administration still had not mastered the requirements of a foreign war.[11]

Charges of extravagance and waste were hurled at the government, and the war's logistical problems were blamed on the mismanagement and profiteering of the administration and its agents. One writer insisted that "Mississippi River Gamblers" had been placed in charge of the procurement of supplies and that they engaged in "wholesale robberies of the public treasury." Opponents of the war were divided on whether the problems resulted from the administration's ineptitude or from its nefarious designs. Many of the difficulties encountered by the government were in fact due to the nation's prosperity. Prices were high and merchants, manufacturers, and shipowners, many of whom opposed the war, sought to make the most of the situation.

Nonetheless, Quartermaster General Thomas S. Jesup, who had served since the establishment of the Corps in 1818, regarded his bureau's accomplishments with satisfaction and justifiable pride. Comparing the achievement with the only recent analogous operation, Jesup reported: "With our depots farther from the sources of supply than Algiers is from Toulon or Marseilles, we accomplished more in the first six months of our operations in Mexico, than France, the first military power in Europe, has accomplished in Africa in seventeen years." While recognizing all the difficulties encountered by the government, regular army officer Henry W. Halleck agreed with Jesup that "no army was better supplied than ours in all matters of subsistence, clothing, medical and hospital stores, and in means of transportation."[12]

Essential to the success of the military operations in Mexico were the personal strength, leadership, and determination of the President. Without any military experience or knowledge, Polk organized and controlled the war almost single-handedly, leaving little to his cabinet officers and devoting long hours to the details of military campaigns and supply. Although unfamiliar with military theory, he followed the rules for carrying on limited warfare down to the last detail. He made mistakes and sometimes he allowed his partisanship to get in the way of good sense, but in spite of these lapses his sense of executive responsibility was of a high order. The experience of the only previous wartime President was a poor guide, for James Madison had exercised little leadership during the War of 1812. It was Polk who first defined the role of the Commander-in-Chief during wartime, and it was this definition that provided later wartime Presidents, including Abraham Lincoln, with the power to meet their own crises. As one recent historian has suggested, it was Polk who "first demonstrated how a strong executive . . . could reconcile civil supremacy and the effective conduct of the war, to the enhancement of both."[13]

The Mexican War did not simply belong to the army or to the government. It also belonged to the American people. It was not the "People's contest" that Abraham Lincoln would later see in the Civil War, although there were some who viewed the Mexican War in that Lincolnian sense. Rather it was a war that touched the people's lives (especially if they were readers), a war that was experienced more intimately, with greater immediacy and closer involvement than any major event in the nation's history. It was the first American war to rest on a truly popular base, the first that grasped the interest of the population, and the first people were exposed to on an almost daily basis. The essential link between the war and the people was provided by the nation's press, for it was through the ubiquitous American newspaper that the war achieved its vitality in the popular mind.

The war coincided with the era of the penny press, a time when technology, marketing innovations, and a dramatic increase in literacy all combined to produce a veritable "print explosion." Although the result was a new demand for the printed word in whatever form, it was the newspaper that became the principal beneficiary of the changes. A "revolution in news" was under way as the newspapers, spearheaded by the large urban dailies, reduced their cost and increased their readership. The combination of cheaper papers and mass circulation placed the news in the hands of all economic and social classes, "common man democracy" at work in the field of journalism. With an emphasis on timeliness, if not on accuracy, innovative techniques in news gathering were developed. The invention of the telegraph just two years before the war began and the use of horse or pony expresses enabled reporters to transmit news to the publishing centers with lightning-like swiftness. Improvements in paper-making and the development of fast steam presses like the Hoe rotary press (1846) made it possible for the newspapers to reach an ever-widening audience.

The Mexican War was the first major event in American history to be reported by the penny press. Satisfying the demand for dramatic and sensational news, the war's coverage was "far more copious than that of any previous war in any part of the world." It was the newspaper, more than any other medium, that influenced the popular attitudes toward the war and molded the popular perceptions of the conflict.[14]

Although an intense competition for war news developed as soon as the war began, the primary role in reporting the war belonged to the

New Orleans press. Because of its proximity to Mexico, its size, and its well-developed port facilities, the Crescent City served as a staging area for troops and as the principal supply depot for the military operations. Its nearness to the conflict also gave New Orleans the advantage in reporting the war. In 1847 the city boasted nine daily newspapers, most of them locked in a bitter rivalry for the news; the *Picayune* and the *Delta* were in the lead but such papers as the *Tropic*, the *Crescent*, and the *Bee* were also active. Because of New Orleans's advantage, these papers served as the primary sources of war information for the entire nation, and their dispatches were widely copied.[15]

The Mexican War was the first conflict in which war correspondents were employed, another outgrowth of the penny press, and it was the New Orleans press that pioneered the practice. Newspapermen were not only among the first to arrive in Mexico but they also on occasion served as fighting men as well. The best known was George Wilkins Kendall, one of the founders of the *Picayune*. Kendall, a member of the ill-fated Texas expedition to Santa Fe in 1842, had been captured and imprisoned in Mexico and finally released because he was a United States citizen. His account of the affair, *Narrative of the Texan Santa Fe Expedition* (1844), became the standard history and one of the important books of the 1840s in arousing American interest in Mexico. When the war began Kendall rushed to the Rio Grande, where he joined the Texas Rangers for a time. Following the battle of Monterey, which he reported in detail, he moved to Tampico, joined Winfield Scott's expedition against Vera Cruz, and accompanied the army to Mexico City, serving part of the time as an aide to General Worth. He was in the thick of the fighting around the Mexican capital and was slightly wounded in the assault on Chapultepec. Kendall's dispatches, noted for their accuracy as well as their human interest and literary quality, were read throughout the country. In the words of his biographer, Kendall was "the first modern war correspondent and the most widely known reporter in America in his day."

Kendall not only served his paper as a correspondent, he also organized a network of reporters that made the *Picayune* the most important source of war news in the country. Agents of the paper were stationed at strategic locations in Mexico and an elaborate staff of correspondents was developed. Among them were Francis A. Lumsden, co-founder with Kendall of the *Picayune*, who served with a mounted company from Georgia, and Christopher Mason Haile. Haile, a native of Rhode Island, had attended West Point and was already known for his humorous sketches in the *Picayune*. During the campaign against Vera Cruz he was commissioned a first lieutenant of infantry.[16]

The number of correspondents in the field was boosted by the fact that so many newspapermen were found in the ranks of the early volunteers. As many as twenty New Orleans printers, for example, joined a single company of Louisiana volunteers. One of these was

James L. Freaner of the New Orleans *Delta,* Kendall's strongest competitor for the war news. Freaner, who signed his dispatches "Mustang," fought at Monterey and accompanied the army from Vera Cruz to Mexico City. He developed a close friendship with Nicholas Trist, Polk's peace emissary, and when Trist was recalled by the President it was Freaner who persuaded him to ignore the order and remain in Mexico. When the treaty was finally signed, it was entrusted to Freaner for the long journey to Washington. Two other *Delta* printers who served as war correspondents were also among the early volunteers, J. G. H. Tobin, whose sketches "From Captain Tobin's Knapsack" ran regularly in the paper, and John H. Peoples, who used the name "Chaparral." Thomas Bangs Thorpe had already established a reputation as a writer of southwestern humor when he acquired an interest in the New Orleans *Tropic* in April 1846 and left for the Rio Grande to report the war.[17]

The New Orleans papers were not the only ones to have active correspondents in Mexico. The *New York Herald* in September 1846 sent five correspondents to Mexico, boasting that the group had more talent than those of any other paper. Other papers followed. The *New York Sun* printed dispatches from the only woman war correspondent and the only one to report the war from behind the Mexican lines. Newspapers all over the country had their "special correspondents," in many cases volunteers who had made arrangements with their hometown newspapers before they left for Mexico. Editors themselves volunteered—sixteen from Massachusetts, five from Harrisburg, Pennsylvania—and dispatched news reports to their newspapers.

Forwarding news dispatches from the field to New Orleans in the quickest time possible was neither safe nor easy. The routes from Monterey and Saltillo to the Rio Grande and from Mexico City to Vera Cruz were infested with guerrillas. Kendall organized the first efficient courier system—"Mr. Kendall's Express"—and other correspondents quickly copied it. To reduce the danger of guerrilla and bandit attacks, Kendall recruited Mexicans to carry his dispatches, paying them high wages and often caring for their families while they were absent. Even so, some were killed or robbed. From Vera Cruz the news reports were carried by ship to New Orleans. Some distance from port the ships were met by a small fast steamer equipped for typesetting and the news was set in type. By the time the ship docked they were ready for the press.

As the news hit the streets, copies of the New Orleans papers were sent northward by express riders, or "pony express." The *New York Herald's* James Gordon Bennett established an express from Mobile, while the Philadelphia and Baltimore papers employed sixty blooded horses to carry the news from New Orleans. The time was shortened as the new telegraph was extended: from Washington to New York by early June 1846, and southward to Richmond, Petersburg, and, by

February 1848, Charleston. Reporters were stationed at the terminus to intercept the express riders and send the more important news over the wire. On February 16, 1848, the Washington *Union* proudly noted that the nation's capital was within three days' communication of New Orleans. The press's "telegraphic era" began with the Mexican War.

The use of the telegraph, however, was expensive, and the instrument was often not adequate to the flood of dispatches. The cost of operating a "pony express," even though shared by three or four newspapers, was high. To reduce the cost and increase the efficiency, David Hale of the New York *Journal of Commerce* proposed that cooperation among the large influential dailies replace their cutthroat competition. Bennett agreed. Early in May 1848, as news of European revolutions began to overshadow the reports from Mexico, representatives of six New York newspapers met in the offices of the *New York Sun* and organized the Associated Press, the first great move toward cooperative news-gathering in America.[18]

Some of the correspondents and printers in Mexico, not content with reporting the conflict for newspapers back home, founded papers of their own in Mexico's occupied cities, the so-called "Anglo-Saxon press." Beginning with the Corpus Christi *Gazette* in early 1846, the papers followed the movement of the army, twenty-five altogether in fourteen Mexican cities, including Matamoros, Monterey, Saltillo, Tampico, Vera Cruz, Jalapa, Puebla, and Mexico City. Most of them lasted only a short time, but some continued to publish until after the war was over. One of the most enterprising publishers was John H. Peoples, correspondent for the New Orleans *Delta*, whose papers in Matamoros, Vera Cruz, Jalapa, Puebla, and Mexico City were supported in part by printing contracts from the army. Following the war he served as a recruiter of volunteers for service in the Yucatan. Another correspondent, William C. Tobey ("John of York") of the Philadelphia *North American*, issued the *North American, Mexico* in Mexico City as an extension of the Philadelphia paper. Usually printed in both Spanish and English on presses acquired from the Mexicans, the papers sent reports of the war to the press in the United States, provided news and entertainment to the soldiers, and poured, as one account put it, "volleys of real first-rate freedom . . . upon the benighted Mexicans." A few of the papers were suppressed for brief periods by the military authorities in response to the demands of the Mexican civilian governments.[19]

The efficient gathering of the war news by the correspondents and its rapid dispatch to the newspapers back home underscored the essentially civilian nature of the war. No longer did the people have to rely on the official dispatches of the military for information; the news was not only more plentiful but also more reliable. Although some complaints were heard from the army, the widespread dissemination of war news became a source of pride and satisfaction. "The thousand prying eyes and brazen tongues attendant upon a free and uncontrolled

Zachary Taylor. From *American Review* (September 1848).

press," complained one army officer, often resulted in the publication of "false and exaggerated accounts of military movements before in propriety they should be discussed at all." But if the reports of the correspondents constituted breaches of military security or resulted in the circulation of sensitive information, very little was done about it. The correspondents continued to enjoy a remarkable degree of freedom, going where they wanted and reporting what they wished. Although some effort was made late in the war to silence those army officers who also served as war correspondents, no move was made to inhibit the activities of the press.

Much more important was the fact that Americans were better informed about their war than any people in wartime had ever been. The episodes of the conflict, the experiences of the combatants, even the intentions and feelings of the enemy, boasted *Niles' Register,* were "more thoroughly known by mankind, than those of any war that has ever taken place." The reporters themselves, being also participants in the conflict, were "better qualified to furnish correct accounts of what transpired." Not only did the people benefit from the comprehensive reporting, the *Register* observed, but America's future historians would also find their task easier as they attempted to discover the true story of the war.[20]

CHAPTER 2

A Dare-Devil War Spirit

"Racial Superiority"

The American victories at Palo Alto and Resaca de la Palma early in May 1846 were as surprising to the victors as they were demoralizing to the vanquished. As the war progressed, commentators pointed to the twin successes as having produced a moral effect on the future course the fighting would follow. For the Americans, the battles provided an "unbounded" self-confidence, replacing uncertainty with a conscious attitude of superiority. They had gained what one writer called the "prestige of victory," an important psychological advantage that would influence subsequent engagements. From those initial triumphs, wrote John Frost, "no American force has ever thought of being defeated by any amount of Mexican troops."

The moral effect of the opening battles worked both ways. The Mexicans too developed exaggerated notions of American military power, often handicapping the efforts of the Mexican commanders. Stories of the superhuman strength of the "barbarians of the North" circulated in the ranks, promoted in part by Mexican leaders who were anxious to explain their unexpected defeats. Some of the speculations, as told to correspondents, approached the ludicrous. One Mexican soldier was sure that the Americans had been fed powder and whiskey before the battles; another suggested that the bean soup on which the Americans subsisted imparted extraordinary powers to the men.[1]

Confidence in their prowess as soldiers quickly merged with the widely popular notion among Americans that they represented a racially superior stock. Indeed, the victories seemed to confirm an attitude of racial superiority. As the American armies penetrated deeper into Mexico, the soldiers expressed amazement that the enemy, often enjoying the advantages of terrain and numbers, did not resist their advance more desperately. The answer seemed simple. The nature of a nation's society, Tocqueville had written, was reflected in the kind of army it had. There were more fundamental reasons than mere military

21

skill and training that seemed to explain the results of the battles. As one of Taylor's soldiers wrote, proudly but crudely, "You may know ere this, that we gave the Mexicans 'jesse' on the 8th and 9th. . . . The Anglo-Saxon never can acknowledge the corn to the cross of negro and Indian."

Americans were harsh in their judgments of the fighting qualities of Mexican soldiers. They found agreeable the observations of George Frederick Ruxton, the English adventurer who traveled through Mexico during the war, although they were indignant at Ruxton's harsh criticism of their own volunteers. The Mexican army, sneered Ruxton, consisted entirely of "Indians—miserable-looking pigmies, whose grenadiers are five feet high." Lacking both courage and discipline, the soldiers displayed a "brutish indifference to death" that Ruxton felt might have been turned to better account by their leaders. The comments of Americans in Mexico followed a similar vein, no less racial in tone. Mexico's private soldier, suggested New Orleans correspondent Thomas Bangs Thorpe, was a "degraded being," a representation of different races "where the evil qualities of each . . .[are] alone retained." Following the battles on May 8 and 9, Thorpe viewed the enemy's wounded in a makeshift Matamoros hospital. "Were these men Mexicans?" he asked. "The Castilian with auburn hair, the swarthy Indian with straight, and the dark negro with kinked . . . lay side by side," their countenances "hideous," their eyes cold-blooded and treacherous. Thorpe found the strange racial mixture "*in one people*" surprising but concluded that it was a fair cross section of the nation's population.

In an effort to lend a certain scientific basis to the racial argument, a Cincinnati phrenologist examined a number of skulls taken from the Palo Alto battlefield. The Mexican soldiers, he concluded in the strange jargon of the "science," were destitute of Comparison, Causality, Constructiveness, Ideality, and Benevolence, while they possessed in abundance Combativeness, Destructiveness, Secretiveness, and Acquisitiveness. To the uninitiated, he explained that the thickness of the Mexican skulls revealed a "very coarse organization, rather animal than intellectual." Even the wolves who scavenged the battlefields were said to prefer the bodies of the Americans to those of the Mexicans (although some said it was because of the spicy Mexican diet).[2]

When citizens of Mobile presented artillery-officer Braxton Bragg with a ceremonial sword following the war, Bragg cautioned them against placing too high an estimate on the American triumphs in Mexico. The enemy, he stated, was inferior in virtually every element of success. Few disagreed. Mexican army officers secured their commissions through political influence or bribery, it was charged, and were often men of corrupt morals and dissipated habits. The foot-soldiers, many of whom had been impressed into service or recruited from prisons, had none of that *élan* so essential to a national army. Poorly armed and trained, they suffered "as much imperiousness and hauteur and even cruelty as the disobedient slaves upon the cotton plantations." It was not the only time that Mexicans were compared unfavorably with slaves in the American South.

While there was wide agreement on the inferiority of Mexicans, not all attributed that inferiority to racial differences. George Wilkins Kendall, reporting the war for his New Orleans newspaper, agreed that Mexicans possessed "few of the instincts which govern other races," but blamed Mexico's rulers for the inferior character of its people. Oppressed by military and religious despots, held in a state of abject ignorance, the people were manipulated and deceived by "high-sounding yet meaningless manifestoes and proclamations." The army, trained primarily for use against the country's own people during a period of almost constant revolution, was incapable of combating a foreign enemy. To historian Brantz Mayer, who served for two years in the American legation in Mexico City, Mexican soldiers were "political engines, designed for the domestic police of cities" rather than for service in the field. The American soldier lived and fought, he wrote, for "practical liberty and progress," fearless yet valuing life and seeking to protect it; the Mexican soldier's existence, on the other hand, was "a mere strife for bread under military despotism." Brave but often imprudent, he exhibited a "Mahomedan fatalism derived . . . from his Moorish kindred."[3]

By emphasizing the racial inferiority and poor military organization of the Mexican soldiers, Americans faced a disturbing dilemma. To heap scorn and contempt on Mexican military capabilities was to rob the American achievements of their lustre. Thus some of the criticisms were tempered by expressions of praise and respect, no matter how grudgingly. "In the praise of our own soldiers," declared a Baltimore paper following the first battles, "let us not forget the foe." The Mexicans fought bravely; to say otherwise would dim the "brilliancy of our victories." Indeed, the courage displayed by the Mexican troops was "worthy of the days of chivalry" and, according to the contemporary historian Philip Young, "redeemed the reputation of the whole nation." What to some Americans had been a worthless and imbecile soldiery became to others the flower of the Mexican army, disciplined veterans who contested every inch of ground with a desperate determination. The most convincing appraisals came from soldiers in Taylor's ranks, but their warnings were often brushed aside. Those volunteers, who were at first unbelieving, learned after Monterey and Buena Vista to respect the fighting qualities of the Mexican soldier.[4]

No respect, however, was offered those irregular horsemen who fought with the Mexican cavalry and engaged in guerrilla activity behind the lines. They were the "rancheros," individuals who not only terrified but also fascinated the American soldiers; indeed, these "hawks of the chaparral" became legendary figures in the lore of the

Mexican War. Likened to Russia's Cossacks, "ever on the alert, never to be surprised, and untiring in the pursuit of the foe when plunder . . . is to be obtained," they were portrayed as little more than banditti who were not always careful to distinguish between their American foes and their own countrymen. Descriptions abounded, in the soldiers' accounts, the press reports, the histories and the novels, until a stereotype emerged that may or may not have borne a relation to reality. Half Indian and half Spanish, gaunt, dark, and of swarthy visage, with ferocious-looking brows and menacing mustaches, they were the "Arabs of the American continent." Feared by their own people as much as by the Americans, they exhibited "but little advance in civilization." They spent their lives in the saddle, and their expert horsemanship aroused the admiration of their enemies. Tough hide leggings, a blanket with a hole in the center and a straw sombrero constituted their costume. Add to this a lance ornamented with red bunting, a horse "as savage and unmanageable as himself," a belt plentifully supplied with pistols and knives, and a lasso hanging from the saddle, and "you have the *Ranchero* as a member of a troop of banditti, or as a soldier in a body of cavalry."

The rancheros were feared because they fought outside the conventional rules of warfare. They were charged with unspeakable cruelties and barbarities, with dispatching wounded soldiers on the battlefields, and with plundering the bodies of the slain on both sides. Treacherous and disloyal, fighting only for themselves, they were described as "cowardly" in an open-field fight but as a formidable enemy "among the chaparrals" or in an ambush. Rancheros, led by Ramón Falcón, were involved in the early skirmishes with American soldiers along the Rio Grande, and later several hundred of them, under Antonio Canales, served as irregular cavalry at the battles of Palo Alto and Resaca de la Palma. Canales, whose very name inspired fear, attempted unsuccessfully to negotiate with the Americans for the separation of Mexico's northern states and the creation of an independent Republic of the Rio Grande. He later led his irregulars in guerrilla activity against American supply trains and, still clinging to the idea of an independent state, exerted a tight-fisted control over much of northern Mexico.[5]

The popular attitude toward the Mexican soldier was summed up by an early military historian of the conflict. With a well-trained and combat-experienced army, led by officers of high reputation, wrote M. C. M. Hammond, Mexico should have held the advantage over America's small inexperienced force. Fighting for home and country against an invader, the Mexican soldier had "all the stimulants of courage and exertion." He fought valiantly and heroically in defense of his hearth, altar, and family. Yet, Hammond asserted, some nations had "a doom upon them," and Mexico was one, a country that made no progress, wasted its treasure, and neglected its resources, easy prey to an adventurous enemy. The abuses of Mexico's civil and religious leaders, their dereliction of duty and indifference to moral precepts, called down upon the hapless nation the "severest judgments of Heaven." For all its valor and courage, Mexico was destined for defeat.[6]

② Citizens Path to Patriotism

However Mexico's troops were to be assessed and for whatever reasons, nothing could dim the enthusiasm of that spring in 1846 when the first reports of victory on the Rio Grande were confirmed. Within weeks of the first call for volunteers, quotas were filled and thousands of young men were turned away. The population was gripped by a martial spirit the dimensions of which surprised even the most sanguine Americans.

"How can this be accounted for?" asked the *New York Herald*, "this almost perfect union throughout the national mind . . . this sublime spectacle of military preparation, and military transition." The *Herald* felt it was a tribute to the power of the press but others had different answers. One in particular echoed a popular refrain: the response to the war was the consequence of the "perfect freedom of our institutions, the equality of our laws, and . . . the determined spirit of the American character." The answer, it seemed, lay in the American commitment to republicanism, an often ill-defined but nonetheless keenly felt conviction that in the United States, where the people were the rulers, the security of the state was in its citizens. Each one who shared the responsibilities and privileges of government experienced an "instantaneous thrill" when the "language of menace, or an act of outrage or insult," was directed toward the United States. An insult to the nation became a personal affront. "Each citizen," wrote Brantz Mayer, "feels that the defence of his native land or of his country's rights depends upon himself." That was in the nature of republicanism and that was what America, the "model republic," exemplified.[7]

The rush of volunteers simply confirmed the superior nature of republican government and proved that even republics could respond quickly and decisively to national crisis. "We had to show the Mexicans that a people, without being military, may be *warlike*." The volunteer system, wrote New Englander Nahum Capen in his analysis of American republicanism, was in harmony with the country's mission and purpose. He found a certain dignity in a people so willing to serve their government. The military power of the United States, he observed, was precisely where it should be, "in the hearts of the people."[8]

The reliance on volunteers gave the Mexican War an immediacy that could be felt by all the people. It was a civilian war from the outset, clothed with all the romance of a conflict that touched the popular imagination. The "passions of the democracy" were aroused, observed an English traveler, and the nation, William H. Prescott noted, was overrun by a "dare-devil war spirit." By identifying the conflict with republican principles, the war's supporters gave it an idealistic thrust.

Even those who had preached the injustice of the war caught the conta-gion, as partisan differences were temporarily erased. "We are now all Whigs and all Democrats," declared one Indiana newspaper. In Bos-ton's Tremont Temple, the son of Daniel Webster pointed out on the war's first Fourth of July that the duty of all Americans was to put their partisan disagreements aside and give the government wholehearted support.[9]

For some the excitement was the inevitable result of a romantic fasci-nation with warfare and military life. Critics of the war were dismayed by the martial literature that formed so large a part of the nation's reading and at a time, as one pacifist stated, when the people "almost universally read," the evil effect could not be minimized. Reformers saw in the nation's response further evidence that a drastic reorganiza-tion of society was long overdue. How did it happen that so many young men of respectable parentage and background had been im-pelled to volunteer and go off to war? A writer in *The Harbinger* was momentarily baffled. The answer, he finally concluded, was to be found in the "unsuitableness of the present methods of labor to the wants of the laborer." Only when the tedium of "protracted labor" had been abolished and the profits of "joint industry" equitably divided, wrote this disciple of Fourierist associationism, would the "greedy cor-morant War" be driven out.[10]

Whatever the explanation, the fact remained. In every section of the country, the volunteers became the object of adulation as communities vied with one another in their show of support to the country's cause. Hyperbole poured in a torrent of patriotic oratory, no words too ex-travagant to describe the honor and glory of those who left their homes "to rally round the standards of their country." The eyes of the world were upon them, they were told, their deeds to be chronicled on the pages of history and "held up to the gaze of millions yet unborn." Go forth, they were urged, and "prove yourselves worthy of the heritage of freedom." Merchants, farmers, mechanics, lawyers, doctors, clergy-men, teachers, planters, all left the security of employment, exchanging the "silken ties and endearments" of home for the battlefields of Mex-ico. For those whose poverty might keep them from enlisting, contribu-tions of money and clothing were raised while donations were made to their families. A Nashville bank pledged a large loan to the state for the use of the volunteers, and in Indiana, volunteers were promised an extension on their tax deadlines. Some states offered land bounties, while in Virginia, Charles James Faulkner—a "sterling Whig" and large landholder in Texas—promised 150 acres of Texas land to men who would join his rifle company. Distraught parents resorted to the courts to prevent their children from running off to Mexico.

When it became clear that more men volunteered than were called for, the question became "who shall remain?" not "who shall go?" There was talk of a draft to determine who would stay behind. Some solved the problem by moving to other states with larger quotas. Three hundred Indianans crossed the Ohio River to enlist in Kentucky companies, Marylanders joined Virginia units, and at least one Mississippi company was mustered under Texas's volunteer quota. Companies that had been organized only to be turned back decided to go to Mexico anyway, at their own expense, to serve as irregular units, hoping they might join the fight and eventually be accepted into the army.[11]

Existing militia and independent companies, whose military experience consisted of weekly drills before the town ladies, volunteered as units, thus boasting a camaraderie that others did not have. Many of the companies adopted awesome and descriptive titles that revealed their geographic origins, their ethnic compositions, and their determination to vanquish the enemy—Wabash Invincibles (Indiana), Avengers of Major Ringgold (Illinois), Jasper Greens (Irish, Georgia), Black Hussars (German, Louisiana). Once they signed up, the volunteers paraded through towns and villages on their way to the camps, where they awaited transportation to the Rio Grande. Everywhere they went they were objects of attention. The ladies of Cincinnati made regular visits to Camp Washington on the edge of the city to present the men with flowers and provide them with ice cream, cake, and strawberries. Factory girls in Pittsburgh gathered around the soldiers "as if they were in love with them," and as the volunteers left they provided the men with their names and addresses. At a special church service just before the troops departed, the choir sang "Gird on Your Armor," and the citizens of the city wished them well in Mexico. As the boats carrying the soldiers pushed into the river they sounded their whistles and the people on shore responded with cheers. Residents of the towns and farms along the Ohio and Mississippi rivers gathered at the water's edge to add their shouts of encouragement as the steamboats carrying the volunteers passed on their way to New Orleans. Flags flew from the dwellings along the banks, and ladies were seen waving "their lily white hands and handkerchiefs" from doors, windows, and rooftops.[12]

The volunteers came from all walks of life and represented a social cross section. "War," wrote one, "makes strange associations." Among the volunteers were individuals from the "best ranks" of society, including sons of Henry Clay and Daniel Webster, a descendant of John Marshall and Edward Everett's nephew, and members of families with proud Revolutionary connections. Well-to-do professional men, merchants, and farmers joined the ranks as common soldiers, "proud-spirited fellows, with just vanity enough to feel that all the eyes and hopes of the country were fixed upon them." From eastern cities came sailors and members of fire companies and fishing clubs, "a wild, frolicsome, reckless set" who often irritated volunteers from the countryside unable to appreciate the "fun of these city fellows." In the western states men came forth who had grown up with muskets or rifles in their hands and who did not have to be taught how to use them. Some volunteers had fought in the War of 1812 or the Florida wars; a large number had been educated in whole or in part at the United States Military Academy. One-third of the volunteer regiments were commanded by former West Pointers, while well over one-third of the field officers boasted some West Point training.[13]

Volunteer companies were often formed out of occupational groups, like the law students in Nashville or the clerks in New Orleans. Several companies were organized by editors and journeyman printers, the one in Philadelphia being dubbed the Press Guards, and many of their members served as newspaper correspondents as well as soldiers. College students caught the excitement, as at Yale, where students held a war meeting, passed resolutions supporting the war, and formed a volunteer unit—the Yale College Regulars. All political persuasions were represented and it was not unusual for a company to have more Whigs than Democrats. "This shows," commented one paper, "that politics had nothing to do with the volunteers."

As one Illinois volunteer looked about him at the rendezvous where the "patriotism" of the state gathered in anticipation of a "grand jubilee in the halls of the Montezumas," he saw

> lead-miners from Galena; wharf rats and dock loafers from Chicago; farmers on unpurchased lands from the interior; small pattern politicians, emulous of popularity; village statesmen, pregnant with undeveloped greatness, and anxious to enlarge the sphere of their influence by a military *accouchement;* briefless lawyers and patientless physicians; and a liberal allowance of honest, hard-fisted "Suckers," whose huge frames, panoplied in muscle, demonstrate their legitimate claims to Illinois nativity.

The volunteer system, a great influence for democracy, "levels up and levels down." There was no aristocracy around the camp-kettle and no place for "professional pomposity or pretended fastidiousness."[14]

The ethnic mix of the country was also represented: English and Irish from the seaports and manufacturing towns of the East, Germans and Norwegians from the West. Some had military experience, like the Germans who had served in the army of the King of Saxony (one claiming to be a classmate of Queen Victoria's consort) and at least one veteran of Napoleon's "Young Guard" who had fought in Russia and at Waterloo. Commanding an Illinois company was a Polish revolutionary, exiled from his native land. And from closer to home was a sprinkling of Indians: Choctaws from Mississippi, Cherokees in the Arkansas units, and Tonkaways from Texas.

One youthful German volunteer became well known. Alexander Kunze joined Company H, Second Illinois Volunteers, because, he said, of his devotion to America's republican system and the opportunity to observe firsthand the Mexican people. A native of Hamburg, he had been educated in German universities before moving to Illinois in the mid-1840s. Although only twenty-seven years old, he was described by his admirers as "probably the most learned man in the army." His knowledge of Latin philology, it was said, enabled him to read Spanish after only one day's examination of Spanish grammar, while his interest in botany led him to collect and study specimens of Mexican plants. When Kunze was killed at Buena Vista in February 1847, his story appeared in newspapers all over the country. "This man died for a country of which he was not a citizen," wrote one correspondent. "Shall it be said that he, the republican son of Germany, was not a true American?"[15]

All the volunteers, regardless of origin or station in life, shared a "restless thirst of adventure." In their own accounts they offered a variety of motivations, most of which reflected their romantic perception of military life in a remote and exotic land. One volunteer had been moved to enlist by Sir Walter Scott's novels, and as he traveled down the Mississippi to New Orleans he dreamed of glory in that fabled land of romance, the land of Cortez and Montezuma. For another, pride and patriotism were important but above all, he confessed, was the romance of fighting in a foreign land. A Massachusetts volunteer likened the conflict to the "fictions of romance and chivalry" that had filled his youthful hours. It was not simply the impulse of patriotism, concluded still another, but the "spirit of enterprise and curiosity" as well. "With light hearts and bounding pulses," he wrote, "we left our homes . . . in quest of wild adventures in that far-famed land."[16]

Not only were the soldiers exposed to an alien people and culture in Mexico but they were also thrown into contact with other Americans, individuals of diverse backgrounds from different parts of the country, and this in itself was a broadening experience. While some were highly critical of soldiers from other states—like the Pennsylvania volunteer who described troops from South Carolina and Louisiana as the "filthiest and laziest set of men I have ever seen"—most found in the war a nationalizing influence, a refreshing antidote to the parochialism with which many of them had grown up. Sectional differences were obscured as New Englanders fought by the side of southerners, and volunteers from the Atlantic states mingled with those from the Mississippi valley. One of the best-publicized episodes of the war occurred at the battle of Churubusco, in the environs of Mexico City, when a brigade composed of New York and South Carolina volunteers, commanded by an Illinoisan, turned the battle and swept the enemy from the field. "Here we are," exulted one soldier, "from all quarters of our glorious Union, acting in the same concert as if all were the children of one state or family." Although sectional animosities might flare at home, wrote a South Carolinian, "when fighting a common enemy, in one great common cause . . . we are all united."[17]

The citizen-soldier became a symbol of American democracy, perhaps one of the foremost symbols of the Mexican War itself. Any writer or speaker, it was said, who even hinted disparagement of the volunteers' achievements "would be hissed from the stage or burned in effigy in the streets." Prescott, whose history of the Spanish conquest of Mexico became a source of inspiration to the soldiers, found the American character mirrored in the character of the volunteers. The way the country's "raw militia" carried on the war, he wrote, was little short of miraculous, proof of the "indomitable energy" of the American people. Indeed, they played the role of pioneers of civilization and missionaries of the American idea.[18]

③ Volunteers are proxy for american national character — honor w/ mercy & justice

Americans perceived their volunteers as they perceived themselves: simple, unpretentious, impatient with authority, individualistic, and disdainful of class distinction. The lack of military appearance and demeanor, informal dress and undisciplined manner, surprising to Mexicans and shocking to the army's regular officers, far from being a source of embarrassment, became a matter of pride for they simply confirmed the absence of a military tradition in the United States. Early war legislation stipulated that the volunteers' dress need not conform to that of the regular army, and the result was often a colorful and bizarre mixture of styles, shades, and hues. Some simply wore the regulation bluejeans jacket and trousers and glazed cap; others added their own touches, like the Kentuckians who sported broad-brimmed hats with black ostrich feathers. The rigors of the campaigns and the inability of the government to provide adequate replacement clothing soon reduced the ranks to a motley and tattered appearance. The heat of Mexico's climate and the merciless rays of the sun encouraged the troops to dress more for comfort than appearance. Straw hats, light jackets, and trousers of all colors and conditions (often supplied by Mexican vendors) made it easy to distinguish the volunteer units from those of the regular army. "Some of our regiments," reported one correspondent in November 1846, "begin to look a little like Falstaff's." The improvised clothing, including deerskins, and the heavy unshorn beards recalled descriptions of the inhabitants of some of the remoter regions of Russia. To the Mexicans, they looked like "clowns at a carnival."

To an English soldier who enlisted in the regular army at the opening of the war, the volunteers were the prototypes of the fabled American frontiersmen. Observing them during the occupation of Tampico, he saw "strange, wild-looking, hairy-faced savages of the half-horse and half-alligator breed, who galloped about the streets and plazas mounted on mules and Mexican ponies, and armed with sabres, bowies, and revolvers, and in every uncouth variety of costume peculiar

to the American backwoodsman." For this foreigner, all the folklore of
the American frontier suddenly seemed real.[19]

What amazed the Mexicans was how such a nondescript undisciplined collection of men could have consistently beaten their own pro-
fessionals on the battlefield. When advance units of Winfield Scott's
army entered Mexico's second largest city, Puebla, in May 1847, thousands of Mexicans crowded the streets, doorways, windows, and rooftops to gaze upon the "barbarians of the North," expecting to see men
who were Herculean in stature, invincible, and virtually superhuman in
their power (as the Mexican leaders had described the American soldiers). One South Carolina volunteer feared for the safety of the few
hundred Americans as they shuffled past this "immense cloud of hostile citizens." Perhaps Puebla's citizens were too astonished at what they
saw to react. Weary soldiers in torn and disheveled uniforms, covered
with mud and dust, many simply in shirt-sleeves, stopped in the grand
plaza, piled their weapons and laid down on the stones. Some slaked
their thirst from the fountain, others passed to the market, where they
bought bread and fruit from startled vendors. Oblivious to the danger
which surrounded them, many of the soldiers fell asleep on the pave-
ment. Officers, including one wearing an ill-fitting frock coat and battered straw hat astride an "enormous cart horse," were hardly distinguishable from the privates. The spectators were baffled, unable to
recognize in the muddy and plainly dressed soldiers the "conquerors of
their army." These "coarse and clownish men," badly clothed, filthy,
and utterly devoid of military deportment, wrote one onlooker, could
hardly be hailed as the "Messiahs of our civilization!"[20]

In their treatment of Mexico's soldiers and civilians, the volunteers
were seen as further exemplifying qualities of the American character.
The war was blamed on the machinations of Mexico's military, aristocratic and Church leadership, and Americans constantly insisted that
they held no animosity against the Mexican people or the common
soldiers in the Mexican army. Incidents describing the magnanimity of
the volunteers toward the civilian population filled the popular prints:
soldiers protecting Mexican civilians from bandits, ministering to the
enemy wounded left behind on the battlefields, defending villages
against the depredations of Comanche and Apache Indians, intervening to shield helpless Mexicans from the oppressions of their own military and religious leadership. Much was made of the volunteers' devotion to Mexico's women, whom they usually praised for their beauty,
gentility, and kindness while expressing outrage at Mexican men for
withholding from the women the respect they felt was due. Stories of
efforts to protect groups of women caught in the midst of battle (in
Monterey particularly) became legendary and strengthened the chivalric, romantic perception of the war.

Consistent with this image was an emphasis on America's humane
conduct of the war. The United States fought as republics must fight,

according to the highest principles of humanity. More important than
the army's military success, at least to one writer, was the "chivalric
generosity, that enlightened moderation, and fraternal beneficence"
that linked the nation's soldiers with the "best days of Knighthood."
One critic of the war, overwhelmed by the reports of American "chivalry" in Mexico, concluded that

> no war, in any age or country, was ever waged upon principles so humane,
> so civilized, and . . . so christian as is this war. . . . Our treatment of the
> Mexican people . . . entitles our country to claim the foremost rank in
> modern civilization.

To a speaker before New York's Saint Nicholas Society, the generosity
and compassion of the soldiers amounted to "high moral heroism."

The occupation of Mexico City in September 1847, feminist Emma
Willard pointed out, marked a new kind of warfare. The Mexican
capital had not been conquered "as Carthage and other cities were by
the Roman,—to be destroyed, or to become the sport of petty tyrants
and a lawless soldiery." The city was spared the usual sack and rape by
soldiers who, scorning to take advantage of the enemy's weakness, truly
behaved like "knights of old."[21]

Although exaggerated and often in conflict with the facts, such perceptions had a basis in the government's avowed intention of waging a
war that bore only lightly on Mexico's civilian population. Indeed, to
some of President Polk's critics it seemed to be a war designed to hurt
the enemy as little as possible. From the outset, however, Polk had
made it clear that the fight was not against the Mexican people but only
against their rulers who had made a mockery of republicanism. Every
effort was to be made to conciliate the Mexican populace. Taylor was
furnished by the War Department with a proclamation, to be placed
before the citizens in the occupied areas, that blamed the war on the
"tyrants and usurpers" who controlled the government. "We come to
make no war upon the people of Mexico, nor upon any form of free
government they may choose to select for themselves. . . . We come
among the people of Mexico as friends and republican brethren." A
similar proclamation was issued by Scott on his march to Mexico City.
There was even a phrase for it. The Mexican War was to be a "war of
reconciliation."

The policy was reflected in the military governments established in
the larger towns and cities, America's first experience at governing a
foreign population. No clear program for administering the occupied
areas had been developed in advance, with the result that the American
military governments were often attended by uncertainty and confusion. Their jurisdiction in most instances extended only to American
military personnel, but in some cases the military officers that were
appointed moved beyond that sphere, helping the local governments to

maintain order, enforcing the decisions of the Mexican courts, improving street lighting and sanitation, and maintaining schools and hospitals. In Vera Cruz, General William Jenkins Worth as military governor distributed rations to civilians, established a fair scale of prices for food sold in the city, and paid "liberal" wages to Mexican laborers employed to clear the rubble from the streets. Winfield Scott made a point of interfering as little as possible with the workings of the Mexican civil administrations, beyond a proclamation of martial law for all offenses involving American personnel (an edict that was enforced against Americans and Mexicans alike), and he insisted on paying for all supplies required by his army. He adhered to this policy until late in the war when Polk, impatient with the delay in making peace, ordered him to exact contributions from the population to support the army. Mexican authorities guarded their independence from the military government and protested vehemently when they felt threatened.[22]

Reports from correspondents and soldiers in the field often dwelled on the beneficial aspects of the American presence in Mexico, satisfying many Americans that their war was a just and humane one. Stories of Mexican civilians, especially in the north, welcoming the advancing troops were told in detail. For the first time, it was said, Mexican villagers found political and economic stability, as well as protection from marauding Indians and bandits. In Monterey, the wealthy families appealed to the Americans to remain; when the military governor of Jalapa departed, he was honored by the citizens with a "handsome ball." Aided by the reopening of the ports and the replacement of the high Mexican tariff with modest tariff duties, commerce behind the American lines revived quickly. American goods entered Mexico duty-free and many American merchants opened stores in the occupied cities. Mexico's lower classes, for whose plight the volunteers expressed sympathy, were relieved of the oppressive levies that had been made by both the government and the Church. "Intercourse with our soldiers," one observer speculated, "inspired the descendants of Montezuma with a profound respect and warm affection for the American people."[23]

(4)   *Underlying brutality of troops*

Obviously not all the troops in Mexico behaved in so exemplary a fashion nor did all Mexicans welcome the invaders as the people back home preferred to believe. There was an uglier side to the war which cast no credit on the character of America's fighting men. At the same time, no effort was made to cover up the breaches of conduct; instead, they were often sensationalized, reported as widely as the less exciting stories of American kindness and generosity. Such episodes, however, were always viewed as exceptional; by condemning them quickly and forcefully, Americans reinforced their view that the war was indeed fought in a humane manner.

The warmth with which some of the soldiers were received in Mexico was balanced by a "cold civility" which others encountered. "We can get the service and property of these people for money," wrote an officer in Taylor's army, "but we have not got their good will." Most of the soldiers found the attitude understandable and accepted it, realizing that after all they were an invading enemy. Even where the men were befriended by Mexican families, they were seldom allowed to forget the barriers that existed between the two peoples. As many of them learned, just because some Mexicans opposed their own rulers did not automatically make them friends of the Americans. One well-educated middle-class citizen of Matamoros welcomed American soldiers into his house and entertained them with his family, but he always retained the aloofness of an enemy. As a devout Catholic, he was opposed to the priests, "as a republican opposed to all the recent military Governments, and as a patriot opposed to the Americans."

Mexican attitudes toward the invaders were molded to some extent by the Mexican press and by military and government leaders. The Americans were portrayed as "half savages" and "infidels who worship the devil." Fantastic tales of barbarity and superhuman strength were employed partly to explain the Mexican army's defeats but also to stiffen the resistance of the population. Stories of shiploads of Tampico's citizens being sent to New Orleans as slaves and of soldiers sticking small children on the points of their bayonets in Vera Cruz were circulated, and believed (all the more readily, it was thought, because Mexico's civilians had come to expect acts of cruelty from the military).[24]

Doubtless the stories had some foundation in the incidents of "ruffianism" that marked the behavior of American soldiers as well as in the more shocking (but thankfully more isolated) atrocities. "Scoundrelism exists to a large extent in the best constituted armies," wrote one regular soldier who saw no point in denying its existence among the Americans. Some of the behavior was dismissed as good-natured fun. "Jack would have his 'frolic,'" commented naval officer Raphael Semmes, after exuberant sailors following their capture of Tuxpán reeled through the streets helping themselves to "a glass of grog wherever they found it" and frightening the women with their "awkward love making." When troops lit campfires on the marble floors of country houses, stacked their muskets on rich carpeting, and reclined in their muddy clothing on velvet sofas, their behavior was shrugged off as but part of the hardships of war.[25]

If reports of regular army officers are to be believed, all the offenses committed against Mexican persons and property were committed by volunteers. There was no love lost between regulars and volunteers, and the comments of the former became so venomous as to cast doubt on their veracity. To the volunteers, it was charged, a state of war was a state of license. Matamoros was converted into a "theatre of drunkenness and brawls," property was destroyed, women insulted, and men mistreated. Young Lieutenant George G. Meade complained that volunteers acted more like hostile Indians than civilized whites, robbing the citizens, stealing their cattle, and on their drunken sprees killing innocent civilians "for no other object than their own amusement." The volunteers left destruction in their wake as Daniel Harvey Hill noted repeatedly in his diary: "The vile Volunteers had committed the usual excesses & the lovely town was in good part deserted."[26]

To the regulars, such reports confirmed the folly of using volunteer soldiers during wartime. By contrast they pointed out how well behaved the regulars were. The term *voluntario,* Meade wrote, inspired terror among the civilians whereas it was common to hear Mexicans in the streets "descanting on the good conduct of the *'tropas de ligna.'* ". Such attitudes did little to harmonize relations between the two groups. Volunteers reacted angrily to the accusations and charged that the stories were deliberately falsified in order to discredit them. They carried their indignation into their accounts of the war and continued to harbor resentment long afterward. Even some regulars believed the "outrages" had been much exaggerated.[27]

That the volunteers resented military discipline and often refused to be governed by it was well known. Indeed, many Americans believed that this was but further evidence of the free democratic spirit that prevailed in the United States. Disciplinary problems were most acute in Zachary Taylor's command, for the General was frequently accused of laxness in controlling his soldiers. If only a tenth of the horror stories were true, Winfield Scott reported, there was sufficient cause "to make Heaven weep, & every American, of Christian morals *blush* for his country." When Mexican authorities in Monterey complained of the behavior of the troops, Taylor responded simply by moving the units to new quarters outside the city, at the same time reminding the complainants of the "impossibility of maintaining rigid discipline" among volunteers. In contrast was Scott's strictly enforced martial-law policy. While his Tampico order caused no little consternation in the Polk administration, where the thought of subjecting free American voters to military restraint was disturbing, the policy did work what one writer termed an "entire revolution" in the behavior of the army. If Scott did not succeed in eliminating all incidents of violence between soldiers and civilians, he established an order and discipline unknown elsewhere.[28]

Breaches of discipline that resulted in acts of violence against the lives and property of Mexican civilians were usually confined to individuals or small groups of soldiers. Only rarely did large bodies of men engage in such acts and then only following the physical and emotional strain of battle. After Santa Anna, at the head of 4000 Mexican troops, failed to retake Puebla following a 28-day siege late in the war and withdrew as a relief column approached, the several hundred American defenders (mostly Pennsylvania volunteers) burst into the buildings that had harbored the Mexicans and plundered their contents, setting ablaze the bullring that had served as the Mexican camp. A more serious breakdown of discipline occurred in October 1847 when Santa Anna's troops fired upon advance units of General Joseph Lane's brigade (Indiana and Pennsylvania volunteers) in Huamantla, northeast of Puebla. Among those killed was the popular cavalry officer and former Texas Ranger Captain Samuel H. Walker, one of the heroes of the Mexican War. Walker's death triggered a wave of vengeance that sent the troops on a rampage of looting, destruction, murder, and rape. "All around me was desolation and ruin," groaned one Indianan.[29]

Many of the attacks by American soldiers against Mexican civilians were retaliatory in nature. An American soldier walking the dark streets of a Mexican town at night or staggering from one bar to another or lured by "false representations" into houses was easy prey. In Saltillo, a surgeon with the volunteers noted that "the assassination of our men was of daily occurrence." Following the battle of Buena Vista so many soldiers were killed by lasso-wielding Mexicans that General Wool issued an order condoning the shooting of any Mexican found in the city with a lasso or lariat, but the order was immediately rescinded. In Mexico City, Scott ordered his men not to leave their lodgings unless well armed and in large numbers. The volunteers had more subtle ways of halting the attacks. Armed with knives and revolvers, they feigned drunkenness and, when attacked, had little difficulty in turning the tables on their assailants. The number of assaults on American servicemen dropped considerably.[30]

Relations between American troops and Mexican civilians were further complicated by a rise in guerrilla activity as the war continued. Some routes connecting the armies with their supply depots were unsafe and supply trains were attacked with regularity, most notably on the roads from Monterey and Saltillo northward to the Rio Grande and from Vera Cruz to Mexico City. Guerrilla warfare was regarded as barbaric and uncivilized and orders were issued to deal with it harshly. "The guerilla system," declared Secretary of War William L. Marcy, "is hardly recognized as a legitimate mode of warfare, and should be met with the utmost allowable severity." The guerrillas, the feared "rancheros," proved an elusive and terrifying enemy. Their attacks often aroused feelings that went beyond retaliation, resulting sometimes in outbursts of indiscriminate and bloody revenge. Although both Marcy and Scott insisted that captured guerrillas be held as prisoners of war, the order was not always heeded.

In February 1847, as Santa Anna moved northward to meet the Americans at Buena Vista, bands of irregulars led by Antonio Canales threatened Taylor's supply lines to the Rio Grande. On the twenty-second, the guerrillas, joined by a unit of mounted lancers, ambushed a supply train bound from Camargo to Monterey, over one hundred wagons carrying provisions, ammunition, and specie, stretching for three miles along the road and guarded by an escort of fewer than thirty soldiers. Only a small number of the teamsters survived; the rest were slaughtered by the guerrillas, burned in their wagons, or killed as they fled into the chaparral, their bodies stripped and mutilated. The soldiers were taken prisoner. Weeks later the scene still remained to remind travelers of the carnage; one Cincinnati newspaper correspondent gazed in horror at the bodies strewn along the road and described his feelings in graphic detail. A passing group of volunteers, said to be Texas Rangers, determined to avenge the massacre, descended upon a nearby village and murdered up to forty of its inhabitants (the estimates varied). The action was strongly condemned in the United States, General Taylor "got his steam up," and an immediate inquiry was undertaken. The investigation, however, proved futile and was dropped.[31]

An even more widely publicized—and condemned—episode, also in February 1847, involved the Arkansas volunteer cavalry (known as "Rackensackers"). Employed as scouts and occupying advanced outposts the men had suffered more than others from guerrilla attacks. At the same time, they had the reputation of being a particularly undisciplined lot, "wild and reckless fellows, with the . . . firm belief that their own State could whip the world and Mexico in particular." When one of their number was found murdered, the Rackensackers had had enough. Swearing revenge, they overtook a group of Mexican peasants who had sought safety in the mountains and began an "indiscriminate and bloody massacre of the poor creatures." As many as thirty men, women, and children were murdered before a company of Illinois volunteers arrived on the scene and restrained the Arkansans. Generals Taylor and Wool were outraged. When the attempts to identify the guilty men failed, Taylor ordered two companies of the regiment back to the Rio Grande but withdrew the order when the battle of Buena Vista became imminent. Ironically, many of the same Arkansas cavalrymen fled the field early in the battle and took little part in the engagement.

The incident, reported in the United States, inspired an immediate reaction. One writer was astounded that men who professed to be Christians, "belonging to one of the most enlightened and civilized nations of the globe," could have carried out such a deed. "Let us no longer complain of Mexican barbarity." The episode was recounted in heart-rending and gory detail and even found its way into popular poetry.[32]

The reputation of the Texas Rangers for brutality against the Mexican population, however, was unmatched in popular perception, reflecting perhaps the low esteem in which Texans generally were held outside the Southwest. Already legendary in frontier lore, the Rangers were viewed as wild, dissolute men motivated by a lawless and vindictive spirit, not much better than the Mexican banditti and cutthroat rancheros they opposed. They were hardly the idealized individuals (defenders of the Alamo) celebrated by Walt Whitman:

> They were the glory of the race of rangers
> Matchless with horse, rifle, song, supper, courtship,
> Large, turbulent, generous, handsome, proud, and affectionate,
> Bearded, sunburnt, drest in the free costume of hunters,
> Not a single one over thirty years of age.

The descriptions by those who encountered them in Mexico were quite different. Armed to the teeth with rifle, pistols, and knives, they presented an awesome sight in their "uncouth" costume—buckskin shirts covered with grease and blood, skin caps, bright red flannels, and dust-covered trousers tucked into high boots. Their "bearded faces, lean and brawny forms, fierce wild eyes, and swaggering manners" gave them a "savage appearance." Superior marksmen, expert horsemen, contemptuous of discipline, their idea of fun was an "open prairie-fight with the untamable Camanches."

The Texas Rangers entered the war with a sworn hatred for Mexicans; some had suffered as prisoners in Mexico, and the war offered an opportunity to revenge themselves against their former captors. Their indiscriminate acts of murder and destruction against the Mexicans—called "Texan vengeance"—were strongly censured by other volunteers. The Rangers, wrote one shocked campaigner, "spare none, but shoot down every one they meet." The chaparral was said to be "strewed with the skeletons of Mexicans sacrificed by these desperadoes." The increase in guerrilla activity in northern Mexico was blamed directly on the Texans' disregard for civilian lives and property. General Taylor was appalled at their behavior, charging that they were "too licentious to do much good" but all his efforts to bring the Rangers under some form of discipline were unsuccessful.[33]

Disciplinary problems also resulted from the large number of individuals who moved with the army but who were beyond the reach of military authority. Some men who had been unable to join volunteer units because the quotas had been filled were nonetheless allowed to remain with the army as "amateur" soldiers; others who simply decided on their own to fight in Mexico without any authorization, were commonly known as "adventurers." While both groups were outside military control, they were allowed to draw rations and supplies from the quartermaster. They received no pay, provided their own transportation, and "did no soldiers duties except fight." Furthermore, a large number of so-called army followers flocked to Mexico and accompanied the troops—sutlers, printers and editors who set up newspapers, reporters, actors and circus-riders who entertained the soldiers, gamblers, speculators, and "certain frail but daring ones, *damas cortesanas,*" who ventured forth to face the "dangers of war." The army also employed civilian teamsters, both American and Mexican, and some of the discharged volunteers remained in Mexico to operate bars, restaurants, and hotels for the soldiers. There were moments when the army followers shouldered arms and took part in the fighting, and at least one irregular cavalry unit was organized from their numbers. Many of the "outrages" blamed on the volunteers were in fact committed by these outsiders.[34]

Little effort was made to conceal the "excesses" from public view, if indeed it would have been possible to do so. Swarms of newspaper correspondents combed the campaigns for stories and in the absence of any checks on the publication of war news they inevitably detailed the "outrages" as well as the deeds of heroism and gallantry. Although condemned by the public, the incidents hardly tarnished the belief that America was waging a humane war. The odium cast on the bad actors, a number of whom were to be found in any large aggregation of men, did not ultimately reflect upon "the arms of the republic."[35]

A First Victory

Although there were obvious handicaps in waging war with such a heterogeneous, largely untrained and undisciplined force, the decision to rely on volunteer soldiers in the war with Mexico was not surprising. Indeed, there was really no choice. While Americans had shown a fondness for military pomp and titles and for tales of heroism in battle, their fascination pertained to the citizen-soldier rather than to the professional fighting man. There was a built-in antimilitarism in popular American republicanism that argued against the maintenance of a professional army. As relations with Mexico worsened, over six months before the war was declared, President Polk reasserted America's traditional position:

> It has never been our policy to maintain large standing armies in time of peace. They are contrary to the genius of our free institutions, would impose heavy burdens on the people and be dangerous to public liberty. Our reliance for protection and defense on the land must be mainly on our citizen solders, who will be ever ready, as they ever have been ready in times past, to rush with alacrity, at the call of their country, to her defense.

Polk had already authorized General Taylor to accept a limited number of volunteers from states nearest the border in the event of "invasion or threatened invasion." That Polk came to view a larger regular army as desirable once the war had begun became evident from his support of a modest increase in regular strength in the war legislation of May 1846 and his later authorization of ten new regiments to serve for the duration of the war, but these actions did not signal any change in his basic attitude.[36]

It was the image of the citizen-soldier, the individual who turned from peaceful civilian pursuits to the defense of his country, that captivated the popular mind and confirmed the nation's republican mission. The image was all the more arresting because of the hostility that had flared against the institution that seemed to embody all the negative elements of a professional military force—the United States Military Academy at West Point. In an era of mass democracy and egalitarian aspirations, West Point became a symbol of aristocratic privilege, a potential threat to popular rule, producing "snobbish officers" for a "caste-ridden army." In the Jacksonian attack on monopoly, the Academy was singled out as one of the worst offenders, and repeated efforts were made in Congress to weaken it. The money required to support it, it was argued, would benefit the country more if applied to the "arts of peace" rather than to the "science of war."

As relations with England over Oregon, and with Mexico over Texas, worsened, however, the attacks subsided, and the army's defenders began to speak out. Following the outbreak of the Mexican War, the appeals for a stronger military force became more urgent. Edward Hunt, a professor at West Point writing in the *American Review*, hoped that the echoes of Palo Alto and Resaca de la Palma would silence the "clamor of detraction" that had been carried on by members of Congress, stump orators, and "editors of the slang-whanger school." War, he declared, was an evil of immense proportions, and Americans were morally bound to strive against its occurrence. But until war should disappear it behooved the nation to develop the most thorough and efficient military establishment.[37]

The popular distrust of the professional soldier and the resentment of the regulars against attacks on the military provided fertile ground for a bitter rivalry between volunteers and regulars during the war. The fact that many of the volunteers had either been Academy students or soldiers in the regular army did little to bridge the gulf between the two groups. There were sparks from the very beginning.

To the volunteers the military profession was dehumanizing, its discipline incompatible with democratic freedom and individualism. The regular soldier was little more than a "drilled automaton," a "moving and musket-holding *machine*" whose mentality was limited by "the Tactics and Army Regulations." While the volunteers had been bred to freedom, the regulars were trained to obedience. Unmoved by patriotism, the latter fought because war was their profession, they were simply practicing their vocation. There was a feeling of superiority over the regulars which the volunteers never hesitated to express. When an Indiana regiment was provided with the same blue uniforms as those worn by the regulars, one Hoosier balked: "I'll be blowed if they make a regular of me."

One of the most severe indictments of the regular soldier came from the pen of George C. Furber, a young Tennessee attorney who joined a volunteer cavalry regiment early in the war. Furber was baffled that any man of intelligence could be induced to enlist in the regular army, for a regular soldier required only "so much brains" as would enable him to stand erect, keep his clothing clean, understand the commands, and handle a musket. Beyond this, he needed only enough language to ask for his "eatables" and, when out of the hearing of the officers, "to swear freely." The pay was poor, the prospect for promotion virtually hopeless. There was no reward for this grim existence, Furber believed, unless it be the fact that soldiers were fed and clothed "without thought or care to themselves."[38]

The regulars responded in kind. Derisively labeling the volunteers "Mustangs" or "Mohawks" or the "Continental Army," regular officers angrily rejected the popular romantic image of the volunteers and the tendency to credit them with the war's victories. "If the brave volunteers should all run at the first fire," protested a cynical young lieutenant, "they will nevertheless come out heroes." The volunteers didn't know the butt of a musket from its muzzle. "They are useless, useless, useless,—expensive, wasteful—good for nothing." When the young George B. McClellan, fresh out of West Point and full of conceit, arrived on the Rio Grande he suffered the momentary indignity of being ranked by a "confounded Voluntario . . . a miserable thing with buttons on it."[39]

If the volunteers reflected the national character and the superiority of republican institutions, thought the regulars, then woe unto the nation's future. But it was precisely because the volunteers were so thoroughly American that the English adventurer George Frederick Ruxton found them wanting. Ruxton's observations reinforced his anti-American feelings and his distrust of democracy. "The American can never be made a soldier," he wrote. "His constitution will not bear the restraint of discipline, neither will his very mistaken notions about liberty allow him to subject himself to its necessary control." America's use of the volunteer system proved the impossibility of building an effective military force in a country where the lower classes are free of society's restraints. Ruxton's criticisms, however, applied equally to the regular service, where he noted that the inducements for enlistment were so poor that only the indolent and those of bad character could be attracted. The United States, he believed, was saved from military disaster only by the fact that the ranks of its regular army were filled mostly by foreigners, Germans, English, and Irish.[40]

Some regulars expressed concern that the volunteers' ignorance of military organization would have serious consequences in camp and on the march. Henry W. Halleck, author of a textbook on military science, warned that the use of volunteers would "necessarily be attended with an immense sacrifice of human life." Battle casualties were not his only worry. Knowing little of camp discipline and cleanliness, sanitation, and proper diet, they would be more susceptible to disease than the regulars. Halleck was not the only one to express concern. Winfield Scott made the point in telling fashion in a letter to the Secretary of War as he was preparing for the assault on Vera Cruz:

> A regiment of regulars, in 15 minutes from the evening halt, will have tents pitched & trenched around, besides straw, leaves or bushes for dry sleeping; arms & ammunition well secured & in order for any night attack; fires made, kettles boiling, in order to [have] wholesome cooking; all the men dried, or warmed, & at their comfortable supper, merry as crickets, before the end of the first hour . . . Volunteers neglect all these points; eat their *salt* meat raw (if they have saved any at all) or, worse than raw, *fried*— death to any Christian man the fifth day; lose or waste their clothing; lie down wet, or on wet ground—fatal to health, &, in a short time to life; leave arms & ammunition exposed to rain, mud & dews . . . In a short time the ranks are thinned, the baggage wagons & hospitals filled with the sick, & acres of ground with the graves of the dead!

The concern for the volunteers was confirmed by the casualty figures. Over six thousand died from disease and exposure, about ten times the number killed in action. Even McClellan was alarmed at the suffering of the volunteers: "They literally die like dogs." At the same time, the confidence in the regulars expressed by Scott does not seem to have been well placed, for their ranks were depleted by disease as well. Although figures vary, a higher percentage of regulars apparently succumbed to disease than did volunteers.[41]

One of the most objectionable features of the volunteer system was the practice of electing officers. Elections became political or popularity contests (indeed they often were simply extensions of the political rivalry back home) and individuals who had neither knowledge nor qualification were elevated to positions of responsibility. The officers knew that at the end of their enlistments they would again be the equals and companions of the men under their command and consequently dared not exercise a tight disciplinary control over them. Command of a volunteer unit was often a ticket to political office, so the officers who harbored political ambitions were careful to remain popular with their men. Some efforts were made to overcome their ignorance of military life by establishing "schools of instruction" at various localities in Mexico, a kind of basic training commanded by regular officers. The training of volunteers in drill and infantry tactics seemed a hopeless task to most. "A more heterogeneous, undisciplined compound of material called soldiers," wrote one officer, "never before was brought together in any Army."[42]

A number of critics protested that it was not only wrong but dangerous to wage a foreign war with such material. Volunteers were useful in a support capacity but, it was said, had no business on the battlefield.

The view was shared by the army's top commanders. "Volunteers," wrote Zachary Taylor, "were never intended to invade or carry on war out of the limits of their own country." Winfield Scott tried unsuccessfully to have only regulars assigned to his expeditionary force against Vera Cruz and Mexico City. The volunteers felt they were deliberately being relegated to inactive garrison duty and kept out of action, charging that it was all part of a plot to crush the volunteer system and secure an expanded regular army. Resentment ran deep among the regiments camped on the Rio Grande as they observed company after company of regulars sent forward to meet the enemy. Left behind "to be the victims of disease and death," some units threatened mass desertion if they were not sent into action. An irate Indianan, whose regiment spent virtually the entire war camped on the Rio Grande, warned Taylor that the volunteers "are not the serfs of a plantation who adore the lord of the soil and crouch at his command." As Taylor's candidacy for the Presidency began to build, he cautioned the general to treat the volunteers with greater respect and fairness if he expected their votes.[43]

Bad feeling between the volunteers and the regulars persisted throughout the war, but in the general praise that was directed toward the military achievements in Mexico the distinction between them was often blurred. The victories belonged solely to neither group, and the more perceptive observers saw the results as an example of democracy's ability to coordinate regulars and volunteers in a single cause. The ultimate recognition of this union was the selection of Alexander Doniphan as a member of West Point's Board of Visitors and his invitation to address the cadets in June 1848. Doniphan had been elected Colonel of the First Missouri Mounted Volunteers soon after enlisting as a private. He became not only one of the war's truly romantic heroes but also a symbol of the citizen-soldier's courage and hardihood. His celebrated march through northern Mexico over barren and inhospitable terrain, cut off from supply, fighting several victorious engagements and experiencing considerable hardship, became legendary in the lore of the Mexican War. While his appearance at West Point raised some eyebrows, he reflected none of the volunteers' disdain for the regular army, emphasizing instead the importance of West Point's educational mission.[44]

There is no doubt that the Mexican War enhanced the prestige of the Military Academy and confirmed its value to the nation. It was West Point's first war, the first to be fought by the United States in which large numbers of graduates took part. That the Academy acquitted itself well, all agreed. Its usefulness, "in the hour of our country's danger," had been proved and the question of its permanence was "settled for ever." In his eulogy of the Academy, Edward D. Mansfield, himself a graduate, emphasized West Point's role in fostering the independence of the American mind from dependence upon Europe. Its success as an educational institution, placing its graduates in civilian as well as military roles, had amply repaid its cost. "The *Independence* of our country consists in the *Independence of its Minds*," Mansfield declared. By sending forth individuals trained in discipline and intelligence, familiar with the highest civilization and equal to any emergencies, the academy had strengthened the republic. "It is MIND which gives success to an Army, strength to a Nation, and perpetuity to a Government." To commemorate its contribution to the Mexican War, the "triumphs of our arms" on the fields of Mexico were chiselled into the rocky cliffs near West Point, a reminder "in the beauty and charming wildness of its romantic scenery" of the Academy's role as a "nursery of heroes."

The highest tribute to America's fighting force, both volunteers and regulars, would be a "proper history" of the war, suggested the *Southern Literary Messenger*. Lacking that, the writer returned briefly to the question of how to explain the "extraordinary facility" with which masses of untrained citizens were converted into an effective force. He found three explanations: that the physical standards of "soldiership" were more easily attained in America than anywhere else; that the "spirit of man" was more generally infused into the population; and finally—and the explanation he preferred—that the officers had been more skillful in uniting science and art with military affairs than had ever been done before. For this, West Point was responsible.[45]

CHAPTER 3

The True Spirit of Patriot Virtue

symbols: flag music eagle (handwritten)

Meaning of True Patriotism (handwritten)

Commenting on the victories at Palo Alto and Resaca de la Palma, a Baltimore paper argued that the battles proved there was "something in the American soldier—something in the cause he espouses—something in the name he bears and the country he defends, which makes him more than an equal for any common foe." Another writer identified that "something" as a "much higher degree of patriotism" than any other people had ever exhibited. It became a familiar refrain: the great advantage enjoyed by America's fighting men over their Mexican foes was their superior devotion to cause and country, their patriotism.[1]

Patriotism, then as now, was one of those words more used than understood, employed so often and so loosely that it tended to lose its meaning, or more accurately, assumed many meanings. At the same time, it was a concept intimately connected with America's search for identity as a nation and as a republic. Thus it became an essential element in both American nationalism and the republican ideology that justified that nationalism. Merle Curti has defined patriotism as "love of country, pride in it, and readiness to make sacrifices for what is considered its best interest," linking it with both nationalism and republicanism in a way that would have satisfied mid-19th-century Americans. Curti's definition mirrored the more cryptic meaning assigned by Noah Webster in the 1845 edition of his *American Dictionary of the English Language:* "Love of one's country; the passion which aims to serve one's country."[2]

For years patriotism provided the theme for Fourth of July orations, political speeches, learned addresses, and sermons. The nature of patriotism and the duties it imposed upon Americans had been examined, dissected, and exhorted by orators, scholars, politicians, prea-

land = manifest destiny (handwritten)

45

chers, editors, and writers of school texts long before the confrontation with Mexico on the Rio Grande. But it was war—as Curti suggests—that became the significant test of national loyalty, the catalyst that gave point to all the sermonizing. Patriotism, observed Charles Lanman in 1848, "generally lies dormant in the 'piping times of peace,' and is developed only at epochs of national danger or distress." It is not surprising that the 1840s, a decade marked by the threat of war with Great Britain and the reality of war with Mexico, should have witnessed a rising crescendo of patriotic fervor as well as a serious examination of the meaning of patriotism to America's burgeoning nationalism. One journal in fact argued that it was precisely the "cheap popularity of professing patriotism" that encouraged the "rashness" of the government in carrying the nation to the brink of war with Britain and over the edge with Mexico.[3]

With the Mexican War, patriotism left the realm of abstraction and assumed a practical importance that left its meaning more muddled than ever. The word, and presumably the sentiment, was tied to the enthusiasm that followed the outbreak of the conflict. Support of the war (enlistment as a volunteer was even better) became that popular test of one's patriotism. Nurtured on patriotism in their schoolbooks and in the children's literature to which they had been exposed, the volunteers not surprisingly attributed their enlistments to lofty patriotic ideals. "I am engaged in the Service of my country from a love of . . . [her] institutions," wrote a young Kentuckian, "and I shall endeavor by my example to make that service promotive of her real honor & true glory." Another, not yet eighteen, was turned back when he attempted to volunteer; he went to Mexico anyway and was eventually accepted into a volunteer unit. His "young and patriotic heart" had been fired because he had heard that the nation's soil "was desecrated by an impious foeman's tread." The soldiers were lauded for their sacrifice of home and family for the dangers of the battlefield, and when some of them also paid the supreme sacrifice it was said that their patriotism was glorious indeed, a shining example to all their countrymen. One of the books the soldiers carried with them to Mexico was John E. Lovell's elocution text, *The United States Speaker,* containing "patriotic speeches about the defence of one's country [and] the sacred rights of one's own land." Passed from hand to hand in the camps, the book further strengthened notions of patriotism in the soldiers' minds. To one cynical officer, the book helped only to explain the fierceness of Mexican resistance. The fire of selfless devotion to the nation, however, did not always burn so brightly, and patriotism itself was sometimes a transitory thing. Praised for their patriotism when they marched off to war, the volunteers were denounced for their lack of it when they preferred discharge to re-enlistment. Scott's army was stalled for weeks in Jalapa, on the invasion route to Mexico City, when the twelve-month volunteers chose to go home. Having just fought the battle of Cerro Gordo they had glory enough and needed no more.[4]

"True patriotism," wrote Lanman following the war, "is a noble virtue, although it has a name which is nearly worn threadbare." Undaunted by its "threadbare" nature, however, scholars, clergymen, and literary figures probed the meaning of "true patriotism" in a period that seemed threatened not only by international crisis and war but also by a rampant materialism that dulled the citizen's sense of obligation to his country. The republic, it was felt, was in danger of being put off its track by what Philadelphia clergyman, poet, and academic George Washington Bethune termed a "narrow, unthankful spirit" that brooded over its imperfections and sighed after greater material advantages. The true spirit of patriotism, he believed, was in decay, a condition he attributed to the vastness of the nation, the unprecedented prosperity, and the "licentiousness" of party rivalries. In a republic, where the people are the only sovereign, patriotism was less easily grasped, more abstract, and hence more difficult to maintain than in a centralized system where the ruler is a "visible, tangible object." Patriotism, the loyalty bred by love of country was nontheless important in a republic, for it was patriotism that balanced the centrifugal forces unique to republics and prevented the nation from flying apart in a "chaos of fragments wild, jostling, and mutually destructive."[5]

Like Bethune, New England scholar George Perkins Marsh felt that America's diversity, the plethora of local interests and the divided loyalties fostered by the federal system actually handicapped the development of a true patriotism. Without "dim traditions" and "hoary fables" and a popular reverence for a "glorious past," Americans lacked those elements that unified and strengthened love of country. Patriotism, Marsh insisted, was a "less tenacious impluse" in a republic and therefore all the more in need of constant nurture. For Dartmouth College professor Charles B. Haddock the task of nurturing a genuine patriotism belonged first to the nation's scholars, who were best equipped by their perspective and understanding of the past to protect society from its own rash impulses and to give sobriety to the public judgment. Orestes Brownson, with customary petulance, dismissed all the speculation with the observation that the United States was too young, its population "too recent, too floating, too little fixed to any particular locality" to be capable of a true patriotism. The outspoken editor announced his distrust of any American "who makes loud pretensions to love of country." Brownson's was a minority judgment.[6]

It was clear to midcentury Americans that patriotism was an essential prop to republicanism. Without a "generous patriotism," Marsh had said, there could be no "private virtue." At the same time they were aware that patriotism was all the more difficult to maintain because of the very nature of the republicanism it supported. If the circumstances of American history and geography seemed to rule out a strong attachment to place, in a country where the republican system provided no visible centralized object toward which patriotic sentiment could be directed, then patriotism, like the United States, must assume a unique form—that of loyalty to a principle. "A man's country is not a certain area of land, of mountains, rivers, and woods," New England thinker George William Curtis declared, "but it is a principle: and patriotism is loyalty to that principle." Patriotism to an American "is simply fidelity to the American idea." Boston's well-known Unitarian minister and one of the most popular lyceum lecturers of the time, Thomas Starr King, placed American patriotism within the context of an American romanticism. Every nation, he believed, had a "representative value," and true patriotism "is pledged to *the idea* which one's native country represents." The patriot "must express the genius of his land in miniature." In America, he stated, each citizen down to the lowliest individual was touched by it and each in turn, by sharing in the mission of the American people, experienced an "enlargement of his being" as a consequence. In a land where the people were the rulers, patriotism became all the more vital to the survival of the nation itself.[7]

This view, linking the concern for a stronger if not purer republicanism with the tenets of popular romanticism, most appealed to the Mexican War generation. To many, perhaps most, Americans, loyalty to the "American idea" required a support of the war, for the war was being fought to promote and strengthen the principle for which America stood. To others, like the New England pacifist Edwin H. Chapin, patriotism demanded opposition to the war, for it was the "wrong method" for achieving the same end. For each group, the conflict with Mexico was a test of patriotism but it was the collective voice of the former that proved the louder and more persistent.

Patriotism, commented the *American Literary Magazine* midway through the war, was rooted in the Americans' love of liberty. Its expression was instinctive, a product of the heart instead of the head and of the memory of America's own struggle for independence. No matter how much it might be put aside or be pushed into the background by more selfish pursuits, the love of country "springs into phrenzy at the approach of peril." Four years before the war began, Haddock outlined the responsibilities of the "patriot citizen." Among them was support of the republic in time of war. "You may be summoned to fight your country's battles," he told a New Hampshire audience. "If so, you may not refuse to die. . . . Dear as life justly is, there are occasions, on which the sacrifice of it is a duty. Patriot soldiers, in our own annals, show you how to conquer, and how to die." It is not certain that Haddock would have applied his admonition to the Mexican War, but it was typical of patriotic oratory on the eve of the war, and its sentiments were echoed after the fighting had begun. Patriotism and the responsibilities of a citizen of the republic were merged, as in the statement of one journalist only a month after news of the first battles had reached the Northeast: "One of the highest tests of a good citizen, is the readiness or reluctance with which he yields his personal liberty, and the good or ill grace with which he submits to the restraints of discipline, when at his country's call, he leaves his private pursuits and enters the field to fulfill the highest obligation a citizen owes his country."[8]

The serious inquiries of men like Bethune, Haddock, Marsh, and King into the nature of patriotism in republican America contrasted sharply with the boastful exuberance and rhetorical flourishes that characterized the popular use of patriotism in the latter 1840s. Yet each level of expression shared more than might have appeared at first glance. Both rested on a common perception of America's uniqueness and of its peculiar "genius"; both agreed on the principle that defined America and gave meaning to its mission. And both held firmly to the conviction that behind the principle and the patriotism it inspired was the guiding hand of Providence that united all Americans with God's plan for the world.

Patriotism and Providence were closely linked in the 19th-century mind by the belief that the United States was God's favored nation, its inhabitants God's favored people. Because God had willed America's progress, its progress was foreordained. Americans saw God's agency in virtually everything that took place. "Following the guidance of Providence," wrote essayist Edwin P. Whipple, "we had no chance-work . . . There was a motive, a purpose, an end in every thing." This belief, he stated, "is the most general, pervasive, ineradicable feeling in the hearts of our countrymen." The deepest feeling in the American heart, another writer declared, "springs from a conviction that Providence had presided over the . . . progress of this country." It was providential guidance that awakened in Americans their unique capacity for building "a fabric of civilization," and it was providential guidance that "has given us our best institutions, and, above all, created a spirit in our country that has signalized itself in education, philanthropy, and patriotism." Whipple was not prepared to recognize the "doctrine of a Providence in human affairs" in what was termed Manifest Destiny, that "tempestuously-furious patriot," but if Whipple was not, there were many others who were.

The cause of liberty and democracy, the "American idea," was God's cause and, as so many Americans pointed out, it was the United States that was charged with bringing to fruition God's plan for all mankind. This was the object to which all true patriotism tended. The idea of a guiding and protecting Providence, a recent scholar has suggested, "was *characteristic* of American patriotism." All those who analyzed the quality of patriotism, from Bethune to Whipple, rested their cases ultimately on God's will. Similarly, the expressions of popular patriotism, which Whipple demeaned as "plentifully bedizened with metaphors of . . . [the] stars and stripes," the "all-for-glory" patriotism, assumed the existence and significance of God's guiding hand.[9]

On June 1, 1846, in a field outside Matamoros, Captain R. A. Stewart, Methodist clergyman, sugar planter, and commander of a company of Louisiana volunteers, delivered what purported to be the first sermon preached on Mexican soil by an American minister. Stewart's remarks were directed to the "sunburnt veterans" in his congregation who only three weeks before had fought the war's first battles. His text was taken from the book of Jeremiah, vii, verses 6 and 7: "If you do not oppress the alien, the fatherless or the widow, or shed innocent blood in this place, and if you do not go after other gods to your own hurt, Then I will let you dwell in this place, in the land that I gave of old to your fathers for ever."

Stewart began by reminding his listeners of the "beautiful spectacle" that was being shown to the world by their presence, a conquering army extending its laws, "more benign, more liberal, more protecting" than those of the country they displaced. Their mission was to "shed light over the dark borders of Tamaulipas," to enable its inhabitants to embrace "the blessings of freedom" and to reveal to them "the degradations of their own government." All this, he pointed out, was the "order of Providence," for God intended the Anglo-Saxon race not only to take possession of all North America but also to "influence and modify" the character of the entire world. The American people, "passive instruments" in the hands of an overruling Providence, were the "children of destiny." Stewart concluded with an "eloquent burst of patriotism" in which he reminded all that it was the Christian duty of every American to stand by the country and to support it "so long as a single foe remained in arms against her." According to one observer, the soldiers greeted his sermon with "deep, silent, powerfully-suppressed feeling."[10]

It was not happenstance that America's fighting men were thought to be endowed with a superior patriotism, for it had been willed by God. The fact of victory was proof enough that Americans were inspired by a patriotic ardor that surpassed other peoples. The Mexican War was seen as a further revelation of God's benign guidance of republican America.

Among those whose emotions were stirred by the mass demonstrations that followed the victories in Mexico was the young editor of the Brooklyn *Eagle*. "There is hardly a more admirable impulse in the human soul," wrote Walt Whitman, "than *patriotism*." The large gatherings swelled his admiration for " 'the common people,' who form the great bulk and strength of the state," and convinced him that the Mexican War was a great democratic mission. Like most Americans, Whitman deplored war's "evil moral effects" and argued that military superiority by itself was no sign of national greatness. The triumphs in Mexico, however, "must elevate the *true* self-respect of the American people" to a point commensurate with "such a great nation as ours really is." He was thoroughly caught up in the patriotic fervor. "Cold must be the pulse, and throbless to all good thoughts . . . which cannot respond to the valorous emprise of our soldiers and commanders in Mexico." No "true American," he felt, could resist "this pride in our victorious armies."[11]

The patriotism Whitman admired in the common people was reflected in those who were fighting in Mexico. Many of the soldiers were convinced that they were instruments of an overruling Providence. "God had a work . . . to be accomplished," wrote one volunteer, and the war was His plan for achieving it. A company of German volunteers, about to leave St. Louis, was exhorted to "spread truth, liberty and light" in Mexico by an army chaplain who hoped to see Mexico "whipped into wisdom, justice, and good behavior." It was God's will that it be done. For some the war assumed the character of a latter-day crusade. Indeed, one popular writer dubbed it "The Crusade of the Nineteenth Century" and the soldiers "the army of the New Crusade."[12]

Obviously not all the men who fought the Mexican War shared these patriotic impulses, but enough of them did, or said they did, to give credence to the popular perception of the war as an important episode in the American quest for national identity. All "scruples of conscience," party feelings, and sectional interests, declared an optimistic Tennessee volunteer, were swept away by a mightier issue, as justice, pride, and patriotism demanded that every American sustain his country. John Hughes, one of Doniphan's Missouri volunteers, reported that "there was a *national* feeling" in the army; every soldier thought of himself as "a citizen of the MODEL REPUBLIC." Writing home to his family, a veteran of the hard fighting in Monterey described the pride he now felt in his country and its institutions, then added: "We think more of these subjects here than you do at home."

When young Indiana volunteer Frank Scribner observed his twenty-first birthday in Matamoros in September 1846, he paused to reflect on what it meant to be an American. He had reached the age of political responsibility and, as he felt all should do who reach that age, he sought to understand and appreciate the "genius" of his country and the "high and glorious privileges" it bestowed upon its citizens. Freedom of thought and the right to share in the nation's governance placed Americans above all other peoples and secured blessings that were not enjoyed "by any other nation under heaven." Pride and patriotism, he wrote, "account for this day finding me a soldier upon the borders of Mexico."[13]

The symbols of American nationhood were the tangible representations of the principle to which the fighting-men owed their patriotism, and like patriotism itself the symbols played a uniquely significant role in fostering American nationalism. National symbols were slower to develop in a republic than under more absolute forms of government, primarily because they evolved out of popular belief and expression—a "folk product," as Ralph Gabriel suggested—rather than being imposed from above. By the 1840s America's national symbols were just beginning to achieve the sanctification that came with the maturation of American nationalism, and the Mexican War was the first national conflict in which they played an important part. The soldiers, like their countrymen back home, saw in their symbols—the flag, the bald eagle, the national songs—objective representations of the nation's democratic faith. To some, they were visible demonstrations of the power of American's destiny and mission, as to the soldier who saw in the planting of the flag on the banks of the Rio Grande a "silent but impressive" proclamation that the "Area of Freedom" had been extended. To others, the symbols conjured a variety of sentimental associations, evoking thoughts of the land, of home, and of family. As objects of reverence and devotion, they even (as some campaign accounts testified) stirred the soldiers to greater feats of courage on the battlefield. The responses were always highly emotional; it was a romantic time and the men felt no embarrassment in recording their feelings.[14]

Of all the symbols, it was the flag—the Stars and Stripes—that was the most inspirational. Its military use was fairly new, for it was not until 1834 that army regulations first specified the flag's design and proclaimed it the official banner of the armed forces. The Mexican War was the first war in which American soldiers fought under the Stars and Stripes; in earlier engagements the troops had followed their various regimental and unit flags. Flag presentations became important ceremonies as the volunteers prepared to leave for Mexico, for it was the flag that not only inspired the men with patriotism but also linked the soldiers with their home communities. The flag became an ever-present reminder of the responsibilities the volunteers carried upon their shoulders. In the first flush of war excitement in May 1846, a popular actress in a New York theatre interrupted her performance to present a flag to a company of volunteers in the audience. "With feelings of true American pride," declared Julia Dean, "I present you this sacred symbol of our country, and enjoin upon you, wherever destiny may lead it in your hands, to keep untarnished its every stripe, undimmed its every star."

To carry the national flag into battle on a staff (or, as one Mississippi volunteer did, attached to the back of his uniform), to be the first to raise it over Monterey or atop Cerro Gordo or from the battlements of Chapultepec, was an honor for which both regulars and volunteers vied. The rivalry among branches of the service and among state regiments was frequently bitter and where conditions permitted was often settled by compromise, as when a soldier and a sailor jointly raised the flag over the Mexican fortress of San Juan de Ulloa. To the volunteers, the honor was especially dear for it mingled national pride with state loyalty and proved the patriotism of the citizen-soldier.

The first American flag in Monterey, according to one report, was carried by Baltimore's battalion but the claim was disputed by others. In the height of the battle, amid the smoke and din, as the soldiers fought desperately through the streets and from building to building, a Baltimore volunteer thrilled at the sight of the "glorious stars and stripes." Despite the carnage that surrounded him, he wrote, "a thrill of pleasure shot through me and I felt as if I could die." One officer, observing the battle from a height overlooking Monterey, suddenly caught sight of the flag: "A glow of honest pride lit up my face, and I thanked God I was an American, and that he had endowed my own country with so much to love and venerate." Another, standing on the same vantage point, was reminded of America's earlier struggle, when he viewed "that most beautiful of all flags, its colors dyed in the blood of our fore-fathers, and re-dyed in that of their sons."[15]

The sight of the national flag as it was "flung out to the breeze" over Vera Cruz in March 1847 or raised atop the National Palace in Mexico City later in the year was exhilarating to the battle-weary volunteers. When the Stars and Stripes at last flew over the fabled "halls of the Montezumas," a 19-year old Pennsylvania volunteer jotted in his diary: "It is a proud and gratifying sight to us poor, used up boys, who have left home and country and every thing dear, to witness this sight."[16]

Enhancing the symbolism of the flag was the music that almost invariably accompanied it. No military unit, volunteer or regular, was without its brass band; by the 1840s, a band was regarded as essential to military life. It became a part of daily routine, was required for ceremonial occasions, offered entertainment to the soldiers, and not infrequently urged the troops on in battle. The band's lively strains drove away "all melancholy thoughts," diverted the attention of soldiers on the march, and brought thoughts of home in the evening hours. Most important as symbols of national patriotism were the so-called "national airs." *The Star-Spangled Banner*, although played with increasing frequency in Mexico, was not the most popular of the national songs. Its acceptance by Americans was slow during the first half of the 19th-century, and it was not until the Civil War that it became the country's unofficial national anthem. More popular was the spirited *Hail, Columbia!*, written in 1798 by a Philadelphia lawyer and played so frequently on ceremonial occasions that many people believed it to be America's anthem. Neither song, however, could match *Yankee Doodle* for popular acceptance as America's foremost national air.

All three tunes were often played together to commemorate America's moments of glory and to remind the soldiers of their obligations to sustain that glory. When the fleet of troopships and men-of-war gathered at Anton Lizardo off Mexico's coast in preparation for the landing of Scott's army at Vera Cruz, the bands of the different regiments played the three national airs from shipboard. Later, as the men clambered into the surfboats and as the boats pulled toward the beach, the regimental bands played *Yankee Doodle* and *Hail, Columbia!* Then in the final moment of triumph, as the soldiers waded through the surf and planted the Stars and Stripes in the sand, the bands struck up the *Star-Spangled Banner* in unison. As the notes carried across the water in the warm evening air, there were few soldiers who did not experience the thrill or appreciate the importance of their landing on the Mexican shore.[17]

No song was more popular among the American soldiers in Mexico than *Yankee Doodle* and no tune was so effective in arousing thoughts of home and country. Perhaps it was the song's association with the American Revolution, with which the Mexican War was so frequently linked. Or perhaps it was *Yankee Doodle*'s identification with the spirit of young, inexperienced and undisciplined volunteers. Whatever it was, there is no doubt that *Yankee Doodle* had become America's most widely sung national air by the 1840s.

Yankee Doodle, as one volunteer remarked, was "the Americans' 'fightin' tune," played in battle by musicians who risked life and limb to arouse the fervor of their units and who often suffered casualties for their pains. It was played as the men of Scott's army neared the Mexican shore at Vera Cruz, when "every one's face paled with excitement" and "pure unadulterated patriotism flowed at every pulse." When Doniphan's Missourians marched into Chihuahua their band played *Hail, Columbia!,* but as they reached the public square *Yankee Doodle* celebrated the occasion. The effect of the song was described by an army correspondent at the occupation of Matamoros, the first Mexican town to be entered by the Americans, when the notes of *Yankee Doodle* suddenly burst forth. Writing to the *Spirit of the Times,* he asked,

> Did you ever hear it, Mr. "Spirit?" I reckon you never did, in a foreign land, just conquered, by good, honest, hard blows! If you did, you never heard such an honest cheer as arose from the gallant fellows on the opposite bank, when the drum and fife gave us that air, which fills, at all times, an American's breast with the purest patriotism! All was excitement, and every one boiling over with "amor patriae"!

The effect was repeated at Monterey, at Buena Vista and on countless similar occasions throughout the war. When the fighting ceased, it continued to evoke an electrifying response as the soldiers marched to its notes on their way home. Nor was the effect limited to the Americans. When soldiers attending a musical performance at Mexico City's Teatro de Santa Anna called for *Yankee Doodle,* the Mexican orchestra obliged. The song ran through the audience "like an electric shock," and one Mexican civilian commented, "It is no longer a source of surprise to me that we have been so easily conquered."[18]

To say that *Yankee Doodle* won the war for the United States would obviously stretch credibility. Nonetheless, it is clear that America's national symbols were important to the morale of the fighting men and on some occasions inspired the soldiers to victory. Perhaps the most celebrated incident was that reported by Doniphan's Missouri volunteers. Deep inside Mexico, cut off from the rest of the army, the men formed their ranks and prepared to meet the attack of a superior (in numbers) Mexican force at the battle of Sacramento, near Chihuahua. From out of the sky, a large bald eagle suddenly swooped and began circling the field, slowly and majestically. It was immediately recognized as "America's bird," and the words "an omen, an omen" passed from one soldier to another. Forgetting that the eagle was also Mexico's national bird, the volunteers viewed it as a herald of victory. Inspired, Doniphan's outnumbered Missourians drove the Mexicans from the field. To some of the men, the eagle heralded more than victory; it was symbolic of their larger mission as well. "The American eagle seemed to spread his broad pinions," wrote volunteer John T. Hughes, "and westward bear the principles of republican government."[19]

State Pride

The flag, the national airs, the eagle, were reminders of America's past, and it was that past, brief as it was, that lent impetus to the patriotism of both the soldiers in Mexico and those who remained behind. The republic was fresh and young, the story of its beginnings firmly embedded in the national consciousness and inseparably linked with notions of mission and destiny. To Americans in the 1840s the seventy years since the Declaration of Independence proclaimed freedom for mankind represented a new direction in world history. Endowed at birth with a providential design, Americans believed that they "had inaugurated a new time scale."[20] History, like the age, now belonged to the "model republic." While many Americans were convinced that their war with Mexico was unique in the history of the world, they went no further back than the origins of the republic to find meaning in the conflict. It was America's past that gave sanction to the present.

As sources of patriotic ardor, the episodes and heroes of American history assumed significant dimension in the 1840s. Nurtured on tales of America's glory, the soldiers often saw themselves as links between past and future, as actors in a continuing drama that would demonstrate to a doubting world the validity of republican principles. They were remarkably aware of the nation's achievements (a tribute to the quality of the educational system) and anxious that their own not suffer by comparison, anxious that they might at least come up to the mark set by their predecessors.

The last war Americans had fought (not counting the little-known campaigns against the Seminoles) had been the second conflict with Great Britain; consequently it was the War of 1812 that invited comparison with the Mexican War. Indeed, the participation of Zachary

Taylor, John E. Wool, and Winfield Scott provided continuity between the two contests. The popularity of military history which the Mexican War stimulated prompted a number of writers to reexamine America's Second War for Independence. Pennsylvania Congressman Charles Jared Ingersoll bracketed the Mexican conflict with the publication of his two-volume "historical sketch" of the War of 1812, while the popular writer Charles J. Peterson issued *The Military Heroes of the War of 1812* (dedicated to Major-General Winfield Scott) as a companion piece to his similar work on the Mexican War. There were problems with the War of 1812, however, as Peterson conceded, for the war furnished little "to gratify the military annalist" until its close.[21]

No writer needed to remind the American public that the greatest act of that war came at its end and that it was the deed of Andrew Jackson. Only thirty-one years separated the Battle of New Orleans from the opening of the Mexican contest; during that time, the day of the battle—January 8—had become one of America's sacred anniversaries, observed with almost as much ceremony as the Fourth of July. It was, Vice President Dallas had said in 1845, "mingled indissolubly with the thought of the country." The battle and its victor assumed a symbolic importance that provided a strong emotional tie between the volunteers of 1846 and those of 1815 for the victory seemed to make clear that God was indeed on the side of republican America and that ill-trained, ill-disciplined volunteers fighting in defense of republican ideals could defeat a regular professional and experienced army.

The lustre of the victories in Mexico was the brighter because of the analogy with New Orleans. Although Jackson died in the summer of 1845, his spirit was very much alive during the war years. It was after all Jackson who had first spoken of "extending the area of freedom," a phrase that was picked up by the people to justify the extension of the nation's boundaries. To George Bancroft, Jackson's spirit rested upon "our whole territory," from the vales of Oregon to the frontier of the Rio Grande. When Joel Tyler Headley promoted the heroic claims of Winfield Scott it seemed fitting that Scott's biography should be paired with that of Jackson in the same volume.[22]

The battleground outside New Orleans, dubbed Camp Jackson, was used as a staging area for volunteer troops headed for Mexico. It was there that they awaited the transports that would carry them to the Rio Grande or to Vera Cruz. To some soldiers, the mud, fog, and "damp steamy heat" drove out all other thoughts. For others, the association with the spot "where Old Hickory gave the British beans" proved an inspiring and moving experience. One Indiana volunteer, walking over the battlefield, felt a special kinship with the men who had fought under Jackson, when the "flag of liberty and republicanism was reared and successfully defended by an army as patriotic as they were brave." "Our hearts," wrote another, "were filled with the mingled love of glory & love of country." More fortunate were the Pennsylvanians who

happened to camp on the battlefield on January 8, 1847. Not only were
they reminded of the "most desperate struggle for liberty" that had
been waged there but the soldiers also took part in the celebration in
New Orleans, parading to the sounds of martial music and booming
cannon. Nor was the battle forgotten once the men were in Mexico,
although conditions did not always allow the festive atmosphere that
marked the anniversary in Puebla in 1848 when the volunteers staged a
military review and listened to patriotic speeches over a specially prepared meal.[23]

The symbols that moved the soldiers in Mexico—the Stars and
Stripes, the national airs (especially *Yankee Doodle*), even the Battle of
New Orleans—were vivid reminders of the nation's revolutionary beginnings. The Mexican War's most popular and pervasive bond with
the past was with the deeds and heroes of the American Revolution.
There was a persistent appeal to the Revolution that helped stimulate a
war spirit in the country. Having been raised on the tales of America's
struggle for independence, the volunteers saw themselves as merely
continuing the fight, longing to experience "in their own persons" the
excitement of the battlefields about which they had only read. They
were anxious to show that the patriotism of the fathers could still be
found in the hearts of the sons. "I am very anxious to have a chance to
try my spunk," wrote one young volunteer, "I think I have the grit of
'76."

The American Revolution was a continuing revolution, one without
end, requiring vigilance and sacrifice if midcentury Americans were to
prove worthy of their past. Sacredly enshrined "in the heart of every
aspirant for Freedom," it was both an object lesson for the present and
future and a call to action. The fulfillment of the founders' expectations and the preservation of their achievements, Michael Kammen has
suggested, was a persistent theme of the 1830s and 1840s. It became all
the more persistent, and urgent, because the revolutionary generation
was gradually passing from the scene. As the living memory receded,
popular writers, historians, and editors anxiously endeavored to keep
alive the "spirit of '76," to preserve the revolutionary tradition, and to
revive that earlier heroic age. The Revolution assumed new relevance
in the 1840s from the expansionist mood, the confrontation with Great
Britain over Oregon, the stirrings of discontent in Europe, the growing
fears over slavery's divisive effects, and the concern with the materialism that seemed to accompany the nation's economic changes. The war
with Mexico appeared to offer an opportunity to recall Americans to
the ideals of their past and to reinforce the charge which those ideals
placed upon them.[24]

Americans were reminded at every turn of their country's revolutionary origin and of the heroism it spawned, thanks in part to the combination of a romantic interest in the past and the publication explosion
of the 1840s. "The country has been flooded with books on the . . .

subject," noted a writer in *Godey's Magazine*. A large and increasing proportion of the decade's fiction dealt with Revolutionary subjects and themes, while the popular magazines were filled with vignettes, tales, and character sketches drawn from the Revolution. The popularity of America's war for independence prompted novelist John Neal as early as 1825 to see in the Revolution the most meaningful theme for the nation's historical fiction. James Fenimore Cooper published three Revolutionary War romances in rapid succession as the fiftieth anniversary of the Declaration of Independence approached; one of them, *The Spy*, was reissued following the Mexican War with a new introduction by the author that tied the two wars together. The editor of *Holden's Dollar Magazine* found no more pleasing or more timely task for the historian and novelist than the depiction of the "unsullied lustre of patriotism which rests on the memories of Washington and his hero-band."[25]

Midway through the Mexican War, in 1847, Benson J. Lossing's ambitious history of the Revolution appeared, in which the British soldiers "who made war a profession" were contrasted with the colonial troops who were "unused to the arts of war," a contrast that readers would instinctively connect with the Mexican War. Lossing followed with his popular *Pictorial Field Book of the Revolution* (1850), a work, according to Kammen, that did more than any other to foster pride in the American past. Jared Sparks, with his Library of American Biography and his work on Washington; William Gilmore Simms, the chronicler of the Revolution in the South; and the great historian George Bancroft brought the American Revolution to the generation of the 1840s in picturesque and romantic terms; and in the year the Mexican War ended, the prolific Charles Peterson and John Frost further promoted the popular interest with *Military Heroes of the Revolution* and *Lives of the Heroes of the American Revolution*, respectively.[26]

Analogies between the Mexican War and the Revolution were common. The volunteers were regarded as virtually a reincarnation of the "boys of '76." At the first call, young men were urged to "show the world" that they were "chips of the old revolutionary block." Even the "most virulent and prejudiced," it was said, would have to acknowledge that there were just as many "noble and magnanimous spirits" in the army in Mexico as in "that fearless band" that battled during the "dark days of seventy-six." In a paean of praise to South Carolina's Palmetto Regiment, the battles around Mexico City were found to be but echoes of Camden, Eutaw, and Cowpens. The same spirit that had animated Marion and Sumter continued "to stir the blood of Carolina's sons." Writing from the Rio Grande, one volunteer concluded: "The spirit of '76 is still alive." In the art and music inspired by the war, as well as the history and literature, the identification of the "boys of '46" with the "boys of '76" was forcefully drawn.[27]

The ritual celebration of the Fourth of July was as important to the soldiers in Mexico as it was to their folks back home. It was, moreover, a reminder of home, arousing thoughts of loved ones far away as often as it inspired them with patriotism. Sometimes, conditions on the march were not conducive to celebration, as when young George Hartman was on the road to Mexico City on July 4, 1847, suffering from the heat and dust and complaining of the scant provisions and absence of coffee. More fortunate was Jacob Oswandel; quartered in a Mexican village, he and his friends purchased jugs of *pulque* (a potent beverage made from the maguey plant) and had a "little spree." In Matamoros, on the war's first Fourth of July, the day began with the firing of Fort Brown's cannon across the river and the playing of *Hail, Columbia!*. A reading of the Declaration of Independence was followed by a patriotic oration, in which the men were admonished to emulate their Revolutionary forbears, and a military review. A year later, the Massachusetts Regiment serenaded General Taylor at his headquarters in Monterey. Caleb Cushing, the regimental commander, delivered the oration, reminding the men of their part in America's providential mission and urging them to hold in their hearts the "sacred fire of patriotism" and to recall the sacrifices of their forefathers in the Revolution. Taylor responded in kind and in a rare tribute to the volunteers praised them for their readiness to vindicate the national honor on the field of battle. All agreed that the "spirit of '76" burned as brightly in the mountains of Mexico as it had at Trenton.[28]

If the American Revolution provided a link between past and present, it was George Washington who personified its meaning to mid-century America. Washington's presence was felt almost as keenly in the 1840s as if he were still alive. Since the latter days of the 18th century Washington's figure had been molded into heroic proportions by biographers, historians, orators, poets, and artists. He was America's most revered personage, its greatest hero. Had Washington lived in earlier times, observed an English visitor to the United States in 1848, he would have become "the god of America." Indeed, the process of deification had been under way since the early days of the republic. By the mid-19th century his characteristics clearly transcended humanity. Washington's name was invoked as the guiding force in the nation's growth, the source of moral vigor in America's progress toward perfection, God's own agent on earth. "If this confederacy should achieve but half the destinies apparently opening before it," wrote a popular historian in 1848, "he will descend to future ages as the founder of the mightiest republic the world has seen."[29]

Just as the American Revolution seemed to add meaning to the Mexican War so also did George Washington become a model and guardian spirit in the conflict. Washington enlivened American nationhood and its unity, both vitally important in wartime. His birthday was celebrated by the men in Mexico with fireworks, military reviews, artillery salutes, and patriotic oratory. "The Father of American Liberty's birthday," wrote an Ohio volunteer from Puebla, "What pleasant thoughts of the glorious land of liberty does this day bring forth! . . . May we take him as our guide." The scenes of Washington's triumphs in the Revolution were often juxtaposed with scenes of the Mexican War, as in *Brother Jonathan*'s Pictorial Jubilee number for July 4, 1847. It was not simply by chance that efforts to memorialize Washington in marble and stone came to fruition in the late 1840s; perhaps it was because the Mexican War and the national expansion it climaxed stimulated veneration of the country's father. Literary critic and poet Charles Fenno Hoffman underscored Washington's divine mission as the "chosen warrior of the God of Armies!" He found a religious grandeur in "that Christian Soldier" as he moved through the "moral desert of History." He would continue to ride, Hoffman asserted, until God's plans for America had been fulfilled by the "million of humbler instruments." There was little doubt that the Mexican War had a place in this scheme of things.[30]

Authors and publishers, anxious to take advantage of Washington's popularity, added significantly to the body of heroic literature during the war years. Mason Weems's and John Marshall's biographies of Washington were brought out in new editions, and John Frost published a pictorial life of Washington in which he argued Washington's relevance to the late 1840s. "Every step in the onward march of the republic affords new proof of the greatness of its founder." Three volumes with virtually identical titles appeared in 1847, setting off a minor controversy in literary circles: Joel Tyler Headley's *Washington and His Generals;* George Lippard's *Washington and His Generals;* and *Washington and the Generals of the American Revolution,* edited and partly written by Rufus Wilmot Griswold (including a contribution by William Gilmore Simms). Lippard charged Headley with pilfering his "title and whole pages of discription [*sic*]," to which Headley replied in kind, while the publishers of Griswold's collection accused Headley of stealing the idea for his book from them.[31]

By far the most memorable publication was the reprinting of Jared Spark's edition of the writings of George Washington (originally published in the mid-1830s). The moment was thought to be propitious for Americans to commune with "the mind of Washington." His writings, declared the expansionist *Democratic Review,* were especially instructive inasmuch as a "great and perilous stride towards empire is about to be taken." Eight million Mexicans might soon be adopted as the "children of Washington." Furthermore, Sparks's collection provided a source from which the "true spirit of patriot virtue" might be imbibed, and all for the modest price of $1.50 per volume. Americans could share the ideas of that "great mind and noble heart" whom God had charged with laying the foundation for an Anglo-Saxon dominion that would soon cover all of America.[32]

George Lippard, one of the most eccentric literary figures of the period, was anything but subtle in drawing the parallel between

Washington and the Revolution on the one hand and the war with Mexico on the other. He confessed that as he completed *Washington and His Generals*—his "Pilgrimage into the American Past"—he beheld a vision ("at once sublime and beautiful!") of Mexico, where the empires of Montezuma and Cortez were giving way before a new and irresistible force. Even while he wrote, "The children of the Revolution and countrymen of Washington, are thronging the vallies [*sic*], darkening the mountains of this land, bearing in their front amid a tide of sword and bayonet the Banner of the Stars." That banner, he believed, would be planted on the Halls of Montezuma, "thus establishing in the valley of Mexico, a new dominion—THE EMPIRE OF FREEDOM." Shall we not follow the Banner of the Stars, he asked, "from the bloody height of Bunker Hill, from the meadow of Brandywine, to the snow-clad height of Orizaba and the golden city of Tenochtitlan"? At that point, Lippard determined to follow his work on Washington with its natural sequel, a volume on Mexico and the battles of Zachary Taylor.

Few writers matched Lippard for extravagance of language. "Never since the days of Washington," he wrote of the Mexican War, "had an excitement, so wild and universal, thrilled in the souls of freemen." The war would live long in history and children of ages yet to come would thrill to the stories of how "the hosts gathered for the Crusade, in the year 1846." The Sword of Washington, Lippard declared, blazed forth over Mexico, showing the world that the "American People, are in arms for the freedom of a Continent." In a final rhetorical burst, he admonished his countrymen always to heed the "mysterious Symbol of our destiny—THE UNSHEATHED SWORD OF WASHINGTON RESTING UPON THE MAP OF THE NEW WORLD."

Lippard's hyperbole reached the camps in Mexico where his tales of Washington and the Revolution, serialized at first in the press, "cheered the weariness of many a sleepless night." As he was completing his book, Lippard was visited by a discharged volunteer who had fought in Taylor's army. "Gathered round our watch-fire before the battle of Monterey," he told the author, "one of our number seated on a cannon, would read while the others listened." The heroism of Washington and his band of patriots "made our hearts feel warm—they nerved our arms for the battle! When we read of the old times of our Flag, we swore in our hearts, never to disgrace it!"[33]

When the American and Mexican armies met on the field of Buena Vista in the war's greatest battle, Washington's presence was keenly felt by the American force. Santa Anna had decided to engage Taylor's army on February 22, 1847, the one day of the year, commented an American officer, when every American heart was "naturally animated by the purest sentiments of patriotism." A more inopportune moment could not have been selected by the Mexican general. To the volunteers, the decision was propitious for the most glorious celebration ever offered to patriotism's "purest model." As the Mexican troops moved into position, Brigadier General John E. Wool, sixty-three years old and a veteran of the War of 1812, rode along the American line reminding the volunteers of their good fortune in meeting the enemy on Washington's birthday. The country, he told them, had "confided a sacred trust to their valor" and he was confident that the "glory and honor" of American arms would "receive a new lustre" on that day. The troops responded with cheers that "awakened the slumbering echoes" of the surrounding mountains, as the name of Washington— "the sacred battle-cry"—ran through the ranks. The bands struck up *Hail, Columbia!,* and the massed flags were unfurled to the late afternoon breeze. If the people back home could only have witnessed the spirit which animated the soldiers, one of them wrote, they would glow with pride. Washington's name, noted a Massachusetts volunteer, cast a spell which "nerved the hearts of our soldiers" and conjured a host of memories that ran "like the electric fire in the wires of the telegraph" from Mexico's wild defile to the serenity of Mount Vernon. The name apparently worked its magic. Taylor's force, largely volunteers, turned back the attacks of a Mexican army almost five times greater in numbers and was left in control of the field as Santa Anna retreated in disarray.[34]

Even the enemy was impressed with the force of Washington's presence. When William W. Carpenter was taken prisoner by the Mexicans, he was asked by his captors if General Washington would lead the march on Mexico City; they refused to believe that Washington had been dead nearly fifty years. And when the first Americans occupied Mexico's National Palace, they replaced the portrait of the Mexican patriot Iturbide in the grand reception room with one of George Washington. "Amid the greatest enthusiasm, the frowning representative of Mexican greatness gave place to the mild benevolent countenance of the great American hero." The symbolism was complete, as the Father of American Independence was given a place of honor in the enemy's capital; it seemed the "proper sequel" to the campaign's triumphant conclusion.[35]

Patriotism, however defined or expressed, played an important role in forming popular American perceptions of the Mexican War. The symbols of American nationalism assumed virtually an objective existence as they touched the springs of sentiment and belief. Whether Americans, either at home or in the field, were truly motivated by patriotic zeal, many of them at least thought and said they were. It was the way they viewed themselves, and perception often has a way of becoming reality. If they were fooling themselves, they were unaware of it. What counted was their belief that they were acting patriotically; that in itself casts light on the character of America's population at midcentury.

While Americans took pride in the grandeur of their country, they found the United States in all its variety and vastness to be amorphous and difficult to grasp. Hence, they emphasized the republic's "idea" or "principle" as the touchstone of patriotic feeling and insisted on the necessity of national symbols to give that "idea" form and substance. American patriotism, unlike that of other nations, lacked strong attachment to place. It was this that encouraged the New-York Historical Society in 1845 to appoint a "Committee on a National Name" to find a name that would more accurately identify the country than the vague designation United States. "What we want," stated the committee report, "is a sign of our identity. We want utterance for our nationality. We want a watchword more national than that of states, more powerful than that of party." While the committee's choice—"Allegania," after the nation's then most prominent geographical feature—satisfied hardly anyone, the effort revealed the desire to ground American loyalty and patriotism on something more tangible than an "idea."[36]

Much more real, because it was closer, was the American's attachment to locality, to town, county, and state. With improvements in transportation and communication providing greater mobility, this identification was gradually being weakened, but by the end of the 1840s strong local pride still persisted. State loyalty in fact became more intense through a combination of political, economic, and social circumstances that infused new vigor into theories of state sovereignty. Allegiance to state was a natural legacy of America's colonial background, when each colony constituted a discrete governmental unit, and was inherent in the federal system to which Americans pointed with such pride. Indeed, states were regarded as miniature republics, the United States, as *Democratic Review* editor John L. O'Sullivan phrased it, "an Union of many Republics." As republics in their own right, states commanded a basic loyalty or patriotism, not so much competing with national patriotism as supplementing it. The peculiarities of the volunteer system adopted during the Mexican War, whereby the states were responsible for providing soldiers who themselves were accountable to the states from which they enlisted, further deepened an already profound sense of state patriotism. Tied to circumstances of birth, home, and family, local and state allegiances supplied the geographic attachment that was lacking in loyalty to the nation.[37]

When the call for volunteers first went out in May 1846, states vied with one another to meet and exceed their quotas. The alacrity with which young men responded was viewed as a mark of loyalty to the state as well as to the nation; for a state to exceed its quota became a badge of honor which all its citizens could share. Tennesseeans felt they had lived up to their state's designation as the "Volunteer State." "Wherever the thickness of the battle," a Nashville paper declared, "then and there will Tennessee valor be conspicuous." When three times as many Illinoisans volunteered as could be accepted, it was

viewed as proof of the superior patriotism of the state. Even in Massachusetts, where Polk had at first hesitated to issue a quota, the response was linked with allegiance to the Commonwealth. The men,
boasted one of their leaders, would carry with them into the land of the
Aztecs the "principles of patriotism and honor which we have drunk in
at this their fountain-head in our own land of the Pilgrim Fathers of
Plymouth and Massachusetts."[38]

For a regiment to fight with valor in the most dangerous part of a
battle or to be the first to raise the Stars and Stripes over battlement or
town was not only to win glory for the unit but also to bestow honor on
the state from which the men were recruited. Appeals to state pride
were commonly made in battle to rally the soldiers to more desperate
deeds of courage or to bolster wavering lines. When soldiers were
hard-pressed by the enemy and their determination flagged, Zachary
Taylor advised: "Call upon their State pride . . . they will not resist
that." Taylor himself called out at one point in the battle of Buena
Vista, "This is not the way for Kentuckians to behave!" At Cerro
Gordo, when a Kentucky officer turned to his men and shouted "Boys,
remember old Kentuck," one young volunteer felt that he could "jump
headlong into the mouth of every cannon there was in the Mexican
battery." "Illinois to the rescue" became a battle cry for men from the
Sucker State, and at Churubusco the war cry of the Palmetto Regiment
was the state's name. Ohioans were assured that their volunteers had
proudly sustained the state's honor at Monterey, and similar assurances
went out to other states throughout the war.[39]

To be kept behind the lines or to be assigned occupation duty was
not only frustrating to the individual's thirst for adventure but was also
viewed as an insult to the states that were thus deprived of the glory of
combat. Camped in the unhealthy floodplain of the Rio Grande
throughout most of the war, the men of Indiana's First Regiment harbored deep resentment that they were not allowed to represent their
state on at least one "glorious battlefield." Angry charges were hurled
at Taylor for his alleged favoritism in advancing the Mississippi Riflemen (commanded by his son-in-law) into battle at both Monterey and
Buena Vista while allowing other equally deserving regiments to languish behind the lines. Each state from which troops had been enlisted,
urged one soldier, should have at least one unit in the battles. "The
States that raised troops had a right to expect nothing else."[40]

Not all the actions of the volunteers were glorious, and the states they
represented sometimes bore the stigma of less noteworthy episodes. On
a scouting expedition a few weeks before the battle of Buena Vista, a
detachment of Kentucky cavalry under Major John P. Gaines fell in
with a group of Arkansas horsemen commanded by Major Solon Borland. Through negligence and disobedience of orders, the men were
later surrounded as they slept by a larger Mexican force and taken
prisoner. To add insult to injury, a patrol sent out by the Kentucky

regiment to find Gaines's men discovered instead a stock of liquor at an abandoned ranch, became intoxicated, and was itself captured. Still, the individuals involved did not appear to suffer, for Gaines, a Whig, was elected to Congress while he was in captivity, and Borland won election to the Senate following the war.[41]

The most controversial episode involving the "honor" of a state, the echoes of which were heard long after the event, related to the behavior of the Second Indiana Regiment at the battle of Buena Vista. Charges that the regiment had retreated in disorder before the enemy, initially made by General Taylor in his report of the battle, "dishonored a whole state" and for decades afterward held the state "subject to stigma" (the words are those of Lew Wallace, one of Indiana's volunteers). According to Taylor, only a handful of men from the regiment remained on the field, continuing to fight with Jefferson Davis's Mississippians. The incident illustrated one of the principal complaints leveled by regular officers against their volunteer counterparts. The order to retreat had been given by the colonel of the regiment, William A. Bowles, an amiable physician who seemed more interested in collecting botanical specimens in Mexico than in accepting the responsibilities of his command. His election as colonel had been disputed; it was clear that he did not enjoy the full support of his men. Furthermore, he was totally ignorant of military tactics and apparently made little effort to learn them.

A court of inquiry following the battle, while charging Bowles with incompetence, absolved him of cowardice. Contrary to Taylor's charge, the court found that most of the regiment had been rallied and with the Mississippians and another Indiana regiment had repelled the climactic charge of the Mexican lancers (Taylor had credited the repulse solely to the Mississippi regiment). Some of the blame for the retreat was placed on Joseph Lane, former colonel of the regiment who had been promoted to brigadier general early in the war. Lane had continued in effect to command his old regiment, often issuing orders without informing Bowles. At Buena Vista, he had ordered the regiment to charge the enemy, a command which Bowles, on another part of the field and out of touch with Lane, misinterpreted as an order to retreat.

While the court of inquiry largely cleared the regiment of Taylor's charges, Taylor refused to modify his report. Indignation against Taylor among the volunteers exploded, and his treatment of Indiana's regiments was severely censured. Indiana's votes against Taylor in the 1848 Presidential election were said to have stemmed from this incident, although modern scholarship casts some doubt on the assertion. Whether the state smarted under the stigma for a half-century afterward (as Lew Wallace claimed) is problematical, but in 1847 and 1848 the dishonor to the state seemed real indeed.[42]

Patriotism and loyalty, honor and glory, may have played a large part in the volunteers' motivation but the soldiers were also keenly aware of the personal advantages they would gain from their service in Mexico. The two were often found in close combination, not always distinguishable. Such was the nature of early 19th-century patriotism—the identification of the individual with the republic—that advancement of self was frequently inseparable from advancement of the country. When President Polk eulogized the citizen-soldier in his December 1848 message to Congress, he recognized this conjunction of personal with patriotic considerations: "In battle, each private man, as well as every officer, fights not only for his country, but for glory and distinction among his fellow-citizens when he shall return to civil life."

Politics was an important element in the volunteer system. Not only were politicians attracted to the service but the rules by which volunteer units were organized encouraged political activity. State militia units and independent volunteer companies, many of which were translated directly into the army, had served as appendages to state politics, "parapolitical as well as paramilitary organizations." Service in the militia had long been considered an important stepping-stone to political office.

When the call for volunteers was issued in 1846, companies were recruited by locality, often by political figures, and became simply extensions of the political community. Political rivalries in civilian life were carried over into the ranks of the army and frequently determined the outcome of the elections for officers. There were Whig companies, and there were Democratic companies, and sometimes the politics of the officers differed from those of the men, a situation not always conducive to good discipline. William B. Campbell, a Whig, was elected colonel of the First Tennessee Regiment in spite of the fact that a strong majority of the men were Democrats. His role was not always a comfortable one. "Politics," he wrote soon after the regiment arrived on the Rio Grande, "is somewhat in my way as all my field officers are Democrats and are somewhat jealous of any character I may acquire and . . . do not second my exertions to institute rigid discipline."[43]

There was no doubt that in many cases patriotic motives were clearly outweighed by the prospect of political rewards. Too many of the volunteer officers, complained Campbell, regarded their service as simply a "political tour to gain reputation to give them importance when they shall return home" and had no other objective in Mexico than to advance their own political fortunes. Public opinion in their units was more important than army regulations or the demands of military tactics and strategy. "The soldiers are writing home constantly and can annoy an officer very much and then when the short term of service is over he goes back to a society composed in part of his soldiers."

The number of volunteer officers who found participation in the war to be a great boon to their political careers simply confirms the truism that military service has always been a sure pathway to political success in the United States. Perhaps the most obvious example was Zachary

Taylor himself, although he was not a volunteer. Where the appointment of the army's high-ranking officers was left to the President, it is not surprising that a large number of political figures reaped the benefits of the executive patronage. Political preferment, however, was not limited to the general officers. Colonels, captains, lieutenants, and in some instances, non-commissioned officers and privates were the political beneficiaries of Mexican War service. When James Shields, who not only commanded a brigade in Scott's army but had the good fortune to be wounded twice, was elected to the United States Senate by the Illinois legislature, Vice President Dallas observed, "Nothing climbs now-a-days but the epaulette and sword."[44]

Although politics frequently got in the way of military behavior and decorum and distracted some volunteers from their purpose in being in Mexico, it is also likely that the hope of popularity, political or otherwise, motivated the volunteers to fight more desperately and heroically, to demonstrate their patriotism by giving a good account of themselves on the field of battle. Each man, commented the *Literary World,* "fought under the eye of his neighbor, his brother voter, or his political opponent, who was certain to report him at home" if his behavior did not measure up. Public opinion, the "ruling power" in a republic, was as important on the battlefield as it was in the towns back home. The volunteer units were strikingly homogeneous in their composition, recruited as they often were from single localities, political persuasions, professional employments, or ethnic groups, and this no doubt contributed to their success in battle. Personal pride mingled with pride in their regiments and their states, creating a bond that in turn linked them in some often unseen and unspoken way with loyalty and patriotism toward the nation itself.[45]

CHAPTER 4

Visions of Romance
and Chivalry

Visions of Romance & Chivalry

When Nathaniel Hawthorne found a "chivalrous beauty" in the response of the volunteers to the Mexican War and saw in the soldiers the "spirit of young knights," he reflected an important element in the romantic outlook of the early 19th century. Perceptions of the war, by soldiers as well as civilians, were shaped by elements of American romanticism: an idealization of the past that found analogies to the Mexican victories in the world's military annals; a tendency to view the war as moral drama; the quest for honor and glory on the battlefield; and the reverence for heroes, heroism, and the heroic ideal. The Mexican War was a romantic episode in the nation's career. With a spirit of romantic adventure, Hawthorne wrote, America's peaceful citizens sought "by daring and desperate valor, to prove their fitness to be intrusted with the guardianship of their country's honor."[1]

Many of the attitudes toward the war were touched by sentimentality and fantasy but they were nonetheless real for it. The conflict—America's first against a foreign foe, fought in a distant and exotic land and justified by a rhetoric that stressed matters of honor and principle—lent itself to romantic idealization, bringing to life what had only been imagined before. Americans who bemoaned the absence of romantic elements in their new nation—the lack of monuments "mouldering in solitary grandeur," of fierce banditti lurking in the shadows, of "legendary tales of hoary antiquity"—now found them in Mexico. The war not only supplied the prestige of military achievement and new arguments for republicanism but it also offered additional ingredients toward a cultural identity that would enable America to compete with the Old World. Americans viewed their conflict in terms of heroism and romance, in ways suggested by the medieval historian Johan Huizinga, "as a noble game of honour and virtue." No matter how much people might disagree on the "origin and justness" of the Mexican War, observed the *Literary World,* "we all must fall more or less under [its] influence . . . and feel a spell thrown over its wild adventures, its heroic acts of daring, and its splendid achievements."[2]

One of the hallmarks of American romanticism was a nostalgic longing for ages gone by that contrasted sharply with the forward-looking tendencies of the times. The romantic's view of history as a vast stream flowing from past into present and future, fed by innumerable tributaries, emphasized the organic unity of human development. Knowledge of the past, therefore, was essential to an understanding of the present and future. With an awareness of origins or beginnings (what some have called primitivism) came a clearer comprehension of man's progress, that same progress that Americans believed had lead directly and inevitably to the foundation of their republic. To know the past, in other words, was to know themselves. It was all part of the search for a national identity, to find a place for America in the larger scheme of things, to provide a pedigree that would balance the newness of their nation and at the same time confirm its uniqueness. Mexico itself, with its ruins, vestiges of an ancient civilization, and its dramatic conquest in the 16th century, supplied an antiquity that helped satisfy America's romantic yearning, accounting in some measure for the popular interest that was given to the observations of the soldiers who fought there. But the war itself also seemed to provide a link between present and past, not just the brief past of the American republic that became so important to the expressions of patriotism but the past of civilization itself; in the popular mind, the war was tied organically to earlier, simpler times.

There was much about the Mexican War that seemed reminiscent of the campaigns of ancient Greece and Rome, and analogies between the war in Mexico and the wars of antiquity were commonly drawn. The study of classical civilization had become a prominent feature of the country's expanding educational system; as writers of history sought the germs of American development they gave increasing and extraordinary emphasis to ancient times. Classical allusions were commonplace in the accounts of the war, the histories, the poetry, and the fiction generated by the conflict, and it is a tribute to the educational level of literate America that the allusions were familiar to the nation's readers.

It was the Middle Ages, however, that most captivated the American romantic mind. Indeed, "medievalism" was a principal characteristic of romanticism on both sides of the Atlantic. Historians in the United States, however, did not share as fully as their European counterparts in the rediscovery of the Middle Ages, the "medieval revival." Instead, the medieval world entered the stream of American consciousness by what was perhaps an even more effective route, that of the historical romance. It was an "imagined Middle Ages" that gave shape to romantic thought in America.

Sir Walter Scott set the pace. Scott's historical romances have been studied primarily with reference to their popularity in the South; in fact, his novels enjoyed a wide popularity throughout the United States, North as well as South. His influence on the development of a national literature was profound but his impact in molding American romantic thought was just as deep, for he set an entire generation "dreaming and prating about the chivalries of a by-gone age." He inspired a host of imitators, including the English writer Edward Bulwer-Lytton and the unbelievably prolific G. P. R. James, both of whom achieved popularity in the United States, and such domestic writers as James Fenimore Cooper (the American Scott) and William Gilmore Simms. Reviewers complained of the "deluge of historical romance with which the country is flooded" at the same time that they found distinction and high moral purpose in the genre. To throw a "deep romantic interest" around an historical period was to beguile the readers while imparting "useful moral lessons."[3]

The popular view of the Middle Ages, shaped by the romances of Scott and his imitators, was highly stylized and had "little to do with the middle ages as they really were and a great deal to do with the emerging values of primitivism, freedom, and heroic individualism." The Middle Ages were not only an historical period but a state of mind, a "complex myth" that seemed to recall a time of innocence that was fast disappearing before the relentless tide of a new commercialism. It seemed a time of stability when values were strongly anchored in tradition and institutional authority, a heroic age when men fought over ideals. Some in the United States saw the Mexican War as an echo of the Middle Ages that would recall Americans to their ideals and turn them away from the diverting temptations of material prosperity and growth.[4]

To American romantics, the medieval period was an age of chivalry, and it was chivalry that captured their imaginations. That chivalry also represented ideals that, if not totally lost, were rapidly being eroded seemed certain. The age of chivalry, it was said over and over, had passed; a new age of practicality, a "bank-note" age, had taken its place. Edmund Burke's observation was quoted at every hand and applied to the United States: "The Age of Chivalry is gone. That of sophisters, economists and calculators has succeeded, and the glory of Europe is extinguished forever." "The age is becoming far too material," complained a writer in the *American Review*. Men were blinded by their eagerness for "present pleasure and immediate profit." He urged Americans to revive the "spirit of the Past—the chivalric and thoughtful spirit, that prompted to wise counsels and valorous deeds—when worth was not gauged by the standards of wealth and fashion." Such laments were common, yet few people seriously addressed the meaning of chivalry to mid-19th-century America. Like patriotism, chivalry was one of those overused and troublesome words whose meaning was more intuitive than rational. Although it evoked differing sentiments and applications, the concept nonetheless lay at the heart of the romantic response to the Mexican War.[5]

It was Scott again who was largely responsible for bringing notions of medieval chivalry to popular thought in the United States. Charles Mills, whose *History of Chivalry* (1825) was inspired by Scott, declared that Scott convinced the world that "the chivalric times of Europe" could strike the "moral imagination . . . powerfully and pleasingly in respect of character, passion, and picturesqueness of effect." A host of writers, following Scott's cue, paid tribute to chivalric ideals in prose and poetry. A "cult of chivalry" took shape, most forcefully articulated in the South perhaps but influential throughout the United States. Chivalry was taken out of the Middle Ages, out of the "age of eternal broil and battle, and bloodshed" which had spawned it, and was brought into the 19th century, where it was invested with new relevance. One writer, relating the spirit of chivalry to the reform movements of the early 19th century, insisted that "modern chivalry" held a wider scope and loftier aim than it ever had in the Middle Ages for it sought the "redemption of men from *spiritual* as well as *physical* evils." It was synonymous with the spirit of humanity that characterized the period. Describing chivalry as the "most glorious institution" that man ever devised, the popular and often-parodied G. P. R. James concluded that "there is scarcely a noble feeling or a bright aspiration that . . . is not in some degree referable to that great and noble principle." No matter how "overstrained" or "fantastic" the doctrines of chivalry might appear to the 19th century, Scott wrote, "it would be difficult to conceive the existence of virtue among the human race" without them.[6]

Chivalry, however, was closely related to warfare, for it was in war that its ideals were traditionally displayed and tested. Chivalry, wrote Scott, blended military valor with the "strongest passions which actuate the human mind, the feelings of devotion and those of love." Love of freedom and the obligation to maintain and defend it, generosity, gallantry, and an unblemished reputation were all qualities of the "perfect knight." That military devotion might often degenerate into brutality and intolerance he conceded, but there was still nothing "more beautiful and praiseworthy" than the theory on which it was based—the soldier "drawing the sword in defence of his country and its liberties, or of the oppressed innocence of damsels, widows, and orphans." Unmindful of any personal advantage, the young knight must seek out "adventures of risk and peril" and never waver before overwhelming odds. To fight heroically in defense of principle was to fulfill the highest requirement of the chivalric ideal.[7]

For a generation steeped in tales of knighthood and chivalric behavior, it was no great leap of the imagination to see in the Mexican War a modern test of chivalry and a reenactment of the fabled contests of old. Although the victories in Mexico were cause for exultation, gushed one

writer in 1847, "we rejoice less at the success of our army than at that
chivalric generosity, that enlightened moderation, and fraternal beneficence which ally both officers and men to the best days of Knighthood." The struggle, as carried on by America's soldiers, was not one
of "brute force" but rather the "stand of disciplined and nerved men,
at the command of their country—an exhibition of duty to the will of a
government, nobly and unhesitatingly obeyed."

Scott's words lay behind George Lippard's characterization of the war
as the "Crusade of the Nineteenth Century," and they were in the mind
of the gift-book writer who insisted that the war with Mexico was "emphatically a war of chivalry." The "age of chivalry has returned," commented the *Southern Quarterly Review*. Every soldier fought "as if he
were striving to pluck from the 'dangerous precipice,' the glittering
flowers of immortality." The celebrant at the Festival of Saint Nicholas
in New York City paid tribute to the chivalric ideal when he toasted
"Our Gallant Little Army in Mexico": "Rivalling romance in the brilliant reality of its achievements, it needs no eulogy to magnify its well-
tried heroism." And it might well have been the spirit of chivalry that
prompted the government to declare the war a "war of reconciliation,"
fought only against Mexico's tyrants and usurpers in defense of its
people.[8]

There were of course dissenters. Charles Sumner found no chivalry
in a war against Mexico, although he was not so sure about a war with
England. The former would be "mean and cowardly," the latter at least
bold. Honor, the "early child of chivalry," he found to be a vestige of
"an age of barbarism," a concept so "impalpable, so chimerical, so un-
real" as to be of little use. Americans, he charged, "nursed by the
literature of antiquity" had imbibed the "narrow sentiment of heathen
patriotism" which they expressed in their "selfish and exaggerated *love
of country*." He had no regrets whatever that the age of chivalry had
slipped into oblivion. The popular concept of chivalry, wrote a peace
advocate, was more injurious to morality than it was beneficial. Setting
aside the "vulgar use" of the term, he found the highest principle of
chivalry to be "self-sacrifice, for good ends," a meaning that did not
seem apparent in the Mexican War. Such views, isolated and unpopular, made little headway against the more common perception of the
war.[9]

The Mexican War offered young Americans an opportunity to reen-
act the scenes of chivalric conduct and to play the parts of storied
knights. The romance of a distant and legendary past seemed suddenly
to become reality. As a youthful volunteer bade farewell to his small
Pennsylvania town in 1846, he fancied himself going to war to do battle
on behalf of lady fair. Paying tribute to the ladies who saw him on his
way, he vowed that "like true knights" he and his comrades "must
maintain their beauty and goodness against all the knights in Christen-
dom." Marcus Cunliffe has found the image of the soldier as knight, or

Chevalier, a persistent one in the "American military ethos." The battlefields of Mexico, he has pointed out, witnessed "sudden flowerings of the improbably gorgeous blossoms of war," as fabled knights of old seemed to "step out of the pages of romantic literature, endowed for a moment with flesh and blood" and then stepped "back again into make-believe."[10]

The prototype of the knightly image, the figure about whom the aura of medieval chivalry burned the brightest, was the 16th-century French knight Pierre du Terrail, Chevalier de Bayard, *le chevalier sans peur et sans reproche*—the knight without fear and without reproach. Charles Sumner called him the "cynosure of chivalry"; to William Gilmore Simms he was the paragon of "all that is pure and noble in manhood, and all that is great and excellent in the soldier." It was no coincidence that Simms undertook a biography of Chevalier Bayard during the first winter of the Mexican War. Believing that war was "the greatest element of modern civilization," he painted the Chevalier Bayard in such glowing colors as to strain credibility. Courageous, unselfish, generous, and disinterested, his "sympathies were always given to the good; his succor gladly sustained the weak; his bounty helped the indigent." As a soldier, Bayard had learned that obedience and "ardent attachment to his country" were his first duties. His life, Simms wrote with an eye cast toward the war then in progress, "furnishes an admirable example to the soldier, of a career in which the most heroic valor may be blended with the most gentle virtues, with mildness of temper, sweetness of demeanor, generosity without display, and the most humble submission to human and Divine authority."[11]

That the Chevalier Bayard had become the ideal of soldierly behavior even before Simms's biography, was evident from the numerous references to the 16th-century knight in accounts of the war. Analogies to Bayard were drawn indiscriminately to describe the heroism of the nation's soldiers on Mexican fields. Lieutenant Colonel William S. Harney earned the title of "Chevalier Bayard of our army" for his assault on Telegraph Hill at Cerro Gordo; Captain Samuel Ringgold, who fell in the war's first battle, was the "true Chevalier 'sans peur, sans reproche,'—the Bayard of our army"; and Captain George Lincoln, a casualty at Buena Vista, was the "Bayard of the American Army." Winfield Scott was "a second Bayard" for his generosity, amiability, forgiving spirit, and unconquerable courage—chivalric traits all. And even the enemy received the highest accolades of chivalry. Colonel Don Juan Najira, who fell at Monterey while leading his Guanajuato regiment against the attacking forces of General Worth, "was as brave as the Chevalier Bayard, the knight *sans peur, et sans reproche*."[12]

The romantic temperament which discovered chivalry in the Mexican War also found expression in what Cunliffe has called a "craving for glory." The literature of war did not deal solely with accounts of classical conquests or of clashes among medieval knights, although these formed a large part of it. War in general was an important part of the reading of Americans, and an inordinate amount of space was devoted to it in textbooks used in the nation's common school systems. Moreover, Americans saw "an intimate connection between patriotism and warfare, democracy and heroism, progress and military prowess."[13] No matter how dedicated they might be to the true responsibility of republics to foster the "arts of peace," they exhibited a continuing fascination with war in all its romantic garb.

Military history had never been more in vogue than in the 1830s and 1840s. Indeed, the popular interest in military history was blamed for the "war spirit" with which the nation entered the war with Mexico. The war in turn encouraged the demand, and publishers seized the opportunity to satisfy it. "The past has been revived," noted one critic, "and the heroes of every age from Miltiades down to Frederick the Great, have been brought into lively comparison with those whose titles to renown have but just been recorded in history." Reviewers complained of the flood of books that crossed their desks. "The market is already glutted with military sketches," protested one in 1847, "booksellers' shelves and parlor tables are assuming the appearance of one universal, militia, parade day, with so many generals and their staffs in cloth and gilt."[14]

When Zachary Taylor moved his army into Texas and took position along the beach at Corpus Christi, only thirty years had elapsed since the longest and bloodiest war in modern time had ended on the field at Waterloo. This greatest war in recent memory quickly entered the romantic imagination of the early 19th century, its drama unfolded, and its heroism sung in prose and poetry on both sides of the Atlantic. After only three decades, the Napoleonic wars had become covered with a "thick sedimentary deposit of romance."

English historians like Archibald Alison, Charles William Vane, and W. F. P. Napier (the "Thucydides of Modern Times") found ready audiences in the United States for their accounts of the campaigns against Napoleon. Long excerpts from their books were reprinted in the press, and Vane's and Napier's works were published in new American editions during the Mexican War. Drawing an implicit analogy between the Peninsular War and the war with Mexico, the author of the American introduction to Napier's history found France and Great Britain representing the "cause of civilization" (even though enemies) while Spain, bound by the tyranny of superstition and oppression, was in a state of decay.

The analogy was not uncommon. The *Literary World* printed extracts from a mother's letter to her son who had departed for Mexico, warning the young volunteer that "there is good Spanish blood in parts of Mexico, and Spaniards are not cowards, as the Peninsular war will testify." More often Mexicans were upbraided for not coming up to the standard of resistance set by their brethren in Spain. If they had, "the whole scene would be a wonderful representation of the peninsula in 1809."[15]

American feelings toward the Duke of Wellington, the victor of Waterloo, were ambivalent. The publication in the United States of two adulatory studies of the battle of Waterloo by Captain William Siborne (1845) and George R. Gleig (1847) enhanced the Iron Duke's reputation during the Mexican War, and Americans glowed with pride when Wellington reputedly praised Zachary Taylor's military skill and expressed admiration for Taylor's successes in northern Mexico. On the other hand, Americans were too aware of Wellington's aristocratic and antidemocratic bearing to view him uncritically. Furthermore, it became common practice to answer English critics of the Mexican War by pointing to Wellington's brutal campaigns in India and Spain. Winfield Scott's conduct toward the Mexican enemy was more easily defended by contrasting it with the inhumanity of Wellington's tactics. Americans had no doubt which was the greater general. Cold, haughty, and disdainful, thoroughly professional in military matters (attributes shared to a degree by Scott), Wellington simply lacked the requisites for a romantic hero.

It was not the victor at Waterloo, however, who captured American interest but the vanquished. There was romance in the French defeat that was not found in the British victory. French tactics, for example, had influenced American military thought for a long time. Scott, often described as a product of the "French school," trained his officers from a Napoleonic field manual and followed the principles of Napoleon's tactician Antoine Henri de Jomini in his campaign against Mexico City. The brilliant French cavalry commander Joachim Murat, whose two sons had settled in the United States following Napoleon's defeat, seemed to combine the chivalric tradition of the Middle Ages with the titanic Napoleonic conflict. Describing Murat as a "handsome cavalier," the American editor of Napier's history noted that "chivalry, since the time of the crusades, has not had a nobler representative." Headley, writing on the eve of the Mexican War, asserted that Murat, by investing battle with glory and romance, had restored the days of knighthood. To be compared with Murat was high praise for a Mexican War officer. Taylor's dashing, impetuous cavalry officer Charles May became the "Murat of the army," while General William Jenkins Worth (a less likely candidate) apparently earned the title "Murat of the American army" because he sat a horse so elegantly. A more immediate link with the Napoleonic wars appeared in the oft-repeated story of the French veteran of Austerlitz, Jena, the Russian campaign, and Waterloo whose luck ran out as an American soldier at Palo Alto. Felled by a shot from a Mexican battery, with his dying breath he urged on his comrades—the epitome of patriotism and romantic heroism.[16]

It was Napoleon who aroused the midcentury's romantic imagination. He had already been endowed with the proportions of a Promethean hero by such poets as Blake, Byron, and Shelley, a "defiant romantic rebel . . . the benefactor of mankind, a lonely eagle" languishing in forgotten exile. As the embodiment of romantic genius, he became the center of a cult that by the time of the Mexican War was at its peak. Americans were not to be left behind in their devotion to the new Napoleonic mythology. The craving for information about Napoleon, observed the *Southern Literary Messenger* in 1848, had never been more intense. Napoleon was studied and imitated by professional soldiers but his appeal was much broader than that. To Ralph Waldo Emerson, he was the idol of the young and ardent, the agent of the middle class, the "incarnate Democrat," whose real strength lay in his identification with the mass of the people.[17]

The publication in the United States of Thiers's *History of the Consulate and Empire Under Napoleon* (1845) and William Hazlitt's *Life of Napoleon Buonaparte* (1847) enabled reviewers to add their own panegyrics. It was in "his primary character of man and in his relations to the real substantial interests of mankind," commented the *Literary World,* that Napoleon's greatness lay. "This is the American, and should and will be the universal point of view from which to regard him."[18]

The publication of the Thiers and Hazlitt books just before and during the Mexican War gave the Napoleonic campaigns a timeliness, doubtless encouraging the Americans' own war spirit. More effective was the appearance in 1846 of Headley's *Napoleon and His Marshals,* dedicated to Winfield Scott, whom Headley admired and thought would soon become the Napoleon of the Mexican War. Headley, whose blood-and-thunder style brought him widespread popularity, couched his book in terms Americans could not only understand but also endorse, the same terms in which the war with Mexico had been placed. Napoleon's marshals, Headley contended, were all "stern republicans," locked in a bitter struggle between liberty and despotism, equal rights and privilege. There was something almost Jacksonian about Headley's portrait of Napoleon as an "amazing genius" pledged to the advancement of republican principles against the European monarchs who unhesitatingly sacrificed "justice, human rights, and human life to maintain their oppressive forms of government." As with his later work on Washington, Headley's *Napoleon* inspired imitators: the anonymous *Napoleon: His Army and His Generals* (1847) and *Napoleon and the Marshals of the Empire* (1848), edited by Rufus Wilmot Griswold.[19]

The flurry of books on Napoleon gratified "a taste in the public mind for military exploits, which the existing war with Mexico has created." At the same time, the works suggested parallels between the Mexican War and the Napoleonic wars that broadened support of the conflict. The triumphs of Taylor and Scott were commonly compared to those of Napoleon; Scott's march on Mexico City found its counterpart in Napoleon's advance on Moscow (without, it was hoped, the tragic result). Americans were "foaming with excitement" and the demand for works on Napoleon seemed but part of the "spirit of the time."[20]

To those steeped in the tales of medieval chivalry, who thrilled to the exploits of history's great commanders, the Mexican War seemed suddenly to translate romance into reality. Whether it was the Chevalier Bayard, George Washington, or Napoleon, the military figures of the past seemed to envelope the conflict with romanticism. Events that had only been found in the story-books now appeared to be daily occurrences.

Late in 1847, Freeman Hunt, editor of the influential *Merchants' Magazine,* conceded that while he had little sympathy for the war he could not help admiring the courage and heroism which it brought out in the nation's soldiery. "Would to God," he wrote, "that these qualities were directed to nobler purposes; and that the heroic age—the age of American chivalry—had passed away." That the characteristics commonly associated with chivalry *were* passing away was clear to many of Hunt's contemporaries. In spite of the appeals to chivalric behavior and the exhortations to patriotism, honor, and the glory of combat on Mexican fields, there was an uneasy feeling that the nobler qualities which Americans extracted from an idealized past were faltering under the pressure of more mundane, less worthy values.

For all his bombast and pretension, Headley recognized the change and was disturbed by it. To those who charged him with stimulating a war spirit he replied that "we need not fear the effect of stimulating too much the love of glory in this age of dollars and cents." The reign of commerce and trade, already begun, enhanced rather than diminished the risk of war. "Men of peace," he complained, "are straining every nerve to destroy the love of glory in our youth, while every war among civilized nations, probably for the next century, will be waged to secure the privileges of commerce." The qualities of chivalry were being replaced by cupidity; the "chivalric and heroic spirit" was falling victim to the "*grasping* spirit."

Headley's concern was echoed by others but none so succinctly as a reviewer in the *Literary World.* The interests of commerce were taking precedence in the affairs of the world, resulting in what he termed a moral evil—"chivalric deterioration." Individuals had become selfish in the pursuit of trade as they abandoned "more liberal aims." The "legitimate virtues of knighthood"—generosity, courage, and self-sacrifice—were superseded by less noble attitudes. Commerce could alter the face of a country in a short time, "people lonely waters with argosies, and build cities where all was previously a desert," but withal there was no "necessary accession of moral energy or intellectual grace." For these reasons, he concluded, the "memories of brave and disinterested soldiers, adventurous mariners, heroic poets, hardy pioneers, and devoted advocates of truth, should be kept green by the pen of bard and annalist."

To those most disturbed by the changing times, the Mexican War seemed opportune, a last moment to recall their countrymen to the

paths of glory. "War waged for principle," Headley reminded, "is the
same as that carried on by the direct command of heaven."[21]

Fantasies of Chivalry in War

Dreams of chivalry and glory filled the heads of many who marched
off to war in what promised to be a great romantic adventure. Their
image of war was that of the history books, of the historical romances,
and of the tales of heroic deeds on which they had been raised. For
most, war was a distant thing, to be read about rather than experienced. Only those old enough to have served in the War of 1812 or
those who had fought in Florida's swamps against the elusive Seminoles
had had direct contact with the real face of warfare and knew what it
was to confront an enemy in battle. There were words of caution but
they hardly dimmed the excitement. As volunteers gathered on the
Island of Lobos, off Mexico's Gulf coast, in preparation for the assault
on Vera Cruz, a regular officer observed that the men anticipated "a
grand frolic." They would soon learn, he wrote, that there was "more
reality and less romance in it than they thought."[22] Still, the war with
Mexico seemed different, hardly comparable to the earlier struggle
against the mother country or the confusing and little known campaigns against the Indians.

The volunteers that began to arrive on the Rio Grande in the summer of 1846 were eager for battle. The victories at Palo Alto and
Resaca de la Palma, fought largely by regulars, had heightened their
anticipation. Convinced of their superiority over the Mexican forces, if
not in numbers in character and conviction, they were anxious to test
their mettle. Action, however, was not immediately forthcoming. Days,
weeks, even months passed without movement, and their excitement
gradually gave way to disappointment, grumbling, and complaint. Impatience began to manifest itself, impatience with the officers, with the
discipline of training and the routine of the camp, and with the government for permitting delay. The spirits of the volunteers, commented
one officer, were altogether too fiery to await quietly all the details of
planning necessary for a military campaign. When the army finally
moved slowly up the Rio Grande toward Camargo, a Baltimore volunteer confided that soldiering was "just the life I wanted to have a taste
of, and I am by no means disposed to relinquish it," but he also feared
that "we shall have no fight." "I would like to have one chance on a
battle field," he wrote, "if it were only just to see how I should feel."[23]

Spirits revived when it became known that Taylor had made the
"stronghold of northern Mexico," Monterey, his objective. For those
left behind in the disease-ridden camps, on the other hand, there was
only gloom and dismay, if not outright mutiny. Alabama volunteers left
behind in Camargo held a protest meeting and sent a formal remon-
strance to Taylor. It was unfair, they charged, that other units should
be advanced ahead of them. "We only ask to share in the dangers and

horrors of the campaign, whatever they may be." For those who were stuck on the Rio Grande the situation became intolerable. "I did not come here . . . to lay around such a stinken hole as this," an Illinois volunteer wrote from Matamoros. "I wish to see some of the country, and experience some of the *hardships* of warfare." For an Indiana officer, the "glitter & tinsel & romance of war" had worn off.

Some soldiers feared that Mexico would make peace before another battle could be fought. "The prospect of peace," noted a volunteer, "seems to depress the spirits of the troops." Rumors persisted, however, that Mexico would seek an end to the war, if not soon then before the Americans should have a chance to storm the "halls of Montezumas." Peace negotiations at the very least, it was thought, should be put off until the volunteers had accomplished what they had signed up to do, "to conquer the Mexicans."[24]

For those who marched on Monterey in the summer of 1846, the anticipation of battle was exhilarating. Even the scenery that surrounded them added to the romance of their campaign. The strange beauty of the Mexican landscape, unlike anything they had ever encountered, overcame their weariness and impatience and conjured up associations that seemed to link them with warriors of the past. "There are few objects in nature," wrote a volunteer, "resembling in sombre nakedness of aspect and lonely and isolated grandeur, a Mexican mountain." Dominating the horizon were northern Mexico's rugged peaks, gloomy and barren, totally unlike the forest-covered slopes the soldiers had known back home. As they gazed at the wild and contorted crags through the shimmering heat, the peaks assumed fantastic shapes. They became lofty towers and stately pyramids, redoubts, battlements, and castles. "Faint and famished as we were, we caught energy from our admiration of the sublimity which was unveiled before us." The mountains with their sharp points, beetling cliffs, and blue summits crowned with clouds appeared as ruined castles, cities and fortifications. A Maryland volunteer, hypnotized by the sight, dreamed of knightly warfare as he saw in the craggy summits "a never-ending variety of castle, cathedral, palace and spires." The grandeur of the scenery set hearts aflame and imaginations wandering.

The towns through which the men marched were as strange as the landscape. Although some soldiers dismissed them as a jumbled collection of filthy and nondescript hovels, others found an exotic quality in the villages. The opulence of the churches and the contrasting poverty of their surroundings brought to mind scenes from the Middle Ages. In Ceralvo the white walls of the "singularly oriental" looking church, bathed by moonlight, reminded the imaginative observer of the Crusades and of "the stirring events of the Alhambra, when the Spaniards drove the Moors from their elysium homes, and reared the cross where before the crescent waved in sullen dignity." It was not difficult for the writer to imagine himself engaged in a similar crusade.[25]

As the men approached Monterey, their eagerness for battle
mounted. Speculation ran through the ranks, some believing that Monterey would be taken easily, others convinced that "we will have a pretty
tight fight." For one Tennessee volunteer, the principal concern was
that he would "not get an opportunity of shooting at a Mexican." An
Indiana soldier observed incredibly that hard marches and daring adventures filled the citizen-soldier all the more with "patriotic devotion
to his country." As they neared the city, the sound of cannon-fire
ahead steeled their nerves. Men who had begun to lag suddenly ignored their blistered feet and the debilitating effects of the heat,
"straightened themselves up and pressed forward with an eagerness
which showed that their sufferings were all forgotten." The blood
surged and strange hopes ran through their minds. "A city to be
stormed, and glory to be won!"

It was as if the soldiers had been transported back to some medieval
field, facing an enemy drawn up in colorful array before his stronghold.

> The mists still clung around the turrets of its churches, and enveloped its
> commanding heights; but the ascending sun constantly dissipated the veil,
> until palace and hill, barricade and fort, with long lines of tents and pen-
> dant flags presented themselves, as if floating in the pure ether with which
> they were surrounded. All was silent; not a breath of air stirred; dewy
> softness rested upon every thing.

When a Mexican battery opened fire from "one of the bastions of the
citadel," the Americans responded with "a cry of exultation" that
echoed off the mountainsides. An army poet was moved to record the
scene in verse:

> There lay the noble city—its cathedrals, and its towers
> And parapets; its palaces, and gardens bright with flowers—
> With the sunlight falling on it, over tower and dome and spire,
> Through the mellow morning radiance, in a rain of golden fire:
> Never, even in dreams of Orient lands, had Saxon eyes looked down
> On so glorious a country, or so beautiful a town.[26]

The battle for Monterey was a costly struggle, marked by bloody,
desperate street and house-to-house fighting. It was, however, immediately idealized by soldiers, correspondents, and the folks back home.
Print-makers portrayed the conflict in romantic, medieval terms as they
produced lithographs of soldiers storming turreted walls, battlements,
and castles; scenes were drawn of fighting over street barricades that
were reminiscent of Delacroix. On a slope west of the city lay an abandoned bishop's residence, dilapidated and in ruins, that had been fortified by the Mexican defenders; its capture by the Americans was an
important factor in their victory. The attack on the "Bishop's Palace"

Third Day of the Siege of Monterey.
Lithograph by Sarony & Major. From *Pictorial Life of General Taylor* (1847).

Battle of Monterey. Lithograph by Nathaniel Currier. Courtesy Library of Congress.

was immediately invested with romantic elements. The building, observed one soldier, conformed to all he had read of the "old castles of Europe." Another imagined that "many a gay cavalier and lady fair" had been entertained within its walls. One wonders if these men were looking at the same nondescript pile represented by the army's official artist, Daniel P. Whiting.[27]

The capture of Monterey was hailed as one of the most extraordinary feats in the annals of warfare. The city had been deemed impregnable, having withstood a siege by Spain's royal troops during Mexico's war for independence. America's soldiers, "far advanced in an enemy's country, attacking a city of the greatest possible natural and artificial strength, and carrying it by storm," had achieved what those of monarchical Spain had failed to do. There seemed to be some great historical significance in that.[28]

The war continued to arouse the romantic vision of America's fighting men as many of the soldiers fell prey to what one called the "fervid imagination of a wanderer's dream." The sight of his marching comrades, their hair and beards whitened by dust, brought to one soldier's mind Byron's prisoner of Chillon ("My hair is grey, but not with years"); later he gazed on crumbling columns in the chapparal and saw a castle where "some princely retainer of the haughty Montezuma once held his lordly revels." Scenes of banquet, dance, and Castilian maids flashed through his mind. Associations with Cortez and his conquistadors, the remains of Aztec civilization, and the splendor of the Valley of Mexico gave Scott's soldiers ingredients for romance they had never before imagined. Bivouacked amidst the ruins of a "palace" west of Jalapa, the men looked upon solitary columns, decayed woodwork, and half-buried marble floors and surmised that here knights had armed for battle. "Here blushing beauty has listened to the amorous tale breathed in her ear by her warrior lover." Looking down on the "enchanted" Valley of Mexico, the soldiers found that it required little effort "to throw over it an air of romance, far surpassing that of the most fabled lands of antiquity." Conspicuous in the distance was the castle of Chapultepec where once the "irresolute Montezuma" held forth, "and Indian maidens wove their garlands of flowers . . . to deck the brows of the successful braves."

For Illinoisan Samuel Chamberlain, a scouting expedition to Zacatecas was the storybook come to life:

> Some of the scenes reminded me of those described by [Sir Walter] Scott, and G. P. R. James, the ruined white walls of a Hacienda at a distance having a striking resemblance to the Feudal Castle of some bold Baron, and when about noon on rising the crest of a hill "a solitary horseman" was seen on the road coming towards us, I would not have been in the least surprised to have seen him draw up and challenge one of our number to break a lance in honor of "fayre Ladye" and chivalry.

The horseman, however, proved "a recreant Knight" and fled at the sight of the American patrol.[29]

Battle itself was invested with elements of romance. Two overworked words in the soldiers' lexicon were "sublime" and "beautiful," revealing perhaps a familiarity with Edmund Burke's well known and widely read treatise on the Sublime and the Beautiful; with the word "grandeur" they virtually constituted the extent of their romantic vocabulary. Finding his first taste of battle at Palo Alto "truly sublime," a young dragoons lieutenant concluded that war was a "soul stirring and noble excitement." He wasn't so sure the next day, as he walked about the field at Resaca de la Palma surrounded by mangled bodies and the moans and shrieks of the wounded. "I have read many accounts of battles," he remarked, "but never a description of one." It was a telling comment and an important distinction. Yet, to a fellow officer the battle was "sublime and beautiful" even though the head of a soldier next to him had been carried away by a Mexican shell.[30]

A popular image (the "supreme romantic image," according to Cunliffe) was that of the "forlorn hope"—the lone soldier, standing above the battle, fighting off the enemy horde; the single horseman suddenly surrounded by fierce guerrillas; the small select group, picked for some dangerous assignment, contending against superior numbers in what would appear to be a hopeless situation. The image was depicted by artists and sung by poets in their tributes to the heroism of the war; the literature is replete with such instances. At Chapultepec, a small hand-picked force was supplied with pick-axes and scaling ladders and ordered to charge the enemy's advanced batteries and scale the castle walls. "I collected my little party," wrote Daniel Harvey Hill, "and for more than a mile was far in advance of all our troops in the chase of the enemy. . . . 'Twas a sublime and exalted feeling that which we experienced whilst chasing some five thousand men with but little more than a dozen." Doniphan's men penetrating northern Mexico, isolated from supplies and reinforcements; and Scott's army itself, deep inside Mexico, its supply lines under continuous harassment and surrounded by a hostile population, facing an enemy that was superior in strength, were described as forlorn hopes, contending against desperate odds.[31]

Death itself became an object of romantic veneration. The men were of a generation that sentimentalized death in poetry, fiction, and drama, that exhibited not only a spiritual fascination with death but also a belief in death's ennobling qualities. Death was a release from the problems and sadness of the world but it was also the individual's ultimate communion with God and nature, the key to immortality. To die for one's country was the most ennobling of all, for the deceased won an everlasting place in the hearts of his grateful countrymen, a form of immortality in itself. The American soldier, insisted an Indiana volunteer, was not afraid to lay down his life for his country, "when his eyes close upon the stars and stripes, and the shout of victory is the last

sound that greets his ear." Writing to his parents, a young Pennsylvanian confided, "If it should this time be my lot to fall, I hope it will be
at the red-mouthed cannon, with feet to the foe, back to the earth, and
face toward the canopy of heaven." The instinct for survival, however,
was overpowering, and the conviction that death in battle was somehow
ennobling did not cause soldiers to court it. At Buena Vista, a terrified
Indianan, trapped in a ravine, overcome with fatigue and thirst and
facing the murderous fire of the Mexican line, leaned against a rocky
ledge and made up his mind to die. His thoughts went to his mother
and to the effect his death would have on her. "I was involuntarily
aroused . . . made an effort for those I loved and gained the summit"—
and survival.[32]

The hope of his countrymen's gratitude, wrote one volunteer,
spurred the soldier on; without it, "patriotism would die—and our
national honor would become a byword and a jest among the nations of
the earth." The soldier's death in his country's "righteous and victorious" battle, concluded army surgeon Richard McSherry, was a hero's
death, a death of "devoted patriotism and of high renown." Weep not,
declared an orator, for those who baptized their patriotism in blood,
for "we envy their fate."[33]

The dying moments of fallen soldiers were told and retold in the
war's literature, and their last words were offered as evidence of the
patriotic ardor of the men in Mexico. As his life ebbed after having
been hit at Monterey, Philip Barbour pressed his wife's miniature to his
lips and exclaimed, "Tell her I died on the field of victory." When
William H. Watson, commanding Baltimore's volunteers, fell in the
streets of Monterey his thoughts were of his men. His last words, according to one source, were, "Who will dare say now that American
volunteers cannot be depended upon in any fight." In another version,
Watson, already wounded and urged to withdraw, cried out: "Never,
boys! Never will I yield an inch! I have too much Irish blood in me to
give up!" A moment later he was dead. Perhaps the most widely publicized last words were those of Captain John R. Vinton, written to his
family just before he was killed by a Mexican shell in the siege of Vera
Cruz:

> My confidence in the overruling Providence of God is unqualified; so that
> I go to the field of battle assured that whatever may befall me will be for
> the best. I feel proud to serve my country in this her time of appeal; and
> should even the worst—death itself—be my lot, I shall meet it cheerfully in
> the beautiful Roman sentiment, *Dulce et decorum est pro Patria mori.*

To many Americans, Vinton's final message held a comforting reassurance that the struggle so far from home had a larger and nobler
purpose.[34]

For all the sentiment and pathos associated with battlefield death, dying had its horrors as well. After the excitement of the battle, when "the spirit is stirred to a courageous madness" and "all the fierce instincts of our nature are aroused," a sober reaction set in. The romance, heroism, and patriotic ardor were suddenly tempered by the sights and sounds of the battle's aftermath. The disorder of the field, the jumbled masses of discarded equipment, broken guns, battered cannon, and personal effects; the dead horses and mules; the bodies of the fallen soldiers and the piteous cries of the wounded brought the real meaning of war home to the men. Passing over the field at Cerro Gordo immediately following the battle, a regular soldier contemplated the "ghastly corpses [that] but yesterday were as full of life and animation as I was at that moment" and felt a "sickening loathing" at the human sacrifice which poets and historians often dignified in terms of honor and glory. Three days later, a South Carolina volunteer marched over the same field and gazed in disbelief at the "legs and arms, and putrid carcasses of men torn and mangled by cannon balls, and left, half devoured by the beasts and birds of prey." He gained, he wrote, an accurate realization of the war's horrors that contrasted with all that he had read of battles and warfare.

Observing the unburied remains of Mexican soldiers on the fields of Palo Alto and Resaca de la Palma eight months after the battles were fought, an Indiana volunteer asked if "this was indeed glory." The sight spoke more eloquently of war's real horror than all the books and sermons ever written. "The dawn of a bright day is upon us," he wrote in his journal, "when nations shall learn war no more forever."[35]

"Seeing the elephant"

Recounting his experiences on the long trek through northern Mexico as an officer in Doniphan's command, a Missouri volunteer recalled that he and his men had "laboured in the trench, suffered fatigue, privation and thirst, upon long marches, and fought the unequal combat, *and gained nothing by it,* BUT OUR OWN IMPERISHABLE GLORY!" The soldier may have been facetious but his comment did reflect the conviction of some of the nation's fighting men that the honor and glory they had gained outweighed the hardship they had experienced. One of the "wonders of war," commented a volunteer, was that "there is nothing else on earth in which splendor is mingled to a greater degree with misery." A South Carolinian put it another way, following his first combat experience: "Glory and all that is nothing but Fudge, although I must confess that the idea of making the enemy fly is exciting in the extreme."[36]

For many the romance of the war was dispelled by the realities of the soldier's life in a strange and often inhospitable environment. Soldiering in Mexico was vastly different from marching before an admiring citizenry back home. The visions of a romantic war in an exotic land,

dreams of "citron groves or perfumed bowers," quickly evaporated
once the volunteers arrived on the Rio Grande. Describing his camp
near Matamoros, Indiana volunteer Frank Scribner cautioned that "if
you think this a romantic spot, or that there is poetry connected with
our situation, you need only imagine us trudging through a swamp,
lugging our mouldy crackers and fat bacon . . . to become convinced
that this is not a visionary abode, but stern reality." Still, he added, "I
never yet have regretted the step I have taken."[37]

Americans had a phrase for the experience, "to see the elephant." Its
origins are obscure but its meaning was clear to everyone. John Russell
Bartlett in his *Dictionary of Americanisms* (1848) defined it as a southwestern phrase although its use by midcentury was national in scope. "To
see the Elephant," according to Bartlett, was "to undergo any disappointment of high-raised expectations." He cited the Mexican War to
illustrate its usage: "men who have volunteered for the Mexican war,
expecting to reap lots of glory and enjoyment, but instead have found
only sickness, fatigue, privations, and suffering, are currently said to
have '*seen the elephant.*'" The phrase, in its common usage, often went
beyond disappointment to encompass any new, broadening, even
frightening, experience, without necessarily suggesting a negative
quality.[38]

Writing from Mexico City late in the war, Jacob Oswandel assured
his friends that he had seen "considerable of the *elephant,* in fact all of
him that was to be seen since we landed on the shores below Vera
Cruz." A newspaper correspondent in Matamoros announced his intention of describing in his dispatches "what are here called the features of the elephant." A surgeon with Kearny's army, after crossing
the desert on the lower Colorado River, confided, "I have seen the
Elephant and I hope I shall never be compelled to cross it again."
When Scribner published his account of camp life in Mexico he did so
anonymously, "By One Who Has Seen the Elephant." A reviewer in
Godey's agreed that Scribner "certainly did see the huge animal." Indeed, Cornelius Mathews's short-lived wartime effort at humor and
satire, *The Elephant,* insisted that the surest way to get a view of the
beast was "to go to Mexico."[39]

That the elephant could be seen on the field of battle was expected;
where it was not expected was on the march or in the camps. Marching
sometimes as much as eighteen miles a day, under a blazing sun with
an intensity of heat never before experienced, through chapparal or
sand, without adequate water was not uncommon. Men dropped from
the ranks, seeking shelter under trees or among the bushes, not caring
whether they lived or died. "You would scarcely believe that human
nature could endure such privation and exposure," wrote a Maryland
volunteer. Faces became swollen and blistered, lips cracked, and feet
swelled and were bruised. In camp, the men were attacked by "myriads
of crawling, flying, stinging and biting things." Rattlesnakes, lizards,

tarantulas, and scorpions were a constant threat and the mosquitoes were regarded as a more formidable enemy than the Mexicans. "All these small nuisances are universally pronounced in camp as death to one's patriotic emotions," wrote a Georgian who resented having to fight the insects without prospect of "finding their masters, (our enemy)." Mexico, he concluded, must be a rich field for the study of entomology and natural history.[40]

Food was a recurring problem for the soldier in Mexico. "The stomach," wrote one volunteer, "is the regulator of the human machine, and the seat of the motive power; while digestion is the thermometer that measures the rise and fall and indicates the extent of his capacity." Yet in spite of its importance, the efforts of the government to provision the army were often inadequate, inefficient, and weakened by corruption. Daily rations of pork and bacon, flour, salt, vinegar, beans, and coffee were issued to each soldier; it was common practice for the soldiers to join together in "messes," pooling their rations and rotating the task of cooking. That was the ideal. In reality, supply was frequently haphazard, and days (even weeks) would go by without the ration. More often, the food that was issued was spoiled. "Our food is abominable," wrote an Ohio volunteer from the Rio Grande, "when you break a biscuit, you can see it move." Moldy crackers, rancid pork, and bug-infested flour were issued to the men. The government contracted with private individuals for supplies of beef, and herds of cattle were driven with the columns as they marched into Mexico. At the evening's halt, animals were slaughtered to provide meals for the men, but the beef was usually of such a quality that "it took a strong man to stand it." Civilian beef contractors accompanying the army often found themselves shouldering muskets and fighting the enemy, and some of them were wounded in action. In the more established camps, slaughter pens were set up but their proximity created other problems, polluting the water supply and attracting insects. Complaints about the food were common, and most of the health problems suffered by the men were attributed to poor diet. One Illinois volunteer, with tongue in cheek, tried to put the best face on a bad situation. Informing his family that he was "fatter and heartier" than ever before, he boasted that his regiment had plenty of "good hard crackers" (he was convinced they had been baked during the Revolutionary War), "some fine flour when the bugs are sifted . . . gobs of pickled pork and bacon, salty as the deuce . . . devilish good Beans, pickled onions, cabbage and to cap all *Sour Crout*."[41]

Food supplied by the government—lacking in both quality and quantity—was supplemented by whatever the soldiers could acquire from other sources. When artilleryman Francis Collins landed on the beach near Vera Cruz he carried four days' rations in his haversack (sea biscuit and boiled beef); he received no further ration for three weeks. "We were compelled to live almost entirely on the Mexican cattle which we found wandering among the hills and woods in the neighborhood of our camp," he wrote in his journal, but "they were poor miserable things." Cattle, pigs, and chickens belonging to Mexican farmers were frequently seized despite strong protests by the Mexicans to army authorities. Winfield Scott had ordered that all provisions acquired from the native population be paid for, and efforts were made to punish those soldiers who disregarded the order. One wholesale attack on a pen of hogs near Perote so infuriated General Joseph Lane that he ordered all those involved to be bucked and gagged (a traditional form of army punishment). The numbers, however, were so great (including Pennsylvania, Ohio, and Indiana volunteers and regular army men) that the punishment could not be carried out. Near Vera Cruz a caravan of mules laden with seventeen barrels of wine was captured and a nearby herd of 200 head of cattle was seized. The wine and beef were issued to the men, "the first Peninsula touch we have had since the commencement of the war," according to one of the soldiers. Major Monsoon (a character in Charles Lever's Peninsular War fiction), he added, "should have been present to have enjoyed it." Marching soldiers picked fruit from groves along the road (oranges were a special delicacy) and chewed ripe sugar cane. The cane juice, "to the dry throat of a soldier who has been marching through clouds of dust, is the consummation of earthly enjoyments."[42]

From the moment Americans first crossed the Rio Grande, they were besieged by Mexican vendors with wares to sell, mostly fresh fruit and vegetables, bread, milk, and the more spirited beverages that were locally produced from cactus or grain. Mexican civilians (mainly women) established market stalls in the army camps from which they also sold hats (soldiers quickly learned to wear the broad-brimmed straw hats as protection from the sun), other articles of clothing, and souvenirs. The Mexicans became dependable suppliers of food to the army, and depending on whether he had some money the soldier came to rely heavily on their presence to supplement the government-issued rations. Many of the men were tempted to sample Mexican cooking itself, sometimes to their regret. Tortillas became a staple in the soldiers' diet, as they were in that of the Mexicans, but the highly spiced sauce that frequently went with them was more than the soldier could take. "The sauce," observed a Missourian, "caused my mouth to burn to a blister" and later, after having partaken of local whiskey and onion pie, he noted, "the very thought of the mess makes my mouth burn."[43]

Under such conditions, it is not surprising that disease took a heavy toll, accounting for seven times the number of battle deaths. Epidemics swept the army camps (in the United States as well as in Mexico), including measles and the dread *vomito*, or yellow fever, but by far the greatest cost was exacted by those illnesses traceable to unsanitary conditions, strange and unclean food, polluted water, and an often hostile climate. Amoebic dysentery and diarrhea brought death and disability to thousands of soldiers throughout the war.[44] Known to the men as the "blues," diarrhea was not only physically debilitating (and frequently fatal) but also dispiriting to the young volunteers who had rushed off to Mexico in search of romance and glory. Many who suffered tried to carry on. Three days' march out of Vera Cruz, an officer in the Third Kentucky Regiment reported, "My men are feeble . . . with diarrhea. They trudge along, curse the war, obey my orders, but look like they have harder times than they expected." Others were hospitalized and left behind—in Jalapa, in Perote, in Puebla—as their units moved on. When those left at Perote had recovered sufficiently to resume the march, they were mustered together into a unit known as the "Diarrhea Blues" and marched westward to rejoin their comrades. Because of lack of medicine, the crowded hospital facilities however crude, and the harsh effects of the climate, many of the sick were simply discharged and sent home.[45]

Henry S. Lane, whose Indiana regiment remained in camp on the Rio Grande throughout the war, watched his men fall sick and die and meditated on the horrors of war. "Poetry, painting, and eloquence will . . . teach a gaping world the splendid achievements and brilliant results of our victories," he wrote, "but who shall sing the horrors of this campaign?" Thoughts of patriotism, honor, and glory turned to ashes as young men he had urged to enlist lay dying in their crowded tents without ever having encountered an enemy. In the great rush of eloquence that greeted the returning soldiers, some orators sought to do honor to those whose "fiery hearts were extinguished in the dull camp or on the gloomy march." It was easy to die in battle, one speaker declared, but "to waste away with sickness; to be crushed by the blows of an unseen enemy . . . to feel that your name will occupy no place in the bright scroll of fame," this was the "noblest proof of the patriot's devotion." One regular officer early in the war, noting the sickness among the volunteers, warned that the soldier's life was "no sinecure." The "Elephant has been seen by a few," but before the war should end he believed that "some other animal worse than 'the Elephant' will make its appearance."[46]

"Seeing the elephant" penetrated the war's romantic veil for many of the soldiers; others regarded it simply as a necessary hazard to the glory they still expected to find on the battlefield. For the folks back home, the suffering of the soldiers, while reported in the press, was but distantly felt, overshadowed always by the clash of armies in battle and by the rejoicing that followed the victories. Not every battle, however, struck a romantic chord. The bitterly fought conflicts in the Valley of Mexico, while decisive to the war's end, did not fire the imagination as much as the earlier clashes, except for Chapultepec, which involved an assault against a fortified castle on a hilltop. Contreras and Churubusco were confused and costly, the battle of Molino del Rey not only costly but ill-advised. The last resulted in criticism of Winfield Scott's judgment; his decision to attack supposed ammunition works was attributed to an "obstinate pride of opinion." Regarded as the "severest battle of the Mexican war," the only one which was "austerely disapproved," Molino del Rey cost the Americans dearly yet achieved no military result. "The flower of chivalry was uselessly destroyed."[47]

On the other hand, at no time during the war was popular fascination with battle so aroused as in the first months of 1847, when two militarily decisive triumphs burst upon the national consciousness almost simultaneously. There were romantic elements involved in each of the engagements that seemed to confirm the public's perception of the conflict as a romantic war.

Following the capture of Monterey in September 1846, Zachary Taylor gradually extended his army's hold on northeastern Mexico. Victoria, the capital of Tamaulipas, and the port city of Tampico were occupied; to the west the army took Saltillo and by early February had moved its advanced units southward on the road to San Luis Potosi. At the same time, disquieting reports reached Taylor that Santa Anna, at the head of a large body of Mexican troops, was moving northward to challenge his advance.

Taylor's army, it was feared, was not in a strong condition to meet a Mexican attack. Late in 1846, plans were matured to open a second front against Vera Cruz, the Mexican seaport that held the key to Mexico City itself. Winfield Scott was placed in command and in early January drew off large numbers of men, including virtually all the regulars, from Taylor's army. Taylor's protests were unavailing; his ranks were not only seriously depleted but he was left with an army that consisted almost entirely of untried volunteers.

Public attention was divided between the two armies. Scott's force, including new volunteer units as well as regulars, began to gather on the Island of Lobos, southeast of Tampico, and by early March had moved to its appointed rendezvous off Anton Lizardo, 200 miles further south and only a dozen miles from Vera Cruz. In the meantime, rumors of a costly battle between Taylor's army and a superior Mexican force in the mountains south of Saltillo filtered into the United States. The Americans, it was said, had been driven back with heavy losses, and Taylor, with four thousand of his men, was taken prisoner.

"The whole country," noted *Niles' National Register,* "has been . . . in a state of intense and daily increasing anxiety." Taylor's army had been attacked by an enemy force so vastly superior as to render the issue "very doubtful if not disastrous." At the same time nothing had been heard from Vera Cruz, although it was certain that the enemy was prepared "to give us a warm reception on landing." News was expected momentarily of Scott's triumph or defeat, "of blood, and the loss of many lives, beyond doubt." Of the fate of Taylor's army everything remained conjecture and speculation. "How many throbbing hearts," the *Register* commented, "are aching with suspense and yet dreading to hear the intelligence that is expected every hour."[48]

Reliable reports of Taylor's battle did not reach New Orleans until a month after it was fought, and it was another nine days before the news hit the streets in New York on April 1. Two days later, on April 3, New York newspapers announced the bloodless landing of Scott's army at Vera Cruz. The suspense gave way at once to rejoicing. No engagements in the war evoked such a jubilant response as the Battle of Buena Vista on February 22–23 and the capture of Vera Cruz the following month.

Buena Vista's setting challenged the descriptive power of the soldiers involved. Lying in a narrow pass between mountain ranges (known to the Mexicans as La Angostura or The Narrows), the field was dominated by towering peaks. To the west of the road that led through the pass a small stream had carved a network of steep-sided gullies, while on the east a plateau, broken by several deep ravines, rose toward the mountain slopes. The pass lay at the head of a fertile valley that broadened southward toward the hacienda of Agua Nueva. North of the pass, on the road to Saltillo, was a livestock ranch, called Buena Vista because of the spectacular view it commanded, surrounded by acres of well-watered grazing land.

An Indiana volunteer, camping near Buena Vista a week before the battle, found the setting "truly romantic," the view one of the finest he ever beheld. The "huge mountain piles" that overpowered the tented plain, he wrote, excited his "loftiest sentiments." The sight of the craggy mountains bathed in the golden light of the setting sun left him almost speechless. "If the gorgeousness of the sunsets could be transferred to canvas," he suggested, "the painter might be called a wild enthusiast." Several months later, a young lieutenant in the Massachusetts Regiment described the scene as "one of the prettiest places in the world." "We see only three things here. Mountain, sky and plain."

Ordnance officer Charles Kingsbury believed the setting was worthy of the battle's significance, convinced that the men fought more bravely because of the beauty of their surroundings. "Nature was there in her grandeur and her power," he wrote, "and far as the eye could reach, the peaks of the Sierra Madre were towering in the skies."

If Napoleon could excite enthusiasm from the antiquity of the pyramids, . . . the members of both armies might have here drawn inspiration from a higher source. They were in the presence of the pre-Adamites. Around them were monuments of creation, which had risen when the "morning stars first sang together," and which will crumble into decay only, when "the sun shall slumber in the cloud, forgetful of the voice of the morning."[49]

"It was a beautiful battle," reported one officer. An Illinois volunteer thought the scene on the battle's first day the "most grand and gorgeous spectacle" he had ever witnessed. More than 20,000 "victims of Mexican oppression and the myrmidons of Mexican despotism" faced 5000 American soldiers. It was Washington's birthday, a coincidence no American was allowed to forget. The sun glancing from the lances and bayonets of the Mexican troops as they moved into line, the sounds of their bugles, the rattling of the artillery carriages, and the prancing of their richly decorated horses—all gave the moment a color and pageantry that recalled the splendor of storied contests in earlier times. "I doubt if the 'Sun of Austerlitz' shone on a more brilliant spectacle," commented another Illinoisan. Taylor's volunteers watched with fascination as a procession of priests moved down the enemy line with all the "gorgeous paraphernalia" of the Catholic Church while the massed bands played a "solemn anthem." The infantry knelt, the cavalry lowered their lances, and the colors were dropped as the priests administered their benediction. The ceremony over, a puff of smoke rose from a nearby battery, and a thirty-two-pound solid shot fell into the road near the American lines. The battle had begun. Skirmishers on the mountain slopes opened fire, and the entire side of the mountain burst into one sheet of flame. The sight was a splendid one, wrote a volunteer, and "our hearts warmed towards home and country." As the firing spread, the discharges followed more rapidly than the "sounds of the Swiss bell ringers in the fierce fervor of a *finale*," while the artillery volleys echoed through the mountains like an Alpine storm.[50]

Such descriptive flights were not isolated. Writing of the next day's fight, another volunteer wrote of the vivid impression made by the "huge, craggy mountains," frowning gloomily upon the narrow valley where "our little band of iron-nerved and brave-hearted men" awaited the onslaught of the Mexican host. The rattle of musket-fire on the mountain sides and the thunder-tones of the artillery echoing from the "deep defiles and the rocky steeps" punctuated the cold, crisp air. Later in the afternoon, the elements themselves joined the fray. For twenty minutes, a violent rainstorm, accompanied by thunder and lightning, swept the field. The mountains trembled to their centers, and the swirling clouds "strove to veil the bloody scene from the eye of heaven." The mingling of the thunder claps and lightning flashes with the sounds of the battle formed "a union of sights and sounds terrifically sublime."[51]

The presence at Buena Vista of Mexico's elite cavalry, the colorful lancers, enhanced the romance with which the battle was viewed. The lancers had been encountered before and would be met again, but it was at Buena Vista that they were at their most impressive, massed in spectacular array. No other Mexican unit excited so much awe and admiration, their sight alone sufficient to distract the volunteers from their purpose. At Monterey an Ohio volunteer imagined that the "days

Battle of Buena Vista, by Henry R. Robinson. Courtesy Library of Congress.

of Spanish chivalry were revived," so much did the horsemen remind him of the "knights of olden times." Later, confronting a troop of lancers in the campaign against Mexico's capital, a Palmetto rifleman was reminded of the "mailed champions of the days of knight errantry." Armed with eight-foot-long lances, a shortened musket called an *escopeda,* and a razor-sharp two-edged sword, the lancers were employed by Santa Anna at a critical juncture at Buena Vista in a desperate effort to crush Taylor's army.[52]

Shortly after noon on the 23rd, some 1500 lancers, the "chivalry of Mexico," in bright scarlet coats, shiny buttons, and snow-white belts, their horses richly caparisoned, advanced on the American line like knights on a medieval field, crimson pennants and brightly colored banners waving over their ranks. Sitting erect in their saddles, their brass helmets topped with flowing red and black plumes, their lances decorated with ribbons and reflecting the bright sunlight, they moved "at an easy hand-gallop," their lines perfectly dressed, never losing their intervals or breaking their formations. Bugles sounded the charge and the horsemen chanted a song as they moved forward. The movement had a nonchalance about it that recalled the "ideal pictures of the cavalry of olden days."

Standing their ground between two deep ravines were the Third Indiana Regiment and Jefferson Davis's Mississippi Rifles, joined by remnants of the Second Indiana that had been rallied from their earlier flight. The men were formed in a flattened V-formation, the open end toward the enemy, and cautioned to hold their fire. It was "an awful moment," wrote an Indianan. The volunteers gazed on the approaching ranks with wonder and admiration and some were unsure whether they should applaud or fire their weapons. The lancers slowed their progress and as they moved within musket range came to a halt, puzzled that no shots had been fired. At that moment, Brigadier General Joseph Lane, commanding the Indiana regiments, called out, "Now give it to them!" The volunteers opened a murderous fire. Saddles were emptied, horses fell, and the ranks were plunged into disorder.

As the lancers fell back in confusion, the volunteers moved in pursuit, shouting their delight and throwing their caps into the air. "It was, indeed, a glorious achievement," wrote one of the soldiers. For the first time he felt there was glory in war. "I almost thought I could not be killed." To another soldier, "it was a sublime, a terrible sight." The episode was told and re-told, by the soldiers themselves, by newspaper correspondents, by writers and poets, and by orators who found in it the clear superiority of America's citizen-soldiers. The feat performed by Indiana volunteers, boasted a proud and loyal Indianan, was unparalleled in the annals of warfare, while in Mississippi that state's volunteers were credited with achieving what had never been achieved before, the repulse of a cavalry charge by riflemen without bayonets.

Whoever deserved the credit (Zachary Taylor singled out his son-in-law Davis without mentioning the Indianans), the ill-fated charge of the Mexican lancers augmented the romance of the battle and of the war.[53]

As darkness fell on the 23rd the battle subsided. The exhausted volunteers settled down to a cold, sleepless night, confident that Santa Anna would resume his attacks the following morning, and unsure whether they would have the strength to resist them. With the first light of dawn, however, the enemy was nowhere to be seen. To their astonishment, Santa Anna had silently withdrawn his army during the night and started his long march southward, his force depleted by heavy casualties and mounting desertions. Gradually, the realization that the battle was over struck home. In the words of a young dragoon officer,

> a sound went along our lines ever to be remembered. It was but a single cry at first; then a murmur, which rose and swelled upon the ear like the voice of a tempest; then a prolonged and thrilling shout: "VICTORY! VICTORY! VICTORY! THE ENEMY HAS FLED! THE FIELD IS OURS!"

A "long, exultant American 'HURRAH' " rang through the pass.

The eagerness with which the volunteers had entered the contest and the joy they expressed at its end now gave way to feelings of horror as they wandered over the battlefield. The bodies of their comrades, many of them disfigured and stripped of their clothing, were buried, the wounded removed to makeshift hospitals in Saltillo. No distinction was made between friend and enemy. Thousands of wounded Mexican soldiers had been left behind on the field and along the road to the south, adding to the task of the already overworked and crude army medical facilities. Casualties had been heavy: over 270 Americans had been killed and almost four hundred wounded. Mexican losses ran much higher. Buena Vista was the bloodiest battle in American history up until that time.[54]

The Battle of Buena Vista entered the national consciousness almost immediately, and it is not surprising that it should have been celebrated in prose and poetry, in music and in art. "On the mere perusal of an account of this battle," suggested one writer, "the blood courses freer, and all the animal energies are to the utmost aroused. . . . The glory of war is magnified, the daring actors in its scenes of hazard and carnage are exalted in estimation, and we become emulous of their deeds of chivalry." The romantic associations suggested by the soldiers were multiplied in the press back home. Analogies with Thermopylae and with Agincourt, Crecy, and Poitiers became commonplace. The pass at Buena Vista, it was said, would become as familiar in song and story as Roncesvalles Strait, which American readers recognized as the locale of the *Song of Roland*.

"The sublime scenery amid which this memorable battle was fought," predicted a reviewer, "will . . . make it, in future time, an attractive theme for the poet and painter." The poets could not wait and rushed into print with gushingly romantic verses, and songwriters, dramatists, and printmakers joined the scramble to celebrate the triumph.[55]

The Battle of Buena Vista was a battle of volunteers and it was this fact that accounted for much of its popularity. Except for about 200 dragoons and three batteries of artillery, the men were volunteers from Arkansas, Kentucky, Illinois, Indiana, and Mississippi. Only Jefferson Davis's Mississippi Rifles had seen combat before; the rest faced enemy fire for the first time. To an admiring nation, a "handful" of raw, inexperienced citizen-soldiers, fighting in a foreign land thousands of miles from their homes, challenged and defeated a "host" of professional combat-hardened veterans five times their number. The officers that fell on the field—John J. Hardin of Illinois, Henry Clay, Jr., and William R. McKee of Kentucky, Archibald Yell of Arkansas and George Lincoln of Massachusetts—became instant heroes. The battle and the volunteers who won it, crowed Walt Whitman, "will live . . . on the enduring records of our Republic." The victory, wrote another, "confirms our belief in the invincibility and high destiny of the Anglo-Saxon race." History, declared John Frost, had not recorded a harder fought battle or a more brilliant victory. Henceforth, "the highest aspirations of military fame will be fulfilled when it shall be said of any fellow-citizen, *he was at* Buena Vista."[56]

The operation against Vera Cruz contrasted markedly with the dramatic engagement in the mountains at Buena Vista. The result of months of careful planning, the expedition required the skillful coordination of military and naval activities, as well as the collection of vast amounts of *matériel* and stores by the Quartermaster Department. An air of urgency hung over the preparations, for Winfield Scott was anxious to take Vera Cruz before the yellow fever (or *vomito*) season should begin. He originally believed that 15,000 men would be required but soon realized he would have to be content with far fewer. With the regular troops from Taylor's command were several new volunteer regiments (including units from Pennsylvania, New York, and South Carolina) that had been raised in response to President Polk's call in November 1846.

Logistical problems were encountered almost immediately, leading to frustrating delays. A serious shortage of transport vessels threatened to postpone the operation, and the specially built surfboats for landing the troops—double-ended, broad-beamed, flat-bottomed craft—were slow in arriving. The lack of transports delayed the movement of the soldiers to the rendezvous points. In the end, Scott decided to go ahead with what he had. Commodore David Conner, commanding the Navy's Home Squadron, made a reconnaissance of the coastline in the vicinity of Vera Cruz and selected a beach protected by an offshore island, the Isla de Sacrificios, about two and a half miles southeast of the city. The landing was scheduled for March 8 but the threat of bad weather delayed the operation until the next day.

The weather on March 9 could not have been better. The sun shone in a cloudless sky and a gentle breeze rippled the surface of the sea. The soldiers were transferred from their transports to the naval vessels, the surfboats were taken in tow, and the convoy moved to the landing site. The air was charged with excitement. A sailor who witnessed the operation from the foretop of the sloop-of-war *Albany* described the scene:

> The tall ships of war sailing leisurely along under their topsails, their decks thronged in every part with dense masses of troops, whose bright muskets and bayonets were flashing in the sunbeams; the gingling of spurs and sabres; the bands of music playing; the hum of the multitude rising up like the murmur of the distant ocean; the small steamers plying about, their decks crowded with anxious spectators; the long lines of surf-boats towing astern of the ships ready to disembark the troops . . .

By late afternoon, the vessels reached their assigned anchorages in the lee of Sacrificios, and the soldiers in the first wave—a division of regulars commanded by William Jenkins Worth—took their places in the surfboats.

A little before sundown the signal was given, and the surfboats pulled for the beach in one great sweep, the regimental and unit flags flying from their bows. For those waiting on shipboard, it was a thrilling sight. "Time can never erase from my mind the impressions that were made by the scenes that surrounded me," observed a South Carolina volunteer, his regiment assigned to the second wave. "The sky was perfectly clear, and the sun was just disappearing behind the snow-capped peak of Orizaba." A member of Tennessee's First Regiment was moved by the same sensation: "The sky was clear and serene—not a breath of air was stirring—the surf, with slow and measured swell, was sweeping lazily upon the shore—the sinking sun, tipping the far-off peak of Orizaba, flashed with golden light on the burnished arms and white trappings of the troops, who, in their broad line of boats, were striving with emulous excitement to be first on shore." The troops on shipboard watched breathlessly. Mexican cavalrymen who had been observed in the dunes earlier in the day were nowhere to be seen. When the surfboats grated on the sand, the men leaped into the water and ran up the beach. The flag was planted on a sand hill and as the Stars and Stripes unfolded in the evening breeze, wild and spontaneous cheering echoed through the still air. Shipboard bands struck up the

Landing of the Troops at Vera Cruz. Courtesy Library of Congress.

Star Spangled Banner. The second and third waves of troops—General Robert Patterson's division of volunteers and General David E. Twiggs's regulars—followed. Within five hours, more than 8600 men were landed on the beach without a single casualty. Under the light of a bright tropical moon—the kind that awakened "the feeling of romance"—the men regrouped and soon their camp fires extended for more than a mile along the beach. "It is wholly inexplicable to us," wrote a soldier in the Fourth Artillery Regiment, "why the enemy did not oppose our landing."

On following days, horses and mules were taken ashore, artillery pieces and ammunition ferried in the surfboats, and supplies of all kinds unloaded from the transports. Troop ships continued to arrive so that by March 24, two weeks later, more than 12,600 men had been landed.[57]

From the beginning, the operation was charged with historic significance and romantic associations. George Ballentine found the landing so surrounded by "all the glorious pomp and circumstance of war" that he was confident few in the army would have wished to miss it, eager as they all were for "the shadow of glory which the distinction conferred." The action, it was pointed out, exceeded earlier troop landings, especially those of the French at Algiers in 1830 and the English in Egypt in 1801, proving once again the military capability of the American republic. Raphael Semmes, watching the landing from the decks of the *Raritan,* went back 300 years to find its counterpart. Every stage of the operation was reminiscent of that earlier conquest, "tinctured with the romance of that remote period, and emulous of the deeds which had characterized its actors." How curious it would have looked, Semmes speculated,

> had Cortez been able . . . to look down upon our gallant fleet, interspersed with that most wonderful and most potent of all modern machines, the steam-ship, and arrayed in the stars and stripes of an unknown flag! Time, with his scythe and hour-glass, had brought another and a newer race, to sweep away the moldered and moldering institutions of a worn-out people, and replace them with a fresher and more vigorous civilization.

That Scott's army landed at the same spot and on the same holiday (Good Friday) as that of the conquistador heightened the romance.[58]

Within four days of the landing, the troops had completed their encirclement of Vera Cruz. A walled city of some 15,000 inhabitants, guarded on the seaward side by the fortress of San Juan de Ulloa and on the land side by a broad sandy plain, the location was considered to be one of the strongest in North America. Although Scott was anxious to capture the city "before the return of the *vomito,*" he rejected the idea of taking it by direct assault, arguing that such an action would be too costly in the lives of civilians within the city as well as men in both armies.

By March 22, siege batteries were in place for the bombardment, and on the same day Scott made his formal call for the city's surrender. The scene recalled the stories of medieval warfare. With its fortified walls, its skyline broken only by the white domes and steeples of its churches, protected by a castle on the harbor side, Vera Cruz presented an aspect unlike any the soldiers, especially the volunteers (for some of the regulars had fought at Monterey), had ever seen before. Captain Joseph E. Johnston of the topographical engineers was selected to deliver Scott's summons. Accompanied by a bugler and bearing a white flag, Johnston advanced to the city walls, where the notes of "Parley" were sounded. The soldiers in the siege lines emerged from their emplacements and climbed the dunes to witness "the novel spectacle of summoning the surrender of a walled city." To one soldier, it was like "the *gesta* of the knights of old."

The refusal of the Mexican commander to surrender the city was the signal for the bombardment to begin. Late in the afternoon, the mortars in the completed batteries opened fire; at the same time, naval vessels, the navy's "mosquito fleet," moved into position and began shelling the city and its fortress. To supplement the army's firepower (Scott had received only one-fifth of the siege artillery he thought necessary for the operation), guns from several ships were brought ashore and installed in a naval battery. The seamen were ecstatic at the prospect of action, and the crew manning the naval battery was rotated every twenty-four hours to give more sailors an opportunity to participate. "I shall never forget the thrill which pervaded the squadron," wrote one midshipman, when it was announced "that we were to land guns and crews."[59]

As the bombardment began, sailors on the ships anchored offshore crowded into the rigging to witness the sight. "Jonathan had at last awakened from his slumber," wrote one of them, "and had set to work in earnest." "Bomb-shells" flew like hail stones into Vera Cruz; the army's mortars continued firing through the night, providing "one of the most striking displays that I ever beheld." The crash of falling shot, the bursting of the bombs, the "lurid flare" that flashed along the lines was a scene "peculiarly grand and sublime." The American fire was quickly answered by the Mexican defenders with unexpected accuracy. The naval battery, because of its exposed position and superior firepower, took the brunt of the Mexican artillery. A heavy blanket of smoke soon covered the city and the siege lines, punctuated only by the red bursts of the guns and the "long fiery streams" made by the balls. The shriek of the balls as they passed through the air was likened to a railway whistle, bearing "a more intimate relation to the sublime than the beautiful." Carrying the simile a step farther, a soldier suggested that the sounds of an "asthmatic engine at the starting of a train" were like "a strain of heavenly melody" in comparison with the din of the bombardment.[60]

The bombardment of Vera Cruz continued for 88 hours, from late afternoon of March 22 to early morning on March 26. After the initial excitement, some soldiers accepted the action with remarkable nonchalance. For others, the thrill they felt when the shelling began was tempered by thoughts of the Mexican civilians in the city. Once again the exhilaration gave way to a realization of war's horrors. Through the smoke the soldiers could see the effects of their work, burning buildings, others reduced to rubble. Large numbers of civilians gathered on the beach outside the city walls at the farthest point from the American batteries, hoping to save themselves. Individuals were observed on the rooftops "in the utmost consternation and apparent despair." The scene aroused feelings that overpowered even its "sublimity." The bombardment was a sight splendid to the eye; but to the heart it told tales of woe, of trial, and anguish. Had the shelling continued two days longer, remarked a volunteer, the "beautiful city of the true cross" would have been reduced to "one undistinguished mass of ruins."[61]

Negotiations for the surrender of the city began on March 26, agreement on the terms was reached the following day, and on the 29th the formal ceremony took place. Again, American soldiers were moved by the pageantry of war. Under a brilliant sun and cloudless sky, the Mexican troops in brightly colored uniforms filed out of the city gate, passed between the massed soldiers of Scott's army, regulars on one side, volunteers on the other, and deposited their weapons and colors a half-mile from the city walls. "It was a beautiful sight to see," wrote a Pennsylvania volunteer, "the Mexican army with their drums, fifes and bands of music playing and their flags flying in the air, marching out of their doomed city." Marching with the soldiers were large numbers of women and children, the former bearing heavy loads of baggage, furniture, and personal property. The ceremony completed, the Mexicans took up their march inland, carts bearing the sick and wounded bringing up the rear. "It reminded me more of the Departure of the Israelites than aught else I can compare it to," commented a newspaper correspondent.

As the city was evacuated the Mexican flags were lowered. When the last of the defenders had passed through the gate, three artillery companies, with their field pieces and colors, moved into Vera Cruz. Those that remained outside the walls stood motionless, their eyes directed toward Fort Santiago, one of the city's fortifications. Moments later, the American flag rose over the fort, and as "our glorious stripes and stars were unfolded to the breeze," salutes were fired from the batteries and the naval vessels offshore. The regimental bands struck up *Hail Columbia!* and, as a Tennessee volunteer described it, "the enthusiasm of the American army was aroused to its highest pitch." It was a stirring, emotional scene, one that would linger in the imagination long after the reality had passed.

As Scott's men moved into Vera Cruz they saw at firsthand the destructive effects of the shelling. "What a scene of desolation and distress met the eye at every turn!" Scarcely a building still stood that did not show damage. The Mexicans who remained in the city seemed broken in spirit, beaten down by fatigue and fear. As he strolled among the shattered buildings and rubble-strewn streets, the enthusiasm he had felt at the surrender suddenly subsided, the sailor from the *Albany* was reminded of Longfellow's lines:

> Is it, oh man, with such discordant noises,
>   With such accursed instruments as these,
> Thou drownest Nature's sweet and kindly voices,
>   And jarrest the celestial harmonies?
>
> Were half the power, that fills the world with terror,
>   Were half the wealth, bestowed on camps and courts
> Given to redeem the human mind from error,
>   There were no need of arsenals nor forts![62]

Scott's decision to take Vera Cruz by siege and bombardment rather than by storm was denounced as inhumane, especially by critics in England. To George Frederick Ruxton, the English explorer who had passed through Vera Cruz earlier, it was an "unnecessary act of cruelty." The city, he wrote, could have been taken easily by two battalions of Missouri volunteers; the fortress of San Juan de Ulloa was defended by only "seven hundred naked Indians." Ruxton's comment reflected at once his contempt for the Mexicans and his scorn for the American fighting man. The criticism was echoed by opponents of the war at home, spokesmen for peace societies, and others who branded Scott's policy as savage and barbarous. Even some of Scott's younger officers had favored a direct assault on the city, arguing that there was more glory in it for the army. Scott was unmoved, convinced that he had averted a needless shedding of blood. He later recalled the incident with some bitterness, complaining that more attention had been given to Taylor's victory at Buena Vista than to his successful operation against Vera Cruz. "Only a few faint cheers were heard for Vera Cruz." What the nation apparently wanted was a "long butcher's bill"; his casualties had been too low.[63]

Although Scott exaggerated the lack of reaction to his victory, it is true that Vera Cruz did not inspire the tributes to the glory and heroism of America's soldiers that were generated by Buena Vista. To be sure, the landing of the army, the bombardment from both land and sea, and the surrender were commemorated in poetry, song, and art but the volume fell short of Buena Vista's celebration. The operation against Vera Cruz lacked the drama of two armies contending for mastery in a rugged mountain setting. Opportunities for individual feats of courage were limited. American casualties had been unusually light (thirteen killed and fifty-five wounded) and, unlike Buena Vista,

Bombardment of Vera-Cruz. Lithograph by Carl Nebel. Courtesy Amon Carter Museum, Fort Worth, Texas.

did not include heroic officers struck down while leading their men
into combat. To the popular historian Joel Tyler Headley, Taylor had
shown at Buena Vista what hard fighting could accomplish; Scott's
triumph, on the other hand, was one of "skill and modern science," a
triumph of mind over castle walls and well-manned batteries. Buena
Vista, moreover, had been fought almost exclusively by volunteers,
while at Vera Cruz the volunteers' role was limited to constructing the
batteries and holding the lines of investment around the city. Much of
the credit for the operation's success had to be shared with the navy.
Furthermore, accounts of the bombardment in the press were balanced
by sobering reports of the suffering of Vera Cruz's civilian population.

In spite of these differences, Vera Cruz ranked with Buena Vista as a
victory of immense proportions. "A new page in the history of the
war," wrote Raphael Semmes, had been turned and the way "to the
rich and populous plains of Anahuac" had been opened. The fall of
Vera Cruz, the "Gibraltar of Mexico," declared Headley, was an achievement such as "had never been witnessed on this continent." To the
Mexicans, the capture of the city marked the first "signal of alarm" for
the capital of the republic itself. Until Vera Cruz, "the threats of the
United States, to make their flag float over the palace of the Moctezu-
mas, was regarded as a piece of madness."[64]

Although Scott's landing at Vera Cruz followed Taylor's victory at Buena Vista by two weeks, news of the two events arrived in some parts of
the United States almost simultaneously. Reliable reports of Buena
Vista were delayed by a combination of enemy action and the interrup-
tion of telegraphic communication on the Atlantic coast. On the day
Santa Anna engaged Taylor's army, Mexican cavalry cut the supply
route between Monterey and the Rio Grande, in effect isolating Taylor's force. It was not until early March that the route was reopened.
With the first train to get through to the Rio Grande was one of
Taylor's aides bearing the general's official report of the Battle of Buena Vista.

In the meantime, the press pounced on every rumor and fragmentary report. Piecing together scraps of information, New York newspapers announced on March 30 that Taylor had apparently won a
victory over Santa Anna but the paper's scenario was all wrong. Taylor,
it was reported, had fallen back on Saltillo following the Mexican attack. There, in a sharp engagement, his men had repelled a second
attack before falling back on Monterey. From entrenchments at Monterey, the American army had sallied forth and administered a total
defeat on Santa Anna's force. The story, all of it utterly false, demonstrated only the editors' ability to engage in imaginative flights of fancy.

Two days later the account was corrected when a special express (organized by the *New York Herald*) delivered New Orleans newspapers bearing an accurate account of the battle. Appearing on April 1, the news was at first received by skeptical readers as an April Fool's joke.

Suspense over the Vera Cruz expedition continued. On March 25, the *Herald* reported that the Mexican city was probably in American possession; later the paper passed on the rumor that Vera Cruz had capitulated without a shot being fired. On April 3, two days after the news of Buena Vista filled the paper's columns, headlines announced the successful landing of the army and the encirclement of the city; a week later, the paper's "special and extraordinary express" transmitted the "glorious intelligence" that Vera Cruz had surrendered. New Yorkers immediately celebrated. Business was suspended and buildings were decorated with flags. "The *furor* was actually terrific," the *Herald* noted. "Joy, patriotism and satisfaction were pictured on every countenance." A meeting of citizens was called into session and a committee was appointed to plan a public demonstration.[65]

Plans were made in many communities to celebrate the twin victories of Buena Vista and Vera Cruz in early May when the first anniversary of the opening battles at Palo Alto and Resaca de la Palma could also be observed. In South Carolina, where the news of Buena Vista and Vera Cruz had already been celebrated in Columbia and Charleston with torchlight processions, the firing of rockets and cannon, and band music, the governor proclaimed May 6 a day of "Thanksgiving and Prayer to Almighty God." The day was marked in town after town by parades, artillery salutes, and after dark the illumination of buildings.

In New York, on May 7, fireworks and roaring artillery marked the victories. Public buildings and private dwellings were illuminated with candles and transparencies, flags were displayed, and a grand procession moved through the streets. An estimated 400,000 people (surely an inflated figure) took part in the celebration. Even the *New York Tribune* noted grudgingly that the city's illumination was probably "the most splendid scene of the kind ever witnessed in this country." People of all ages—"tottering age, vigorous manhood, happy adolescence, and squalling babyhood"—had turned out to hail the army's achievements in Mexico.

New York's entertainment establishments added to the festivities. P. T. Barnum's American Museum not only provided space for people to watch the parade, with a brass band on the balcony playing patriotic airs, but also offered a special program "in honor of our Victorious Arms in Mexico." The Melodeon advertised a "splendid Panoramic Representation" of General Taylor and the battles of Palo Alto, Resaca de la Palma, Monterey and Buena Vista, "with the flight of the Mexican Army." At the fashionable Park Theatre, the program was highlighted by the singing of patriotic songs before a large transparent likeness of General Taylor while the more popular Bowery Theatre presented a new play entitled "The Battle of Buena Vista and the Bombardment of Vera Cruz" to an overflowing crowd.

On the following day, the national capital celebrated the victories with a fireworks display of "unequalled brilliance and splendor." The night before, news had been received of Scott's victory at Cerro Gordo, providing an additional incentive for the festivities. The names of military and naval officers were outlined in fireworks, rockets were launched, and buildings were bathed in "a universal blaze of light." Names of generals were illuminated in the windows of houses, and at the home of Washington's mayor an elaborate display featured General Scott with the inscription "Vera Cruz and St. Juan de Ulua" on one window and on another a full-length portrait of Taylor, with "Palo Alto, Resaca de la Palma, Monterey, Buena Vista." Because of the fire hazard, President Polk forbade the illumination of government buildings, but the White House and the homes of cabinet members were lit up. A huge bonfire between the Capitol and the navy yard composed of one hundred tar and turpentine barrels in a column forty feet high was lit, producing a pillar of fire that was seen for miles. The celebration was repeated in towns and cities throughout the United States.[66]

CHAPTER 5

A New Stock of Heroes

Leather Stocking

From out of the patriotic enthusiasm generated by the fighting and the romantic prism through which it was viewed were born the heroes of the Mexican War. The time was right for the appearance of a new set of individuals who could stir the imagination and inspire the intellect, a new national pantheon that would celebrate deeds of courage, daring, and leadership. "Our old supply was just thread-bare," one writer declared. One of the beneficial results of the Mexican War, he suggested, was that it augmented "our stock of 'heroes.' "[1]

The sentiment touched a deeper concern among midcentury Americans. With the passing of the Revolutionary generation—Jefferson and John Adams in 1826, Jackson in 1845 and John Quincy Adams three years later, to cite the most obvious examples—Americans felt a loss of contact with their national origins. The scenes of the Revolution, as Abraham Lincoln reminded an audience eight years before the Mexican War began, were fading into memory. While Lincoln urged his countrymen to carve new "pillars of the temple of liberty" out of the "solid quarry of sober reason," others were seeking more emotional means for preserving their links with the Revolutionary era. As the nation matured, its citizens became more aware of their heroic age. Some of the figures of that earlier seed-time for heroes had long since passed into myth, secure in the national ethos, but memories of a host of lesser heroes were kept alive only by a great outpouring of historical and fictional treatments of the Revolution. The Mexican War was of service to this effort for it "freshened the events, becoming rapidly old," of the Revolution and the war of 1812, America's second war of independence.[2]

Hero worship, according to Walter E. Houghton, was a 19th-century phenomenon, nurtured by romantic enthusiasm and meeting some of the "deepest needs and problems of the age." Houghton was writing of Victorian England, but his comment was relevant also to America. The

popularity of medieval romance and heroic legend, fostered by Scott
and his imitators; an obsession with chivalry and the chivalric ideal; the
cult of individualism that sprang in part from America's frontier experience and in part from the dizzying pace of social and economic
change; the fascination with Cooper's man in the wilderness; the cherished perception of the nation's revolutionary beginnings—all supported and strengthened a veneration of heroes. The age was one of
rebellion, a scholar has written, and hence an age of heroes, for heroes
are essentially rebels. Americans, grounding their views in a commitment to republican government and political democracy, saw themselves as rebels against a hostile and insensitive world. To fit the Mexican War into this context required no great leap of the imagination.[3]

A major figure in defining the hero and the heroic to romantics on
both sides of the Atlantic was the British thinker Thomas Carlyle,
whose book *On Heroes, Hero-Worship, and the Heroic in History* (1841) was
influential in directing thought during the midcentury years. Heroes,
Great Men, Carlyle insisted, were the stuff of history. They stood at the
center of human experience. "Universal History, the history of what
man has accomplished in this world, is at bottom the History of the
Great Men who have worked here." Carlyle's heroes were "the leaders
of men," "the modellers, patterns, and in a wide sense creators, of
whatsoever the general mass of men contrived to do or to attain." They
were those outstanding individuals, men of power and genius, who
rose above the mass, demanding and receiving a submissive admiration
and loyalty from the people.

No friend of revolutionary change, Carlyle saw his hero as a rock of
stability against the destructive "cries of Democracy, Liberty and Equality." Hero worship provided a solid foundation to society, an indestructible, eternal cornerstone standing amid the "confused wreck of
things crumbling and even crashing and tumbling all round us in these
revolutionary ages." For Carlyle, the hero was at once the epitome of
romantic individualism and the essential antidote to romanticism's
disorder.[4]

Carlyle's work was known in America as early as the 1820s but it was
not until the 1840s, when publishers in the United States reprinted his
books in American editions, that interest reached its peak. *On Heroes,
Hero-Worship, and the Heroic in History* appeared in 1842, barely a year
after it was published in England. In 1846, the New York publishers
Wiley and Putnam, whom Carlyle had authorized to "print and vend"
his books in the United States, included *On Heroes* in its "Library of
Choice Reading," and two years later Harper and Brothers brought out
its (possibly unauthorized) edition. By the end of the Mexican War,
Carlyle's views of the hero and of heroism were familiar to many
Americans.

"The spirit of Thomas Carlyle is abroad in the land," noted the
Southern Quarterly Review in 1848. Hero worship—"the love of the good

and great in human nature"—was the republic's safeguard, insulating its institutions from the attacks of enemies and the imbecility of friends. Reactions to Carlyle's views, however, were ambivalent. On the one hand, his insistence on deference and submission to the great man of genius, his rejection of democracy, and scorn for reform seemed out of accord with the prevailing mood of mid-19th-century America; on the other hand, his delineation of the hero as an anchor against the tempest of reform and change satisfied the yearning for order and stability. Southerners found in Carlyle's hero a buffer against the caprice of the popular will. "The mass of men have always been dependent on superior mind." Thoreau believed Carlyle's writings were a "gospel to the young of this generation," although he felt there was danger in Carlyle's exaggeration of the heroic in history. Walt Whitman, reading Carlyle selectively, declared him a democrat in the "enlarged sense," a champion of the downtrodden and a foe to tyranny.[5]

Carlyle's concept of the hero had its counterpart in the ideas of Ralph Waldo Emerson. Indeed, the two men carried on a lively correspondence for years following their brief meeting in 1833. Emerson first addressed the question of heroism in the mid-1830s in a series of lectures on biography and continued his investigations in later essays, including his 1841 essay on "Heroism." Beginning in late 1845, he further developed his views in several lectures on Representative Men (published in 1850).

Although Emerson no doubt was influenced by Carlyle, his views diverged from those of his English friend. His hero was indigenous to the dynamic, optimistic, and egalitarian atmosphere of early 19th-century America. The essence of heroism, Emerson had written, was self-trust or self-reliance. The hero was a natural man, guided by the intuition that sprang from his oneness with God; hence Emerson concluded, "heroism feels and never reasons, and therefore is always right." Although he declared that "heroism works in contradiction to the voice of mankind," his hero was not separated from mankind. "All these great and transcendent properties are ours," he wrote, and here was the most important distinction between Emerson and Carlyle. To Emerson there were no common men; every individual was a potential hero. His was a democratic heroism. In this, Emerson was in tune with popular views that always saw a close relationship between the hero and the society of which he was a part.[6]

Emerson, however, suggested only one side of the heroic ideal, mirroring rather than inspiring popular thought. Much more influential was America's most widely read novelist. James Fenimore Cooper, in his tales of sea and frontier, not only reinforced the self-image of Americans but also sketched an heroic portrait to which all could aspire. As with Emerson, Cooper's hero was indigenous, the product of American experience, and again like Emerson, his hero exemplified the virtues of the common man. Drawing on historical fact and oral tradition, Cooper's greatest contribution to America's order of heroes, Leatherstocking, was a figure so real that, as Francis Parkman suggested, the reader was likely to confuse him with memories of his own experiences. To Parkman, he was "an epitome of American history."

Although Cooper was acclaimed as the most American of writers, his hero owed part of his character to the "tradition of chivalric romance" found in the novels of Sir Walter Scott. A knight of old in a wild American setting, Leatherstocking was a man of nature, simple, truthful, and trustworthy, bold, courageous, and unmindful of danger, guided by intuition, one with Nature and God. There was something "admirably felicitous," wrote Parkman, in "this hybrid offspring of civilization and barbarism, in whom uprightness, kindliness, innate philosophy, and the truest moral perceptions are joined." Leatherstocking was the American hero *par excellence*, combining the characters of knight and frontiersman.

Mexican War soldiers, like Leatherstocking, were perceived as embodying both chivalric and frontier ideals and when Americans identified their war heroes, they looked for those who carried these ideals to highest expression. It was part of their continuing quest for symbols that reflected their national identity, that reflected themselves. Heroes, said Henry Giles, not only stood for great deeds, they also stood for great virtues. "In doing them worship, we elevate ourselves."[7]

Midcentury America seemed in need of heroes. Critics grieved over the passing of the "enthusiastic springtime" of America's "kindling youth." The nation's "age of chivalry" was at sunset. "The age of heroes is over," lamented Edward G. Parker. "A brazen age, anti-sentimental, succeeds . . . when sordid, calculating interest rather than conscious merit dares to run after renown." In spite of the insistence of men like Lorenzo Sabine that the times were no more degenerate than earlier periods, writers of all kinds and classes searched for new fields of endeavor on which new heroes might be raised. "What battle-field with courage now Shall ardent minds inspire?" asked poet Henry T. Tuckerman, "Upon what shrine can youth devote Its wild yet hallowed fire?"

> Must the bold heart ignobly pine
> Far from heroic strife,
> And win no trophies to adorn
> This cold and fleeting life?

Tuckerman's prescription for heroism—resisting "Opinion's tyrant bands" and remaining true to oneself—hardly satisfied the popular desire. While war was scarcely in the minds of most commentators, it was nonetheless the Mexican War that heralded a new age of heroes, reminding Americans that patriotism, chivalry, and self-sacrifice were not outmoded after all.[8]

"Heroes are created by popular demand," Gerald Johnson has written, "sometimes out of the scantiest materials, or none at all." The sentiment echoed the statement of a Philadelphia orator in 1847, who complained that "we live in an age when the public taste requires that all should be in heroics." Indeed, he declared, "we are on the very verge of mock-heroics." The Mexican War filled a need and in doing so provided a bright side even to those who opposed the conflict. While deploring the fact that the heroes in the "moral world" usually pass unrecognized, Freeman Hunt's antiwar *Merchants' Magazine* conceded that the "annals of war do not furnish more brilliant examples of courage, than those brought to light in the unfortunate contest between the two great North American republics." In his analysis of heroism in all its various guises, Edwin P. Whipple found compensations in the hero as soldier. War, he believed, was a passion that "in nobler natures" was "consecrated by the heart and imagination," acknowledging an "ideal aim" and inflaming "the whole man with a love of the dazzling idea of glory." It was this heroic element in war, he added, that "palliates its enormities" and "humanizes its horrors," proving the soldiers "to be men, and not tigers and wolves." The discovery of heroes and heroism in the Mexican War made the conflict all the more palatable, especially to those who were not always certain that warfare was compatible with the goals of the republic.[9]

The heroes of the Mexican War were those whom Emerson called "heroes of the hour," those of a "faster growth . . . in whom, at the moment of success, a quality is ripe which is then in request." Each victory contributed a "column" of new names to the roster of heroes until there were so many that their feats were in danger of being trivialized, evoking admiration but hardly surprise. "If the Mexican war should produce no other result," wrote poet-editor Park Benjamin, "it has made for us . . . an army of heroes, of whom the nation have a just right to be proud." He took issue with those who had been moaning over lost virtues: "We believe the genius of our institutions is favorable to the fullest development of the loftier attributes of our nature, and that there is no lack of heroes amongst us." As for those who made disparaging comparisons between the "illustrious men of our revolution" and the soldiers in Mexico, Benjamin insisted that America's victories demonstrated that "the sons are worthy of their sires."[10]

Who were the heroes of the Mexican War? Popular perceptions varied but one thing was clear: in a republic where sovereignty rested with the people, the heroes were drawn from the popular ranks. The egalitarian view of heroism—every man a hero, at least potentially—was reinforced by reliance on the citizen-soldier, the ultimate expression of republican virtue. The celebration of heroes became linked with republicanism itself.

> True republican virtue in the *citizens* consists in the prompt sacrifice of comforts, interest, and even life, for the nation. True republican virtue in the country consists in the recognition of merit in the sacrifice of the citizen, and a public demonstration of gratitude to those who renounce *self* for the country.[11]

In one sense, all Americans who put aside the comforts and security of civilian life to take up arms on behalf of the republic were heroes.

But heroism also depended upon certain individual qualities and unique circumstances that elevated some men above the rest. Heroism, on its more meaningful level, was bred in battle, for it was in the drama of combat that deeds of daring and courage were most easily recognized. There were no heroes among the poor unfortunates who spent the war languishing in idleness in the disease-ridden camps, although efforts were made to recognize their sacrifice. Heroes were molded and cast in the battle reports, the dispatches of newspaper correspondents, the soldiers' letters, and the plethora of publications which the conflict generated. Their stories were told and retold until they became independent of reality. Their deeds were celebrated in poetry and song and were reenacted on the stage. When they were martyred, they were mourned with striking intensity. The first encounters with the enemy in May 1846 produced the war's first heroes and virtually every engagement after that added to the list.

The guns of Palo Alto and Resaca de la Palma hardly cooled before writers and publishers raced to meet the public demand for information. The production of books and articles continued unabated for the rest of the conflict. "Next in importance to the interest excited by the performance of heroic deeds," explained one author, "is the curiosity . . . to learn something of the life, character, and general qualifications of the men who have shared the glories or perils of these deeds." Books designed to meet this curiosity were rushed into print, providing capsule biographies of the war's leaders and accounts of their heroism, with the usual "numerous anecdotes" and "personal adventures." Compiled largely from newspaper reports, usually without attribution, the information was often fragmentary, exaggerated, and inaccurate, but this did not diminish the eagerness with which they were received by an excited reading public. Popular writers like Charles Jacob Peterson and the prolific historian John Frost joined New Orleans correspondent and southwestern humorist Thomas Bangs Thorpe ("Tom Owen the Bee Hunter") in churning out publications that offered Americans a body of heroic lore.

In identifying the war's heroes, writers cast a wide net, gathering not only those whose valor seemed worthy of recognition but also, in some instances, virtually every high-ranking field officer in the army. (The navy played only a limited role in the war and, except for Peterson's sketches in his history of the United States Navy (1856) and some scattered biographical notices, naval figures were ignored.) The presentation of heroes to a receptive public also became a matter of some urgency, lest the passage of time dim the lustre of their deeds. Fears were expressed that heroism might be overlooked in the excitement of the moment:

> The war with Mexico has added a most interesting page to American history; it has called forth new energies, and unexpected displays of exalted character. Many of the most interesting details of great events are lost in the succeeding ephemeral excitements; and examples of patriotism, of bravery, and of fortitude, worthy of all emulation, are engulfed in oblivion.

Presumably it was better to be undiscriminating in the search for heroes than to pass over some deserving individual. Furthermore, heroism often served some larger cause. To find heroes among the regular army officers was to prove the value of West Point, while singling out heroes from the ranks of the volunteers demonstrated the wisdom of relying on citizen-soldiers. The stories of heroism on Mexican fields were viewed as inspiration to those who had been left behind, reminders that the republic was well served by its citizens. Heroes were the instruments by which Americans could be recalled to a true sense of their patriotic responsibilities.[12]

Patriotic devotion to the republic, a willingness to sacrifice even life itself for the nation, and chivalry, that knightly ideal that united courage in battle with decency and humanity, all were prime requisites for heroism. Indeed, they seem to have been passed from one generation to another, for most of the heroes (according to the popular descriptions) were descended from patriots who fought in the country's earlier wars. Grandfathers who served in the Revolution, fathers who were veterans of the War of 1812, and sons who distinguished themselves in Mexico established a direct link between the Mexican War and the past, a strong and emotional tie between the "boys of '48" and the "boys of '76." Chivalry, Frost insisted, ran in the blood.[13]

The Mexican War's quintessential hero was Zachary Taylor, Old Rough and Ready. An obscure army colonel holding a brevet as brigadier general, with an undistinguished career behind him, sixty-two years old, Taylor burst upon the scene with unexpected suddenness in the spring of 1846. "There probably has never been . . . a time of such intense general excitement," declared one writer, "as that immediately preceding the first engagement between the Americans and the Mexicans in the present war." It was then that the nation looked, in a "moment of breathless anxiety," to the Rio Grande and asked, "Who is General Taylor?" Authors, publishers, editors, correspondents, all scrambled to provide the answer. A race to produce the first biography of Taylor resulted in the almost simultaneous appearance of two books early in August 1846: C. Frank Powell's *Life of Major-General Zachary Taylor*, carrying Taylor only through Resaca de la Palma, and the anonymous *Life and Public Services of Gen. Z. Taylor*, which ended with the occupation of Matamoros, a book that "should be in the hands of every citizen."

It was only the beginning. Taylor was a man "neither Mexicans nor biographers" could put down. When it became apparent that he would achieve political as well as military fame, the number of works multiplied rapidly, some "mere catchpenny affairs" published in haste and showing it. Taylor, it was said, had more lives than a cat and one critic felt that the General could recruit an entire battalion out of the authors "who have *attempted his life*."[14]

Taylor sprang into fame "as a fabled personage of mythology came into being, the instant creation of a perfect hero." He had served his country as a soldier for almost four decades, yet remained unknown. As a representative man and counter-agent to his times, Taylor appeared to be "the American whom Carlyle would recognize as 'a hero' worthy of his pen's most eloquent recognition: THE MAN OF DUTY in an age of Self!" He was likened to Alexander, Caesar and Hannibal, Cromwell and Frederick the Great. Standing below medium height and inclined to corpulency, he recalled Napoleon. But it was to George Washington that Taylor was most often compared. Their lives, it was said, were parallel, their characteristics similar; indeed, to his generation Taylor seemed the "inheritor" of Washington's virtues. In moderation, fairness, caution, fatherly regard for his troops, repugnance toward war, it was obvious wrote Walt Whitman, that "our Commander on the Rio Grande, emulates the Great Commander of our revolution."[15]

Americans did not have to look far to find the sources of Taylor's heroism. The blood of some of the oldest and most distinguished families of Virginia flowed in his veins. His father had fought both British and Indians during the Revolution. Patriotism ran in his family and even showed in his face, as a practitioner of the new "science" of physiognomy pointed out. Nurtured on Kentucky's "dark and bloody ground," Taylor grew up in the woods. His nursery tales were stories of Indian butchery; as he grew older he heard often the "shriek of the maiden . . . the crack of the rifle . . . the fierce conflict between the father and his savage foe." There was no better school for a warrior. "There is something in the very air of Kentucky which makes a man a soldier." A man of the wilderness, Taylor imbibed the freedom, independence, and strength of the forest. He was, in short, of the same mold as Leatherstocking.[16]

Taylor's character and personality were as important to his popularity as the victories he won in Mexico. Known affectionately as Old Rough and Ready or Old Zach or simply "the old man," Taylor's simplicity and lack of ostentation endeared him to the men under his command. Mounted on Old Whitey, wearing a large straw Mexican sombrero and a loose brown frock-coat his appearance belied his authority. His costume was so well known that he became known as the "old man in the plain brown coat." Without visible indications of his rank, he was frequently mistaken for an aging private soldier. Those who saw him sitting alone in front of his tent, spectacles on his nose, mending his britches, could not believe that he was the "old hero, with whose name and fame the country was then ringing."

The contrast between Taylor and his Mexican counterparts, in their brightly colored uniforms, gold embroidery, huge epaulettes, and collections of medals and ribbons, was so striking that witnesses could not resist drawing an analogy between the two nations they represented. The headquarters tent (or pavilion) of Mexican General Mariano Arista, overrun by American troops at Resaca de la Palma, seemed to be that of an Oriental satrap. The large gaily striped marquee housed richly figured ornamental chests, bright satin wall-hangings, intricate tapestries, and the General's own personal silver plate. It was a "vision of a fairy land" to the open-mouthed soldiers who encountered it. Taylor slept in a regulation army tent with no outward markings to distinguish it from all the others; no sentinels were posted to screen the General's visitors. Furnished only with camp stools and a couple of rough chests that served as a table, the tent was surrounded by an array of barrels, tubs, and pails, with Taylor's favorite tin dishes and "good old coffee pot." Only the presence of Ben, Taylor's personal slave, revealed that the occupant was no ordinary soldier. The "semi-barbaric splendor" of Arista's tent seemed to bespeak the pomp and despotism of the Mexican government, while Taylor's abode reflected the democratic simplicity of America's republican institutions.[17]

Taylor's insistence on being in the midst of battle and his coolness under fire matched his informality and served as inspiration to his men. Stories of his close calls abounded, many of them no doubt exaggerated. For example, measuring the speed and direction of an oncoming cannon ball at Buena Vista, Taylor rose in his saddle at precisely the right moment, allowing the ball to pass between him and his horse; when his coat was pierced by canister shot, he exclaimed, "These balls are growing excited." True or not, Taylor's apparent indifference to his own safety bolstered the confidence of the men around him. At Buena Vista he was described as "calm as a summer's morning." All eyes were turned toward him and "as long as he continued to rest easy, we were all satisfied, for never did Napoleon . . . possess in a more unbounded degree the confidence of his men and officers."

The old General's laconic remarks, uttered in battle were widely quoted. Some became legendary. Best known was his comment to young Captain of Artillery Braxton Bragg at Buena Vista, as Bragg brought his pieces to bear on the Mexican line: "A little more grape, Captain Bragg!" When an appeal was made for reinforcements to meet

SIMPLICITY OF OLD ZACK'S HABITS.

Simplicity of Old Zack's Habits. From *Yankee Doodle* (July 31, 1847).

a Mexican charge, Taylor calmly replied, "I have no reinforcement to give you but Major Bliss and I will support you." Both statements became important bits of Tayloriana, even though Bliss, Taylor's adjutant, later insisted they were apocryphal. Some of Taylor's remarks appeared in more than one version, and some were viewed as vulgar and profane, as when he urged his men to "stand to your guns and give them h---!" Taylor, however, prevailed and his terse, pithy statements evoked admiration and respect. During the war and after, "Give 'em Zack!" held unmistakable idiomatic meaning for Americans.[18]

When Taylor returned to the United States in December 1847 he was received as a conquering hero. The citizens of New Orleans greeted him with one of the wildest and most lavish celebrations ever mounted in the Crescent City. Speeches of welcome, before thousands of people, were followed by a triumphant procession in which Taylor, spurning the offer of a carriage, rode on Old Whitey. Spectators plucked at the horse's mane and tail for souvenirs. That evening, buildings were illuminated and transparencies were hung, depicting Taylor "in the old brown coat" and repeating his by now famous command to Captain Bragg. A sumptuous banquet followed at which toast after toast was drunk, each accompanied by appropriate music from a brass band. The festivities continued through the next day, and it was not until the third day finally dawned (a Sunday) that Taylor was able to journey up the Mississippi to the peace and quiet of his home in Baton Rouge.[19]

Taylor's heroism was celebrated not only in the outpouring of biographies and military histories. Engraved portraits by the score were executed and placed on sale; painters committed to canvas the record of Taylor's achievements in Mexico; and statuettes were sculpted. "A great variety of portraits, of all ages, sizes, faces and costumes as diverse as imagination could paint them," remarked the *Scientific American*, all purported to be "correct likenesses of Gen. Taylor." Collected, the writer thought, the portraits "would form an interesting curiosity for a museum." Countless poems, from humorous doggerel to effusive sentimental verse, appeared in books, newspapers, and magazines; and music, such as *General Taylor's Gallop, General Taylor's Grand March, General Taylor's Quick Step,* and the *Rough and Ready Polka,* was composed, sold, and performed. Taylor's sobriquet became a household phrase: Post and Lemon's Manhattan Fresh Milled Effulgent Horse-Radish Sauce adopted the motto "Rough and Ready" ("Our Country, Horse-Radish and Liberty!"); straw bonnets became known as "Rough and Ready straws"; boots and shoes were advertised as "Rough and Ready."[20]

In contrast with the adulation of Taylor, the public response to the war's other (and ranking) commander was ambiguous at best. Winfield Scott's credentials as a hero seemed uncertain. Comparisons were common but, while efforts were made to clothe Scott with the same heroic raiment, they usually placed him at a disadvantage. "If the Hero of Buena Vista nobly commenced the present war with Mexico," began one account of the conflict, "the Hero of Chippewa has not less nobly completed the second Conquest of Mexico." The comment was characteristic. Scott's heroism was of an older order, dating from the War of 1812.

Charles J. Peterson tried rather clumsily to pinpoint the difference between the two men. "Scott," he declared, "has more of the General in his composition, and Taylor more of the hero." Which is to say that Taylor's bearing and personality more clearly befitted a romantic hero than did those of Scott. A Tennessee volunteer informed his family that "old Zack has the manners to please all, being so plain, and easy and affable." That could not have been said of Winfield Scott. Taylor appealed to the popular imagination; Scott did not.[21]

The difference lay partly in the fact that, unlike Taylor, Scott was well known when the war began. He did not have the advantage of Taylor's "instant heroism"; indeed, he got off to a rather bad start. Although he was the army's ranking officer, he appeared reluctant to take the field against the Mexicans, thus incurring the administration's displeasure at the outset. His problems were compounded by indiscreet remarks in a letter to Secretary of War Marcy in which he complained of the President's attitude, charging that he faced "a fire upon my rear, from Washington, and the fire, in front, from the Mexicans." The allusion did not help matters; instead, they worsened when Polk removed Scott from active command against Mexico. Stunned, Scott once again allowed his emotions to get the better of him. The President's order had arrived, he wrote, just as he was sitting down to "a hasty plate of soup." These two remarks—the fire upon his rear and the hasty plate of soup—invited ridicule and caricature that persisted throughout the war.

Scott's behavior offered clues to his personality and forecast later difficulties with both the Polk administration and officers in his command. Emotionally volatile, often surrendering to what his biographer has called his "black mood of martyrdom," he was quick to commit to writing sentiments that were better left unsaid. Furthermore, his disdain for Taylor was well known, which only hurt Scott the more. Taylor on his part took a "violent dislike" to the commander, especially after Scott gutted his force for the Vera Cruz operation. The old soldier thought Scott lacked the qualifications to be a great general.[22]

Judged solely on his military achievements, Peterson insisted, Scott must be considered the greatest general America had produced. His youthful triumphs in the War of 1812 were matched in old age by his victory over "the myriads of Mexico." Writers who advanced Scott's cause summed up his achievements in three words, "skill, science and strategy." "Science guided and protected" his daring invasion; his direction of the battles in the Valley of Mexico exhibited a happy blend of genius and skill. Scott's successes proved that "science in war is not a less potent instrument than headlong valor or the most indomitable constancy." There was, however, little of the romantic in that, little of the stuff of which heroes were made.[23]

If Winfield Scott did not qualify as a romantic hero, elements of romance were nonetheless found in his accomplishments. Indeed, Scott himself believed it. When his aides chided him for understating his triumphs in his official reports, he replied, "If I tell the whole truth, they may say, 'It is all a romance!'" In a laudatory address following the war, Sir Henry Bulwer, Britain's minister to Washington, suggested an analogy between the General and his Scottish namesake: "If Waverley and Guy Mannering had made the name of Scott immortal, on one side of the Atlantic, Cerro Gordo and Churubusco had equally immortalized it on the other. If the novelist had given the garb of truth to fiction, had not the warrior given to truth the air of romance?" That Scott simply completed the conquest of Mexico that was begun by Cortez more than 300 years before seemed plausible. A 19th-century conquistador, Scott, like Cortez, was directed by "an invisible spirit" and, like Cortez, advanced the mission of "Divine Providence on earth." No general in history, it was claimed, had fought so successfully against such overwhelming odds, losing fewer men, making fewer mistakes, and creating less devastation in proportion to his victories.[24]

Scott ended the war as he began it, under a cloud of suspicion. He quarreled first of all with Nicholas Trist, the emissary sent by Polk to accompany Scott's army with the authority to negotiate with the Mexicans for an end to the war. Scott, convinced that Trist's mission was a deliberate effort on the part of the President to compromise his authority, fumed. Next he became embroiled in a feud with three of his officers, including the respected General William Jenkins Worth and the infamous political appointee General Gideon Pillow. Several public letters critical of Scott's conduct of the war's final campaign were traced to the trio. It was well known that Pillow, a close friend and former law partner of President Polk, had tried to advance his own career by discrediting Scott. Instead of allowing public opinion to do its work, Scott reacted with customary haste and indiscretion. His effort to discipline the officers backfired, and instead charges were brought against him. Relieved of his command, Scott was forced to return to the United States to vindicate himself.

The episode became very complex, but one thing was clear: the conqueror of Mexico was forced to defend himself before a court of inquiry. Mexicans were shocked, the soldiers in his army were indignant, and the Whigs back home were outraged. Some Mexicans hoped that Scott would defy the administration, remain in Mexico, and accept their nation's leadership. If the Presidency was not in his grasp, the emperorship of Mexico seemed to be. Scott, however, returned to New York in May 1848, where he was greeted by a public celebration and parade. Songwriter George Pope Morris honored the occasion:

> Victorious the hero
> Returns from the wars;
> His brow bound with laurels
> That never will fade
>
> Huzza! huzza! huzza!
> The hero forever!
> Whose fame is the glory
> And pride of the land!

Scott's treatment at the hands of the administration did little for his public image, and the efforts of his partisans to make Scott the mar-

tyred hero of the Mexican War fell short. Gideon Pillow was exonerated by the court of inquiry, and all other charges were dropped,
leaving Scott angry and bitter. To top it off, Taylor, his subordinate
officer, was promoted by the voters in November 1848 to be Scott's
commander-in-chief.[25]

Taylor and Scott were obvious candidates for heroism. Less obvious
(and less creditable) were those officers whose claims to heroic status
were based simply on the fact that they held high rank and responsibility during the war. Heroes only in a very superficial sense, they
achieved notoriety not because of public admiration or esteem but because of the publicity they received at the hands of the war's annalists.
"Why," asked one officer, "must every general be praised as a hero,
greater than Napoleon?" Men of "tried courage, of patient endurance,
of exactness, punctuality, and system," there was little of romance
about them.[26]

William O. Butler, former Democratic Congressman and one of Polk's
political generals, was reared in frontier Kentucky, descended from
fighters in the Revolution, experienced in fighting Indians and British,
and a veteran of the Battle of New Orleans—good credentials even
without service in the Mexican War. But Butler had fought at Monterey
where he suffered a leg wound and became a hero. He was with Scott in
the last stage of the war, and when Scott was recalled he assumed command. One looks in vain for the Homeric qualities that were assigned to
Butler—"brave as an Ajax," "circumspect as a Nestor." In an embarrass-
ingly gushy article, Francis Preston Blair found the Kentuckian's heroism sufficient to justify his nomination for Vice President on the Democratic ticket in 1848. John Ellis Wool, the army's third-ranking officer,
commanded a force made up largely of Illinois and Arkansas volunteers.
Crabbed, petulant, and "old-womanish" (as Josiah Gregg described
him), Wool was a stern and severe disciplinarian, known to his men (who
heartily disliked him) as "the old Woolly Devil" and "Old Granny Wool."
The fact that he whipped the unruly volunteers into an effective force
seemed heroism enough, but Wool in addition selected the site for the
Battle of Buena Vista and directed the troops before Taylor arrived on
the field. To one writer, he was "the hero of a defeat," for the battle had
been going badly until Taylor's arrival.[27]

William Jenkins Worth, in the army since the War of 1812 and a
brigadier general when the Mexican War began, was reputed to be the
one who first planted the Stars and Stripes on the banks of the Rio
Grande. Narrow, self-centered, and quarrelsome, he missed the first
battles (to his later regret) because he resigned his commission in a
dispute over seniority. Realizing that there was glory to be won in
Mexico, he rushed back to rejoin Taylor's force. He participated in the
attack on Monterey and, assigned to Scott's army, in the assault on
Vera Cruz and all the subsequent battles. In spite of his faults (and
some said, lack of patriotism early in the war), Worth was cast as a

Winfield Scott. From *Graham's Magazine* (April 1848).

John E. Wool. From *Democratic Review* (November 1851).

romantic hero, the Murat of the American army whose handsome features and dashing courage recalled that "impetuous prince, the Roland of Napoleon's army."[28]

The list of war heroes compiled by popular historians, magazine writers, and newspapermen revealed a lack of discrimination that only clouded the meaning of heroism. Local pride often dictated the selection, for no area that supplied soldiers felt it could afford to be without a hero. David Twiggs, dubbed "Old Orizaba" because of his white hair, was lauded for his bravery; Persifor Smith earned fame as the "hero of Contreras"; and Illinois's James Shields, twice wounded, displayed a heroism that was "as proverbial as his chivalrous sense of honor." Bennet Riley, idolized by his men, had the face of the *"beau ideal* of a veteran soldier," complete with scar and whiskers "trimmed up to his eyes." The Indianan Joseph Lane rallied his volunteers at Buena Vista and later, while chasing guerrillas between Vera Cruz and Mexico City, became known as the "Marion of the Mexican War." And finally there was even the hapless Franklin Pierce, thrown from his horse and injured at Contreras and disabled by dysentery through Molino del Rey and Chapultepec. Nathaniel Hawthorne found gallantry and leadership in this, and a New Hampshire newspaper immortalized Pierce's "heroism" in verse.[29]

Aside from Taylor, the commander who most captured the public's esteem and admiration was the outspoken congenial frontier lawyer from western Missouri, Alexander W. Doniphan. Doniphan, leading his Missouri volunteers against Navajo Indians, traversing the barren desert wastes of northern Mexico, and fighting two battles against superior Mexican forces and winning, became *the* hero to the citizen-soldiers. "When the deeds of the citizen soldiery shall be appreciated," wrote one volunteer, "then will the deeds of Doniphan and his gallant men shine forth with a brilliancy not to be surpassed." It was Doniphan who demonstrated to all critics the wisdom of entrusting the nation's defense to its citizens. His long and arduous march was "one of the most romantic episodes" of the war; his victory at the battle of Sacramento, north of Chihuahua, recalled the "heroic ages of antiquity." Called from his law practice, untutored in the art of warfare, Doniphan combined the heroic qualities Americans most admired, the upright simplicity of the frontiersman and the courage and patriotism of a chivalric knight. History, wrote Peterson, "will preserve his name to latest posterity"; in future generations, his achievements would be cited "as proof of what Americans were 'in the brave days of old.'" It was in Doniphan that Americans found assurance that their heroic age had not passed.[30]

On May 23, 1846, thousands of Baltimore's citizens gathered in Monument Square for what was described as an "immense war meeting."

Ten days before, Congress had recognized a state of war between the United States and Mexico. Taylor's army was on the Rio Grande, and Baltimoreans had been crowding the newspaper offices for late news. The meeting was called to consider the "hostile position of the two countries" and to adopt such measures as might be necessary for the "honor and welfare" of the country. The principal speaker was Reverdy Johnson, prominent attorney, Whig leader, and United States Senator, who delivered "one of the most eloquent and patriotic addresses that was ever listened to." Following Johnson on the platform were Texas Senator Sam Houston and William L. Yancey of Alabama.

As Houston spoke he was interrupted when a messenger handed a note to Baltimore's mayor, who promptly revealed its contents to the audience. General Taylor had defeated the Mexican army in two decisive engagements north of the Rio Grande but his victories had not been achieved without cost. Among the casualties was Baltimore's own Major Samuel Ringgold, who fell at Palo Alto while directing the fire of his artillery. With the mention of Ringgold's name, "every head was uncovered, and many a manly cheek was suffused with tears."

Ringgold's death dampened the celebration of the victories. On the next day, flags in the city and on the ships in the harbor flew at half-mast; buildings were draped in black crepe. "His loss is deeply mourned," wrote a correspondent. As he adjourned the Baltimore County court, the judge noted that Ringgold had died while defending the honor of his country and the integrity of its soil and in dying had added "another brilliant page" to its history. Samuel Ringgold was the Mexican War's first martyr.[31]

Ringgold's family background was right, his father a veteran of the War of 1812 and his mother descended from an officer in the Revolution. "Inheriting on both sides the blood of patriots," he was destined for heroism. A member of West Point's first graduating class, Ringgold was commissioned in the artillery, where in 1838 he organized an experimental company of flying artillery that was designed to move swiftly from place to place. His men, trained to perfection, advanced their battery at full gallop, unlimbered, fired, remounted, and whirled off to a new position. On the field of Palo Alto, Ringgold pushed his pieces to within a hundred yards of the enemy, maintaining a "murderous fire" in a scene that "approached the sublime" until he was hit by a Mexican cannon shot. As he fell he waved his men on, crying, "Don't stay with me; you have work to do—go ahead." Carried from the field, he died three days later.[32]

Ringgold's death was followed by a wave of eulogy. To the Philadelphia *North American* he was "the Bayard of the age—the star of the war . . . the soul of chivalry and honour . . . lofty as a patriot, beloved as a man." He died for his country, and his memory would be "gratefully cherished so long as honour has a victory, freedom a hero, or his country a name." The details of his death were recounted over and

over; soldiers in their letters home and in their diaries interrupted
their own recollections with praise for Ringgold's heroism. Americans
everywhere read of the calm with which he faced death, of his admonition to his men, and of the tenderness with which he handed his watch
to a fellow officer to be sent to his sister. His name was invoked by
defenders of West Point as proof that the Academy brought distinction
to the service. Even Abraham Lincoln, four years later, could still recall
with "mingled sensations of pride and sorrow" when American valor
trumphed at Palo Alto "and the noble Ringgold fell."[33]

As soon as news of his death was received, poets rushed forward with
their tributes, no less sincere for their sentimentality. Ringgold's name
was linked with the heroes of the Revolution and he was accorded a
place of honor among the agents of America's destiny, to be held in
grateful remembrance

> When the era of freedom has so far increased,
> That its bounds can be traced on the ocean alone.

Struck down at the moment of victory, he had earned the immortality
that is reserved for those who die in battle:

> Thou'rt of the chosen few who die,
> To be immortal by their death.

Ringgold's heroism was confirmed by his death in the face of his country's enemies; if there was an ascending scale of heroism, Ringgold had
achieved the highest stage.

> But Death! thou art more glorious,
> When the youthful hero dies,
> With the flag of Freedom waving
> Like a meteor o'er his eyes!

Verse was put to music as Americans mourned the martyred artillerist
to the doleful notes of the *Lament on the Death of Maj. Ringgold,* the
music and words of which were printed in a popular woman's magazine.

The dramatic scene on the Palo Alto battlefield was recreated countless times by printmakers, and no two reproductions were alike. The
imaginations of the artists roamed freely, although most of them dupli-
cated the arrangement popularized by Benjamin West's classic painting
of the death of General Wolfe. They mirrored the romantic perception
of soldiers in battle, ranging from the stiff, immaculate depiction by
James S. Baillie to the melodramatic composition of Louis Nagel that
caused one viewer to exclaim, "Grand Opera!" The popular illustrator
Felix O. C. Darley, the Italian-born Luigi Persico (whose work adorned

126

The Fall of Major Ringgold at the Battle of Palo Alto. From *Columbian Magazine* (July 1846).

the United States Capitol), the careful battle-artist Tompkins H. Matteson, whose exquisite mezzotint was probably the most lifelike, all offered versions of Ringgold's moment of triumph.[34]

On the stage, Ringgold was a hero even before his death. Four days before the word was received, a false report reached the east coast that Ringgold's artillery had reduced the Mexican town of Matamoros to rubble, killing seven hundred of its inhabitants. In what must stand as a record of dramatic production, "a great national drama" reenacting the bombardment was written, rehearsed and performed within five hours of the moment the news reached Philadelphia. Later, when accurate reports of the opening battles were circulated, the stage play "Palo Alto" provided audiences with a glimpse of the conflict in which Ringgold was struck down, while a more pointed production, a "panoramic sketch" titled "The Death of Ringgold" attracted theatregoers through the summer of 1846.

Ringgold's horse, a thoroughbred racehorse known as Davy Branch, was mortally wounded by the same Mexican ball that hit his owner and was mourned in sporting circles throughout the country. William Tylee Ranney, a painter well known for his frontier scenes, commemorated the animal in a "powerful and startling" canvas titled "The Dead Charger."[35]

After its defeat at Palo Alto on May 8, the Mexican force regrouped on the following day, blocking Taylor's advance at Resaca de la Palma, a dry shallow ravine some three miles north of the Rio Grande. The point at which the road crossed the *resaca* was protected by Mexican artillery whose fire was particularly effective in halting Taylor's progress. Lieutenant Randolph Ridgely, who had assumed command of Ringgold's battery, pushed his guns forward to challenge the Mexican barrage. Taylor, fearing for the safety of Ridgely's men, summoned Captain Charles A. May's squadron of the Second Dragoons to charge and silence the Mexican artillery. May and his men moved out at full gallop, dashing down the road in a column of fours, and a new hero was born.

Thomas Bangs Thorpe described it as a "soul-stirring sight." Stripped of every encumbrance, brandishing their weapons and raising a shout that "rang above the din of battle," the dragoons raced toward the Mexican line. All eyes were fixed upon the figure at the head of the column. May, over six feet tall and standing in his stirrups, seemed to be a "living messenger of death." The charge carried the dragoons through the battery and beyond. Exposed to grape and canister from the guns they were charging as well as the fire of the Mexican infantry on the flanks, the squadron suffered heavily and became disorganized. Wheeling about, May rallied six of his troopers for another charge on the guns. As he passed through the battery the second time, in a last stroke of bravado, he captured a Mexican general, Romulo Diaz de la Vega, who was servicing one of the artillery pieces. The guns were silenced and Taylor's army swept the Mexicans from the field.[36]

May's name, like Ringgold's, was instantly on everyone's lips. The story of his charge against the Mexican guns grew as it was repeated until its details became lost in fantasy. No one questioned that it was one of the most heroic exploits ever recorded in history. May suddenly became the "personification of a knight of the ancient days of chivalry," his exploit matching in dash and romance the "knightly deeds of old." Sang one poet,

> Twine garlands for our Cavalier,
> The gallant Captain May!
> A knight without reproach, or fear—
> A Bayard in the fray!

May's appearance, "straight as an Indian," the "beau-ideal of the dashing cavalry officer," and an air of mystery about his background (there was no evidence, for example, of any Revolutionary War forebears) added to his popularity. Described at the height of his charge— "his face all covered with beard, his hair streaming behind him, like a

Cumanche Indian, and his eyes glowing like a comet"—it was no wonder that General de la Vega thought him a "spirit from the other world." May's long hair and beard, unusual for an officer in the regular service so early in the war, resulted, it was hinted, from an unhappy love affair and his vow never to allow a razor to touch his chin or a scissors his locks.[37]

Poets, printmakers, songwriters, and eulogists, as they did with Ringgold, rushed to put their tributes to May's heroism before the people. The dramatic moment when May overpowered the Mexican gunners and captured General de la Vega presented a vivid action-packed picture and, with only the vague and often-conflicting newspaper accounts at hand, artists and engravers produced almost as many versions of the incident as they did pictures. Nathaniel Currier offered a choice, one depicting a clean-shaven May, the other a much hairier hero. Painter John L. Morton's version was the most moving, the Mexican general cowering before the upraised saber of the dragoon, becoming a fine mezzotint in the *Columbian Magazine.* New York's well-known print publisher Henry R. Robinson executed full-length figures of a neatly uniformed and well-trimmed May standing beside his horse, Old Tom. Park Benjamin's poetic tribute to Resaca de la Palma appeared in his *Western Continent* soon after the battle, complete with May's "high heroic heart," his flowing beard and hair, and the swarthy Mexican cheeks grown pale. Music publishers were soon advertising *Capt. May's Quick Step* and the *Resaca de la Palma Quick-step;* more ambitious was a complex "battle-piece" titled *The Battle of Resaca de la Palma* that included movements describing General Taylor's march, Captain May's charge, General de la Vega's surrender, and the Mexican retreat.[38]

Even General de la Vega became a hero of sorts, presumably for his good sense in surrendering to May. Lines to be sung to the tune of *Yankee Doodle* lauded the Mexican general for his action. Mrs. Sarah Anna Lewis used the incident in her antiwar poem "Lament for La Vega," in which the General wails "I am a Captive while my Country bleeds" and calls upon the spirits of Cortez and Montezuma to rescue his distracted nation. Few Americans, however, felt sorry for Vega. Following his capture he traveled to New Orleans where he was lionized by society, a favorite with the ladies. "The fire of their eyes," he declared, "was more fatal to the heart than even the fire from the American artillery." Indeed, it was reported that he quickly became engaged to a New Orleans woman. The General was granted permission to spend the summer months in the cooler environment of the Kentucky mountains but, alas, he was shortly exchanged and returned to the Mexican army (only to be captured a second time at Cerro Gordo). Before he left the United States, he publicly thanked the people for their kindness toward him.[39]

Ringgold and May, the war's first battlefield heroes, were unequaled in adulation through the rest of the war. They were participants in the nation's first battles against a foreign foe and that fact alone explained much of their notoriety. Their actions on May 8 and 9 seemed all the more heroic, coming as they did on the heels of uneasiness and apprehension over the fate of Taylor's army. Furthermore, Americans believed that Mexico, its army now humbled, would be brought speedily to the peace table; the heroes of Palo Alto and Resaca de la Palma became the instruments for the victorious termination of the war. Ringgold in the long run was more fortunate than May. His heroism, after all, was unquestioned for he had suffered that most noble and patriotic of deaths. May was not so lucky. The heroic expectations raised by his charge were unfulfilled in later engagements. He missed the fighting at Monterey and was kept out of Buena Vista by Taylor. Although he was promoted (by brevet), presented swords by admirers, and feted on a tour of the United States, questions were raised about the authenticity of his heroism. His claim to have silenced the guns was disputed by others. May's dragoons, it was said, had become so disorganized that Taylor, in disgust, sent his infantry to take the battery. The real captor of General de la Vega was a bugler. Justin Smith, writing in 1919, characterized May as a "newspaper hero" and a "cowardly sham."[40]

The American victories at Palo Alto and Resaca de la Palma did not end the war. The conflict continued, more battles were fought and more victories were won, and still Mexico appeared reluctant to concede defeat. The army's triumphs became almost monotonous. The soldiers, one editor observed, "are hardly upon the battle ground than they are masters of the field." Battles legendary in military annals no longer seemed unique as their modern counterparts became common occurrences. "The days of the old French fields such as those of Creçy, Poitiers, Agincourt, are nothing compared to the fields that we hear of every day." Americans, he suggested, hardly recover from their surprise at one victory before they hear of another even greater. "The lustre of the army of the United States is either very great and almost astonishing, or else their adversaries must be pusillanimous wretches."[41]

The celebration of heroes continued, although on a diminished scale and without the spontaneous flow of eulogy that had greeted Ringgold and May. Heroism, perhaps, was taken for granted and no longer aroused such a passionate response. Perhaps the people had become surfeited with heroes or, as one correspondent suggested, there were just too many heroes to enumerate. To describe all the "individual instances of heroism would be but commencing an endless task." Some became downright blase, like the writer in the *Literary World* who confessed that gallantry among the soldiers had become so common "that we read their exploits, with admiration indeed, but hardly with surprise." Or it may be that Americans by the summer of 1847 were growing tired of the war. While the battles fought by Scott in his campaign against Mexico City were as hard-fought and as costly (indeed more so) than any in the war they did not stir the public response that followed Taylor's victories in the north. The war had gone on too long, and the Mexicans did not seem to know that they were beaten.

At the same time, the celebration of heroes moved from the national to the local level, where heroism contributed to local pride and symbolized the roles of the state and community in the war. When Alexander McClung, second in command of the Mississippi Rifles and wounded at Monterey while leading his volunteers in a charge against a Mexican fort, returned home he was received as a glorious hero. His "daring exploit" was recounted "at every fireside, and little children listened with . . . staring interest," but it is doubtful that he was well known beyond Mississippi's borders.[42]

Family connections and a Revolutionary War background still remained important in the identification of heroes. Schuyler Hamilton, grandson of Alexander Hamilton and great-grandson of Revolutionary War general Philip Schuyler, became a hero when he drove off a body of lancers, although wounded, while on a reconnaissance mission in the Valley of Mexico. By itself, the incident was not of great significance (Hamilton had to be rescued by a fellow officer) but his gallantry forged another link between the Mexican War and the Revolutionary War and seemed to prove the popular contention that heroism ran in the blood.[43]

Death in combat against the enemy remained the surest path to admission to America's sanctum of heroes. William H. Watson, commanding Baltimore's volunteers, fell at the head of his troops in the bitter street fighting in Monterey and was immediately hailed as an exalted patriot distinguished for his "generosity and goodness of heart" as much as for his "bravery and Chivalry." No single battle of the war, however, produced so many martyred heroes as the Battle of Buena Vista. The titanic dimensions of that clash, the romantic landscape in which it was fought (itself, it was said, inspiring heroism), the odds faced by the American army and the initial uncertainty of the battle's outcome all lent themselves to celebratory treatment.

"Other and abler pens will do justice to the character and memory of the illustrious dead," wrote an army correspondent the day after the battle, "whose devotion to the Republic they have written with their blood and sealed with their lives": the gallant Lincoln, "of pure heart and generous impulses, and worthy of his revolutionary lineage"; Yell, "quick to see the right and ready to pursue it"; Hardin, "one of nature's noblest spirits, a soldier tried and true"; McKee, "wise in council and brave in the field"; and Clay, "the young, the brave, the chivalrous—foremost in the fight—the soul of every lofty sentiment."[44]

Three of the men were regimental commanders, William R. McKee of the Second Regiment of Kentucky Volunteers, John J. Hardin of the

The Charge of Captain May at the Battle of Resaca de la Palma. From *Columbian Magazine* (September 1846).

First Illinois Regiment, and Archibald Yell of the First Regiment of Arkansas Cavalry; Hardin and Yell had served their states in the lower house of Congress. Yell, courageous but imprudent (much better suited to politics, according to Gregg), had served in the War of 1812 and the Seminole War. Upon hearing of Hardin's death, a correspondent was moved to quote Napier: "None died that day with more glory than he—yet many died, and there was much glory."

In a class by themselves, their heroism sealed by family ties and background, were George Lincoln, native son of Massachusetts and captain in the Eighth Infantry Regiment, and Henry Clay, Jr., second in command of Kentucky's Second Regiment. Lincoln, scion of one of the Bay State's oldest and most prominent families, son and grandson of governors, and descended from Revolutionary War soldiers, was assigned to Taylor's staff following a distinguished performance at Resaca de la Palma, an honor, according to Thorpe, that was like "the accolade" which "a king, in the old chivalry, laid upon the neck of the doer of gallant deeds." Felled by a Mexican bullet while charging the enemy at full gallop, he immediately acquired the sobriquet "Bayard of the American Army." His body was returned to Boston for a hero's burial in one of the grandest funeral ceremonies the city had ever

witnessed, and his heroism was soon after commemorated in a stage
play, "The Battle of Buena Vista, The Yankee Volunteer, or, The
Heroic Death of Captain Lincoln."[45]

The second son of the Kentucky politician and statesman, Henry
Clay, Jr., had resigned his commission soon after his graduation from
West Point in 1831. With the outbreak of the Mexican War, he joined
his state's volunteers and was elected lieutenant colonel of the Second
Regiment. His death at Buena Vista was among the most dramatic and
heart-rending recorded. Wounded while repelling an attack by Mexican lancers, his comrades attempted to carry him from the field. As the
enemy closed in, the soldiers found their way so rough and steep that
Clay ordered them to leave him behind. He asked that his sword be
placed in his hand, then, giving his pistols to one of the men, he asked
that they be sent to his father. "Tell him," young Clay murmured, "that
I used these to the last." Moments later, Clay was seen sitting up,
slashing at the enemy with his sword while their lances pierced his
body. "He fell in the flower of his age . . . and has left no worthier
name behind him." His death was widely mourned in the army and at
home. Zachary Taylor's condoling letter to Clay's father was reprinted
in the press throughout the country. Inspired by Clay's heroism, wrote
the General, the "sons of Kentucky" had proudly upheld the honor of
their state and of the country. The moment of Clay's death was relived
not only in prose and poetry but also in countless prints. "Notwith-
standing a deep-seated conviction that all war is a madness and folly,"
declared the *Union Magazine's* editor Caroline Kirkland, "there is something in our nature which causes the blood to stir and the eyes to fill
with sympathetic tears, as we read of gallant self-devotion, or call up
before the fancy such a scene."[46]

Scott's campaign seemed to lack the excitement that had characterized Taylor's engagements in the north. Scott himself, aloof, pompous,
more military in his bearing, hardly fired the imagination. As his army
moved inland from Vera Cruz, the conviction spread that Mexico was
already defeated and that it was only a matter of time before the
fighting would cease. The public's impatience to see the end mounted.
Scott's victories were reported in detail, but there was something missing. The wild and rugged mountainous terrain in which the battle of
Cerro Gordo was fought in April 1847 was not clothed with the veil of
romance that had been applied to Buena Vista. Even though the soldiers traversed treacherous mountain paths, scaled peaks under fire,
and turned an apparently impregnable Mexican postion, the battle did
not produce heroes on the scale of Taylor's earlier battles. The long
hiatus in Puebla, as the twelve-month volunteers departed for home
and new regiments were awaited, dulled the public's interest in the
campaign. When a false report was circulated that Scott's army had left
Puebla and marched quietly "into the city of the Montezumas" in mid-
July, Americans were ready to celebrate the end of the conflict.

The battles in the environs of the Mexican capital, marked by heavy casualties on both sides, produced few heroes. Pierce Mason Butler, colonel of South Carolina's Palmetto Regiment, fell at Churubusco, covered "with the glory of an American Hero." Mourned principally in South Carolina, Butler's death assumed a larger significance for at least one national journal. Reminding its readers that Butler was the son of a Revolutionary War soldier, the *Spirit of the Times* concluded that "it is such spirits that redeem an age from degeneracy, and exalt a nation to renown." At the disastrous battle of Molino del Rey, Charles F. Morris, a lieutenant in the Eighth Infantry Regiment, was fatally wounded, a circumstance that would not have attracted special notice had not Morris been a grandson of Robert Morris. His honor, it was said, "was chivalrous, his respect for women romantic"; he was a knight in the true sense of the word.[47]

Although severely criticized for their brutal treatment of Mexican soldiers and civilians, the Texas Rangers provided drama and romance to the Mexican War in ways that other soldiers could not. Distance tended to obscure their more unsavory characteristics and, while their acts of cruelty and ruthless vengeance were fully reported, they still assumed a picturesque, almost fanciful image that appealed to the popular imagination. To a generation nurtured on tales of frontier adventure, they seemed to embody all or most of the essential qualities of the western frontiersman—wild and undisciplined, independent, daring and courageous, bred to the saddle, and inured to hardship. If they did not conform fully to the Leatherstocking image they came close. They were, in short, "of the stuff which fills the moulds of heroes."[48]

The Texan was a legendary figure even before the war. The settlement of Texas, its revolt against Mexican rule, the ill-fated Santa Fe and Mier expeditions were dramatic episodes in America's western experience,[49] and for a people that looked to the frontier for that which was uniquely American, the figures involved in them assumed mythical attributes. The Texan became a new American hero, pursuing his adventures across the pages of cheap popular fiction and travel accounts. "A braver and a fiercer spirit never surveyed the desert or pitched his tent in the wilderness!" "The Texan Soldier" was celebrated in poetry as the true examplar of the Anglo-Saxon race, "as ever true to thoughts that might a Harold grace." William Gilmore Simms found in the "Texian Hunter" the qualities of knighthood and chivalry. Even Walt Whitman sang the glories of "the race of rangers."[50]

That the Texas Rangers should enter the lists of Mexican War heroes was inevitable, for the war offered a new arena for their "deeds of daring and reckless chivalry." Their outlandish dress, dark beards and long hair, and awesome weaponry (a rifle and as many as four pistols) not only terrified Mexicans but also enlarged their romantic image. Their often indiscriminate acts of brutality were sublimated to a "desperate yet chivalric method of fighting." John Coffee (Jack) Hays, slight, raw-boned, with a "Roman face," recalled the legendary tales of knights-errant. Ben McCulloch, with weatherbeaten features and cool calculating demeanor, was celebrated for his skill in tracking the enemy. Both Hays and McCulloch fought at Monterey "like enraged tigers," where some Texans made a game of shooting Mexicans off the rooftops. No Mexican in sight was spared, the "sharp crack of the Texian rifles" mingling with the shrieks of women. It was, wrote Thorpe, a "terrible sight."[51]

Daniel Drake Henrie was a hero straight out of the storybooks whose widely told adventures inspired tales that were more legendary than factual. An Ohioan who fought in the Texas Revolution, Henrie was captured at Mier in 1842 and held in the dread Perote prison until his escape a few month later. Eager for vengeance against his former captors, he attached himself to the army as an irregular soldier soon after the Mexican War broke out and because of his familiarity with northern Mexico and his knowledge of Spanish became a guide in General Wool's division. Late in January 1847, while leading a detachment of Arkansas cavalry on an intelligence mission in the vicinity of Buena Vista, Henrie was captured a second time (along with the Arkansans and a unit of Kentuckians).

He had good reason to fear for his life, having been a prisoner of the Mexicans earlier, and tried unsuccessfully to conceal his identity. Aware that he had been recognized, Henrie made another daring escape, eluding his pursuers and narrowly averting capture by Mexican scouting parties, rancheros, and Comanche Indians. He rode through deep gorges, scaled mountains, and traversed deserts until his horse expired. Continuing on foot through chaparral and prickly-pears, subsisting on desert rats and what little water he could find, he finally reached the American camp, his clothes in rags, shoes worn out, hair and beard matted, skin withered, and his hands and feet covered with cactus thorns.

Henrie's story, for which he was the only source, was first described by newspaper correspondents, then confirmed in soldiers' letters, and finally picked up by writers at home. The tale grew in the telling. "This reckless and daring ranger," wrote Charles Wilkins Webber in the *Democratic Review,* "has probably passed through a greater number of perilous and singular adventures than any other man of the same age." Henrie's hatred of the Mexicans was "of the most savage and deadly character," his hatred for Indians "refreshingly orthodox." Otherwise a "light-hearted mortal," he had a "careless knack" for getting into scrapes and then fighting his way out "with the most dashing gallantry." Henrie's name was known throughout the country as a true representative of "the brave Texan Ranger."[52]

Samuel Walker. From *Gra-
ham's Magazine* (June 1848).

"Time and opportunity make men," wrote Fayette Robinson, "and high talent in any profession or sphere of life is valueless unless called into action." Robinson was writing of Samuel H. Walker, the Texan whose claim to heroic status was more solid than any other; indeed, Walker was the last hero of the Mexican War. A native Marylander, veteran of the Seminole War, and like Henrie a Mexican prisoner following his capture at Mier, Walker escaped his captors, joined Hays's company of Texas Rangers, and fought an engagement against the Comanches. Utilizing his experience, he became acquainted with the arms manufacturer Samuel Colt, designed the so-called Walker Colt revolver, and persuaded the War Department to supply the army with the weapons.

At the time hostilities with Mexico began, Walker headed a company of scouts in Taylor's army. When he and his men rode through the Mexican army north of the Rio Grande to report the enemy's movements to Taylor, he became an instant celebrity. An account of his feat was immediately published, titled *The Brave Ranger,* in which he was portrayed as so valorous and his achievement so daring that one correspondent feared no reader would believe it. As far away as New York, theatregoers relived the adventure in a new drama, "The Campaign on the Rio Grande or Triumphs in Mexico," in which Walker was a leading character. After fighting with distinction in Monterey, he was given a captain's commission in a new regiment of mounted riflemen and sent to the east coast to recruit his men. Wherever he went he created a sensation.[53]

Assigned to Winfield Scott's army and given the task of keeping the line between Vera Cruz and Mexico City clear of guerrillas, Walker carried out his mission with a vengeance. "Should Captain Walker come across guerrillas," wrote a Pennsylvania volunteer, "God help them for he seldom brings in prisoners." While pursuing a force of lancers in October 1847 he met his death in the town of Huamantla, near Puebla. Some accounts had him shot from behind by a marksman in a nearby building; others insisted he was run through by a lance. Dying, he shouted to his men, "Yield not an inch—not one inch!" (or words to that effect, there are several versions).

Walker's death at a time when Americans believed the fighting to be over was deeply mourned. Eulogies became commonplace. His deeds, wrote Thorpe, had become part of "our national glory"; his career demonstrated the courage and fortitude of the American character. Prints depicting the Texan in buckskins and fur hat, leaning on his long rifle, were reminiscent of Daniel Boone and Leatherstocking. The moment of his death at the hands of an ugly, grimacing Mexican was illustrated. Charles Deas, a prominent painter of the frontier, exhibited his painting of Walker killing an Indian who was about to lift his scalp. This "star of freedom's chivalry," it was said, was worthy of the heroes of the Revolution, while soldier-poet Henry Kirby Benner found in Walker the true qualities of heroism,

> For a braver, or a better, or a more chivalrous knight
> Never put his lance in rest in the days when might was right;
> And he had the fox's cunning, and the eagle's restless eye,
> With his courage, to see danger, and that danger to defy.

It was to men like Walker that America must look to "grasp the brand" and "Westward and Southward, point the way."[54]

At a time when the traditional roles of women in society were coming under attack, it might be expected that women should participate in the Mexican War in more ways than simply by exhorting their men to patriotism or by sewing flags and uniforms or even by working in the ammunition factories. There were instances, although few, of women who volunteered to fight as soldiers, though they could do so only by disguising themselves as men. Those who did strive to join the combat, moreover, did so less from patriotic motives than from the desire to follow a lover or a family member into the service. Invariably they were discovered at the first inspections.

One who remained undiscovered, if her story can be believed, was Eliza Allen Billings, a native of Maine, who not only volunteered as a soldier but also served in combat and was wounded at Cerro Gordo. Even then, she insisted, her sex was not revealed. Following the war, she recounted her experience in *The Female Volunteer, or The Life and Wonderful Adventures of Miss Eliza Allen, a Young Lady of Eastport, Maine,* a dramatic tale of unrequited love, narrow escapes, battlefield carnage, shipwreck and rescue, and finally (the happy ending) marriage and the "termination of all her trials and sorrows."

Others had no need to hide their identities but accompanied the army in more or less official capacities. Among these were the army laundresses, often the wives of enlisted men. They were issued rations and bedding, assigned quarters (where that was possible), and on occasion provided with arms. They frequently served as cooks, maintaining messes to which both officers and enlisted men contributed their rations.[55]

Mexican women likewise were drawn into the conflict, and some found themselves thrust suddenly into combat roles. Mexican army units customarily traveled with large entourages of female camp-followers, wives, daughters, or lovers of the soldiers, often with babes in arms, who marched with the men and carried their packs and household goods. The sight aroused wonder and no little anger among the American soldiers, who complained that Mexican women were treated as "slaves of the men." There were times when they also fought alongside their men: at Bracito, Doniphan's men observed women attending the Mexican cannon; women were found among the Mexican casualties following Cerro Gordo; and in the defense of Mexico City, women "fought like heroes." It was in the bitter street fighting in Monterey, however, that the role of Mexican women assumed legendary proportions.

Commanding a company of lancers, Dos Amades, as she was known, "unsexed herself" (in the words of an American officer), donned the uniform of a captain of lancers, and swore that she would never yield until the "Northern barbarians" were driven from her country. After exhorting her men to fight with fierce and unrelenting courage, she led her lancers in a devastating charge against the Americans. Her American enemies responded with feelings of admiration and respect. "There's an example of heroism worthy the days of old!" exclaimed one officer, "It has remained for Mexico to produce a second Joan d'Arc." She survived the battle. Following the suspension of hostilities, Dos Amades doffed her uniform and returned to her family. Nothing more was heard of her, while in the United States her story continued to circulate in the press.[56]

Heroism of a different sort during the desperate house-to-house fighting was acclaimed when a beauteous young Mexican señorita was observed carrying water and food to the wounded soldiers of both armies, at great peril to her own life. As she cared for the men, binding their wounds with bandages torn from her clothing, she was struck by a bullet. The volunteers who watched were distraught. "I heard the crack of one or two guns," one of them declared, "and she, poor good creature, fell; after a few struggles all was still—she was dead!" She was buried by American soldiers "amid showers of grape and round shot." Later identified as Maria Josefa Zozaya, she was celebrated as a hero of the Mexican War, the "beau-ideal of heroism," the "Heroine Martyr of Monterey."

> Far greater than the wise or brave,
>   Far happier than the fair and gay,
> Was she, who found a martyr's grave
>   On that red field of Monterey.[57]

The involvement of women in the war, on both sides, was an index of the world's advancement, *Godey's Magazine* maintained, for after all, the "civilization of the world is to be the work of woman." The editor cited reports that companies of women had been raised and armed in Switzerland and that Mormon women had formed a regiment, showing that "a sort of petticoat ascendancy seems coming about." The *National Intelligencer,* noting that women were serving in the Mexican ranks, urged (less seriously) that the United States recruit members of "the (miscalled) softer sex" for service in the army. "Men can no more encounter women, when once fairly aroused, than they can so many tigresses." Women of the Spanish race, moreover, fought like "so many born devils" when defending their firesides (as witness the Maid of Saragossa, a heroine of the Peninsular campaign). Women, the paper asserted, were *"instinctive* soldiers"; to enlist them in the war with Mexico would merely conform to "the great 'tendency' of the age."[58]

That women could be heroes (or heroines) in war had been shown in earlier conflicts, but their heroism, as Dixon Wecter has pointed out, usually resulted from their "imitation of the stronger sex." In the Mexican War they were recognized rather for doing what some Americans would argue women could do best, gathering intelligence from the enemy and transmitting it to the American forces, or serving as ministering angels, dispensing food and drink and binding wounds during battle. Ann Chase, the Irish-born wife of the American consul in Tampico, remained behind when her husband was expelled at the beginning of the war. Protected by her British citizenship, she supplied the U.S. Navy for months with information regarding troop movements and harbor defenses. When American naval units, acting on her information, moved against Tampico in November 1846, she anticipated their arrival by raising the Stars and Stripes over the city. Mrs. Chase was honored throughout the United States as the "Heroine of Tampico."[59]

No woman, however, was accorded as much attention as the "heroine of Fort Brown," an Irish laundress whose identity and background are now shrouded in the mists of legend. Sarah Borginnis (or Bourdette) was known simply as The Great Western because of her size—six feet tall (some said six feet two inches), "a remarkably large, well-proportioned strong woman, of strong nerves, and great physical power." Married to a soldier in the Seventh Infantry, she not only did the wash but also served as a cook for a group of young officers. Furthermore, she had been reportedly "enlisted" in the army at Jefferson Barracks six years before in a mock ceremony, giving her a status not enjoyed by the other laundresses. The Great Western attracted notice even before Taylor's army reached the Rio Grande. While the women employed by the army were taken by sea from Corpus Christi to Point Isabel, the army's staging area near the Rio Grande, Mrs. Borginnis insisted on traveling overland with the men, driving her donkey-cart laden with cooking utensils and supplies and displaying qualities which the "best teamster in the train might have envied." When the men hesitated on the banks of a small stream, expecting its crossing to be disputed by Mexicans, The Great Western drove her cart to the front and prepared to cross the river, swearing that she would whip "every scoundrel that dare show himself."

During the Mexican bombardment of Fort Brown, erected by Taylor on the Rio Grande opposite Matamoros, the eight or ten women attached to the garrison sought safety in bombproof shelters. Not so The Great Western. She set up her tent near the center of the fort and provided food and hot coffee to the exhausted soldiers. Her specialty was bean soup, that same bean soup which some Mexican soldiers claimed was the basis for the Americans' "invincible spirit." Ignoring the shot that fell around her, she continued to supply food to the soldiers, bind their wounds, and load their guns. One enemy bullet pierced her bonnet, another shattered her bread tray, but she persevered. As she moved among the men in the fort during the seven-day bombardment, "no belle of Orleans . . . ever met a more gracious reception."

When the fort was relieved following the battles of Palo Alto and Resaca de la Palma, The Great Western was given her due. She was toasted by the soldiers, and her heroism was told in detail by newspaper correspondents, repeated in soldiers' letters, and published in their campaign accounts. One correspondent went further than the rest when he praised her for her virtue as well as for her heroism, seeking to quiet the "tongue of slander" that had been directed at her character. Her fame did not end on the Rio Grande. She marched with Taylor's army to Monterey, although she was not involved in the assault on the city. At Buena Vista she was on the field, making car-

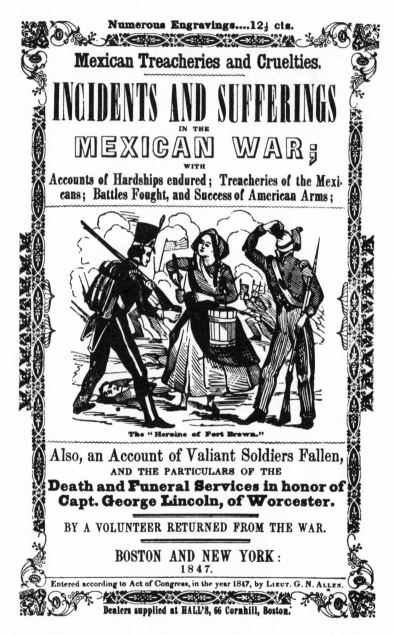

Numerous Engravings....12¼ cts.

Mexican Treacheries and Cruelties.

INCIDENTS AND SUFFERINGS

IN THE

MEXICAN WAR;

WITH

Accounts of Hardships endured; Treacheries of the Mexicans; Battles Fought, and Success of American Arms;

The "Heroine of Fort Brown."

Also, an Account of Valiant Soldiers Fallen,

AND THE PARTICULARS OF THE

Death and Funeral Services in honor of Capt. George Lincoln, of Worcester.

BY A VOLUNTEER RETURNED FROM THE WAR.

BOSTON AND NEW YORK:
1847.

Entered according to Act of Congress, in the year 1847, by LIEUT. G. N. ALLEN.

Dealers supplied at HALL'S, 66 Cornhill, Boston.

The Great Western, Heroine of Fort Brown. From *Incidents and Sufferings in the Mexican War* (1847).

tridges, caring for the wounded, and bolstering the nerves of the soldiers. Her subsequent activities become vague. She apparently forsook the infantry for the dragoons, resided for a time in Saltillo, and operated a hotel in Monterey. It was said that General Winfield Scott himself later ordered that she be made a pensioner of the government. Following the war, she settled at Fort Yuma, where she kept a saloon and where she died in 1866. Buried with full military honors, The Great Western ended a long career with the army that had reached its peak within the walls of Fort Brown—the unchallenged Heroine of the Mexican War.[60]

In midsummer 1847, the men who had marched and fought with Doniphan on the incredible trek through the deserts of northern Mexico were on their way home to Missouri. With their long beards, buckskin costume, and uncouth appearance, the volunteers attracted attention wherever they went. Word of their return preceded them as they moved up the Mississippi, and crowds gathered on landings and housetops to cheer their passage.

By early July several hundred, including Doniphan, had arrived in St. Louis, where elaborate preparations had been made to honor their return. Church bells rang as fire companies and military units paraded through the streets. Behind them marched the "heroes of Bracito and Sacramento," carrying their bullet-riddled flags, displaying several captured Mexican banners (including the famous black death's-head flag carried by Mexican troops at Bracito) and dragging eleven Mexican cannon festooned with flowers. The procession ended in a grove on the edge of the city, where several thousand people gathered to hear Thomas Hart Benton praise the deeds of the volunteers as "among the most wonderful of the age." Following Benton, Doniphan paid tribute to the men in his command. A Whig, he expressed chagrin at the attitude some in his party had adopted toward the war and charged that antiwar politicians like Thomas Corwin had in fact prolonged the conflict. Americans, he declared, had shown conclusively that not only could republics create heroes but that they also knew how to honor them. It was not the generalship, he modestly suggested, that had determined the outcome of their battles. Rather, "the victories of Bracito and Sacramento . . . belong to the *rank and file!*"

In a ceremony that would be repeated throughout the country, the returning volunteers were hailed as heroes, their achievements "worthy of the greatest heroes of antiquity." Ruxton, in St. Louis when the soldiers arrived and no admirer of the Americans, grumbled that the townspeople had "converted these rowdy and vermin-covered veterans into perfect heroes."[61]

And so it was, in towns and cities across the land as the soldiers returned to their homes. We want the world to know, commented the *New York Herald,* that the "gallant band of heroes who have fought their way to the Halls of the Montezumas" have returned "in victorious guise and dignified majesty." The celebrations began in New Orleans and Mobile, where the returning veterans were greeted as they left their ships. The volunteers, declared a former Congressman, were "worthy of the genius of this great republic." The taunts heaped upon "our citizen soldiers" had been hurled back into the teeth of European generals and diplomats. Alexander Beaufort Meek's eulogy was typical for its romantic imagery and rhetoric. Greeting the soldiers in Mobile on July 4, 1848, the lawyer-poet linked their heroism to the "sainted fathers of our land." Lighting anew the "fires of freedom," they had unfurled the "standard of the stars above those lofty palaces where once floated the golden gonfalon of Cortez, and was heard the wild music of the teocallis of Montezuma."[62]

For the western volunteers, the journey up the Mississippi was a triumphal procession. Their reception, according to an Indiana volunteer, was ample repayment for "seeing the elephant." As the vessel carrying the First Pennsylvania Regiment moved upriver, towns along the banks were crowded with cheering people. At Cairo, the townspeople fired a cannon. The scene was repeated on both banks of the Ohio; at Cincinnati, where the boat docked, people crowded the waterfront for a glimpse of the soldiers and the men paraded through the city in response. As they approached Pittsburgh, it became obvious that the welcome in their home state would exceed all that passed before. Escorted to the dock by boats with bands on board playing *Home Sweet Home,* the regiment marched through streets so crowded the men could barely move. As they crossed the state by train, the veterans were greeted in one town after another, until they arrived in Philadelphia. There businesses were closed, the buildings decorated with flowers and flags, and the streets jammed. More eulogies and a banquet for the regiment were followed by a brilliant fireworks display. A song of welcome was especially composed and sung for the occasion:

> Ye braves, whose bands on Mexico's plain
> > Hath struck the blow for country's right,
> We bid ye welcome home again
> > From the dark turmoil of the fight.

One volunteer was convinced that the people must really believe that "the second conquerors of Mexico" were men of extraordinary strength and power. "Who wouldn't be a soldier of the Mexican War?" he asked.[63]

In New York the city militia units which had not seen active service escorted returning volunteers up Broadway, as thousands lined the street. Ladies threw bouquets of flowers at the feet of the men. The entire city, noted Horace Greeley's *Tribune,* bore a festive appearance. The air was filled with excitement and an eagerness to hear of the volunteers' adventures, for the New York Regiment had borne the brunt of much of the fighting around Mexico City. The city, observed one citizen, was "full of our returned Mexican heroes, and we should not be surprised if hero-worship should be the order of the day in the fashionable world the coming winter." Women were bound to ask those who would seek their favor, what have you done? "Then will the siege of Vera Cruz, the wild terrors of Contreras, and the consummate brilliance of Churubusco, glow in martial picturesqueness through their romantic fancy."[64]

Not all was picturesque and romantic, however, as the rigors of the campaigns were often evident in the depleted ranks, shabby and worn clothing, and the wan appearance of some of the battle veterans. To Horace Greeley, the appearance of the soldiers testified to the "ruin and terrible devastations of WAR." The hard-fought fields that had brought the volunteers such an abundant harvest of laurels were dramatically apparent in the faces and frames of those weary men who marched through the cheering crowds. Some never returned at all. "What a contrast between the return of the living and dead," wrote editor Ann Stephens. "The one comes back, with brows wreathed in victory" while the "other is brought home in sadness, in silence, in tears." But all, living and dead, were revered as "Patriot-Warriors," all were hailed as heroes. "A free people," noted *Godey's,* "have no lives to barter away, and those who offer themselves in the hour of their country's need, should be honored through life and lamented in death."

A nation's heroes are but manifestations of those qualities most esteemed by the people. Americans saw themselves, or what they most wanted to see in themselves, in the characters of the heroes they venerated. Steeped in notions of romanticism, they merged the traits of chivalry and medieval knighthood with the ideal of the rugged, self-sufficient frontiersman to produce an image (a self-image) they believed to be truly and uniquely American. The heroes of the Mexican War, indeed "this *army of heroes,*" had proved worthy of America itself, redeeming a generation so often charged with forgetting its inheritance. After thirty years and more of peace, Americans had proved that "the blood of the men of Seventy-six had not degenerated in their veins." Their true monument was in the "enhanced reputation of their country, and in the increased moral power of their countrymen."[65]

CHAPTER 6

Travelers in a Foreign Land

From the very first days of the war, Americans exhibited a "voracious appetite" for news, a demand for information that remained high throughout the conflict. The interest was an index of the war's popularity, an attitude that was separate from and at times contradictory to more fundamental views of the rightness of the war as public policy. The Mexican War was popular, a recent military historian has suggested, because it "responded to a national mood of self-confident expansion and romanticism." Americans found their military actions against Mexico appealing, no matter how alien many of them felt the war was to the purposes of a republic or how unnecessary in its origins. Questions of national identity and mission, never far below the surface of American thought, were mixed with a romantic outlook that sought gratification in tales of patriotic sacrifice, of heroes and heroism.

There was, however, another element in the war's romantic attraction, for it coincided with a growing popular fascination with remote and exotic lands. The world was shrinking; improvements in transportation and communication brought Americans closer to the distant areas of the globe. It was a period of "reaching out," not only in terms of economic and commercial expansion but in intellectual and scientific ways as well. Government-sponsored exploring expeditions were dispatched to Antarctic and Pacific waters, to the jungle interiors of South America and Africa, and to the fabled Levant. Their reports were eagerly consumed by a reading public anxious to learn more of strange lands and their even stranger inhabitants. Every person, observed James Fenimore Cooper, "has a longing to see distant lands," to gratify a natural impulse to observe the "peculiarities of nations" and to ascertain the "differences which exist between the stranger and ourselves."[1]

The Mexican War reflected this longing, expanding the horizons of Americans and providing one more window on the world through which they could view a foreign land and culture. Thousands of

144

Americans left home to experience at firsthand the sights and sounds of a strange land. Those who remained behind shared their perceptions vicariously. Through the experience, Americans both in Mexico and at home sharpened their views of themselves; the war was another step in their own quest for national identity.

The war's impact on American popular thought and perception was aided by the "publishing explosion" of the 1840s, when technology and the "universal itch of authorship" it spawned brought low-priced reading material within the reach of the masses. The press was "as busy with Mexico as our army." No war had ever been fought, noted *Niles' National Register,* "of which there were so many historians."

> If its very minutiae are not known to every man in this country, it will not be for want of either free pens or free presses. The avidity of all classes for news from the army, places in constant requisition some thousands of printing presses, & mails, expresses, steamboats, locomotives, magnetic telegraphs, are flying in all directions. In order to keep the *supply,* fairly up to the mark, some thousands of ready writers are required. The army and its retinue promptly meet the demand.

To the *Register* this phenomenon revealed America's democratic character. The "republican habit" of writing and speaking what one pleased was so "universally indulged" that it was no surprise the habit was carried into the army. Critics of the war despaired at the flood of books that flowed out of the Mexican experience, but they could do little to halt it. They were, the critics conceded, "books for the times."[2]

The tales of Mexican adventure that poured from the pens of the soldiers, complained *Holden's Magazine* in 1849, often treated matters that were inherently grave and serious in an inappropriately light-hearted manner; too many such books were "waggish and rollicking" and written in a "pantagruellian" style. It was a tendency that characterized travel literature in general. To blame, the writer felt, was the English writer and traveler A. W. Kinglake, whose account of travel in the Middle East, *Eōthen,* was published in England in 1844 and immediately reprinted in the United States (there were seven American editions between 1845 and 1850). Kinglake's imitators among the authors of Mexican War books, he claimed, were legion. The outburst was directed toward Henry Augustus Wise's *Los Gringos; or, An Inside View of Mexico and California.* Wise, who also wrote adventure stories under the pseudonym Harry Gringo, was a young naval officer who served in California and on the west coast of Mexico during the war. In the spring of 1848, he carried dispatches from Mazatlan to Mexico City and back, traveling in disguise and encountering a number of close scrapes with brigands, Mexican authorities, and beautiful young ladies.[3]

Holden's analogy between the soldiers' accounts generated by the war and travel literature was an apt one. Observing the sights and sounds of this strange land, the men thought of themselves as travelers as well as soldiers. Army service for some was one way of satisfying curiosity, of probing the mystery and experiencing the enchantment that clung about the ancient land of the Aztecs. "Mexico! land of romance and boyhood's waking dreams!" exclaimed a volunteer in Taylor's army. "What American youth is there whose veins have not swelled with a warmer current, as he pored over her early history." Curiosity vied with patriotism and the spirit of adventure. Mexico, a *terra incognita,* was to be opened to the gaze of Americans. "What cared the youthful blood whether the war were a righteous one or not." Mexico was a country "replete with wonder and instruction."

Next to the "classic shores of the Mediterranean," confessed an Ohio volunteer, Mexico had been of greatest interest to him. Prescott's history was responsible, kindling, as it did for so many others, a strong desire to visit Mexico's "grand and beautiful scenes." The war provided the opportunity.

> To revel among the intoxicating perfumes and flowery plains of the *tierra caliente;* to wander among the verdant fields and fruits of the *tierra templada;* to gaze upon the magnificent scenery and wonderful exhibitions of Aztec civilization displayed in profusion throughout the *tierra fria!* To conquer the descendants of the Spanish conquerors, and to plant the flag of our young republic upon the capital reared centuries ago above the ruins of Montezuma's palaces! What prospect more captivating to the youthful imagination?

While not all the soldiers were able to wax so ecstatic at the prospect of penetrating Mexico's mysteries, the sentiment was widely shared. Mexico was "a fabled land . . . almost an earthly paradise," its story partaking more of romance than of the "sober lessons of historic truth."[4]

America's horizons were expanded. Thousands of uniformed Americans poured into Mexico, their observations filling the "unwritten void" of Mexican history. They brought home what could not be acquired from books, a "current knowledge of the country and people." The war-worn veterans, wrote historian Brantz Mayer, would long remember the "delicious land, amid whose valleys and majestic mountains they had learned . . . to admire the sublimity of nature." Because of them, Mexico had become the "most interesting portion of the world."[5]

Travel and the literature it inspired were basic outlets for the romantic temperament. As a literary genre, travel narratives have suffered neglect yet travel-writing was one of the most popular literary forms in the 18th and 19th centuries. It combined instruction with pleasure, satisfied a yearning for knowledge about foreign lands and peoples and heightened the romantic's sentimental attachment to nature and land-scape and fascination with the vestiges of a dim and forgotten past. The love of the beautiful in nature and the veneration of the "accumulated treasures of historic lore"—crumbling monuments that speak of a people and a grandeur that passed away centuries ago—were not only requisite to travel but also inseparable from its purpose.[6]

It was precisely this romantic appeal that accounted for the popularity of travel books in the United States during the midcentury years. "Everybody travels now-a-days," complained a reviewer, "and everybody that travels writes a book." Yet the quality of the books was not always commensurate with their popularity. "The art of travelling," wrote James Fenimore Cooper, "is far more practised than understood." Two travel books became models of the genre, Kinglake's *Eōthen* and Herman Melville's fictional narrative of his sojourn in the South Seas, *Typee.* The latter, published early in 1846, achieved a popularity that few books were able to match. A "new chapter in book-making," it inspired imitation among travelers, including soldiers in Mexico. Before *Typee,* travel writing concentrated on facts, observations, and opinions, "everything but the *picturesque.*" Melville supplied the missing ingredient.

To the love of the picturesque and the excitement of adventure, the travel literature of mid-19th-century America added other elements of the romantic temperament: the quest for roots in a distant past and the search for national identity. The campaign accounts of the nation's soldiers in Mexico—travel books in a larger sense—both revealed and met these desires.[7]

Popular interest in Mexico ran high long before the outbreak of the war; indeed, the interest was one of the reasons for the war's popularity. The attention devoted to America's southern neighbor in the mid-1840s had its beginnings early in the century. Alexander von Humboldt has been credited with the 19th century's discovery of Mexico. His monumental study of New Spain (1811) was translated immediately into English and remained a classic for decades afterward, while Humboldt himself was recognized as the world's leading authority on Mexican politics, society, antiquities, and culture. No wonder that Americans glowed when the aged Humboldt expressed his admiration for the achievements of Taylor's army in 1846.

The winning of Mexico's independence from Spain, the opening of a lucrative overland trade between Missouri and the upper Rio Grande, and the settling of Texas by Americans turned popular attention to the south and southwest. Santa Fe traders and Texans published their impressions of Mexican life and society and helped to shape American attitudes toward Mexico at a time when relations between the two countries were deteriorating. Many of the Mexican War's volunteers carried with them perceptions first derived from these works. Archaeologists John Lloyd Stephens and Benjamin M. Norman shared their discoveries of Mexico's antiquities; diplomats Joel R. Poinsett, Waddy Thompson, and Brantz Mayer offered their observations on Mexican life and culture to the American public; and travelers like Frances Calderón de la Barca (whose *Life in Mexico* was published in 1843 at Prescott's suggestion) and the scientifically oriented Albert Gilliam drew attention to the land, its people, and its resources. Most of these works reached American readers just before the war, and many of them were brought out in new editions during the war. Still, Mexico to most Americans remained a land of mystery and legend. It was not until America's "victorious legions" had traversed Mexico "from Palo Alto to Chapultepec," one soldier insisted, that accurate knowledge of Mexico was received in the United States.[8]

"Every American soldier in the present war considers himself in some degree its historian," John Frost observed in his *Mexican War and Its Warriors*. Regulars and volunteers not only supplied their families and friends with detailed accounts of their adventures but they also served as correspondents for their hometown newspapers. Nearly every soldier in the ranks of "*our* army," according to *Niles's*, was capable of writing an account of what he sees, hears, or does, and for every platoon there was at least one newspaper back home ready "to speed to the four winds of heaven whatever is written." Following the struggle for Monterey in September 1846, the volume of letters received in the New Orleans post office from Taylor's army swelled to over 14,000 pieces, about twice the normal figure. The implication was that the soldiers were doing little else but record their battle experiences for the benefit of those left behind. Indeed, one gathers that letter-writing was their most popular pastime.[9]

Not all agreed with the editor who maintained that the thoroughness with which the war was reported also involved accuracy. "The thousand and one letters from the Volunteer privates and others," protested one correspondent, "are not unfrequently downright *Munchausens*." Many of the items carried in the papers under "Incidents of the War," he insisted, had no basis in fact. Some letter-writers were suspected of being overly anxious to puff their own deeds. The "tickle-me-and-I'll-tickle-you" system often seemed more widespread than imagined, and even high-ranking officers (General Gideon Pillow for one) were not above employing letter-writers to "blow the trumpets" of their patrons. Readers back home were warned to be on their guard; the "unadorned truth" was extraordinary enough to satisfy even the "most wonder-loving reader."[10]

Many of the earliest volunteers were young men of education who were motivated by idealistic and patriotic considerations. The Civil War has been said to be the first war in which significant numbers of literate men served as common soldiers. While statistics are obviously sketchy and incomplete, that claim might be made for the Mexican War. Some volunteers moved directly from the classroom into the field, expecting to find a campaign in Mexico more appealing than a "recitation in Thucydides or Juvenal." A remarkably high proportion were college graduates or individuals who had attended college, medical students, and students of the law. "Of what consequence was a license to practise law?" recalled an Indiana volunteer, when there was glory to be won on Mexican fields. A company of Tennessee volunteers was formed from Nashville law students. Two companies of Mississippi volunteers consisted of planters and planters' sons, all persons of education. Philip Kemble Garrick was only one of a number of actors who left the stage to join a company bound for Mexico.[11]

That many of the soldiers were exceptionally well-read was apparent from the letters they sent home, the journals they kept, and the accounts they published. The literature is sprinkled with literary and historical allusions that reveal a familiarity with classical writing, contemporary fiction, and works of history. References to Shakespeare, Defoe's *Robinson Crusoe,* the works of Sir Walter Scott and Charles Dickens and the Peninsular War fiction of men like Charles Lever testify to the continuing popularity of English literature in midcentury America. Soldiers found the small towns of northern Mexico reminiscent of *Don Quixote* and felt their observations were more meaningful because they had read the novels of James Fenimore Cooper.

The soldiers not only called upon their earlier reading experiences but also continued to be avid readers while campaigning in Mexico. Reading material was in great demand and short supply. In the aftermath of Buena Vista, one volunteer complained that "books cannot be had for love or money." A Tennessee volunteer reported that an unnamed novel which had fallen into the hands of one of the men had been passed around the camp until it was hardly readable. Early in the war, a group of New York publishers contributed a library to the army on the Rio Grande to meet the demand for reading material, but the effort was not repeated. Soldiers carried books with them in their knapsacks when they marched into Mexico, received books in the mail from their families (often asking for specific titles), and sought out booksellers in the Mexican towns. Before they left for Mexico, many volunteers had received Bibles from the American Bible Society and from their local communities with the result that the Bible was probably the most widely read book among the soldiers. Indeed, some read it as a travel book that would aid in their understanding of Mexico itself. Scenes in the small Mexican towns sometimes seemed but reenactments of Biblical scenes.[12]

Selection of books was not always possible, so the soldiers had to be content with whatever was available. Stuck on the Rio Grande, an Indianan found himself reading Rufus Wilmot Griswold's *Poets and Poetry*

of America, "a great treat here but at home no great shakes of a book."
An extraordinary case was that of the regular officer who filled his
off-duty hours studying Spinoza's *Ethics,* at the same time correspond-
ing with Longfellow on such topics as "Rossetti's mystics and their
esoteric writings." Shakespeare was popular, as were Byron (especially
Childe Harold, which some not only read but quoted in their journals)
and Shelley. Commentaries on Mexican history and society by Brantz
Mayer and Waddy Thompson and Madame Calderón's *Life in Mexico*
were read for what they could tell the soldiers about the land they were
then experiencing. By far the most popular book read by the men in
Mexico, if they could get their hands on a copy, was Prescott's *History of
the Conquest of Mexico.* Many had read it before and now reread it with
new insights; for others, the book was new and fresh. It not only served
to provide the Americans (especially those in Scott's army) with a sense
of historical purpose but it also served in a more practical way as a
guidebook to the sights along the route to the Mexican capital. Soldiers
carried copies with them into Mexico, while some purchased the Mexican edition to help them learn Spanish. At the beginning of the war,
the Secretary of the Navy ordered Prescott's book to be added to every
ship's library.[13]

Newspapers were even scarcer than books, so scarce that soldiers
often fought over them. The arrival of a newspaper in the mail, wrote
a South Carolina soldier, created so much excitement that the fortunate recipient was forced to "sneak off behind some hill" to read it or
risk being involved in a brawl. One of the most sought-after papers was
William T. Porter's weekly sporting and literary journal, *The Spirit of the
Times.* No fewer than thirty army correspondents were sending letters
to Porter, providing his paper with some of the most detailed and
complete information available on the operations in Mexico. Copies
were jealously guarded, passing from hand to hand through the ranks,
and reading the *Spirit* took precedence over most chores. One of Scott's
soldiers no sooner landed on the beach near Vera Cruz when he seated
himself on the sand and drew out his copy of the paper, a sight that
seemed incongruous with the military bustle that surrounded him.

The delivery of newspapers to the army was haphazard at best, and
the postal service was roundly condemned for its failures. An Illinoisan
wondered if there was an army regulation that made it "criminal for
soldiers to read newspapers." Some units published their own camp
newspapers, like the *Picket Guard* put out by Illinois volunteers in Saltillo, but they were a poor substitute for the hometown newspaper.[14]

Writing materials were as much in demand as books and newspapers;
indeed, they became essential items of military equipment. Some volunteers outfitted themselves with portable desks containing paper, pen-
cils, pen and ink, and blank notebooks. When Marylander William H.
Richardson joined Doniphan's Missouri volunteers, he included a "writing apparatus" among his "regimentals." Months later, near El Paso, he

lost his journal, a greater blow to him than any the enemy might have inflicted; it was recovered only after his captain threatened to search every soldier in the command. Soldiers from privates on up carried notebooks in their pockets or attached to their belts, so it was not unusual for them to fall out of the line of march to record their observations. Writing tools and paper were treasured items, for once lost they were not easily replaced. Camp sutlers sold writing paper at what the men complained were outrageous prices, but sutlers were not always at hand nor could the Mexicans be relied upon as a source of supply.[15]

In camp, writing became a popular means for filling the time that often lay heavily on the soldiers' hands. When they were not drilling or cooking, wrote a young volunteer from his camp at Brazos Santiago, there was nothing to do "but scribble, of which I think there is a vast deal done, as pens, ink and paper are in constant requisition." Left with a few idle hours, a soldier on the Rio Grande felt there was no better way to fill the time than to record the "facts and fancies" that fell within his observation; another, wounded at Buena Vista, relieved the pain and tedium of his sick bed by writing an account of the army's campaign. Conditions for writing, however, were not always so ideal. Jotted down on the march or in the midst of battle, the notes were rough and hurried. Apologizing for the cryptic nature of his record, a dragoon officer noted that "there is no time here for poetry." Even in camp, complained a regular, letter-writing was "no trifle." The heat of the Mexican summer sun, "enough to bake one's brains," and the constant torment of mosquitoes, gnats, and other "blood-thirsty" insects that were attracted by his single candle rendered letter-writing difficult if not impossible.[16]

The humor magazine *Yankee Doodle* caught the importance of letter-writing to the soldiers in a cartoon showing men in battle, seated on the ground, on camp-stools, or drum-heads, busily writing while their comrades were firing at the enemy that surrounded them. An Illinois volunteer serving as a correspondent for a St. Louis newspaper left a vivid word-picture of the soldier-writer at his task: "This thing of writing letters for publication, in camp, is neither so pleasant nor so easy as might be imagined. Draw the picture of a man of common size sitting cross legged on a blanket spread on the ground, with his portfolio on his knee, and an old broken lantern holding a piece of candle, propped on a well-worn leather trunk, and an earthenware inkstand on the ground close by, covered by the by, with a small tent in which old boots, old cloth[e]s, old guns, swords, pistols, are strewed around in the back ground, all striving to withdraw themselves from notice—and you will have an accurate daguerreotype of the writer and his ranch." To which another added: Cramped and uncomfortable, without benefit of table and chair, "one feels after writing a letter as if he had been mauling rails all day."[17]

Latest from the Army. From *Yankee Doodle* (December 12, 1846).

The soldiers who marched into Mexico were travelers in a foreign land. It was their first exposure to an outside world they had only imagined before. Travel indeed was offered as an inducement for volunteering by recruiters who promised a visit to Mexico and the Southwest with all expenses paid. A stopover in New Orleans and the sea voyage from New Orleans to Brazos Santiago, Tampico, or Vera Cruz was novelty enough, but it was Mexico—different in so many ways—that cast its spell on the soldiers. "So soon as you cross the Rio Grande," remarked Kentucky volunteer Cassius M. Clay, "you feel yourselves in a foreign land." The sights were so unexpected that many of the soldiers decided to "blot" them all down with a "running quill." Raphael Semmes, a young naval officer attached to Scott's headquarters, was so struck with curiosity about "this *terra incognita*" that he later published his notes just so Americans could learn something of their southern neighbor.[18]

The literature generated by these new travelers to Mexico was of the class which one English critic found peculiarly American, the literature of the forest and prairie, of the Indian camp and backwoods settlement, a literature of travel and adventure that was neither rivaled nor imitated anywhere else. Some of those who fought in Mexico were already experienced writers of travel and exploration. Fitch Taylor, the navy chaplain whose book *The Broad Pennant* combined a narrative of the Gulf Squadron's role with a broader sketch of the war, had authored an account of a round-the-world voyage that went through at least five editions by 1845. Josiah Gregg, whose chronicle

of the Santa Fe trade *Commerce of the Prairies* was already regarded as
a classic, built on this earlier experience in his dispatches from General Wool's division.

Among the correspondents of the *Spirit of the Times* were several
soldiers who had contributed to its columns in earlier years. James
Henry Carleton, an officer of the First Dragoons, had published accounts of the dragoons' expeditions to the high plains before the war
and continued to send dispatches from the army in Mexico. In 1848,
Carleton published the most detailed, reliable eye-witness account of
the Battle of Buena Vista. Pierce Butler, colonel of South Carolina's
Palmetto Regiment, had contributed stories of frontier experience and
backwoods humor before the war, and Albert Pike, an officer in Arkansas's volunteer cavalry, had been a regular writer for the paper.

The best-known of the *Spirit*'s army correspondents was William Seaton Henry, an 1835 graduate of West Point and captain in the Third
Infantry. Henry began sending letters to the paper before the war
began. Writing under the mysterious *nom de plume* G** de L***, Henry
sent back firsthand accounts of the battles and marches from Palo Alto
to Monterey, as well as vivid descriptions of Mexican life and scenery.
His letters bore a sense of dramatic immediacy, for he had been in the
thick of combat, winning brevets and commanding his regiment at
Monterey when all his senior officers were killed or wounded. In 1847
his letters were published by Harper and Brothers under the title *Campaign Sketches of the Mexican War,* and Henry (whose true name was
used) became an instant celebrity. "Julius Caesar," wrote George Ripley
in *Harbinger,* "was not the only great captain who could handle the pen
as skillfully as the sword." Novelist Henry William Herbert concluded,
after reading Henry's book, that the "best travels, the best journals of
discovery, and many of the best histories have emanated from the pens
of soldiers."

The War Department was less thrilled. Reviving an 1825 regulation
forbidding regular officers from writing for publication letters relative
to military movements and operations, the army command tried to
discourage the practice in the Mexican War. The *Spirit*'s correspondents, writing under pseudonyms, were not easily identified—but
Henry was. Shortly after his assignment to Scott's invasion force, Henry
was suddenly transferred to recruiting service in Vermont. The reason
for the transfer was never revealed but it seemed clear that the army
was displeased by his dispatches to the *Spirit of the Times.*[19]

The Missouri schoolteacher and chronicler of Doniphan's expedition,
John T. Hughes, intended his work to provide "entertainment for the
curious, truth for the inquisitive, novelty for the lover of romance,
instruction for the student of history, [and] information for the general
reader"—an ambitious expectation but one that was typical of midcentury travel narratives. Corydon Donnavan, whose *Adventures in Mexico*
abounded with romantic incident, hair-breadth escapes, and descrip-

tions of the Mexican government and people, supplemented his work
with a panorama of Mexican scenes which he painted and took on tour
in 1848. Publishers as well as critics recognized the popularity of the
soldiers' accounts as travel books. Benjamin Scribner's *Camp Life of a
Volunteer,* the straight-forward journal of an Indiana soldier, was advertised as "a rich, racy, and piquant chronicle of the glories of Mexicans
and Musquitoes, Grenadiers and Guerillas, Stoccadoes and Senoritas,
Jungles and Jackasses, Rancheros and Revolvers." There was no doubt
that the accounts of Mexican War soldiers touched a popular nerve,
and their number multiplied. "We thought the Peninsular war was the
cause of as much spilling of ink as blood," groaned a reviewer in
Godey's, "but we bid fair to go as far beyond our across-the-channel
friends in this as we do in other matters."[20]

Commenting on the travel literature of the mid-19th century, Henry
T. Tuckerman observed that "Antiquity, Nature and Society" were the
principal "fields of observation revealed by the records of travel."
While the soldiers in Mexico fell short of the ideal requirements
Tuckerman thought essential to good travel-writing—a foundation of
historical and scientific expertise and familiarity with "mental philosophy," for example—their lack of scholarship was more than compensated for by those characteristics Tuckerman believed made Americans
the most perceptive of travel writers: the lack of roots in the soil, the
restlessness and accustomed mobility ("the American is by nature locomotive"), curiosity, the power of adaptation and that pioneer enterprise
that was a staple of their history. These characteristics the fighting-men
shared in abundance. Furthermore, they possessed the two qualities
essential to any successful traveler: an instinctive spirit of adventure
(which Tuckerman believed to be a form of heroism) and the enthusiasm of discovery.[21]

"Mexico," wrote one editor shortly after the outbreak of the war, "is to
us an unknown country." Earlier travelers had been restricted to the
principal highways and the larger towns, their observations limited and
superficial. "We know in fact nothing of the country." It remained for
the nation's soldiers, in their capacity as travelers, to make up the
deficiency. Travelers, however, had other limitations besides those imposed by geography, for they often saw more than existed in reality.
"What they saw was shaped by their deepest needs and values." The
soldiers shared the romantic longings of their generation, and this
often colored their accounts. To them Mexico went far in satisfying
their fascination for antiquity, remoteness in time; for nature, landscape, and the majesty of the picturesque; and for the people of
strange and distant places, remoteness in space.[22]

It was in Mexico that Americans encountered the ruins "mouldering in solitary grandeur," the "ravages of desolating conquests" and the hoary antiquity which their own country lacked. Americans, wrote one of the soldiers were hard up for antiquities and consequently likely to "make much" of broken pottery, eccentric hillocks, and adobe ruins; such vestiges were invariably "pressed into the service of American archeology."[23] As they marched and fought, they felt the presence of the past, their sense of history (shaped largely by Prescott) came alive. It was only a small imaginative leap to see themselves as successors to the 16th-century conquistadors, as participants in one of the world's great events.

As they marched inland from their landing at Vera Cruz (carried out, like that of Cortez, during holy week), the men in Scott's command were always aware that the "second conquerors of Mexico" were following the path of the first. An Illinois volunteer reported an "unaccountable feeling" as his mind went back to the days of Montezuma and Cortez. Pierre G.T. Beauregard, a young engineering officer, experienced the same feeling as he rode one day over the route of Cortez's flight from the Aztec capital during the "Noche Triste" over 300 years before.

Soldiers sought out the locations of Cortez's battles. "The entire route," wrote E. Kirby Smith, "is full of interest, many points being the scenes of severe contests of Hernando Cortes." Every foot of the road, he believed, held some historical interest. Buildings erected by the Conqueror, like the church in Jalapa that bore the date 1556, were described in detail as "relics of the heroic Spaniard." Following the bloody engagement at Churubusco, a battle-weary volunteer proudly noted in his journal that Cortez had defeated the army of the Montezumas on that day 326 years ago and had entered the Aztec capital. "We have conquered Santa Ana's army," he wrote, adding ruefully, "but cant get into the City yet."[24]

America's soldiers also became aware of a presence that was considerably older than that of the Spanish. The ruins of the Aztecs touched their imaginations. The army of Napoleon, they felt, fighting in the shadow of Egypt's pyramids, could not have experienced more awe. The "race" that built Egypt's monuments was well known to history. What of the Aztecs? For centuries whole cities have "mouldered in the forest," their people now "mingled together in undistinguishable dust." The soldiers strained their imaginations to catch "but one glimpse" of life in these ancient communities. The lack of knowledge only heightened the romance: "The bloody tale of tragedy, or the softer one of a princess's love, breathed forth under the waving woods of Aztec, had no historian to transmit them to the future."

Mystery hung over the ruins like a shroud. "By moonlight," wrote one soldier, "one of these ruined cities is an impressive spectacle," the gaps and irregularities obscured in the shadows, the stones in fanciful shapes, and the richly ornamented architecture surmounted by ancient trees. In the half-light, all appeared new and fresh. Few of the men looked upon the remains without bending forward to catch a glimpse of the inhabitants.[25]

Acting the part of tourists, the men in Scott's army frequently made side-trips to view the vestiges of Aztec civilization. Following the occupation of Mexico City, soldiers roamed widely through the region to search out the reminders of Mexico's past. Charles Hamilton, a regular officer, led a group to the ruins of the temple of Xochicalco, described by Prescott and appearing just as he had portrayed it. To Hamilton, the mysterious carvings pointed to a "history of events which went beyond the memory of man." Even the inhabitants they encountered in the vicinity of the temple were objects of curiosity, for Hamilton claimed they were pure-blood Aztec Indians "whose history had been lost in the past."[26]

No site attracted more attention or was visited more often by more soldiers than the ancient pyramid of Cholula, several miles from the city of Puebla. When Scott halted his army at Puebla in May 1847 he provided his men with the opportunity to examine one of Mexico's best-known Aztec monuments. Although the danger of Mexican attack always existed, excursion parties were organized. A thriving Aztec city dominated by the pyramid and its temple dedicated to the god Quetzalcoatl, Cholula was destroyed and its inhabitants massacred by the Spanish invaders, a story that was familiar to all who had read Prescott's history.

Overgrown with vegetation and surmounted by a 17th-century Spanish chapel, the pyramid (as one Indiana volunteer put it) linked the present with the "hoary centuries which have passed." The soldiers allowed their imaginations to roam as they speculated on the pyramid's ancient purposes, some insisting that it was the original Tower of Babel, others that it was the tomb in which the Aztec kings lay buried, still others that it was the spot where the Aztecs made human sacrifices to their gods. The dimensions of the pyramid were taken (by Beauregard among others) and compared with those in Humboldt and Prescott. For a moment, the war seemed far away as the soldiers stood atop the pyramid and gazed on the ruins of Cholula's ancient city. The horizon in two directions was dominated by majestic snow-capped peaks, Orizaba to the southeast and Popocatepetl to the west. Jacob Oswandel, from the mountains of Pennsylvania, was certain that it was the "most beautiful and romantic" scene ever beheld by human eyes.

The spot teemed with historic associations. "I felt as if I were standing upon the classic tombs of by-gone generations," wrote a South Carolinian, where Cortez himself had stood and where the bones of his slaughtered victims rested beneath his feet. Now the air was filled with "Anglo-Saxon voices" and the clanking of steel, announcing the arrival of a new army on the summit of Cholula. In the distance, the stars and stripes could be seen flying over Puebla. A nation not even dreamed of when Spain's glory was at its height was following the path of Cortez to the "Imperial City of the Aztecs"! An army band gathered on the pyramid's highest point and played America's three national airs, *Hail Columbia!*, *Yankee Doodle*, and *The Star-Spangled Banner*. For one volunteer, the music was a moving finale to "one of the best-spent days" he had ever experienced.[27]

Like all travelers, the soldiers were avid souvenir hunters. At Cholula, they carried off bricks with which the pyramid had been constructed, or purchased from Mexican vendors small clay figures that had been recovered from the debris surrounding the pyramid. One wonders how many such items found their way into American homes. Newspapers frequently reported the arrival in the United States of pieces destined for museums—two antique idols complete with sacrificial basins, a statue of an Aztec woman in rough stone, a set of Castilian armor. When one paper reported the discovery near Durango of a "million" preserved mummies, with the same wrappings and ornaments as those found in Egypt, the editor concluded that "America will become another Egypt to antiquaries" and that the discovery proved "that the ancestors of the Montezumas lived on the Nile."[28]

In Mexico City's National Museum, the soldiers stood in the presence of Mexico's past, as they viewed the large collection of Aztec objects, stone idols and paintings, as well as the armor of Cortez and the massive bronze equestrian statue of Charles IV. The most awesome display was the "great sacrificial stone altar" that once rested atop the *teocalli*, or Aztec temple, on which, the astonished volunteers were told, 20,000 humans had been sacrificed to the Aztec war god in a single year. On the site of the ancient temple in the center of the city stood the great Cathedral, where the Aztec Sun or Calendar Stone attracted the soldiers' attention (General Scott was said to have considered the Stone's removal to the United States should Mexico not agree to peace terms).[29]

For the men in General Kearny's Army of the West, marching through the deserts of New Mexico on their way to take possession of California, the remains of Indian and Mexican antiquity held further interest, for the soldiers assumed that the country would be annexed to the United States. Many of the ruins had been described by mountain men and Santa Fe traders and were already known to Americans. Gregg's recently published *Commerce of the Prairies* served as a guidebook and copies were carried by some of the men. Still it was Prescott and archaeologists like John L. Stephens who gave perspective to the soldiers' observations, even though the scenes they described lay thousands of miles away. The Spanish conquest remained the common reference point and it was to the struggle between Cortez and Montezuma that the soldiers most often referred when they tried to fathom the secrets of the crumbling towns and villages they encountered.

When Kearny's army was organized, William H. Emory, a young

lieutenant in the topographical engineers, was designated as the expedition's chief mapmaker. He was assisted by two other officers, Lieutenants James W. Abert and William G. Peck, and together the three men provided detailed notes on what would soon be the American Southwest. Their observations, submitted to Congress in 1848, were published in the same year. Emory, who maintained close contact with the nation's scientists, possessed the "eye of a scholar as well as soldier." His widely reviewed report familiarized Americans with their newest acquisition and stimulated a scientific interest in American ethnology and antiquity.[30]

The first ruins encountered by the army, and hence the ones most fully described, were those of the ancient town of Pecos, lying east of Santa Fe along the Santa Fe trail. When the army camped in the vicinity many of the soldiers explored the remains, accompanied by guides from a nearby village. The town, they were informed, had once been inhabited by Indians claiming to be lineal descendants of Montezuma, about whom many legends were told. An immense serpent, it was said, had been kept in the pagan temple, to which human victims were sacrificed. A sacred fire, "the eternal fire of Montezuma," supposed to have been kindled by the great Aztec Emperor himself, had been kept burning for centuries, as the Indians awaited his promised return. Emory wandered through the "dark and mysterious corners" of the ruined Spanish church, where he imagined many a maid had "sighed out" her confessions, and admired the elaborate carvings and well-hewn timbers that marked its construction.[31]

The Indians living in the pueblos of the upper Rio Grande, the soldiers noted, held similar traditions regarding Montezuma, still expecting him to appear from the east to free them from "Mexican bondage." Montezuma's name, wrote Emory, was as familiar to the Indians as that "of our Saviour or Washington" was to Americans (an interesting coupling), for it was in their image of Montezuma that they united the qualities of divinity and patriot. Except for those in Taos, who mounted a short-lived revolt against the American occupation, the Indians viewed Kearny's army as a liberating force.

The soldiers visited their villages, describing in detail the buildings of sun-burnt brick, the terraced stories, the lack of ground entrances, and the accessibility by ladders through holes in the roofs. The towns and their inhabitants had not changed since the Conquest, so the troops felt an even stronger link with the Spanish conquerors who had preceded them. The Taos pueblo, noted Abert, was "a curious relic of the Aztecan age"; Acoma, perched high on its mesa top, was reminiscent of the fortresses "observed by the army of Cortez," undoubtedly one of Coronado's Seven Cities of Cibola. When Doniphan visited Zuñi, following his expedition against the Navajos, he believed he stood in the presence of the ancient Aztecs.[32]

As Kearny's dragoons followed the twisting course of the Gila River westward, Emory noted they were "now in the regions made famous in olden times by the fables of Friar Marcos, and eagerly did we ascend every mound, expecting to see in the distance . . . the fabulous 'Casa Montezuma.' " The reference was to the early reports of the Spanish priest Marcos de Niza, who had penetrated present-day Arizona in 1539 and later accompanied Coronado. There were ruins in abundance along the Gila, surrounded by immense quantities of broken pottery and obsidian fragments which Emory (recalling Prescott's description) thought had been used by the Aztecs to cut out the hearts of their sacrificial victims. The identity of the people who once lived in these towns was lost in mystery. "In vain," Emory commented, "did we search for some remnant which would enable us to connect the inhabitants of these long deserted buildings with other races."

On November 10, 1846, as Kearny's men approached the villages of the Pima Indians, the soldiers wrote excitedly that the "Casa Montezuma" had at last been found. Camped a few miles from what is now known as Casa Grande, the soldiers explored the best-preserved ruin they had encountered thus far. A three-story adobe building with the remains of hewn cedar rafters, the edifice appeared to be the work of a people well advanced in civilization. The Indians were unable to account for its age or its inhabitants, but they were convinced that it had been the work of an ancient race descended from "the first man." With only Prescott's history at hand, the men sought evidence that would connect the ruins with the Aztecs to the south. "Who were they?" asked Emory. "And where have they gone?" On one thing all agreed: "A knowledge of the true character of these nations is a great desideratum."[33]

The remains of vanished civilizations not only had a romantic appeal. They also stimulated a scientific inquiry into the origins of North America's ancient peoples. "Glimpses are given us," noted the *Southern Quarterly Review,* "of the ruins of unknown cities—the vast and curious abodes of unknown and extinct nations—and of living races of which we have scarcely heard the names before." The progress of the armies was followed closely by members of the American Ethnological Society (founded in 1842), and reports from the soldiers were frequently read at the society's meetings. Although the society's founder and president, the aged Jeffersonian Albert Gallatin, strongly opposed the war, he as well as others in the organization saw America's penetration of Mexico as advantageous to the field of ethnology. One of the nation's leading anthropologists, Ephraim G. Squier, incorporated Emory's observations in his work on the "aboriginal" inhabitants of New Mexico and California and later presented new information regarding the Aztec Calendar Stone. However one might view the wisdom of the Mexican War, Squier was convinced that it contributed materially to knowledge of the continent's ancient peoples. Archaeologist Benjamin M. Norman displayed casts of Mexican antiquities at the society's meeting in May 1849 and later that year acknowledged, in a new edition of his *Rambles in Yucatán*, the "fresh impulse" which had been given to the study of American antiquity by the visit to Mexico "of so many intelligent observers, connected with our noble army." He paid tribute to these soldier-travelers who had combined "pride of country; characteristic curiosity; a natural love of the marvellous; a generous ambition to enlarge the boundaries of human knowledge: [and] an adventurous spirit of enterprise" to broaden America's horizons.[34]

Comparing American and European scenery, James Fenimore Cooper conceded that the "grandeur" and "wild sublimity" of Europe's mountains gave the Old World a "countenance" which America could not match. America's scenery, he wrote, was of a different sort—abundant forests, a blending of the agricultural with the savage, the "freshness of a most promising youth," and a natural radiance that produced landscapes of "extraordinary beauty and grace." A passion for landscape, in the mode of Sir Walter Scott, found expression in Cooper's work. It was a time when a feeling for nature became a "touchstone of sensibility"; it was an "age of landscape," and Cooper was one of its principal spokesmen. Nature evoked an emotional, even a moral, response. The "vogue of the picturesque," an enthusiasm for romantic landscape, supplied the lens through which Americans viewed and judged their natural environment.[35]

To a generation nurtured on an appreciation for the picturesque, Mexico offered a new and wondrous field for observation. As it supplied the ruins and antiquity for which Americans yearned, putting on nature what Cooper called the "impress of the past," so also did it present a landscape that was quite unlike anything ever experienced before. The same romantic impulse that caused soldiers to pause in the midst of battle to admire the beauty of their surroundings also motivated the soldier-travelers to enter descriptions of the countryside in their journals and letters.

"God has not made a more magnificent land than Mexico," wrote a soldier in the fall of 1847. The valley of the Rio Grande was the "Eden of America!" Beauty was found even in the dense chaparral that covered the plain, "bowers that surpass . . . art's fairest handiwork." On the road to Monterey soldiers found the countryside "nearer the idea of *fairy land*" than any they had ever seen, its "picturesque beauty" exceeding their "most romantic dreams" of nature's charms. The meandering course of a stream reminded a Maryland volunteer of the "graceful curve of Hogarth's line of beauty."[36]

The novelty of the Mexican landscape often distracted the soldiers from their military mission and many of them recorded moments when the war seemed far distant. Lieutenant Thomas Whipple, captured by

Mexican guerrillas near Vera Cruz, was "so lost in admiration" of nature's glories as he was led over narrow pathways through dense tropical forests that he momentarily forgot he was a prisoner. Pursuing guerrillas on a night expedition, Daniel Harvey Hill took time to note that the wild scenery and pale moonlight gave his journey "a romantic tinge" which he would never forget. But the war was always there, ready to intrude and to shatter the reveries into which the men sometimes fell. One officer, lulled by the pastoral tranquility of the Rio Grande valley, was jolted by the sight of a "*high pressure steam boat*" moored along the bank, disturbing "nature's rich and solemn silence." A classic reminder of the "machine in the garden," it also seemed symbolic of the intrusion of American technology into a primitive environment. The Mexicans themselves frequently spoiled a proper contemplation of the nation's natural wonders. "If those cursed Mexicans did not shoot at one so hard," exclaimed a young lieutenant, "Mexico would be a delightful country to be in."[37]

The dry rarefied atmosphere of the high elevations, the remarkably transparent and refreshing air, the towering mountain ranges that appeared much closer than they actually were, and the bright winter sun had an enervating effect on the troops. Nature seemed to be in sweet repose. There was a "dreaminess of the air, earth and sky" that produced a "luxuriant lassitude, a delicious disinclination to do anything." Standing guard on Christmas night, an Indiana volunteer forgot all discomfort as he observed the unclouded sky "all bespangled with brilliant stars, and the silvery moon riding forth in the midst of this beautiful scenery." "Everything," he remarked, "is filled with romance." Others were eloquent in their descriptions of a Mexican mountain sunrise. One colonel roused his men early so that they might by a forced march reach the point where the rising sun was at its most spectacular. "I was struck dumb with admiration and amazement," wrote one of the soldiers, by the flaming hues with which the mountains were bathed as the first light of the sun struck them. "What a country to dream in!"[38]

The abundance of fresh fruit was a new experience, especially for soldiers from northern climes. Oranges, a rare treat back home, were consumed in "hundreds of thousands." Apples, peaches, apricots, figs, and "alligator pears" (something new and strange) supplemented the meager army fare. Orchards along the march were stripped and village markets depleted, often without regard to the ripeness of the fruit. Army doctors blamed the excessive consumption of fruit for the dysentery and stomach disorders that prostrated so many.

The strangeness of the landscape also excited a scientific interest among the soldiers, many of whom described the plants and birds they encountered. "I regretted very much while in Mexico," recalled an Indiana volunteer, "that I was not a botanist." The maguey or century plant, from which a fermented drink called *pulque* was derived, the yucca or Spanish bayonet, the varieties of palm trees, the "cragged and

thorny" chaparral, and the "eternal cactus," all found place in the soldiers' notebooks. Much of the vegetation, beautiful in a strange sort of
way, gave the land an inhospitable aspect. "Every bush, tree, plant and
every insect and serpent here," observed a Tennesseean, "has a sting or
thorn."

Soldiers gathered seed from plants and flowers and sent them home
in their letters. Others carried specimens home with them when they
returned to the states, like the navy lieutenant who deposited some
thirty or forty native Mexican plants in the museum of the National
Institute. Information from soldiers' letters found its way into the
pages of the nation's scientific literature, thus adding a further dimension to the war experience. Few, however, surpassed Josiah Gregg, the
erstwhile Santa Fe trader, who regularly sent botanical and mineral
specimens to scientific friends, including some 200 varieties of plants
which he had collected in the vicinity of Saltillo alone. Much of Gregg's
collection was eventually deposited in the Academy of Natural
Sciences.[39]

The birds of Mexico, brightly feathered and strangely melodious, not
only struck the soldiers' fancy but often eased the ardors of the march.
The sights and sounds of colorful parrots, parakeets, and mocking
birds, noted an Illinois volunteer, "lend much to the day." It was not
uncommon for the men to carry parrots with them; when an Ohio
regiment was ordered on a forced march with reduced baggage, many
of the soldiers carried rudely constructed cages containing parrots instead of more useful articles. Sketches and specimens of Mexican birds
were sent by the scientifically curious to John James Audubon, then in
the last years of his life, for identification. At least one army officer
published descriptions of birds that he felt had not been adequately
recognized. Mexico's four-footed creatures were equally astonishing:
coyotes, viewed with mingled interest and fear as they stalked the
marching columns; monkeys hanging by their tails from tree limbs;
and the bizarre armadillo, "an odd-looking animal . . . of the kind I
have never seen," according to a Pennsylvania volunteer.[40]

Of all the features of the Mexican landscape, none was more picturesque or struck the soldiers' senses with more power than the country's mountain ranges and peaks. There was nothing in the volunteers'
experience that could compare with the rugged beauty of Mexico's
mountains. New England's granite peaks, the spiny ridges of Pennsylvania, the rounded contours of Kentucky and Tennessee, all seemed
tame in contrast. Mexico's wild, rocky, and desolate aspect brought to
mind the paintings of Salvator Rosa, the 17th-century Italian painter
whose "rocks, chasms, caverns and . . . riven trees" were popular with
American romantics. Mountain scenery held special place in the romantic imagination and was often invested with therapeutic qualities
("a perfect tonic," as one soldier put it). Of all types of scenery, wrote
E. L. Magoon, mountains exerted the "greatest and most salutary

power." Beauty and sublimity were "interfused" and "commingled" with the body of the beholder. Mountains were also the "nursery of patriotism"; heroism and moral excellence were fostered "where rocks and wilderness are piled in bold and inimitable shapes of savage grandeur."[41]

If the grandeur of Mexico's mountains did not seem to be reflected in the character of its people (a puzzle to many of the soldiers), it had a profound effect on the emotions of the Americans. A Kentucky volunteer, captured by Mexican cavalry on the eve of Buena Vista, gazed with open-mouthed astonishment at the snow-topped peaks that ringed the Valley of Mexico. Never, he wrote, had he been so "spell-bound!" Confronted with the same prospect from a different direction, a captain in the regular force was literally prostrated by the sight. "I know not whether I am more susceptible to the effects of fine scenery than others," he confessed to his wife, "but this . . . was by far the most glorious picture of nature I have ever beheld . . . and I dropped on earth to breathe a prayer and a thanksgiving to a good God who had made such a glorious world."[42]

One of the first sights to greet Scott's expeditionary force as it sailed toward Vera Cruz was snow-capped Mount Orizaba, over three miles high and visible at sea long before the Mexican shoreline came into view. To a Marine surgeon, Orizaba seemed to float in the air; and for an Indiana volunteer, "all was poetry from the time we saw it until we dropped our anchor in the harbor of Vera Cruz." The mountain continued to dominate the horizon as the army marched inland and the column was often halted to enable the men to gaze upon the peak. Early in 1848 a party of soldiers and sailors scaled Orizaba. The men suffered headaches, nausea, nose-bleeds, and swollen lips, but as they stood on the summit they all agreed that the climb had been worth the effort. The star-spangled banner, planted on the highest point, was saluted with three hearty cheers. Polk, the cabinet, the Congress, a correspondent later wrote, could make whatever treaties they pleased but the American flag would continue to wave over Mexico, "for who will go up there to pull it down?"[43]

The route of the army along the Spanish-built National Highway carried the men over higher elevations than they had ever imagined, over high mountain passes and through narrow defiles, which, to their amazement, the Mexicans had neglected to fortify. The "serrated outlines and fantastic shapes" produced a scene of "perfect wildness," which one officer noted "gave wings to the imagination." The troops found themselves marching in the clouds, "immersed in a vapor bath" that soaked through their uniforms. When the clouds lifted, they beheld scenery so magnificent that words were inadequate to describe it.

Few sights evoked so many superlatives as the soldiers' first view of the Valley of Mexico in mid-August 1847. From its camp on Rio Frio, high in the Cordilleras surrounding the valley, the army wound its way through the thin frosty air to the 10,000-foot summit. "From thence," wrote an aide of General Shields,

> we commenced descending the mountains, and after passing several miles through a dense forest of pine, a full and unobstructed view of the peerless valley or basin of Mexico, with its lakes and plains, hills and mountains, burst upon our astonished sight, presenting a scene of matchless prospective that would bid defiance to the pencil of the most gifted landscape artist of any land.

Spread before the soldiers' gaze far below were glittering lakes, cultivated fields, and gleaming white villages. In the distance could be seen the spires of the city of Mexico, dominated by the awesome snow-clad volcanoes, Popocatepetl and Ixtaccihuatl. It was from the same point that Cortez had first gazed upon the ancient city of Montezuma. The comment of the Spanish soldier Bernal Díaz del Castillo as he looked down upon the shining temples of Tenochtitlán that the enchantment of the view was like things seen only in dreams was echoed in the reactions of Scott's men. It was a "panorama of fairy-land," "an illusion of the senses, a dream." Although he had read much of Mexico, commented a Pennsylvania volunteer, "no book's opinions or correspondence of tourists" could capture the romance of the scene.

No matter that, as the army descended, the lakes became marshes and the villages collections of mud huts. The Valley of Mexico retained its magic and even some of the hardest fighting of the war failed to dim the enthusiasm. "What an Eden this is!" exclaimed a volunteer.[44]

Throughout their stay in the valley, the Americans were aware of the "stern" and "haughty" presence of the two mountains that guarded its eastern approaches. The peaks, clad in the garb of eternal winter, seemed "to preach of eternity." The story that Cortez had made an unsuccessful attempt to scale Popocatepetl prompted a number of Americans to make the effort in April 1848, motivated, as one of them noted, by "national pride and a spirit of emulation." The group, which included Ulysses S. Grant, was turned back by storms, swollen eyes, and snow-blindness but several of them later returned to the task. They reached the top, looked down into the dark sulphurous crater, and planted the stars and stripes on the highest peak, an act of symbolic importance. The national flag, wrote one of the party, had been placed where it would receive the sun's first rays as it rose from the Atlantic and its last beams as it sank into the Pacific.[45]

After describing in ecstatic terms the beauty of a Mexican sunset, the grandeur of the mountains, the softness of the climate, and the purity of the air, one soldier confided to his family that Mexico would surely be "an earthly paradise" if only its inhabitants were civilized. Mexico's

Entrance of the Army into the Grand Plaza at Mexico. From Edward D. Mansfield, *The Mexican War* (1849).

picturesque landscape seemed incongruous with the condition of its people; to many of the soldiers, the contrast was puzzling. Although the beauties and wealth of Mexico almost defied description, wrote a Tennessee volunteer, there was a "dark side" to the picture, for "nine-tenths of the inhabitants of this delightful clime" were "more degraded than the African race among us." That the soldiers should perceive the Mexican people as uncivilized revealed their confidence that America represented the highest stage of world civilization. The notion was widely shared at home and indeed lay at the heart of American popular thought. Those societies that differed, they reasoned, were somehow inferior. Inexperienced in the world's ways, provincial in their outlook, the men suddenly found themselves thrust into what one writer has called the "maze of a complex and totally alien culture." That it should appear uncivilized was less a commentary on the state of Mexican society than it was on that of the United States.[46]

The Rio Grande was a diminutive stream, winding, narrow, and shallow, a disappointment to the soldiers who had expected of the controversial boundary something more imposing; but it represented a wide cultural gulf. By crossing the Rio Grande, wrote a Kentucky volunteer, the men mingled for the first time with a people "speaking a different language . . . and with manners and customs as totally different, as though they lived in another hemisphere." Matamoros, the first Mexican town encountered by the soldiers, both repelled and fascinated them. Narrow dusty streets were lined with one-story flat-roofed adobe buildings that seemed always in need of repair. While many of the buildings were windowless, others, like the homes of the well-to-do, had iron-barred windows that gave them a prison-like appearance. Rude hovels, which an Indiana volunteer thought inferior to the Negro huts he had seen along the Mississippi, seemed more like hogpens than living quarters. On the town's plaza stood an unfinished "cathedral," fast falling into decay. To Captain Henry, Matamoros was the "meanest looking and filthiest city" he had ever seen; to the more romantic eye of a fellow officer, it was reminiscent of Old Spain, with scenes that seemed straight out of the pages of Cervantes.[47]

As the army marched into Mexico, the soldiers looked beyond the "dirt, slovenliness, and misery" to discover picturesque qualities in the towns and cities. Monterey with its towers and Moorish domes had the appearance of an Oriental city, its luxuriant gardens (especially that of the Mexican General Arista) reflected an Eastern opulence. After fever-ridden Vera Cruz, lying in ruins from the American bombardment, the high healthful city of Jalapa, with its gardens, orange trees, and fountains, inspired one soldier to exclaim: "There can be no other place on earth more nearly approaching Paradise." Indeed, Jalapa seemed more like home; it was easy, wrote a Pennsylvanian, to "imagine ourselves in some thriving Yankee town." Puebla, Mexico's second city, was judged to be prettier, neater, and cleaner "than any of our American towns," but Mexico's capital evoked the highest praise. Mexico City was the goal of all American soldiers, not only for its historical associations and symbolic importance but for its beauty as well. "I am at last in Mexico," wrote an officer in the Ninth Regiment, "the great city of Montezuma, of Cortez, of the Spanish viceroys, of Mexican pride and of American conquest." It seemed like a "fairy land," differing from the rest of Mexico and almost European in its aspect. Here, in Mexico's interior, the soldiers felt they could observe "the true Mexican character and customs more perfectly" than in the country's small miserable frontier towns.[48]

To journey into Mexico was to journey back in time. To the Americans the country seemed centuries behind, a "fragment of the medieval world" with a society that was feudal in spirit. Progress appeared to have been minimal since the days of Cortez; indeed, the soldiers felt that the ancient Aztecs had manifested more energy and were more advanced in the "arts of civilization" than their 19th-century descendants. The reason? "They are a conquered race," wrote a soldier. "They have been crushed by oppressors, and rent by factions until they are entirely a different people from their noble ancestors." To the volunteers who had left farms in Illinois, Ohio, or Kentucky, Mexican agricultural practices seemed unbelievably crude. Farming tools had changed but little since the Spanish conquest. Missing was the spirit of inventiveness and technological development, the go-ahead temperament that defined America's age of steam. As they surveyed the Mexican scene, they also began to see their own country in a new light.

Racial explanations for Mexico's condition came quickly to mind. Mexico's racial mixture, it was said, had resulted in a mongrel population that was innately inferior to the vigorous and enterprising Anglo-Saxon. But racial explanations were too easy and too restrictive. No matter how backward the people of Mexico appeared to be, they were always regarded as capable of improvement. A more common explanation, in the judgment of the soldiers, was the grinding oppression under which most of the Mexicans seemed to live and labor. Standing on picket duty one moonlit night at Buena Vista, a volunteer listened to the mournful songs of the Mexican soldiers nearby. The music, he felt, was the "dirge of souls in bondage, the cry of an oppressed race."[49]

The American soldiers carried their convictions of political equality and economic opportunity with them into Mexico, and if anything their beliefs were sharpened by what they observed there. Matters they had taken for granted now assumed new importance. They were astounded, even shocked, to discover that such notions did not prevail in a nation that professed to be a republic. They found incomprehensible the power which state and Church exerted over Mexico's common folk, and they were baffled by the apathy with which most Mexicans seemed to accept their authority. The Mexican attitude, they felt, was incongruous with what they had all assumed was an age of progress and freedom.

The role of the Catholic Church in the lives of the Mexicans was especially difficult for the volunteers to understand. The priest, viewed by the average Mexican "with an awe amounting to idolatry," became a sinister figure, fostering superstition, ignorance and bigotry while at the same time growing rich off the masses. The contrast between the opulence of the cathedrals and the poverty of the people was described in tones of anger and frustration. Indeed the Church was blamed by some for fomenting resistance to the American occupation, for it was believed the Church had the most to lose by the extension of republican principles.

There is no doubt that the growing anti-Catholicism of the 1840s lay behind many of the complaints the soldiers leveled against the Church. Although many Catholics served in the regular army, especially Irish and Germans, and some volunteer units were recruited from among Catholic groups, most of the volunteers encountered Catholicism for the first time when they entered Mexico. Not all the reactions were negative. The Church, with its ritual and customs (burial customs seemed particularly fascinating), was but one more exotic feature in a foreign land. Some found the public displays of worship refreshing when compared with the lack of religious feeling found among many Americans. Soldiers billeted in monasteries found the monks to be a "jolly set of fellows, not at all backward in drinking or *gambling* with our men." There was something even romantic about being quartered in a monastery.[50]

The Church was not alone held responsible for the condition of the Mexican people. Although ostensibly a republic, Mexico's governmental system was unlike the republicanism with which the soldiers were familiar. It quickly became apparent that the mass of the people with whom they came into contact had little voice in the direction of their government and, even more amazing, didn't seem to care. The power of the government, like that of the Church, appeared to be absolute. Mexico, observed Raphael Semmes, groaned under "an unmitigated military despotism." The frequent changes of government, the prevalence of revolution and intrigue, the power of the military, and the tendency to dictatorship belied Mexico's republican pretensions. Revolution had become such a way of life that some Mexicans believed that Zachary Taylor was simply another Mexican leader who had declared against the government and was marching on the capital. "Is it strange, then," asked an Ohio volunteer, "considering this vampirism of church and state, that the principal productions of the country should be *pronunciamentos, priests,* and *prickly-pears?*"

The Mexican people were judged unfit for self-government, not because of inherent racial characteristics but because they had been held in virtual bondage for centuries. To the Americans, for whom equality had become a watchword, the class structure in Mexico was an unpleasant discovery. "It is utterly impossible for any one who has not seen it," declared one of Doniphan's soldiers, "to imagine the difference which exists between the rich and the poor in this wretched country." The nation's wealth seemed concentrated in the hands of the few, while the masses were kept in a state of "ignorance, vice, and poverty."[51]

Some of the soldiers reacted with anger to the social conditions they found in Mexico. Education, they believed, was vital to republican government, yet, as one volunteer fumed, not one person in ten could read and write. The statistic may have been faulty, but his outburst was nonetheless sincere. The Mexican people, he raged, were held in a state of "slavish ignorance," degraded to the "level of beasts," and held in "moral bondage." Suddenly brought into contact with conditions that seemed frightful compared with those at home, the Americans felt that their real enemies were the "religious and civil tyrants who lord it over this fair land" and that it was their mission to bring enlightened and free government to Mexico. "We are fighting the Army and the Aristocracy," insisted Daniel Harvey Hill, "*not* the people of Mexico."[52]

Still, the soldiers found the people, their manners, and their customs fascinating, as they sent home vivid descriptions of cock fights, fandangoes, gambling dens, and bull rings. Life in Mexico seemed looser, more carefree, less rigidly proscribed by moral restrictions and convention. Discoveries were made and adopted, like the "cigarrito" seen dangling from the lips of virtually every Mexican. The food provided sensations never before experienced—the ubiquitous red pepper, the chili that caused tears to stream down Lieutenant Emory's cheeks ("rather hot for uninitiated palates," according to a South Carolinian, but "quite a savory dish when one becomes accustomed to it"), the tortillas that substituted for eating utensils.[53] The civilian dress was recorded in detail, the men in buckskin or velvet pantaloons studded with silver buttons, colorful sashes, wide-brimmed sombreros, and the common *serape* thrown casually over their shoulders. And the women! Like soldiers in all times and places, America's fighting men in Mexico observed, described, and befriended the women more than any other element in the population.

As soon as Taylor's army arrived on the Rio Grande, the men realized that Mexican women were different. Standing on the river bank in early morning or evening, they gaped as the young women of Matamoros came down to the river, disrobed without hesitation or embarrassment, and plunged into the stream. Swimming and splashing, their long black hair floating behind, oblivious to the spectators, they seemed like mermaids to one volunteer, "the only live animals of that fabled creature" he had ever seen.

The soldier was rare who did not rhapsodize over the beauty of Mexico's women. "Nearly all of them," wrote Captain Henry, "have well-developed, magnificent figures . . . [and] dress with as little clothing as you can well fancy." Many were barefoot, their ankles in view. A colorful skirt or petticoat, a loose chemise cut lower than would be socially acceptable in the United States, and a bright red sash completed their dress. "Their bosoms," commented a sharp-eyed Indianan, "were not compressed in stays . . . but heaved freely under the healthful influences of the genial sun and balmy air of the sunny south." There was a natural grace about their movements and gestures. The ladies of Jalapa were the "ethereal embodiment of all that man has learned to love and admire"; in Puebla, women in full dress, coquettish with flashing large dark eyes and raven tresses, were such "magnificent creatures" that no man could possibly resist their charms.[54]

Once they became convinced that the Americans were not the "barbarous and murderous Yankees" their leaders had led them to expect, the women overcame their reluctance to fraternize with the soldiers. They conversed with them through their iron-grated windows and frequently, with their families, invited them into their homes. They flocked to the camps to sell food and drink, clothing and souvenirs. They cared for the sick and wounded, often in their own homes, and served as cooks and laundresses. The most popular spot in Jalapa was the *lavandero,* where the women washed their clothes in a stream that flowed through the city. The soldiers were drawn to the site, where they soon were "taking lessons in Spanish and love making, while their shirts were being washed." The soldiers enjoyed the companionship of Mexico's women on picnics, sightseeing excursions, at dances, and in the theatre. Commented the *Spirit of the Times:* "Some of our Yankee boys, who have 'listed in the Mexican service, appear to be having 'tall times' among the pretty señoritas."

More serious relationships were also formed. Some of the soldiers married Mexican women and took their discharges in Mexico. Others took Mexican war-brides home with them. Correspondent Thomas Bangs Thorpe found that encouraging, from a racial standpoint: "It seems . . . to be in the order of Providence, that these women, so justly to be admired, are to become wives and mothers of a better race."[55]

The soldiers' perceptions of the role of women in Mexico mirrored the culture in which they had grown up. They regarded Mexico's women as superior to the men, more industrious, more humane, and more keenly sensitive to human needs. At the same time, they were indignant at the attitude of contempt in which the women seemed to be held by the men, and they charged Mexican males with treating their women as little more than slaves or beasts of burden. By contrast, women's lot in the United States seemed idyllic. American women, suggested one soldier, might well feel proud of their country for "it is the only land in this wide world" where women were considered man's equal! On the other hand, Mexican women appeared to be content with their roles, a comforting thought to some of the men. "Perfectly feminine in character," wrote Raphael Semmes, "they are indeed the vine to cling around the oak, which nature designed the sex to be." They would be shocked "at the idea of holding public meetings" or discussing "in open forum, the equal rights of women, as unsexed females sometimes do in other countries."[56]

To many Americans, the soldiers in Mexico were more than travelers in a foreign land, broadening horizons and bringing knowledge of the unknown into their homes. They were also pioneers, carrying the tenets of republican government and extending the bounds of American civilization. For those who marched with General Kearny's Army of the West, the pioneering role was perhaps more clearly discerned. On the eve of his departure for the Far West, Philip St. George Cooke viewed his "wilderness-worn dragoons" as pioneers about to take a great leap into the darkness of "wild plains and mountains," there to found a Pacific empire. When Jonathan Stevenson's regiment of New York volunteers was recruited, it was charged with a colonization as well as a military mission. Known as the California Regiment, the men were carefully selected (at least that was the intention) to provide the nucleus of a "mighty Anglo-American population" on the shores of the Pacific, a mission that was only partially successful. Doniphan's Missouri volunteers, wrote Charles J. Peterson, were moved by the same spirit that drove the Normans into France and sent the Spaniards on their voy-

ages of discovery. Those who penetrated central Mexico were pioneers
no less, fulfilling the mission of "our adventurous Anglo-American
race."[57]

To historian William H. Prescott, whose influence in shaping the war
spirit was so great, the soldiers were the "pioneers of civilization"; it did
not matter whether they fought the "bear and the buffalo, or the wild
Indian or the Mexican." Few expressed the soldiers' pioneering role so
well as the writer in the *Democratic Review:*

> Wherever our victorious arms have been carried, the arts of peace have
> followed them. Instead of destroying, we have built up commerce; instead
> of impoverishing, we have enriched the country with our enterprise and
> our wealth. The pitching of our tents proclaimed the reign of law and
> order; and the watchword of our sentinels was 'protection to life and
> property.' In vain may the annals of history be searched for a similar war.
> It was not the Goths and Vandals invading the fertile plains of an edu-
> cated people; but the pioneers of civilization exploring a country of
> boundless wealth, teaching and persuading as they went on.

The volunteers, the "most enterprising class of a race unequalled for
energy," were only clearing the way for the "no less adventurous
settlers."[58]

With the American invasion of Mexico, two distinct and dissimilar
cultural traditions came into contact—and conflict. Both sides made
efforts to learn the ways of the other, but the mixing of the cultures
never went beyond the superficial, and in the end the gap between the
two remained unbridged. Soldiers mingled with the Mexican people,
were invited into their homes, ate their food, adopted their clothing
styles and tried, in some instances, to view the war through their eyes.
"Strange, indeed," wrote a Missouri volunteer following the march into
Santa Fe,

> must have been the feelings of the citizens when an invading army was
> thus entering their home . . . all the future of their destiny vague and
> uncertain—their new rulers strangers to their manner, language and hab-
> its, and, as they had been taught to believe, enemies to the only religion
> they have ever known.

The invaders, non-Catholics as well as Catholics, attended religious
services in Mexican churches, participated in church ceremonies, and
marched in funeral processions for fallen Mexican officers. They purchased Spanish grammars and studied the Spanish language, often
employing tutors to assist them; an ability to speak the language, wrote
one correspondent, was "exceedingly useful" to travelers in a strange
land. In the larger cities, they attended Mexican concerts and theatrical
productions and mingled with the Mexican people in the parks and on
the streets.[59]

Mexicans, on their part, served the Americans in a myriad of ways. They were employed by the army as guides and teamsters and supplied the troops with mules, cattle, and corn, for which they were remunerated. Contacts between the soldiers and the Mexican civilians became so close and commonplace that one officer, while marching on Victoria, confided to his family that "it was hardly possible to believe we were marching through a hostile country." The indifference of many civilians toward the war astonished the soldiers; the deference paid to them by Mexicans who assumed that the military played the same role in the United States as it did in Mexico was bothersome, especially to the volunteers.[60]

The Mexican people quickly discovered that it was not only through their contacts with American soldiers that they were exposed to American "civilization." Indeed, the soldiers were never very far from elements of their own familiar cultural environment even as they advanced into Mexico's interior. They were but the vanguard, pioneers in a true sense, for in their wake came large numbers of American civilians, entrepreneurs of all sorts eager to furnish the soldiers—and the Mexicans—with goods and services to their own profit. In the process, Mexican communities seemed about to be "Americanized," a development that some saw as a first step toward Mexico's cultural absorption.

Matamoros was the first Mexican town to feel the impact of the American cultural invasion. Businessmen from New Orleans and Texas followed Taylor's army across the Rio Grande, setting up their shops and marketing their goods, whatever they might be. Printers arrived to establish an American press and daguerreotypists moved in to record the occupation. An American air seemed to pervade the town. The dollar, reported a correspondent, had unlocked the doors "of many a citizen, whom the conqueror would not disturb." "This species of warfare," wrote another, "is rapidly converting the people over to American notions."[61]

The pattern was repeated in city after city. In Monterey, American stores, American goods, American drinks, and American faro drove out Mexican shopkeepers and gamblers. Vera Cruz was transformed. Wharves and depots were built to accommodate the flow of military personnel and supplies, the channel was marked and buoyed and Chesapeake pilot-boats plied the harbor waters. Forges and workshops were established and "Yankee hotels, Yankee auction houses, Yankee circus companies, and Yankee ice houses, are starting up at every turn of the corner."

Mexico's capital seemed so changed following its occupation that a "stranger let down among us without a knowledge of recent events, would be sadly puzzled to know into whose kingdom he had fallen." Already cosmopolitan, with a large European population, the city now assumed an American appearance. At every hand were signs announcing the American presence in large bold capitals: Union Hotel; Mush and Milk at All Hours; American Dry Goods; United States Restaurant; St. Charles Exchange; Egg-Nogg and Mince Pies For Sale Here. The Mexicans themselves hastened to join the trend. "The tailors' shops," wrote a resident, "which had been called Mexican, were converted into American; and tailors, barbers, storekeepers, bar-keepers, and hotel-keepers, felt the influence of the language of the conqueror, and hastened to substitute for their signs and advertisements other signs and advertisements in the English language." The city, remarked a visitor, was "almost entirely Americanized." The "great fondas and sociedads" were all under the "dominion of Yankees," with American signs, manners, habits, and customs "as if the city had been from time immemorial Yankeefied all over."[62]

Professional theatre companies joined the influx of entrepreneurs, following the army through Mexico and establishing theatres in the occupied cities. Foremost among them was that of Hart and Wells, a company that included for a brief time young Joseph Jefferson, soon to become one of America's great actors. From Matamoros, the players performed in Tampico, Jalapa, Puebla, and Mexico City, carrying productions of Shakespeare and the popular "The Lady of Lyons," "Rob Roy," and "Timour the Tartar" to Mexican and American audiences alike.[63]

The American soldier in Mexico as traveler and pioneer filled an important cultural role, expanding America's familiarity with its southern neighbor, introducing into the American consciousness an awareness of the dimensions of a foreign culture and carrying elements of his own heritage, for good or ill, to the Mexican people. Although some of the soldiers entered Mexico with prejudices already formed, derived principally from earlier travel accounts or works by Texans and Santa Fe traders, for many others contact with the Mexican people and their ways was a fresh and enlightening experience. They were persuaded, moreover, that they had done Mexico some good by being there. "Society in Mexico," remarked one of the troops, "received a great impulse from the American occupation." "Castilian customs and traditions," he believed, "could not resist the go-ahead-ism of the victorious Nort' Americano." While this perception reflected the wishful thinking of an ingrained ethnocentrism, it was later echoed by an English traveler who visited Mexico following the war. Wrote Lady Emmeline Stuart Wortley: "I think the Americans have done good to the country and the people in some respects."

For the soldiers who served in Mexico, and for those at home who shared their experiences, the sojourn contributed to national self-awareness. America was still a nation in search of itself. That some of the soldiers discovered America's meaning in Mexico is apparent. "Mexico," wrote a Pennsylvania volunteer "is no doubt one of the best places for an American to feel proud of his nationality." Henry Tuckerman insisted that no writing was more characteristic of the

American mind than those accounts written by America's travelers. What he said of travel writers in general was also applicable to the military travelers in Mexico: "What they see they know how to describe, and what they feel they can express with courage and animation; so that, in the memorials of other lands, the native mind often reflects itself with singular force and fervor."[64]

CHAPTER 7

A War-Literature

While traveling on a train in the summer of 1849, the popular writer Grace Greenwood (Sara Jane Clarke) observed a lady reading Alphonse de Lamartine's *Raphael,* "seemingly with great interest." Greenwood watched as the lady put down the book and took up "with as much apparent satisfaction, a miserable Mexican war story, with diabolical wood cuts and some such title as 'The Knight of the White Feather,' or 'The Hero of the Bloody Jack Knife.' " Greenwood was not only surprised but shocked. The traveler obviously "read for the sake of the story alone." The incident prompted Greenwood to ponder the taste of American readers: "Some people seem to have a sort of love for the beautiful, existing with propensities for the commonplace and the low; as cattle devour roses and cabbages with the same coarse relish."[1]

Greenwood, antislavery and an opponent of the war, had herself written a Mexican War tale to show the deleterious effect the conflict had on those who volunteered, and a poem, "Illumination for Victories in Mexico," in which she recounted the cost of glory in death and bereavement.[2] Her comment accurately reflected the state of American letters at midcentury. Critics returned to the theme again and again: American literature was changing in the 1840s, and the "cabbages" seemed about to drive out the "roses."

Reading among Americans had never been so popular or so widespread. The expansion of public education, one of the highest (if not the highest) literacy rates in the world and an increase in leisure time brought on by industrialization created a growing demand for reading material. Foreign visitors were amazed at America's addiction to print, observing, as did Alexander Mackay who toured the United States during the Mexican War, that the nation's expanding readership rendered it unique in the world. Reading was no longer an aristocratic or intellectual pastime; the age of the common man had also heralded the rise of the common reader. A "democracy of print" had become indispensable to political democracy.

Technology enabled publishers not only to meet the demand for printed material but to stimulate it as well. The development of steam-powered cylinder presses, improved techniques in the manufacture of paper and in binding, and new systems of distribution enabled them to mass-produce low-priced books on an unprecedented scale. One result of the new mass market was the nation's first paperback revolution. Beginning with such weekly periodicals as *Brother Jonathan* and the *New World*, in both of which Park Benjamin and Rufus Wilmot Griswold were associated, and extending to book publishers by the early 1840s, the demand for inexpensive reading material brought a profusion of paper-covered books, costing as little as twelve and a half cents each.

By the end of the forties most of the publishers were engaged in the production of "cheap literature." Leading the technological explosion, called by one authority the "first great leap forward since the fifteenth century," was America's foremost publishing house, Harper and Brothers. With a list that included pirated editions of British works (there were no international copyright laws) and an expanding number of American writers, Harper's boasted twenty-two presses, nineteen of them worked by steam, printing over 33,000 sheets a day, the equivalent of 6000 octavo volumes of 500 pages each per week. The firm's influence was mind-boggling, for it wielded "the lever of Archimedes, which moves the world." "Every where," noted a visitor to the New York establishment, "on the wings of every wind, are their publications disseminated," to the refined lady in her boudoir, the pioneer in the silence of the backwoods, and the volunteer in the interior of Mexico.[3]

It was not only an "age of book-making," it was also an "age of universal authorship." In striking understatement, Henry T. Tuckerman noted that "there is no danger of an intellectual famine from scarcity of books." Literary pursuits were no longer a pathway to distinction, he observed, for "not to have written a book is now something to boast of." Where books were "so cheap and multitudinous," some feared, the "art of reading" itself would be threatened. There was no way an individual could keep pace with the offerings of the country's authors and publishers. "How can poor common-headed people keep up with the age?" The age of steam "in things mechanical," as southern author and critic George Frederick Holmes put it, had indeed introduced "an age of steam in things intellectual."[4]

The rise of the common reader brought the rise of the common book. Some critics were harsh in their strictures against the popular literature of midcentury America. The "sublime and the beautiful" had given way to the "horrible and startling." Tales of Gothic romance, "ergots of a diseased brain," with their "flaring title-pages, cheap, eye-destroying editions, flash composition, horrible murders, improbabilities and personalities," had captured the market. Shallow, mawkish, divorced from reality, the popular books, it was said, insulted the imagination, stultified the mind, and stained the heart, producing a generation of "moonstruck sentimentalists" who sighed "for a return of the chivalrous days of Richard and the knights errant." Protests were raised against the "vending of trashy books" lest the literary profession fall under the sway of "young authorlings . . . who attempt paths in which their feet were never designed to tread." That such writers should enjoy popularity was "a libel on the intelligence of the country." Hawthorne's famous complaint against "the scribbling women" was only one voice in a broader fear for the future of American letters.[5]

Virtually all agreed that the popular literature simply reflected what was loosely termed the "spirit of the age." "The age has too much haste," commented the *Christian Examiner*, "and too little stopping to take breath." Literature had assumed the characteristics of the utilitarian, "busy-driving" commercial spirit of the nation, where men measured their attainments "by an arithmetical computation"; the "ethics of humbug" had replaced the moral precepts of old. Mammon toppled Minerva as the patron saint "in our Pantheon of intellect."[6]

When J. D. Whelpley, editor of the Whig *American Review*, wrote that "literature has gone over to the people," he did so derisively. American letters, he complained, had become "democratic and revolutionary," so completely were writers swayed by the "republican spirit of the age" and so desperate to make the individual equal, even superior, to kings. That public opinion, to which authors bowed, was the "greatest scourge of true, heaven-born genius." Caroline Kirkland, noting that the spirit of the time was adverse to the "deification of literary heroes," found relief when she turned "from Kossuth and Pio Nono, the Sikhs and the Mexicans" to Washington Irving's biography of Oliver Goldsmith.[7]

Some who mourned the passing of romanticism in the face of the "conventional, the analytic, the utilitarian tendency" of the age looked to the romances of the past—Scott's "mediaeval clarion" or Byron's "Greek fire"—to counter the "sordid, grovelling, earthy sensations" of the "money-getter."[8] Romanticism, however, had not so much waned as changed its shape. It too had gone over to the people. The movements of the early 19th century—political, economic, and social—awakened a romantic mood in the people that was strengthened by the publishing explosion and rise in readership. "Popular romanticism," according to a recent scholar, owed its success in part to the remarkable changes that were taking place in writing, publishing, and reading. "A new generation of authors," James Smith Allen has written, "learned to profit in the literary marketplace: their intellectual maturation and commercial apprenticeship . . . fostered the vogue of popular romanticism." The popularity of their works demonstrated that "romanticism was good business." When Whelpley attacked the vulgarization of American writing he was attacking popular romanticism. Although his attitude was hostile, he caught the meaning of romanticism better than many of his contemporaries. The current literature, he insisted, imparted a "feeling, a secret conviction of the dignity and liberty of the individual; of man in his objective and separate individuality, setting at defiance the opposition of nature, of fate, of *society,* and even of Divinity itself." Inferior novels, vaudevilles, and melodramas all taught, falsely, that "the spontaneous sentiment, the agreeable impulse of the moment, the dictate of the heart, unassisted by reason, or by considerations of the general good, is the great and truly divine law." The poor, the uneducated, and undisciplined, he feared, were being impressed with dangerous feelings of "self-estimation" and a hatred for "every species of control" that did not emanate from the individual. As the good Whig he was, Whelpley firmly believed that literature's true mission was to check and restrain the "corrupt desires and ungoverned passions" of the common people, not encourage them.[9]

Writing in *Holden's Dollar Magazine,* the eccentric New York critic Charles Frederick Briggs (better known as Harry Franco) defended the cheap literature that deluged the land. Far from corrupting the common people, he maintained, the cheap books actually benefitted them. They were, after all, eagerly devoured in spite of their "bathos, balderdash, and bad grammar," their "ultra-romantic scenes and heroes . . . puerile philosophy, and maudlin morality." They were "pulse-feelers" and "appetite-sharpeners," implanting a taste for reading in minds that before had none. Instead of condemning "the scribbling tribe," Briggs urged his fellow-critics to thank them for fostering the literary taste of the people "with their caudle and pap" and for preparing the public for the "appreciation of better food." The popularity of cheap literature would one day be recognized as the precursor of "our literary sunrise."

If Briggs's comments were meant to be satirical, they nonetheless struck a sympathetic chord in the columns of that outspoken defender of the popular interest, the *Democratic Review.* While recognizing the "triumph of enterprise over romance" and of the "literature of utility and progress over the literature of fables, and gods and battles," the *Review* insisted that the success of writers demonstrated that the people were the "only audience worth having." Going one step further, the *Review* asserted that the cheap books marked an advanced state of American society; by exposing the people to the world that lay outside their immediate experience, they elevated the intellectual level of the mass. Cheap literature might even accomplish peaceably what the Mexican War was trying to do militarily: "If our neighbors of Mexico could be induced to read, with interest, the cheap publications, in the proportion in which they are devoured here, a speedy reformation in the whole structure of society might be looked for." Mexico would be brought into the 19th century.[10]

"Roses" and "cabbages" both were important to the midcentury literary scene; indeed, the "cabbages" may have been the more nourishing for American readers. The Mexican War, it was predicted, would form a distinct "epoch" in the history of American letters, providing writers for years to come with all the elements of romance and drama they would need. Expectations were high that the war's literature would put the nation back on track, recalling the virtues of an earlier romanticism, counteracting the deadening tendencies of materialism, and strengthening the foundations of a truly national literature.

Mexico was not unknown to American fiction before 1846. Writers had shared the same romantic interest in Mexico that had attracted travelers in the early 19th century. It was an ancient land, strange and mysterious, still exhibiting vestiges of that chivalric past Sir Walter Scott described so dramatically. It was the closest Americans could come to the Old World without leaving American shores. Its ancient civilization, its legends and ruins, were near enough to be claimed by Americans, thereby satisfying the desire for an antiquity of their own. Mexico's struggle for independence, moreover, was fresh in memory, and the analogy with America's own revolution clear and obvious. Bonds of interest and ideology linked Americans with their southern neighbor. Indeed, the first American novel with a Mexican setting, Timothy Flint's *Francis Berrian, or The Mexican Patriot* (1826), dealt with Mexico's revolt against Spain. Mexico lay on the nation's frontier, and the first American contacts were western contacts, led by those who had already entered the romantic imagination—mountain men, traders, pioneer settlers. The land carried with it all the fascination of "romance and adventure and danger."[11]

Flint explained the attraction in the opening pages of his book: "It is so long since I have heard of nothing but dollars and cents, the mere mercenary details of existence, that I languish to be introduced to another world." That other world was the world of romance, and Mexico was its locale. "Poesy and romance," Flint continued, "are the higher and holier matters of the intellectual world." Without them "the love of glory and of fame, the feelings of benevolence, the thrill of affection and tenderness, are all extinguished in the heart . . . the dreams of patriotism, the willingness to devote all, and die for our country, become the idle extravagance of insanity." Flint, twenty years before the war began, established the character of Mexican War literature. The romance, the 19th century's substitute for the ancient epic (according to William Gilmore Simms), became the vehicle by which the war entered American literature.[12]

Flint found romance in Mexico's war for independence, but most writers who were attracted to Mexico went further back in time. More than any other episode in New World history, Spain's 16th-century conquest of the Aztec Empire captivated American romantics. Prescott was only one of those (and not the first) who sought to chronicle Cortez's great triumph. All the elements of great moral drama were there: civilization pitted against what seemed at best only semi-civilization, and Christianity against paganism; two towering figures, Cortez and Montezuma, locked in mortal combat, the one representing the future, the other symbolizing the past. On the one side were the Aztecs, the cynosure of romantic eyes, colorful, mysterious, primitive, and—like the American Indians—children of nature: pure, simple, and virtuous. As with the Indians, however, romantics expressed an ambivalence toward the Aztecs which they never resolved, for Montezuma's people also represented despotism, cruelty, and sanguinary religious practices. On the other side were the Spanish, carriers of civilization and Christianity, exhibiting all the glories of knighthood and chivalry but motivated by greed and avarice. "There is so much of romance in the . . . Spanish conquests of America," explained Edgar Allan Poe, that they possess "the charm of the most elaborate fiction" while bearing the "marks of general truth." "These adventures," Poe asserted, "occurred during the age of chivalry" when personal valor was regarded as the "pre-eminent quality." An epic struggle in a remote and shadowy past, fought in an exotic and mysterious land that seemed to have changed little during the intervening three centuries—it is little wonder that the Spanish conquest became so familiar to Americans by the 1840s that they almost considered it a part of their own past. When their own army trod the path of Cortez the link was complete. For thousands of young Americans the opportunity to experience the romance of the Conquest, to "revel in the Halls of the Montezumas," was at hand.[13]

One of the earliest writers to be captivated by the drama of the Conquest was young William Gilmore Simms, whose poem *The Vision of Cortes* (1829) portrayed the Aztecs as freedom-fighters against an ambitious and greedy Cortez. Cortez's Aztec adversary was endowed with all the characteristics of a "hero in Romance, fully worthy of the middle ages." The Aztec's curse hurled at the Spanish conqueror, yet "Hangs o'er the race, the name, the land, Of that fierce, base and murderous band." The exploitation by American romantics of the Conquest, however, did not really begin until five years later when Robert Montgomery Bird published *Calavar; or, The Knight of the Conquest: A Romance of Mexico* (1834), the first fictional treatment of the Conquest. Poe judged it the best American novel he had read, aside from a couple of Cooper's works, and he predicted that Bird would find position in the first rank of America's writers. The importance of Bird's work cannot be minimized; it brought him immediate fame and pointed to a new direction for writers of historical romance. *Calavar,* moreover, influenced American perceptions of Mexico at a critical moment and played a part in stimulating the popular "war spirit" after 1846.[14]

A Philadelphia physician with a medical degree from the University of Pennsylvania, Bird had already established a reputation as a successful playwright. His plays, the most popular of which were "The Gladiator" and "The Broker of Bogota" (both written for and performed by Edwin Forrest), united the popular interest in Indians, Spanish-American subjects, and America's mission to advance the cause of liberty over despotism. Bird had a keen sense of history and used it to promote an awareness of the political and social problems of his own time, pampering the romantic self-image of Americans and focusing on the struggles of a patriot-hero against the forces of oppression.

In turning to the Spanish conquest of Mexico, Bird discovered a subject which, "while still being American, had all the strangeness and exotic qualities of Old World romance." His purpose was twofold: to prepare himself for a history of Mexico which he hoped to write; and to illustrate "the most romantic and poetical chapter in the history of the New World." The demands of history were united with the "requisitions of romance," and the result was impressive even to Prescott. The great historian later vouched for the accuracy of Bird's research and suggested that Bird had done for the Aztecs what Cooper did for the Indians, "touched their rude features with the bright coloring of poetic fancy."[15]

For many Americans who later responded to the Mexican War, *Calavar* was a first exposure to the country whose history Bird had said was itself "a romance." A land of Edenic charm, of "strange deeds of renown," over which the "mysteries of backward years" still brooded— this, he suggested, was "the proper field for romantic musings." Bird followed *Calavar* with a sequel, *The Infidel; or The Fall of Mexico* (1835), but it fell far short of *Calavar*'s success. He then turned to the American frontier and to the Indians for his themes, publishing in 1837 his best-known work *Nick of the Woods*.

With the outbreak of the Mexican War, Bird's interest in Mexico revived. The landing of Winfield Scott's army at Vera Cruz focused attention on *Calavar* once again, and in 1847 Bird's publisher, anxious to capitalize on the popularity of the war, brought out a new edition. In his preface, Bird compared Scott's invasion to that of Cortez; both followed the same route, attacked the same city "in the same most magnificent of valleys," and fought the same "petty forces" with the same "daring intrepidity." *Godey's*, for whom Bird had earlier written sketches on Mexican and Peruvian history, pronounced *Calavar* a book everyone should read while "we are at war with the nation where the scene is laid."[16]

Bird's interest in the war carried him even farther. He began collecting materials for a projected history of Texas annexation and the Mexican War and made plans to publish a novel, to be titled *The Volunteers*, that would celebrate the bravery of the nation's citizen-soldiers at Buena Vista and other battles. In the meantime, Bird had acquired an interest in Philadelphia's Whig newspaper, the *North American*, and assumed its editorship. At the suggestion of John J. Crittenden, Kentucky's Whig Senator whose son served on Taylor's staff at Buena Vista, he wrote a campaign biography of Zachary Taylor, published first in the columns of his newspaper and later as a pamphlet. The Mexican War, he charged, was a "new element of political intrigue" that went awry for it redounded more to Whig than to Democratic benefit. This time it was Taylor whom Bird compared to Cortez. His victories were the "joy and happiness" of the American people, his triumph at Buena Vista unmatched in modern times. American superiority over the "mongrel Mexican" had been demonstrated beyond doubt, with consequences that reached far beyond the New World.[17]

The success of Bird's *Calavar* and the immense popularity of Prescott's history of the Conquest (published in 1843) inspired a number of imitators. Edward Maturin, Irish-born teacher of Greek and Latin and son of the reputed master of the Gothic novel, Charles Robert Maturin, published *Montezuma: The Last of the Aztecs* late in 1845, a book the *New-York Mirror* described as "a *sensation*." Dedicated to Prescott, the novel relied heavily on the historian and on Bird's work. Maturin's sympathies were with the Aztecs—"he has thrown over the career of the Mexican Prince, the warmth of his Irish sympathies," commented the *Democratic Review*. Cortez, his chivalry debased by avarice, was a bird of prey about to despoil "this chosen Eden." Like other writers of his generation, Maturin seemed to be calling attention to the conflict in his own time between the love of gain and true knightly virtue. His tale was replete with Gothic excesses, in the tradition of his father, which no doubt was just what the public wanted. *Montezuma* was almost immediately adapted for the stage and in the fall of 1846 opened in New York "in a style of costly magnificence."[18]

In the same year, Joseph Holt Ingraham, a New England-born professor at a Mississippi college and a prolific "penny-a-line scribbler" of the "cheap and nasty school," published his *Montezuma the Serf; or, The Revolt of the Mexitili. A Tale of the Last Days of the Aztec Dynasty*. Although Longfellow had once called him a "tremendous ass" and the writer of the "worst novels ever written by anybody," Ingraham knew the prescription for success. Early in 1846 he boasted that he had written eighty novels, from which he earned more than $3000 a year. *Montezuma the Serf* was an expansion of a story he had published in the *Southern Literary Messenger* in 1839, an obvious effort to capitalize on the growing interest in Mexico. The Spanish conquest does not appear in the book; rather it is the tale of Montezuma, the "low born bondman," and his struggle to free the Aztecs from their "degrading servitude" to a ruthless and powerful monarch. "Let us break our chains, and elevate our condition to that of freemen," Montezuma cried. "I will be true to my country, and strike the first blow for her liberty." It was a common theme for the 1840s. The work, moreover, had a strong medieval tone, full of knights, chivalric virtue, and courtly love. There was no doubt that Ingraham had found the formula.[19]

William W. Fosdick, a Cincinnati lawyer and the only writer of Conquest literature to have traveled in Mexico (whether as a soldier or a civilian is uncertain), published *Malmiztic the Toltec; and the Cavaliers of the Cross* three years after the war had ended. Fosdick's hero, an Indian whose people had been displaced by the Aztecs, joined Cortez, although scorning the Spaniard's moral weakness. The story was a comment on Fosdick's own changing times: Cortez represented the "last sparks of chivalry" in a dying age of knight-errantry and symbolized, by his passion for gain, the dawning of a new age. Mexico, for Fosdick, was a land of enchantment where the "Spirit of Romance . . . glides among the ruins" and where the echo of "long-lost voices" could be heard in the "hollow depths of the buried temple and the broken arch."[20]

The degree to which the literature of the Spanish conquest contributed to the formation of a national literature, as reviewers maintained, is problematical. That it bore all the marks of popular American romanticism is more certain. Its importance lies rather in its impact on popular thought during the midcentury years; through its successful appeal to the reading public, it promoted an awareness of Mexico's past and provided a yardstick by which the "second conquest" could be measured. By painting the Spanish conquest in heroic shades, Bird and his followers helped shape a mood that allowed Americans to accept their own conflict with Mexico more readily and to perceive their war in the same reflected light of romance and history. Many of the volunteers in Mexico caught that "Spirit of Romance" of which Fosdick wrote and standing amidst the ruins of Mexican antiquity heard those same "echoes of long-lost voices." By sympathizing with the Indians of 16th-century Mexico against the despotism of their Aztec masters and by portraying Cortez and his men as grasping individuals whose knightly virtues had been replaced by love of gain, the writers were speaking to their own time. Chivalry was sullied by avarice—a lesson and a warning that some Americans felt bore a special relevance to the comparable venture on which they embarked late in the 1840s.

A second stream of literary activity that turned American attention toward Mexico flowed out of the nation's southwestern frontier. The Santa Fe trade and the settlement of Texas provided points of contact between Mexicans and Americans that found expression in imaginative literature as well as in travel books and the accounts of traders, explorers and other adventurers. Flint's *Francis Berrian* was as much a tale of the borderlands as it was of Mexico's struggle for independence. The Texas Revolution, the subsequent expeditions against Santa Fe and Mier, and the growing issue of annexation, brought the area into the public eye, adding elements of social conflict to the already captivating romance of frontier adventure. A new literature of the southwestern borderland gradually emerged as part of that "literature of the forest and the prairie, of the Indian camp and backwoods settlement" that *Blackwood's Magazine* found so characteristically American.

One of the new writers, Charles Wilkins Webber, explained the fascination this border region held for Americans. "Events now taking place in the region of Texas and Mexico," he wrote in the fall of 1845, "the peculiar position of our Government toward those countries, and the near prospect—if not of a long war—of numerous fierce skirmishes at least, among the strange mixture of wild Indians, Mexicans, negroes, half-breeds, Spaniards, and Americans, inhabiting that region—united with the singular magnificence and freshness of the vast scenery—combine to form a field, at this time, of equal attraction to the sketcher and interest to the American reader."[21]

Experience on the border led some writers into service in the Mexican War. Albert Pike, a native New Englander, short-time student of the classics at Harvard, and schoolmaster, drifted to St. Louis in 1831, where he joined an expedition bound for Santa Fe. He stayed in New Mexico for about a year, later publishing his observations of Indians and Mexicans in his *Prose Sketches and Poems Written in the Western Country* (1834). Unlike Flint, Pike had seen the country about which he wrote. His judgments of the people were harsh: the Indians were "mean, cowardly, and treacherous," the Mexicans were a "lazy, gossiping people, always lounging on their blankets . . . living on nothing, and without labor." Pike later settled in Arkansas, where he followed careers in journalism and the law. There he fell under the spell of the English romantics, especially Byron, became interested in the Spanish conquest, and planned a romantic novel to be set in 16th-century New Mexico, a project he quickly abandoned. With the outbreak of the Mexican War, Pike joined Arkansas's "Mounted Devils," the state's volunteer cavalry regiment, was elected captain, and became famous for his poem "Buena Vista," written on the battlefield.[22]

Anthony Ganilh, a French-born Roman Catholic missionary and teacher who came to the United States early in the 19th century, was the reputed author of the first Texas novel, published anonymously in 1838 under the title *Mexico versus Texas* and reissued four years later under the pseudonym A. T. Myrthe as *Ambrosio de Letinez, or The First Texian Novel*. Ganilh's theme anticipated later perceptions of the Mexican War. The conflict between Mexicans and Americans, he contended, sprang most of all from the "spirit of adventure and ardent love of freedom" that rendered all Americans "mortal foes to arbitrary rule." The Texas Revolution was a crusade against the "antiquated prejudices and narrow policy of the middle ages" which governed Mexico. It was the "fourteenth century pitted against the nineteenth." With the help of the Americans, Ganilh hoped the Mexican people could make a successful transition from despotic to republican government.

Indeed, he sought a role in that transition, for according to one source he served as an officer in Zachary Taylor's army during the Mexican War.[23]

Two European writers were influential in providing Americans with early impressions of Indians, Mexicans, and Texans: the English traveler Frederick Marryat and the Austrian ex-priest Karl Anton Postl. Marryat's novel, *Narrative of the Travels and Adventures of Monsieur Violet, in California, Sonora, and Western Texas* (1843), was published in London and immediately reprinted in pirated editions in the United States. Although stridently anti-American in tone (and clouded by charges of plagiarism), the book was well received for its tales of romantic adventure in the Mexican borderlands. Postl, who used the name Charles Sealsfield, had published travel accounts and novels dealing with Mexico and Texas. His work, the most popular of which was *The Cabin Book; or, Sketches of Life in Texas*, was reprinted just before the war. While some critics condemned his writings as "pure trash," others found in Sealsfield an "exponent of Young America." His point of view was summarized by one periodical: "the land is too good for the lazy 'greasers,' who must incontinently absquatilate, and make way for better men."[24]

By 1845, accounts written by the survivors of Texas's expedition against Mier three years earlier began to appear. The suffering of the prisoners taken at Mier, the notorious "lottery of death," and the imprisonment of many of them in the castle of Perote aroused indignation against Mexico and provided a ready audience for the accounts. William P. Stapp's *The Prisoners of Perote* (1845), the first to appear, was based on a journal kept while Stapp was a prisoner, although it also contained considerable romantic embellishment. No doubt Stapp's characterization of Santa Anna as an "infuriate Attila" bent on exterminating the "gallant opponents of his usurpation and despotism" fixed an image in the minds of Americans that carried over into the Mexican War. The story of the Mier prisoners became a familiar one, and the grim fortress in which they were incarcerated was a popular tourist attraction for the soldiers in Scott's army.[25]

As the Texas issue bubbled to a boil and the United States and Mexico moved closer to hostilities, stories of Texas and the Mexican borderlands became common fare in the popular magazines. Among them, those of Charles Wilkins Webber assumed a special veracity because of Webber's involvement in the turmoil of the Texas-Mexico frontier. Leaving his native Kentucky for Texas in 1838, he fell in with the legendary John Coffee Hays and his Texas Rangers and spent the next few years "in singular adventures" clashing with Indians and Mexicans. After returning to the United States, he joined the *American Review*, the Whig party's magazine, as joint proprietor and associate editor.

Webber published extensively in the early numbers of the *Review*—

articles on ornithology, essays on American literature, and a number of adventure stories. In a series of six sketches he recounted his experiences with the Rangers and informed his readers of the peculiar circumstances that existed on the Texas frontier. Populated by a "mongrel" collection of whites, Mexicans, and Indians, the region, he concluded, lacked all the stable elements of society. The Mexicans were singled out for his "deadly and unutterable scorn," but he was hardly less severe on the Texans he had come to know. The latter were consumed by an "exterminating hate of domineering brutality," destitute of magnanimity, and motivated by a "cut-throat ferocity." As a Whig editor on the eve of the Mexican War, Webber helped to strengthen public concern over Mexico and to shape the perceptions of Mexican character. He urged his party to espouse a deeper patriotism than that suggested in the "epithets of war" with which oratory had been stuffed. The war, he felt, was "disgraceful." Like Robert Montgomery Bird and William H. Prescott, steadfast Whigs both, Webber exhibited a fundamental irony with respect to the war—a staunch Whig opposed to the conflict yet one who through his writings fostered a spirit that made the war all the more popular.[26]

The literature of the Spanish conquest and that of the Texas-Mexican borderland defined the milieu into which the fiction inspired by the Mexican War would fall. The former provided an historical and medieval-romantic background for the confrontation with Mexico, while the latter supplied all the excitement of frontier adventure. When the guns of Palo Alto and Resaca de la Palma marked the opening of hostilities, a new direction for American letters was opened. The "scribbling tribe" entered the fray and publishing's social and technological advance gave the warriors a perfect medium for their romantic fancies.

Among the literary innovations of the 1840s was the inexpensive paperbound adventure story, precursor to the "dime novel" but more commonly called "novelette" in this earlier period. The novelette had its beginning in the story-papers that appeared in the 1830s and 1840s to meet the increasing demand for reading material. Issued weekly (usually on Saturday in order to provide Sunday reading) in newspaper format and selling for only a few cents a copy, the papers at first offered the latest British novels serially, but as competition became keener they began printing complete works in a single issue. As the market expanded, the publishers of story-papers commissioned works by domestic authors and then reprinted the tales in cheap paperbound form; their success attracted established publishing houses and before long a new literary (or sub-literary) genre was born. Bound in bright yellow paper covers, embellished with an eye-catching woodcut, printed on rough paper in double columns and rarely exceeding 100 pages in length, the novelettes swept the country.

Although some story-papers had circulations approaching 100,000 and the novelettes were frequently published in editions of as many as 60,000 copies, few of these early productions have survived. They were read and reread, passing from one person to another until they were literally used up. Written for both people and profit, they reflected the attitudes, prejudices, and aspirations of the mass more clearly than most other types of literary output. Their themes were necessarily those that had the widest possible appeal. They were, as Merle Curti suggested, the closest thing in America to a true proletarian literature, that is "a literature written for the great masses of people and actually read by them."

Nor were the novelettes read only by the common people. Their popularity was not a function of class, for they appealed to more refined readers as well (as Grace Greenwood discovered). A traveler on a western railroad in 1847 (the novelettes seemed to be especially popular on trains) was momentarily dismayed "to see with what avidity 'yellow covered literature' is here as elsewhere, devoured by travelers. . . . Numbers of well dressed and sensible looking ladies and gentlemen, with foreheads of respectable dimensions, have busied themselves for hours today . . . in perusing, page by page, the contents of some shilling romance."[27]

The Mexican War boosted the popularity of the new paperbound books. Soldiers bought them in quantity and carried them to Mexico in their knapsacks. They became standard reading fare on the long sea voyages from eastern ports and broke the monotony of the camp. Publishers, with their eyes on sales, solicited authors and tailored their lists with the military market in mind. The war provided the settings and plots for scores of works that, like the penny press, carried the conflict into households throughout the country. "This war-literature has circulated through the newspapers and cheap works over the whole land," moaned a critic of the war. "It is so diffused, that it enters every nook and corner of the land."[28]

New York's Jonas Winchester published one of the most popular story-papers, *The New World* (edited by Park Benjamin and others), and at the same time became a leading publisher of novelettes. Webber's Texas sketches and Marryat's and Sealsfield's works appeared in *The New World* just before the Mexican War. Winchester's chief competitors were three firms which, with Winchester, virtually monopolized the market: Williams Brothers in New York, and Boston's Gleason Publishing Hall and Jones Publishing Office. Frederick Gleason and Justin Jones also issued widely circulated story-papers, *The Flag of Our Union* and *The Star Spangled Banner* respectively. Almost all of the novelettes with Mexican War themes were published by these firms; indeed, so many were issued by Gleason and Jones that Boston became the publishing center of Mexican War fiction.

Justin Jones not only published scores of paperbound tales of romance and adventure but also wrote many of them himself, using the pseudonym Harry Hazel. Among his works were at least three thrillers on Mexico and the Mexican War, whose titles reveal the Gothic character of the war fiction: *The Rival Chieftains; or, The Brigands of Mexico. A Tale of Santa Anna and His Times* (1845); *Inez, the Beautiful; or, Love on the Rio Grande* (1846); and *The Light Dragoon; or, The Rancheros of the Poisoned Lance. A Tale of the Battle Fields of Mexico* (1848).

Jones was only one of a large number of writers who found profit in Mexican War themes. "Everything connected with the Mexican war," commented *Godey's*, "is replete with interest," and the fact was revealed by the quantity of books that were published to exploit that interest. Many of the writers were (and still are) obscure. Nothing, for example, is known of the person who used the name Harry Halyard when he wrote *The Chieftain of Churubusco; or, The Spectre of the Cathedral* (1848); *The Mexican Spy; or, The Bride of Buena Vista* (1848); and *The Heroine of Tampico; or, Wildfire the Wanderer* (1847), each carrying the subtitle "A Tale of the Mexican War." Two others, including *The Warrior Queen; or, The Buccaneer of the Brazos* (1848), were billed as Mexican Romances. Charles Averill was the author of *The Mexican Ranchero; or, The Maid of the Chapparal* (1847) and *The Secret Service Ship; or, The Fall of San Juan D'Ulloa* (1848). Others were A. S. St. Clair (*Senora Ines; or, The American Volunteers*), Arthur Armstrong (*The Mariner of the Mines; or, The Maid of the Monastery*), S. H. Boynton, Jr. (*The White Dart; or, The Cruiser of the Gulf of Mexico*) and the pseudonymous Lorry Luff (*Antonita, The Female Contrabandista*). John Tuel's *The Prisoner of Perote: A Tale of American Valor and Mexican Love* (1848) was inspired by Stapp's earlier account. Robert F. Greeley, a popular magazine writer who had won acclaim for his *Old Cro' Nest; or, The Outlaws of the Hudson*, published two Mexican War novelettes in 1847: *Arthur Woodleigh: A Romance of the Battle Field in Mexico*, and *The Bloody Nuptials; or, A Soldier by Chance: A Tale of the Mexican Campaign.*[29]

Joseph Holt Ingraham, the "Professor," followed his success in *Montezuma, the Serf* with the publication of *The Texan Ranger; or, The Maid of Matamoras* (1847), one of twelve books by Ingraham that appeared that year. The title was descriptive—heroic Rangers putting to rout numerically superior Mexican cavalry, a love interest that overcame national and cultural differences. Ingraham's publisher, Williams Brothers of New York, also issued the novelettes of Newton Mallory Curtis, one of the most popular yet least known of the writers. A schoolteacher and editor of a political paper in a small New York town, Curtis exploited local settings in tales of the French and Indian War and the American Revolution, although he also wrote a series on "Life in the Great Metropolis" (influenced by Eugène Sue's revelations of life in Paris). Three of his works dealt with the Mexican War: *The Hunted Chief; or, The Female Ranchero* (1847); *The Prairie Guide; or, The Rose of the Rio Grande* (1847); and *The Vidette; or, The Girl of the Robber's Pass* (1848).

The most notorious of the novelette writers was Edward Zane Carroll

Judson, whose pseudonym Ned Buntline became a household name and whose sensational stories remained a mainstay in the dime-novel market for years to come. Judson's own life read like those of his fictional heroes; in fact Judson himself had difficulty distinguishing between his own past and that of his characters. He ran away to sea at an early age, served in the Navy for four years, fought in the Seminole War, roamed the western plains, and survived a succession of shootings, lynchings, and riots. Judson began writing stories based on his experiences for *Knickerbocker* and his own periodicals, *Ned Buntline's Magazine* and the *Western Literary Journal*. He wrote his first novelette for the Jones Publishing Office in 1847, moved to Gleason soon afterward, and later switched to Williams Brothers. It was the beginning of a long and lucrative literary career, during which he is said to have written more than 400 novels. Judson's great disappointment was that he had never served in the Mexican War, although he later insisted that he had and even claimed battle scars from the experience. His participation in the conflict was limited to two novelettes, both published in 1847: *The Volunteer; or, The Maid of Monterey* (Gleason's "100 Dollar Prize Tale") and *Magdalena, the Beautiful Mexican Maid: A Story of Buena Vista* (which also contained Whittier's poignant poem "The Angels of Buena Vista").[30]

The Mexican War novelettes, like the genre they represented, do not rank high as literary efforts. They were for the most part potboilers, hastily written and printed in cheap, shoddy form in order to capitalize on the popular interest in the war. Their very titles convey hints of their contents, and if there was a similarity among them it was deliberate. They bore all the characteristics of formula-fiction, in one of its earliest manifestations. Their authors were not artists but professional writers—hacks—whose talents were shaped by the demands of the marketplace. Ingraham admitted that writing novels had become "merely mechanical" with him, while Judson later confessed that in order to make a living he had to "write 'trash' for the masses."[31] They were passive reflectors of notions and attitudes that were current, popular, and salable, rather than innovators or leaders. Their portrayal of the war reinforced the way many Americans saw, or wanted to see, the conflict: the stark contrast between the "superior," good, and patriotic American volunteer and the dark, skulking, "inferior" Mexican ranchero; the dramatic and bloody encounters on the battlefields; the American soldiers on their mission of rescue, displaying tenderness and sensitivity toward the enemy and seeking to redeem innocent civilians from the stifling oppression of state and church; the incredibly beautiful *señoritas* and the love that ultimately overcame all obstacles—all this played out against the backdrop of an exotic tropical clime.

At the same time, the novelette writers exhibited a knowledge of Mexico and the war that could only have been acquired from at least a modicum of reading. Virtually all the novelettes were published in

1847 and 1848, and it is clear that their authors had the advantage of the many travel narratives, campaign accounts, and soldiers' letters that had appeared in print by that time. Their own renderings paralleled those of the soldiers, revealing the same attitudes held by the latter toward the land and its people. Reflecting the popular, romantic convictions of American uniqueness and superiority, they provided, as one recent writer has pointed out, "a significant reinforcement" of those stereotypes of Mexico and Mexicans that were so widely held in the 1840s.[32]

The heroes of the novelettes were often thinly disguised Natty Bumppos. Ned Buntline's Kentuckian, "a noble specimen of a backwoodsman," in *The Volunteer,* informs his mother of his duty to raise a company and join General Taylor—"It were better for me to fill a brave man's grave, than to live in a coward's place." With all the mystery, concealed identities, and mistaken motives of a Gothic novel, Buntline spun a tale of action and suspense in which good ultimately triumphed over villainy. The "deep dyed villain," a Texas Ranger who is in treacherous contact with the Mexican enemy, is frustrated in his designs against the hero. A fiercely patriotic Mexican officer, captured at Monterey, turns out to be a woman who, without conceding the justice of the American cause, falls predictably in love with the Kentucky volunteer. The villain meets his fate at the hands of a combined American-Mexican force, and the two lovers are married by a Mexican regimental chaplain in the camp of General Urrea, eventually returning to Kentucky to begin their lives together. In Curtis's *The Vidette* the hero is the scion of a wealthy and respectable New England family, seized with the desire "to enter upon a life of adventure, and perhaps of glory, in the far famed land of the Aztecs." After ministering to a mortally wounded Mexican officer on the battlefield of Cerro Gordo, he sets out to find the officer's family. Assigned to the pursuit of Mexican guerrillas and bandits, he is captured, wins the favor of his captors, locates the officer's family, defends its members against the evil intentions of a bandit-priest (the "hoary-headed villain"), and falls in love with the young daughter ("he had never looked upon one so beautiful"). All ends happily. The villainous priest is executed, and the lovers are married; rescued by American forces, the hero resigns his commission and carries his bride with him back to New England.

In both stories, the Mexican side of the war is given full treatment. Buntline's Mexican heroine-officer denounces the invaders of her country and predicts continued bloodshed as long as Americans remain on Mexican soil. For Curtis, it is the priest, in one of his sympathetic moments, who inveighs against the "northern heretics" who have "invaded our land, devastated our dwellings, murdered our fathers, brothers, and friends, and destroyed our commerce." Both sides eventually unite in recognizing the folly of war, as Buntline's Kentuckian swears it is the last time he will leave his country "to seek for glory."

Although Mexico is held responsible for the war, there is no rancor against the Mexican people, a characteristic separation of rulers and ruled that appeared throughout the literature of the Mexican War. The American soldiers are cast as redeemers, striving to free the people from the bondage imposed by government and Church, to regenerate the nation, and bring it to a state of true republicanism. In the end the mission is triumphant, American soldiers and Mexican civilians discover their common humanity, and the tales close on a hopeful note of reunion and harmony symbolized by the mutual love and intermarriage that signal the beginning of a new relationship.[33]

The novelette writers experienced the war vicariously, through the published accounts of travelers, soldiers, and newspaper correspondents and their own fertile imaginations. There were others, however, who fought in Mexico, knew the war at firsthand, and used that knowledge for later excursions into fiction-writing. Their works, blending fiction with autobiography, assumed an authenticity which the novelettes lacked. One of the best known was the Irish-born adventurer Thomas Mayne Reid, who emigrated to the United States in 1840.

Reid's first two years in America were spent on the frontier, where he encountered "buffaloes, grizzly bears, and Indians on the warpath." In 1842 he began his literary career, first in Pittsburgh, then in Philadelphia, where he formed a close friendship with Edgar Allan Poe. His poems and prose sketches were published in such popular magazines as *Graham's*, *Godey's*, and the *Spirit of the Times*. In the summer of 1846, he was in Newport, Rhode Island, reporting the social season for the *New York Herald*.

When the New York Regiment was formed later in 1846 he joined it as a second lieutenant. He took part in the landing at Vera Cruz, chased guerrillas during the siege of that city, missed Cerro Gordo, and fought with his regiment at Churubusco. Reid's greatest claim to fame was in the assault on Chapultepec. A member of the storming party, the "forlorn hope," he led the final effort to place scaling ladders on the castle walls until a Mexican bullet in his thigh stopped his progress. He was cited for heroism in the battle reports, and the story of his daring circulated through the army. Back in the United States after the war he tried unsuccessfully to raise troops to aid German and Hungarian revolutionaries, finally returning to England in 1849.[34]

As a correspondent for the *Spirit of the Times*, Reid published his "Sketches by a Skirmisher" (using the pseudonym Ecolier)—eyewitness accounts of the battles at Vera Cruz, Contreras, Churubusco, Molino del Rey, Chapultepec, and Mexico City. Some were written with such flair (his encounters with guerrillas and girls, for example) that they moved beyond reality into romance. Writing from the sand hills surrounding Vera Cruz during the bombardment, Reid described his situation:

> If you suppose that we write on an elegant desk, with gold pen, and superfine post, you are just off the track. But thus: Half buried in soft sand—our left elbow "dug" in so as to form a support—for a desk we are using a huge old book, stolen (we fear) from a Mexican Ranche. What? Holy mother! *"La vida de la Santa Maria."* . . . I scribble in the midst of sweets and bitters, of heaven and hell, and to vary the monotony around, am obliged at intervals to drop my pencil, throw myself flat on the sand, to escape being chucked off by the fragments of a shell, or "cock" my ear at the whistling of a grenade, in order to get clear of its course.

His sketches later served as the basis for a series of fictionalized tales (each subtitled "A Sketch of the Late Campaign") published in *Graham's Magazine.*[35]

Before he left America for England, Reid wrote the first of his full-length novels, published in New York as *War Life; or, The Adventures of a Light Infantry Officer* (1849) and the following year in London under its better-known title, *The Rifle Rangers; or, Adventures of an Officer in Southern Mexico.* Several more followed during the fifties, including *The Scalp Hunters; or, Romantic Adventures in Northern Mexico* (1851), the story of trappers and Indians in New Mexico, and *The War Trail; or, The Hunt of the Wild Horse* (1847), a tale of the American invasion of Mexico in 1846.

There was Gothic romanticism in Reid's work, combined with a deep respect and admiration for the democratic mission of his adopted country. Reid's Mexico was a strange land of wonders, of exotic vegetation and animal life, of crumbling castles and beautiful maidens. He had a keen eye for landscape, and his stories conveyed the beauty and terror of the countryside in romantically charged language. Into this paradise—"Bright land of Anahuac"—war intruded, violating the serenity and innocence of the landscape. The field at Chapultepec, littered with the carnage of battle and revealing "heaps of mangled carcases" with their "swollen limbs and distorted features of decomposition," presented a frightening contrast to the surrounding beauty of the Valley of Mexico.

Strangely, the intruders are not the American soldiers but the dark and scowling Mexican guerrillas, treacherous, brutal, fiercely jealous, and—when confronted with danger—cowardly. More often than not it is the American officer who protects the innocence of Mexican maidenhood from violation by the half-savage guerrilla. The guerrillas are bands of robbers, "committing every species of outrage" upon the country's peaceful inhabitants. The Mexican army, a "rabble soldiery," is little better, and its leader, Santa Anna, a "cowardly despot" with a "dark, malice-marked face" that was "furrowed by guilt." But when

The Wounded Guerrilla. Illustration for a Mexican War story by Mayne Reid. From *Graham's Magazine* (January 1849).

they triumph over their Mexican adversaries, the Americans fall captive to the charms of the *señoritas.* As the "conqueror dallies in the halls of the conquered," Love is the victor after all, "and the stern soldier, himself subdued, is transformed into a suing lover . . . on bended knee, whispering his soft tale in the ear of some dark-eyed *doncella,* Andalusian or Aztec!" The *Rifle Rangers* closes with the young American officer and his Mexican sweetheart strolling through the lush gardens of Jalapa, lingering in the shadows of orange trees, gazing upon the moon and listening to the "soft notes of the tropic night-birds."[36]

Reid's work was directed toward a more sophisticated audience than were the novelettes, although many of his later stories were published as dime-novels. There were, however, similarities: his plots, characterizations, and the exaggeratedly romantic style. Contemporary critics noted his propensity for "literary and moral pyrotechnics." "This is a farrago of fierce adventure in Northern Mexico," wrote a reviewer of *The Scalp Hunters,* "full of skirmish and intrigue, outlawry and blood, traffic and terror—all sorts of fabrication—wild, startling, grossly improbable, yet spirited, lively, and full of interest." It was written in a style that "out-herods even that of Dumas and Sue." Reid himself described his work as "fact, enamelled by fiction—a mosaic of romance and reality," and it was this mix that set him off from the writers of sensational cheap fiction.[37]

A more serious writer of Mexican War fiction was John Ludlum McConnel, a law graduate of Transylvania University and son of one of Illinois's pioneer lawyers. A volunteer in the First Illinois Regiment, McConnel was wounded twice at Buena Vista before he was mustered out in 1847. His first novel *Talbot and Vernon* (1850) followed his experiences in Mexico and became in effect McConnel's campaign account. He lauded the spirit that impelled thousands of young Americans to volunteer. "Not a man that went upon that campaign and came back," he wrote, "would not go again and again." The war, he felt, was an "emigration as well as an invasion." Like many other soldiers, he was harshly critical of upper-class Mexicans and the leaders of the Church and the government who, he believed, kept the people in a perpetual state of poverty, ignorance, and superstition. Only the "gradual leavening of the loaf with Anglo-Saxon blood" could save Mexico from eventual ruin and decay.[38]

The Mexican War can hardly be said to have inspired a *great* literature. In his study of Civil War literature, Daniel Aaron has suggested that the Civil War probably inspired more writing than all of America's wars combined; it was a war that "seemed designed for literary treatment." Perhaps the attraction of the Civil War may explain the paucity of literary expression that emerged from the conflict that ended just thirteen years before. The Mexican War, while it possessed many of the ingredients regarded as necessary for a worthy war literature, became so entangled with what were commonly assumed to be the causes of the Civil War that it virtually lost its identity. Indeed, the Mexican War itself became one of those causes. In the anxious years of the 1850s, as Americans confronted the increasingly explosive slavery issue, the enthusiasm and romantic idealism with which they had viewed the Mexican War was swallowed up in the national consciousness by the divisive issues it apparently unleashed. Any literary impulse which the war may have inspired was snuffed out by its troublesome aftermath.

Although critics and reviewers believed that the Mexican War would be to American letters what the Peninsular War was to English literature, the fact remained that the latter, the greatest of the world's wars before the American Civil War, did not enter the stream of English literature until two or three decades after its conclusion. The biographer of one of the first writers to exploit the Peninsular War in fiction has attributed the lag to an absence of war correspondents, insufficient newspaper coverage, and a lack of literary talent among the soldiers. All those elements, however, were present in the Mexican War (one might question the literary talent), and still the conflict failed to move America's major writers. Just as Sir Walter Scott and Jane Austen "seemed oblivious" to the Peninsular War, so also were America's literary leaders (with few exceptions) untouched by the Mexican War. Yet even the Civil War, which touched people's lives more intimately than any previous conflict, disappointed those who looked for something grand and lasting in the literature it inspired. One 20th-century critic has questioned whether any war since the Crusades really lent itself to epic treatment; another has blamed the mediocrity of Civil War fiction on the sterility of the American literary imagination. It may be, Aaron suggests, that "national convulsions" simply do not provide "the best conditions for artistic creativeness." Perhaps too much is expected. Perhaps Americans should be content with a less distinguished literary expression, with even the kind of sub-literature represented by the novelettes, for it is *that* literature that often provides a more accurate measure of the war's impact on the people.[39]

In 1862, John Weiss, a Boston Unitarian minister, explored the relationship between war and literature. "A war," he wrote, "must be the last resort of truly noble and popular ideas, if it would do more than stimulate the intelligence of a few men, who write best with draughts of glory and success." War must awaken something spiritual, high and pure, in the people. "There must be a great people before there can be a great character in its books." But, he cautioned, "we must carefully discover what a war was about, before we can trace it, either for good or evil, into the subsequent life of a nation." Weiss believed he knew what the Mexican War was about: it was a conflict precipitated by Slavery in which the power of the republic was employed to advance a conspiracy on behalf of Slavery's extension, a conflict promoted by that spirit "which lusted for the appeal to arms."[40]

Weiss's strictures against the Mexican War reflected the views of New England's religious and literary intelligentsia (which also may explain the absence of a great Mexican War literature); but not all Americans would have agreed with his judgment. To those who linked the war with nationalistic and patriotic sentiments, the conflict was an appropriate subject for literary celebration. The same convictions of national mission and destiny that shaped their attitudes toward the war also encouraged the demand for a distinctive American literature. The two were closely interrelated, for the war, it was thought, would play a major role in the development of a national literature. One of America's leading critics, William Alfred Jones, argued that America's literature must be a faithful reflection of its people, democratic in character and appeal, but he also insisted that it must be "penetrated and vivified by an intense and enlightened patriotism," qualities which many thought were supplied by the Mexican War.[41]

The novelettes, while expressing popular attitudes toward the war, fell short of supplying the national literature Young America yearned for. That they dealt with the Mexican War at all may be little more than coincidental. The novelette writers aimed at a popular audience; the war simply became an element in their formula, alongside such other topics as the American Revolution, the mysteries of urban life, frontier adventure, piracy on the high seas, and so on. Clearly, if the Mexican War were to occupy a significant place in the development of a truly national literature, something more was needed.

Those writers now considered to be major literary spokesmen of mid-19th-century America contributed little toward a relationship between the Mexican War and a national literature. For example, Herman Melville gave the war little notice. Writing to his brother late in May 1846 from the small New York town where he then lived, he observed (with some surprise) that "people here are all in a state of delirium about the Mexican War. A military ardor pervades all ranks . . . and 'prentice boys are running off to the wars by scores.— Nothing is talked of but the 'Halls of the Montezumas.' " Unswayed by the enthusiasm, he sought some clue to the war's meaning. While he expressed pride in the gallantry of the nation's soldiers, he felt the war "is nothing of itself." Something great was impending but he didn't quite know what; at any rate, he did not think it was the war. Melville's literary response to the war was limited to a series of seven unsigned comic articles, "Authentic Anecdotes of 'Old Zach,' " published in Cornelius Mathews's humor magazine *Yankee Doodle,* in which he subjected General Taylor to biting satire. In his allegorical romance *Mardi,* published in 1849 and described by one modern scholar as a "lecture" to his countrymen, Melville was said to have registered his shock and disgust with the war but if he intended his "lecture" to be effective, he badly missed the mark. The work was so thickly wrapped in allegory that with few exceptions reviewers, yearning for the straightforward narrative of *Typee* and *Omoo,* were baffled, either praising it as a "purely imaginary record of adventures" or denouncing its "grossness and utter improbabilities." In either case, none found in it a comment on the Mexican War, allegorical or otherwise.[42]

Nathaniel Hawthorne's response to the war, written four years after its conclusion, was a campaign biography of his old friend Franklin Pierce, a brigadier general of volunteers during the war and Democratic candidate for President in 1852. More interested in boosting his friend's record than in commenting on the war, Hawthorne made free use of Pierce's wartime journal and did his best to cast him in an heroic mold, no easy task but a necessary one considering that Pierce's opponent was Winfield Scott. As a loyal Democrat, Hawthorne probably supported the war, but if so there was no hint of it in his work.[43]

Three of the most popular writers of fiction in midcentury America were Henry William Herbert, George Lippard, and of course James Fenimore Cooper. To classify Cooper with Herbert and Lippard may seem bizarre and injudicious, but each touched the public's nerve in his writings, and each was in turn touched by the Mexican War. Herbert, whose prolific production defies belief, was the most varied in his talents. Born in London of aristocratic parents and educated at Eton and Cambridge, he came to America in 1831 to escape his debts. He taught

Latin and Greek, edited a literary magazine, and published his first novel in 1835. During the next twenty years, work literally poured from his pen—historical novels, poems, translations of the work of Eugène Sue and Alexandre Dumas and of the plays of Aeschylus and, under the pseudonym Frank Forester, a spate of articles and books on hunting and fishing. Herbert's fiction ranged from ancient Rome through medieval knighthood and the English Civil War to the American Revolution. "Mr. Herbert," wrote one critic, "has a quick and accurate eye for the picturesque features of the romantic Past" and "pursues the study of history with the soul of a poet." A "romancer of the old school," he was sometimes *"grandiose"* but always capable of "delineating a heroic portrait with truth."

In 1848 Williams Brothers published Herbert's excursion into the Mexican War, *Pierre, the Partisan: A Tale of the Mexican Marches.* The hero was a Natty Bumppo-type character, a "rover of the wilderness" for whom the joys and perils of forest life were dearer than "all the charms of civilized society." Pierre happened upon a unit of American dragoons somewhere in the Mexican borderland (the geography is vague), guided the soldiers out of danger, eluding "blood thirsty" Mexican lancers and "wild Camanches," rescued a beautiful maiden "of the once mighty Gothic race of Spain" from the evil designs of the lancers (he had defended her once before against drunken Texans), and finally bested the enemy in battle, dying "in the arms of love, religion, honor." Pierre was a man of many talents; with the "eye of a painter, and the imagination of a poet," he entertained his companions with tales of "wild adventure, or rude chivalry, as stirring to the soul as the high feats recorded in the old French of Froissart, or Comines."[44]

In a commentary on Charles Deas's painting of the trapper "Long Jakes," Herbert had glorified the "man of energy, and iron will, and daring spirit" and despaired of his own time when manhood seemed on the decay. The love of country had been quenched by "selfish greed and the base love of gain"; chivalry had become a "mockery on the lips of the truckling trader." Even war, Herbert wrote, was welcome if it could teach the multitude that "patriotism and glory" still existed and that mammon was not the "whole aim and intention of man's life." Presumably, Pierre was one of those "wild and dauntless spirits" who could still appreciate feelings of honor, patriotism, and chivalry, a hero straight out of the Leatherstocking mold.[45]

War in general, however, held no attraction for Herbert. "When the hounds of war and havoc are let slip," he wrote in *Pierre*, "the fiercest and most savage passions of the most fierce and untamed men are released from the restraints of society and law." "Hot animal courage" was alone regarded as a virtue and even "delicate and lovely women, vie with each other in bestowing honors and praise . . . and love itself on those whose sole title to their approbation is written in the blood of fellow beings." The war with Mexico, however, was different, if not a little ambiguous. It was not idealism alone that induced Pierre to join the fight. Memories of Mexican brutality in Texas burned deep ("Texas was *my* country," he declared). More importantly, it was "the wild spirit of adventure" that urged him on, and the belief that his presence in the field might allay "the atrocities of national animosity." The aristocratic Margarita, who fell in love with Pierre after her rescue from her own country's soldiers, breathed haughty defiance against the American invaders and vowed never to be conquered. Strong men, she declared, have always "preyed upon the substance of the weak" and mighty nations have despised the rights of small nations. Her counterpart, the wife of the dragoons officer, the "perfection of the glorious glowing womanhood of the all-conquering Anglo-Norman strain," conceded that "noble and just and wise hearts" among her countrymen questioned the justice of the war but fought to maintain their country's honor nonetheless. Besides, she asked, "are you free, Margarita?" She had heard much of the tyranny of Mexico's military rulers and of the misery and degradation of her people. Margarita rejected the notion as irrelevant, pointing out that the Mexican people had all the freedom "they are fit for." Although Herbert's biographer has characterized *Pierre, the Partisan* as "hack work to cater to the Mexican War interest," there was clearly more to it than that judgment would allow.[46]

George Lippard has been described as "America's most widely read novelist" between 1844 and 1854, a representative American who expressed widely held social, political, religious, and literary principles, "one of the most fantastic creatures in the whole American literary menagerie."[47] After giving up plans for the ministry and the law, in each case because the vocation fell short of his ideals of social justice, Lippard took up journalism and quickly became an ornament in Philadelphia's literary circle. In the early 1840s he began writing fiction and, in 1844 at the age of twenty-two, published his most successful (and sensational) novel, *The Quaker City; or, The Monks of Monk Hall,* a Gothic exposé of urban life in Philadelphia modeled on Eugène Sue's *Mysteries of Paris.* The book sold 60,000 copies within a year and appeared in twenty-seven editions within five years. Skirting the edge of mid-19th-century decency and convention in his discussion of sex, seduction, and violence, Lippard cried out against the decline of republican principles and the betrayal of the American Revolution by the power of wealth and avarice.[48]

With long dark curls, blue-velvet coat, sword-cane, and exaggeratedly romantic air, Lippard's appearance matched the eccentricity of his writing. Critics were not always kind. A writer in *Holden's Magazine* found his style sophomoric and the Gothic trappings of his novels too much to bear. "Murder, incest, fraud, and superstition, are materials too horrible . . . even for a yellow covered romance." Too much of his writing, complained the *New York Tribune,* seemed to be written "in the highest state of unhealthy excitement." On the other hand, Theodore Parker found traces of "superior abilities" in Lippard's outrage against the "wrongs of the world."[49]

While his novel of urban horrors attracted most of the attention, Lippard was also moved by the Past—"the glory and gloom of the age of chivalry" and the American Revolution—if only to recall America to the promise of its birth. "To love chivalry, genius, greatness, fills the heart with fire," he wrote, "and lifts the soul into a purer light." He promised to "wander forth into the awful shadows of the Past," to "evoke the spirits of that giant time" against the fraud and imbecility of his own time. In 1846 he published his most successful Revolutionary War novel, *Blanche of Brandywine,* and in the following year, *Washington and His Generals: or, Legends of the Revolution,* which he described as an effort to "embody the scenes of the Past" and to bring forth "some of the brightest gleams of poetry and romance, that illumine our history." Recognizing a link between the Revolution and the conflict with Mexico, Lippard ended the Washington book with an announcement that he would soon bring out a companion volume on the Mexican War.[50]

Legends of Mexico: The Battles of Taylor (1847) was to be the first in a series that would encompass "ancient and modern, from the era of Scott and Taylor, back through the mists of ages, to Cortez and Montezuma." A "rhapsody on the romance of war," the work contained only a thin veneer of historical fact. "A legend," Lippard wrote, "is a history in its details and delicate tints, with the bloom and dew yet fresh upon it, history told to us, in the language of passion, of poetry, of home!" Although the book was advertised, incredibly, as a "faithful history" of the war, it revealed Lippard's inability to distinguish between history and romance more than anything else.

The *Legends of Mexico* (from Palo Alto to Buena Vista) was marked by all the Gothic devices that identified his work—voluptuous Mexican maidens, ghostly apparitions, seduction, murder, and so on. The characters were drawn in extravagant contrast. The chivalric American soldiers, displaying generosity to the vanquished foe and capturing the hearts of the *señoritas,* confront "crouching rancheros," their dark eyes shining with the lust of plunder, "who cut a throat to give them appetite." The volunteers—hardy mechanics, sturdy mountaineers, pale students, and tanned farmers—meet the flower of Mexican chivalry, the fabled lancers in their gilt buttons and spangles, glittering helmets and brightly colored plumes; the plain old man in the faded brown coat confers with his officers before a small simple tent, while his Mexican counterpart resides in a pavilion ablaze with Oriental magnificence, surrounded by silken curtains, drinking champagne. America's star-studded banner of Freedom, shedding its light over the benighted land, is contrasted with the "Superstition, Ignorance and Crime" symbolized in Mexico's tri-colored flag.[51]

Four years before, Lippard had expounded on war in general and it is evident he saw the Mexican War in the same light:

War is the great prompter of high deeds, the originator of noble impulses and generous actions. War is the great corrector of civil sloth, servile luxury, and national licentiousness . . . Luxury stalks around in the apparel of broadcloth; temples of magnificence are peopled by an enervated people; dissipation shatters the lives of the young, and avarice curses the souls of the aged. . . . War tries the mettle of men's souls. . . . War requires nerve, courage, fortitude. War rouses up all that is noble or good in man's nature. . . . There is sublimity in battle.

The Mexican War was a new Crusade that "aroused a People into arms, and startled Europe, its Kings and Slaves, into shuddering awe." It was the extension of the American Revolution, decreed by God and sanctified by the blood of the patriot fathers to lead the nation to higher purposes, possess the continent, drive out "all shreds" of monarchy, and build "the Altar, sacred to the BROTHERHOOD OF MAN." Like Herbert, Lippard saw the war as a cathartic, cleansing America of "civil sloth" and "servile luxury."[52]

George Lippard was not finished yet. In 1848 he published a Mexican War novel, *'Bel of Prairie Eden*, a story that moved from the "wild prairie" of Texas to Scott's landing at Vera Cruz and finally to Philadelphia for its climactic scenes. Again Lippard employed the language of spooky Gothic imagery and vivid sexuality. The landing of Scott's army was recounted in dramatic detail, with a flashback to the landing of Cortez 300 years before. Planted in the sands by the chivalric General Worth, the "Banner of the Continent" announced: "There is a doom upon the land, the hardy children of the North are here."[53]

Lippard was hardly typical of midcentury writers, although his popularity would suggest that his views appealed to many Americans. His romantic extravagance, sentimentality, and sensation outdid even the novelette writers. In his view of the Mexican War as an antidote to decline in civic virtue, honor, and public morality, however, Lippard was far from unique. The "crusade," he believed, was double-faceted, bearing on the one hand the promise of America's revolutionary mission and on the other the redemptive qualities needed to awaken Americans from the sleep of avarice and dissipation.

George Lippard dedicated his first Revolutionary War romance to James Fenimore Cooper, but so far as is known the two men never met. Like Lippard, Cooper looked favorably, if with much less bombast, on the Mexican War. His interest was flavored by a lifelong devotion to a strong navy and to a well-developed (and romantic) doctrine of maritime nationalism, both offshoots of his own early experience as a midshipman. By the late 1840s Cooper was nearing the end of his career; his last works were not equal to his reputation, and critics sadly noted their decline in quality. F.D. Huntington felt not only that Cooper's talent had degenerated but that he also seemed "strangely determined to persevere in forfeiting his title to fame." While Cooper's novels no longer met the standard established in his early work, his faith in America, its institutions and its mission remained vital, shaken only by the fear that republicanism was being eroded by forces that turned people away from civic responsibility and patriotism. The Mexican War, according to one scholar, apparently "renewed, in part, his confidence in the spiritual strength and unity of the Republic."[54]

Writing in the *Democratic Review* in 1842, Cooper asserted, "We are not the advocates of war, except in cases in which the nation is clearly right." An appeal to war could be justified only if it was sustained by moral principles; policy alone as an excuse for fighting was not sufficient. Still, he continued, "we firmly believe that the dignity of a nation is inseparable from its policy, and we see an intimate connexion between the maintenance of this dignity and the maintenance of its rights." Cooper was writing with reference to a possible war between the United States and Great Britain, but the sentiment also suggested a basis for his support of the Mexican War. As early as the summer of 1845, he expected a war with Mexico over Texas that would force the United States to "act on the defensive." The conflict might have been averted, he felt, by buying Mexico off: "Money would have done it, and money we have and might so easily have paid." By 1845, however, that alternative was no longer available. Once the war began, he supported it enthusiastically. "The nation is aroused, and goes into it, with great good will," he observed, with only some Whigs opposing it because of the popularity it would give to the Democratic administration. He later believed that the Whig opposition had needlessly prolonged the war.

Cooper's support of the Mexican War did not mean he was uncritical of the way it was carried out. "I do not like the management of the war," he wrote early in 1847. It had been pressed too fast for the good of economy, "the lives of our people" and "the great ends of the war." The volunteer system in which Americans took such pride had in fact not proven adequate to the task; to employ volunteers in a "war of invasion" was a "blunder." By increasing the size of the regular army and delaying the invasion until a more healthful season "all that has been done could have been done at half the cost, in a fourth of the time, with a loss of life scarce worth mentioning." Nevertheless, Cooper expressed his admiration for the nation's fighting men, both regulars and volunteers, and voiced the common view that the character of the Mexican soldier could not equal that of the American. "As for fighting," he commented, "we are too much for any of the Spanish race, beyond a question." The volunteers could easily "overmatch the regulars of Mexico" but, he added, the "blackguards would waste more than they consumed, and march only when they were ready."[55]

America's mission in Mexico, Cooper believed, was to break the "crust" that enclosed that country in bigotry and ignorance, and he hoped that the war would, in the long run, bring the "inestimable blessings of real liberty" to the Mexican people. The war's meaning for the United States was beyond argument. The nation, he wrote in an introduction to a new edition of *The Spy*, had passed from the "gristle into the bone"; the war was a giant moral stride in America's progress "toward real independence and high political influence." The guns that thundered in the valley of the Aztecs found their echoes in the revolutions that convulsed Europe.[56]

Cooper was asked to write a naval history of the Mexican War, a companion volume to his *History of the Navy of the United States of America* (1839, revised 1847) and later was urged to write a biography of General Stephen Watts Kearny, to whom his wife was related. Neither received his serious consideration. He was, however, disappointed that the navy did not play a greater role in the war. He followed the movements of the navy closely and corresponded with naval officers, but he could never overcome the realization that the war would be decided on land and that the glory of victory would go to the army. Mexico's navy, he knew, was of no consequence, but he found it inexplicable that Mexico did not fit out privateers to prey upon American commerce. Cooper was not alone. Fears were expressed early in the war, especially in commercial circles, that American vessels would be easy victims of Mexican raiders. The Paredes government issued regulations in the summer of 1846 that would have encouraged privateering operations had they not been ignored. In May 1847 an American schooner carrying a cargo of coffee from Puerto Rico to Trieste was captured by a Mexican privateer in the Mediterranean Sea and taken to Barcelona. Spanish authorities immediately impounded the Mexican vessel, arrested its crew on charges of piracy, and returned the schooner to its owners. It was the only privateering incident to receive much publicity during the war.[57]

Cooper partially overcame his disappointment by writing a Mexican War novel in which the navy played an important role. *Jack Tier; or, The Florida Reef* was the only one of Cooper's novels to be serialized before its publication as a book, appearing in *Graham's Magazine* between November 1846 and March 1848 under the title "The Islets of the Gulf; or, Rose Budd." Graham paid Cooper $1800 for the story, although he later grumbled that the money "might as well have been thrown into the sea" for it brought him no new subscribers. For his characters and incidents, Cooper borrowed heavily from his earlier works, but what set *Jack Tier* apart from those works was its realism. Captain Spike, an aging, coarse, and brutish master of an old and decaying ship, sails from New York with a cargo of flour. What is not immediately known is that Spike is engaged in a treasonable enterprise; at a prearranged rendezvous, the ship will be sold to a Mexican to be converted into a privateer that will plunder American merchant vessels. The flour barrels in actuality contain gunpowder to be smuggled into Mexico for use against the Americans.

In contrast to the unsavory character of the traitorous American ship captain, the Mexican to whom the ship is to be delivered is a gentleman, well-bred, tactful, humane, and considerate. The motives of the former were "of the lowest and most grovelling nature"; those of the latter, earnestly engaged in what he believed to be the cause of his country, were of the highest nature. Cooper's attitude toward the war was revealed in the stilted dialogue between the romantic hero, Harry Mulford, second in command to Captain Spike but unaware of the captain's nefarious plan, and the Mexican *don*, Señor Montefalderon. My country, Mulford reminded the Mexican, "is more powerful than yours . . . and in this it has been more favored of God. You have suffered from ambitious rulers, and from military rule, while we have been advancing under the arts of peace, favored by a most beneficent Providence." But even Mexico, Cooper added in one of his asides, for all her "punic faith, instability, military oppression, and political revolution" had redeeming qualities, not the least of which was that "chivalrous courtesy" found among the descendants of Old Spain. Montefalderon, without demeaning his own patriotism, conceded American superiority. He was surprised at the swiftness of the American victories and by the warlike qualities of the American soldiers. "Little had he imagined," wrote Cooper,

> that the small, widely-spread body of regulars . . . scattered along frontiers of a thousand leagues in extent, could, at the beck of the government swell into legions of invaders, . . . formidable alike for their energy, their bravery, their readiness in the use of arms, and their numbers. He saw what is perhaps justly called the boasting of the American character, vindicated by their exploits . . . He had himself, though anticipating evil, been astounded by the suddenness and magnitude of their conquests, which in a few short months . . . had overrun regions larger in extent than many ancient empires. All this had been done, too, not by disorderly and barbarous hordes, seeking in other lands the abundance that was wanting at home; but with system and regularity, by men who had turned the plowshare into the sword for the occasion, quitting abundance to encounter fatigue, famine, and danger.

Needless to say, Captain Spike's treason was frustrated by the U.S. Navy, his ship foundered on the Florida reef, and Spike expired, hurling curses, blasphemy, and defiance.[58]

Jack Tier was serialized in England simultaneously with its appearance in *Graham's*, and it was published as a book in London at the same time as the American edition, under the title *Captain Spike; or, The Islets of the Gulf*. The work did little for Cooper's reputation. The story's departure from his earlier idealization of nautical life, and the realistic, unromantic turns of the plot discouraged some reviewers. Its charm, according to the *Literary World*, was in its narrative and description, rather than in its "delineations of human character." While the reviewer felt that Cooper's fame would ensure him a multitude of readers, he would need "all the *prestige* of that fame to insure it a good-natured reception from the public." As a statement of Cooper's attitude toward the Mexican War, however, it was important; inasmuch as Cooper's writings were (and are) regarded as a faithful reflection of his own time, *Jack Tier* mirrored the feelings of many Americans.[59]

CHAPTER 8

Poetry and the Popular Arts

The war with Mexico entered the stream of American popular thought and activity in a variety of ways, and one indicator of its importance was the depth to which it penetrated the national psyche. It is not surprising that it should have done so. The war was not a long one—sixteen months after it began, the fighting ended—but it was unique in American experience and, as most people viewed it, gloriously triumphant in its course and outcome. No event in the nation's history had been so widely reported or become so well known to the people. The war was brought into American homes as no other episode ever had; in those states in which large numbers of volunteers were recruited popular involvement in the conflict was even more direct. "There are few persons," suggested Hunt's *Merchants' Magazine,* "who have not had some friend or relative engaged in the [war's] stirring scenes."[1] The names of Mexican battlefields, if they didn't quite become household words (as some thought they would), nevertheless became common to print and conversation. Americans felt a keen interest not only in the progress of their fighting men but also in the strange land in which their men fought. The soldiers' letters, diaries, and published accounts went far to satisfy both concerns.

The soldiers, however, brought back more than tales of military adventure and foreign travel. Exposed to a way of life different from their own, they returned with an awareness of the diversity of civilization. Those at home were anxious to share their perceptions, to experience Mexico even though at secondhand. Interest in America's southern neighbor, already mounting before the war, assumed new meaning with the war, and Americans now sought that meaning through the various forms of popular expression, in their literature, art, music and entertainment. Mexico and the Mexican War, wrote one critic in November 1847, "forms the attractive topic for Historian, Dramatist, and Romancer."[2]

The Mexican experience quickly marked American life and behavior. Returning soldiers sported "immense moustachios" and set a new style of facial adornment among those who wished to be up-to-date. "The passion for hair on the face," complained one writer, "always is consequent on a war" but, he added, men who never saw a shot fired were now "parading a moustache in every thoroughfare throughout the country." The same writer predicted a similar influence on men's dress, following the appearance of some of the returned soldiers, and expected to see the ranchero's striped blanket, broad-brimmed hat, and cow-hide boots on America's city streets. Cloth caps and brown-striped green trousers, in imitation of the dress of Mexican soldiers, were already "much in vogue." For the ladies, *Godey's* carried illustrations of the fashions worn by Mexican women. Of a different sort was the popularity among smokers of the Mexican "cigarrito," described by one soldier as a little cigar made of finely cut tobacco and wrapped in thin cornhusk or paper. Although cigarettes were already known from earlier contacts in the Santa Fe trade and Texas, they were no longer identified only with the frontier; on the contrary, urbanites (men, not women) regarded them as exotic and therefore a badge of sophistication.[3]

The Mexican War brought many more Spanish words and phrases into American speech, a trend that had begun earlier when travelers, traders, and colonists first penetrated the Spanish and then Mexican borderlands. Soldiers used Spanish words liberally in their writing, with definitions often added for those back home. Such words as *adobe, ranchero, chaparral, sombrero, lasso, corral, hacienda, peon, calaboose, fandango,* and *patio* (the list could go on) came into common use. Many of the words had entered the language earlier, but their use was either rare or regional. In 1848, John Russell Bartlett, New York bookseller, historian, and theologian, included the more common Spanish words in his *Dictionary of Americanisms* and credited their popularity to the war. For example, Bartlett wrote that the words *rancho* and *chaparral* "have lately become familiar to us, in consequence of the present unhappy war with Mexico."[4] Many of the same words, with a few not found in Bartlett, were listed in the 1847 edition of Webster's *Dictionary*. The Mexican War soldier, adopting the words of the enemy, played an unwitting part in shaping the American idiom.

Bartlett found further impact on the language in the large number of place-names that commemorated the war's battles and leaders. "Now the Mexican War is over," he wrote, "we shall doubtless have a large fund of names to use in our newly acquired territories, and the new States at the West." The generals of the Revolution would be passed over, and "the span-new heroes of this war will be handed down to the admiration of posterity in the metamorphosed shape of cities, towns, and villages, yet to come into existence." In the second edition of his *Dictionary of Americanisms* (1859), he enumerated eighteen Buena Vistas, sixteen Montereys, nine Palo Altos, and two Resacas, in addition to a host of Taylors and Taylorvilles, Worths and Worthvilles, Pierce and Piercevilles, and Polks and Polkvilles.[5] Iowa became a state in 1846, the year the war began, and may hold the record for Mexican War place-names (with such counties as Polk, Taylor, Worth, Scott, Ringgold, Palo Alto, Buena Vista, and Cerro Gordo), but older states as well, especially those that supplied large numbers of volunteers, were not far behind. Ships that plied the Mississippi bore the names of war heroes and battles, as did vessels launched in eastern shipyards. "Old Rough and Ready takes wonderfully in New England," reported the *New York Herald*. "We shall soon have quite a fleet of General Taylors, Palo Alto, Old Rough and Ready, Resaca de la Palma, Rio Grande . . . and who has a better right than the Americans to these bright and brilliant names!"[6]

Newspaper advertisers used the war to attract notice to their merchandise. Taylor's popularity and his catchy nickname helped sell horseradish sauce, straw hats, and shoes. Readers whose eyes caught the words "War with Mexico" in bold type were informed that "as our armies are victorious over the Mexicans so Dr. LeRoy's Sarsaparilla and Wild Cherry Pills are achieving victory . . . over disease and death."[7] Items from books to camp equipment were touted as war-related and hence worthy of the consumer's attention.

Americans were reminded of their war with Mexico at virtually every turn. Through the reports of newspaper correspondents and the soldiers' letters and campaign accounts, they were able to share the glories and vicissitudes of the conflict and to experience the sights and sounds of that alien land. But it was in the field of popular entertainment that the drama and romance of the war was brought home to the people. The purveyors of popular culture—on the stage, in lithographs and paintings, in the patriotic strains of music and the strident verses of poetry, and in the plots and constructs of sensational "yellow-covered" fiction—identified those elements of drama and romance and made them available to the public in terms that could not be misunderstood.

Barely a month after the war began, a New York newspaper reported that a "poetical mania" was sweeping the land. America's "aspiring poetical geniuses" were "throwing into rhyme every thing connected with the war." Mounting Pegasus, as Thomas Bangs Thorpe put it, the rhymesters poured their sentiments into "*Rough* and Ready" poetry, in verses that jolted the mind "like a stage fiercely drawn across a cordway road." It was an age of poetry, a time when poems filled the columns of newspapers and magazines, of giftbook annuals and countless volumes issued by profit-minded publishers. New books of poetry were announced daily, and it was assumed that their publishers knew they would be bought and read. Never before, commented *Holden's Maga-*

zine, had poets been so honored and poetry so much in request. "There is a love of poetry in the age, if there is not the power of poetry in the people." The Mexican War added a new dimension to this poetic effusion; all the elements of moral drama, romantic pathos, and gushing sentimentality were there—the great clashes between rival armies, overpowering scenery, individual heroism and sacrifice, the separation of loved ones and homesickness, the glory of death on the battlefield and the sorrow it left behind, patriotism and selfless devotion to the country's ideals.

In a country where striding across the Rocky Mountains or "blowing it off" in a Presidential election or laying iron rails across a thousand miles of prairie seemed commonplace, commented the *Literary World,* the need was not for more energy and passion but for taste and elegance of sentiment. Thus the mission of poetry in America must be to "temper mental excitement already existing, with the more genial graces of sentiment," to mellow and refine that "hard self-seeking intellectuality" that tended ever closer to the "most grovelling materialism." Employing the metaphor of military life, the writer contended that the poet's role was not as a bugler sounding the charge but as a musician in the evening bivouac, keeping alive the memory of "some civil graces in the great moving camp." The American muse was not expected to create another *Iliad,* for the whole country was "engaged in acting an Epic." Written in 1847, when America's legions were contesting the enemy in the Valley of Mexico, the metaphor seemed particularly apt. Not all Americans, however, were persuaded that the "true mission of American Musehood" was limited to filling the need for taste and feeling, elegance of sentiment and refinement of expression. To rouse the "torpid soul" from its lethargy, to "crumble the crust of slavish conventionalism," required the call of freedom and the recollection of heroic ages. Either way, the Mexican War supplied the impetus for an outpouring of popular poetry during America's midcentury years.[8]

Although the *Literary World* looked for no new *Iliad* to flow from the poets' pens, some would-be Homers made the attempt to celebrate the Mexican War in grand style. In late 1849, *Knickerbocker* announced a work in progress by an unnamed poet to be entitled *The Mexiad: An Epic in Five Cantos,* but this masterpiece apparently never saw the light of day. Three years later (epic poetry was clearly not a thing of the moment), Sheppard M. Ashe published *Monterey Conquered: A Fragment from La Gran Quivera; or, Rome Unmasked* (1852), a poem in seven cantos that glorified the bravery of Tennessee volunteers in the campaign against Monterey, with strong anti-Catholic overtones. The poet's intention was "to sing his country—her political and religious destiny— her arms and institutions—her unaffected manners, and moral worth," a theme he found so "lofty and difficult" as to be almost "impracticable in a commercial and utilitarian age." The war was again viewed as an appropriate response to an age gone awry, the war's opponents especially singled out as "the base of a degenerate age." The romantic ancestry of Ashe's effort was established by his use of classical and medieval names for the poem's characters: the Tennessee volunteer and his sweetheart were Lycidas and Lavinia, Polk was Augustus, Taylor (when he was not hailed as the "son of Washington") was Godfrey, and so on.

Eight years later, William F. Smith's *Guadaloupe: A Tale of Love and War* (1860) appeared, published anonymously by "One Who Served in the Campaign of 1846-7, in the Late War with Mexico." It was only the first canto of a much longer project but no more were published, probably because of its lack of success. Introduced by a quotation from Byron's *Don Juan,* the 273 stanzas were intended to fill a vacuum in the history of the Mexican War. "Historians," Smith wrote,

> may give us very exact and edifying accounts of the origin and progress of a war;—Partizans, in their eternal wranglings, may give us exaggerated and startling accounts of its glories, its horrors and its cost, and Statesmen may enlighten us as to its remote or immediate affects upon the welfare and destiny of the Nation;—but who will draw a faithful picture of the heroism, the dangers, the privations, the toils, sacrifices, sufferings and triumphs of the actors, if the poet and the painter decline the task?

Only the poet and painter, he contended, could express the "ardor of the hero," the impulsive spirit of battle, the "headlong daring" and cool determination of the combatants; in short, only they could really impart "the living soul of war." Opaque, digressive and obviously incomplete, the poem focused on the opening of the war and the call to arms:

> There was no lack of heroes, and the world
>   Saw, with incredulous wonder and surprise
> That war's dread bolts could be as deftly hurl'd
>   By freemen, conscious of their liberties,
> As by a host, above whose ranks unfurl'd
>   Th' emblazonry of Princes flaunts the skies,
> And that a pure Democracy may own
> A power as great as that which guards a throne.

As a poem, *Guadaloupe* probably deserved its fate.[9]

Neither more skillful nor more lasting was the work of William C. Falkner, great-grandfather of the novelist William Faulkner and one of Mississippi's earliest volunteers. The state's quota was oversubscribed, and Falkner's company was sent home, to the bitter disappointment of the men. In November 1846 a second call for volunteers was issued, and this time Falkner's unit (in which he had been elected first lieutenant) was accepted and incorporated in the Second Mississippi Regiment. The first regiment, the famed Mississippi Rifles commanded by Jefferson Davis, had fought gloriously at Monterey and Buena Vista and came home heaped with honors. In contrast, Falkner's regiment arrived in Mexico too late to fight; for seven months, the men combatted only disease and boredom as occupation troops in Monterey.

In 1851 Falkner left his hometown of Ripley, Mississippi, after being acquitted by two successive juries for the murder of two men, and moved to Cincinnati, where he wrote *The Siege of Monterey*. The poem, 493 stanzas (about 4000 lines) written in a "dog-trot rhythm," has been described as "in all probability the strangest poetical composition in the language." Military leaders from Zachary Taylor on down are portrayed as "Homeric heroes," and the whole is couched in such exaggerated classical analogy that Falkner's seriousness and sincerity might be questioned. Resentment against the glories won by the Mississippi Rifles was only thinly veiled. The volunteers, led by "Jeff the Bold," career across the battlefield in chariots, carrying shields and swords and hurling spears; blood and gore abound and the piles of corpses grow higher and higher. A love story, involving a Mexican girl (who disguises herself as a soldier) and her lover, one of Monterey's defenders, was woven through the account of desperate combat and heroic engagements. Falkner published the poem at his own expense and promised another if this one did well enough to pay the printing bill. It did not. The *Siege of Monterey* was followed, not by a poem, but by a work of fiction, *The Spanish Heroine; A Tale of War and Love. Scenes Laid in Mexico,* a stock romance in which the Battle of Buena Vista played a small part.[10]

At a time when writing poetry was a popular literary pastime, when poetry belonged to the "amateurs," it was not surprising that poets should be found among the war's combatants. While not achieving the level of war poetry in later conflicts, the Civil War, for example, or more obviously, the First World War, the Mexican War soldier-poet did manage to convey an impression, albeit often highly romanticized, of what it was like to be far from home and loved ones, fighting an unfamiliar enemy in an alien land. Most of the soldier-poets, unlike their counterparts in later conflicts, celebrated the battles in which they fought in stridently patriotic language, while the long periods of inactivity and tedium that separated the engagements inspired poetry of a nostalgic even sorrowful mood. Although the quality falls short of standards in later wars, the poems that flowed from the soldiers' pens were heartfelt and sincere. "Hastily written and created for the moment," commented the *Spirit of the Times*, which published much of the poetry, "yet they belong to the army and the age, and . . . should be preserved with the many evidences we have of the spirit and prowess of those who have gone before us."

Albert Pike, captain in the Arkansas cavalry, had written a number of southwestern sketches before the war, but it was his poem "Buena Vista" that caught fire. Written on the battlefield almost before the guns had cooled, the poem celebrated the drama, heroism, and sacrifice of the volunteers, recounting the ebbs and flows of the battle until the final moment of victory. "And thus, on Buena Vista's heights, a long day's work was done . . . And still our glorious banner waves unstained by flight or shame, And the Mexicans among their hills still tremble at our name." George Washington Cutter, a captain in the Second Kentucky Regiment at Buena Vista, had been about to publish his first volume of poetry when he volunteered. With his regiment in the thick of the battle, Cutter assisted the mortally wounded Henry Clay, Jr., at risk to his own life. Following the battle, he penned his "Buena Vista" on the head of a cartridge keg "amidst the confusion of a victorious army." With a sensitive eye to the grandeur of the scenery which surrounded the death and destruction, he found a striking contrast between the excitement of the battle and the sorrow that followed, when the field was shrouded by "sulphur vapors" and the "wounded and dying O'er all thy hills were strewn."[11]

Captain George W. Patten of the Second Infantry Regiment, already known for poems he wrote during the Florida war, greeted the opening of the war with "The Gathering" ("Rally! ye free-born men Arm! with the sword!") and in "Landing at Vera Cruz, March 9, 1847," he captured the moment when the "starry banner" was raised and "our eagle" ruled the "Aztec sky." Arthur T. Lee, lieutenant in the Eighth Infantry, published his "Ballads of the Army" in the *Spirit of the Times,* and Henry Kirby Benner's "Ballads of the Campaign in Mexico" appeared in *Graham's Magazine,* each poem embellished by an elegant battle-engraving.[12]

The war poetry of those who stayed at home hardly differed from the productions of the soldier-poets. The patriotism of the volunteers who set aside their civilian pursuits to answer their country's call and the sadness of those they left behind were perhaps given more emphasis, and, if possible, the sentiments expressed were more openly nationalistic. As the number of casualties increased and as the bodies of those who fell were returned to their communities, memorial odes appeared in the press, contemplating death and the glory of dying for one's country. The men were all heroes, their leaders gallant and brave, and their places in the nation's history deserved and secure.

The justice of the war, the patience America had shown toward an untrustworthy neighbor, the treachery of the Mexican foe, and the need for patriotic Americans to vindicate the nation's honor were all eloquently preached in spirited poetical terms. "The MEXICAN!— where is the heart so dead to pride and shame, As not to feel a patriot's scorn at mention of that name?" asked an anonymous poet in May 1846. "Our cause is just and righteous—meet it with dauntless brow— And may there be no recreant soul to fail or falter now." Lydia Jane Pierson, more accustomed to writing such poems as "To the Blue Violet" for ladies' magazines, was so fired with indignation by Mexico's challenge of Taylor's presence on the Rio Grande that she dashed off several animated stanzas descriptively titled "On the Proposition to Surrender to Mexican Barbarity and Tyranny the Land Between the Nueces and the Rio Grande." Her response echoed that of Taylor himself, an *"emphatic NO!!"* America's mission and responsibility in the crisis were extolled in countless paeans to "Our Country" and to the "Banner of Freedom" whose stripes and stars served "as a beacon for the free, To point the way to liberty!"[13]

The call for volunteers recalled the "glorious days of SEVENTY-SIX" and Americans were urged to answer the summons like "True heirs of sires of '76." "Shall we shame our fathers?" asked poet, novelist and editor Thomas Dunn English. "To the battle then, my countrymen . . . Arouse and arm and onward swarm." Opponents of the war received rough treatment at the hands of the poets. Whig Senator Thomas Corwin, whose denunciation of the war distressed soldiers and civilians alike, was advised by one embarrassed Ohioan to go to Mexico but with different intent: "Traitor to thy country—go! Haste thee quick to Mexico!"[14]

From the first engagement at Palo Alto to the actions in the Valley of Mexico, the dramatic encounters on Mexico's alien ground provided the poets with their most popular themes. Some of the contributions were too sanguinary for the public's fastidious tastes. *Knickerbocker* rejected a poem on Resaca de la Palma because it was "revolting." "It is not minutely-described horrors that convey the most forcible pictures of a battle-field," the editor advised. "Accessories, naturally cited, are more effective," by which he meant that the blood and gore were best left to the imagination. There were so many poems entitled "Monterey," complained another editor, that it was difficult to keep them apart, but even Monterey was soon eclipsed by Buena Vista, the most celebrated battle of the war. Vera Cruz, Cerro Gordo, Contreras, Churubusco, and Chapultepec all found their bards. One of the widely read poets of the day, Alfred B. Street, celebrated "The Day of the Three Fights," a long narrative poem of a volunteer who survived Contreras and Churubusco, returned to Puebla, and there claimed his Mexican sweetheart for his bride. The volunteers fought as knights on a medieval field—"Bugles sounding, armor clashing, Kindled with the charger's neigh"—and the verses were thick with chivalry. The heroes were given their romantic due in William H. C. Hosmer's tribute to Captain May at Resaca de la Palma:

> Twine garlands for our Cavalier,
> The gallant Captain May!
> A knight without reproach, or fear—
> A Bayard in the fray!

The smoke and dust, the cannon's roar, the reddening earth, filled the poetry columns of the popular press. The God of Battles was repeatedly invoked, and the spirit of America's revolutionary legacy perched on the country's guns.[15]

The prayer of a young lady for the safety of her soldier-brother and the plaintive words of D. W. Belisle's "The Dying Soldier to His Mother" were poetic reminders of the dangers faced by the volunteers. The anonymous "Written on Hearing of the Battle of Buena Vista" focused not on the gallantry of the soldiers but rather on "the mother's moaning deep, The orphan's wail, the wife's low sob." Many more soldiers died of sickness and disease than died in battle, but their deaths seemed less noble, or at least more difficult to glorify poetically. An exception was the tribute to "The Dead at Lobos," which urged the nation to provide a "little place on memory's scroll of gold" for those who never made it to the battlefield. The number of poems dedicated to the deaths of individuals was legion, especially if an aura of heroism had gathered about the fallen soldier. The poetry linked the local community with the larger struggle, commemorating its contribution to the war by eulogizing its citizen-soldiers. Ranging from the "Lines, On the Death of Col. Pierce M. Butler" by Charleston's poet Paul Hamilton Hayne (later to achieve renown as a poet of the Confederacy) to "Captain Taggart's Dying Words" by an anonymous Indianan, the tributes mirrored popular attitudes toward heroism, death, and patriotism.[16]

Mexican War poets were for the most part individuals whose names and identities have been lost, or like Park Benjamin, Alfred Street, William H. C. Hosmer and Thomas Dunn English, they were individuals whose reputations were greater in their own day than in ours. An exception was William Gilmore Simms, the South's most popular literary figure. Simms had been attracted to Spanish and Mexican historical themes early in his career and as a young man wrote at least two plays and several novels with Spanish settings. Not only did he read widely on the subject but he also maintained close contact with like-minded individuals, including Robert Montgomery Bird (whom he hoped to emulate), Joel R. Poinsett, and Waddy Thompson (fellow South Carolinians who had served as ministers to Mexico), and the historian Brantz Mayer. Closely identified in the 1840s with literary nationalism, Simms was a steadfast proponent of a distinctively American literature that would breathe the democratic spirit of the age and encourage patriotism in the people.

Simms supported the war with Mexico from the beginning, viewing it as necessary to America's progress and to the security of the South. It must be, he wrote in 1847, "a war of conquest." Americans who saw the war in deepening romantic hues drew encouragement from Simms, for he reminded them of the importance of chivalry and knightly virtue, especially in his biography of the Chevalier Bayard and his collection of poems *Areytos: or, Songs of the South* (in which *Godey's* found the "true, loyal feelings of the American heart").

In July 1848, the return of South Carolina's volunteer regiment was

celebrated in Charleston, and Simms honored the event with a collection of verses, *Lays of the Palmetto: A Tribute to the South Carolina Regiment, in the War with Mexico.* "These songs," Simms wrote, "are almost
improvisations, the outpourings of a full heart, exulting in the valor
and the worth, and lamenting the misfortunes and losses, of the gallant
regiment whose career they seek to honor." Simms was almost apolo-
getic for their quality: "They may be rude, but they are earnest; the
lyre of the poet may be wanting, but the feeling, which it sought to
declare, can suffer from no reproach." The poems carry the regiment
from the initial call to arms through the battles of Contreras, Churubusco, and Chapultepec, where the soldiers fought with distinction.
The analogy with the Revolutionary War was drawn throughout; the
volunteers carry forward the legacy left by such heroes as Moultrie,
Marion, and Sumter. "We've a right from ancient valor," insisted the
regiment's commander, "To be first in ranks of danger." The poems
were laced with the chivalric ideal and the valor of knights, and full
play was given to Simms's convictions of racial superiority over the
"mongrel Mexicans." The glory, however, had not been won without
cost. Simms mourned the deaths of South Carolina's sons; those who
returned were "wan and few," relics of the proud youthful band that
had marched off to face the "Mexic lance." The verses seem crude in
comparison with Simms's other work, which may account for their
omission from later collections of his poetry.[17]

Charles Fenno Hoffman, poet, novelist, and editor, was, like Simms,
a persistent advocate of an American national literature. A concern for
the American scene, both in its historical and natural aspects, pervaded
his work, and it was no doubt this "ardent love of Americanism in art
and letters" that brought him a popular reputation and the admiration
of his fellow literati. He was a "sterling republican" whose affection for
his country was clearly visible in his writing. In 1845 Hoffman was
among those appointed to the New-York Historical Society's committee
to select a new national name for the United States. His influence on
literary development was enhanced by a series of editorships, from
Knickerbocker in 1833 to the *Literary World* in 1847. His work exhibited
strong romantic influences (reminding some critics of Rousseau and
Tom Moore) with a liberal dash of heroism and chivalry.

Hoffman did not have a great deal to say about the Mexican War but
what he did write made a pronounced impression. His poem "Monterey," written in November 1846, was one of the most popular of
Mexican War poems, depicting in six brief stanzas the proud spirit of
the volunteers, their steadfast courage in the face of danger and death,
their steady determination against overwhelming odds, and the glory
that lingered over the graves of those who fell.

> We were not many—we who stood
> Before the iron sleet that day—

> Yet many a gallant spirit would
> Give half his years if he then could
> Have been with us at Monterey.

Romantic heroism and patriotic pride also appeared in Hoffman's "The Men of Churubusco," written almost a year later. He was not a great poet but he was a popular one. "His verses linger in the ear," wrote one critic, because of "their light, common-place, *popular* nature."[18]

Hoffman was also responsible for at least two poems that made the rounds of the press purportedly written by "the popular Mexican poet," Don Jose Maria Joacquin de Ho Axce de Saltillo. "Rio Bravo, A Mexican Lament" and "The Field of Buena Vista" provided readers with a Mexican perspective on the battles. Hoffman claimed to have discovered and translated the poems but in fact they were the work of Hoffman's own pen. Their true identity was revealed when the *Literary World*, which Hoffman edited at the time, pointed out that "Ho Axce" in the poet's name was to be read "Hoax," but this revelation did not appear until after the authorship of the poetry had been taken seriously by other editors. The poems credited American arms with superiority and bemoaned the example set by the poet's "inglorious countrymen." The Mexican defeats at Palo Alto and Resaca de la Palma were compared with "the field of Roncesvalles" where was "Sealed the fate of many a knight!" At Buena Vista the "proud Aztec" met the "brave Alleghan" but quailed before the stars and stripes ("those fearful meteor-bars") and the awesome war-cry of "Old Zack."[19]

A recent study has insisted that Hoffman's "Ho Axce" verses were "daring" and an "invitation to the charge of treason." There was nothing so melodramatic about them; to suggest that Hoffman's authorship bordered on the treasonable is to ignore the range of popular reaction to the war. In fact Hoffman's lines assumed the popular belief that Mexico's soldiers were inferior to the American volunteers, and the latter emerge as more glorious and heroic in their triumphs than before. It was not uncommon for poets to write from a Mexican perspective or to laud the heroism of individual Mexican combatants.[20]

While many of the war's poets were celebrating the deeds of America's soldiers and extolling the glory of America's victories, others were denouncing the war, condemning the nation's leaders, and praising the valor of the enemy. The most outspoken opposition to the Mexican War came from the abolition movement (under the mistaken notion that the war was being fought to extend the area of slavery) and the peace movement, although the latter displayed a curious ambivalence toward the conflict.

William Lloyd Garrison's abolitionist journal *The Liberator* was one of the principal vehicles for antiwar poetry. Garrison himself set the tone with his verses, "The War for Slavery":

> If ever war was waged for basest ends,
>   By means perfidious, profligate and low,
>   It is the present war with Mexico,
> Which in deep guilt all other wars transcends.

The slave-power of the South was blamed for the war (by John Quincy Adams in "Slavery and the War" among others) and the administration's determination to vanquish Mexico was attributed to that country's earlier abolition of slavery. Mexico's weak and defenseless condition invited sympathy and cast dishonor on "our proud Bird of Freedom." For those who volunteered to fight in Mexico there was only bitter condemnation:

> All those who have the power to kill,
>   Without a heart to fear,
> Can bid adieu to home and friends,
>   And volunteer.[21]

The antiwar poetry of *The Liberator* was blunt and, however sincere, bordered on the shrill outpourings of those who saw villainous slavemasters behind every action. The war was reduced to a single exclusive issue. The appeal of the poems was limited to the already converted and had little impact on popular perceptions of the conflict. On a different, and perhaps higher, plane were the two foremost abolitionist antiwar poets, John Greenleaf Whittier and James Russell Lowell. Their work assumed a higher level of sophistication and commitment and hence was recognized outside the immediate abolitionist circle.

Two weeks after the war broke out, Whittier, already well established as a poet of reform, wrote that he was "heart-sick with this miserably wicked Mexican War." There was no doubt in his mind that it was being waged to strengthen and expand slavery. As Taylor's army moved southward, the "clank of chains mingles with the music of their march" and the plaza "of every conquered Mexican village becomes a market-place for human flesh." Early in 1847, Whittier became an editor of the abolitionist weekly *National Era,* and it was there that he published many of his prose pieces on the war.

Whittier's first poetic response to the war was also his most curious: "Palo Alto," allegedly written by the "popular Mexican poet," Jose de Saltillo. Whittier had taken the fictitious name used by Charles Fenno Hoffman and extended the hoax to register his own strong opposition to the war. The poem urged Mexicans to be true to "ancient Tenochtitlan" and heed "Arista's bugle-call." "On they come, the mad invaders," leaving "Slavery's blackened waste" behind them. Fighting for "Freedom, Faith, and Home," the Mexicans, with "the saints and holy angels" on their side, had the ultimate advantage.[22]

In "Yorktown," Whittier followed the familiar practice of linking the

Mexican War with the American Revolution, but he did so with a difference. The bond that tied them together was the hated institution of slavery. Noting that a large number of slaves present at Yorktown were returned to their masters by the Americans following the British capitulation, he charged, "Ye spared the wrong; and over all Behold the avenging shadow fall!" The legacy of that act, so inconsistent with the revolutionary cause, was clear, for he asked:

> Where's now the flag of that old war?
> Where flows its stripe? Where burns its star?
> Bear witness, Palo Alto's day,
> Dark Vale of Palms, red Monterey,
> Where Mexic Freedom, young and weak,
> Fleshes the Northern eagle's beak . . .

"Slavery's flag" was unfurled over America; Old World tyranny no longer had anything to fear from the promise of the New.

Shortly after the appearance of "Yorktown," Whittier published his most enduring Mexican War poem, "The Angels of Buena Vista." The poem was based on the report that a number of Mexican women hovered near the battlefield to give aid to the wounded; one woman, surrounded by "the maimed and suffering" of both armies, was seen ministering to their wants "with impartial tenderness." The poem had a romantic appeal that virtually assured popularity, and, if it was Whittier's intention to arouse an antiwar protest, it was lost in the sentimentality. Its theme was a favorite among the war's poets, the courage and sacrifice of women who neither shared nor understood the belligerent roles of their loved ones, who in a sense stood above the fray and fulfilled one of the primary womanly functions, that of serving as angels of mercy. The incongruity of their presence on the battlefield brought into bold relief the horror of war itself.

Whittier conveyed the din and confusion, the clouds of smoke, the dead and dying, through the eyes of Ximena, one of the Mexican "angels." As the smoke lifts, she

> can see the wounded crawling slowly out from
>   heaps of slain.
> Now they stagger, blind and bleeding; now they
>   fall, and strive to rise;
> Hasten, sisters, haste and save them, lest they die
>   before our eyes!

Ministering to a dying American soldier, "fair and young," who mistakes her for his mother, Ximena hurls "A bitter curse upon them . . . who led thee forth, From some gentle, sad-eyed mother, weeping, lonely, in the North!" As the battle ends, the "Mexic women" continue their "holy task" and it is from their devotion that Whittier drew his lesson:

> Not wholly lost, O Father! is this evil world of ours;
> Upward, through its blood and ashes, spring afresh the Eden flowers;
> From its smoking hell of battle, Love and Pity send their prayer,
> And still thy white-winged angels hover dimly in our air!

The poem, unlike his earlier attacks on the slavery-inspired war, ended on a hopeful note.[23]

Like Whittier, James Russell Lowell was a dedicated abolitionist; also like Whittier, he viewed the Mexican War as a "national crime committed in behoof of Slavery, our common sin." It was this conviction that inspired his writing of what some critics have considered Lowell's best work, *The Biglow Papers*. He wrote little else in response to the war.

Angered at the sight of recruiters in Boston attempting to enlist a company of volunteers shortly after the war began, Lowell penned the first of Hosea Biglow's letters, employing the "homely" Yankee dialect of just "such an upcountry man" as he had often seen at rural antislavery gatherings. Encouraged by its success, Lowell published several more during the war, each written rapidly and often at a single sitting; by the end of 1847 he had decided to put them into a book. They appeared anonymously, for, as Lowell wrote, he wished "Slavery to think it has as many enemies as possible." In addition to his own observations, Biglow rendered into verse the remarks "at an Extrumpery Caucus" of the politician Increase D. O'Phace and the letters from Mexico of Birdofredum Sawin, a private in the Massachusetts Regiment who found that army service was not all that he had been led to expect.

Hosea's first epistle, sent to the *Boston Courier* by his father Ezekiel, summarized Lowell's attitude toward the war. In his covering letter, Ezekiel (or Zekle as he called himself) noted, "Our Hosea wuz down to Boston last week, and he see a cruetin Sarjunt a struttin round as popler as a hen with 1 chicking, with 2 fellers a drummin and fifin arter him like all nater." Hosea began his poem with a response to the sergeant's arguments:

> Thrash away, you'll *hev* to rattle
>   On them kittle drums o' yourn,—
> 'Taint a knowin' kind o' cattle
>   Thet is ketched with mouldy corn;
> Put in stiff, you fifer feller,
>   Let folks see how spry you be,—
> Guess you'll toot till you are yeller
>   'Fore you git ahold o' me!

Hosea (Lowell) then moved to a consideration of the war itself:

> Ez fer war, I call it murder,—
>   There you hev it plain an' flat;
> They may talk o' Freedom's airy
>   Tell they're pupple in the face,—

> It's a grand gret cemetary
>   Fer the barthrights of our race;
> They just want this Californy
>   So's to lug new slave-states in
> To abuse ye, an' to scorn ye,
>   An' to plunder ye like sin.

Private Birdofredum Sawin, introduced in the second letter (published in August 1847), complained that "This kind o' sogerin' aint a mite like our October trainin'." He resented the arguments of those who had persuaded him to volunteer, arguments

> About the Anglo-Saxon race (an' saxons would be handy
> To du the buryin' down here upon the Rio Grandy),
> About our patriotic pas an' our star-spangled banner,
> Our country's bird alookin' on an' singin' out hosanner.

The poor food, the bugs, the Mexicans lurking with their lariats convinced Birdofredum that

> This 'ere's about the meanest place a skunk could wal diskiver
> (Saltillo's Mexican, I b'lieve, fer wut we call Salt-river).

He was, however, hopeful that his situation might soon change, for

> . . . arter I gin glory up, thinks I at least there's one
> Thing in the bills we aint hed yit, an' thet's the GLORIOUS FUN;
> Ef once we git to Mexico, we fairly may persume we
> All day an' night shall revel in the halls o' Montezumy.

Lowell's sarcasm spared no one—politicians, officers of the army, newspaper editors. "Mr. Biglow," he wrote in September 1848, "has a thousand readers for my one, & . . . he has raised the laugh at War & Slavery & Doughfaces to some purpose."[24]

   Although it has ranked high as a classic of American political satire, as a statement against the Mexican War *The Biglow Papers* had little influence on Americans' perception of the conflict. Lowell himself expressed ambivalence toward the war when he recalled the circumstances surrounding his authorship of *The Biglow Papers*. The Mexican War, he stated in 1859, had been "a war of false pretences," for it was fought to extend the power and influence of slavery. At the same time, however, he argued that "it is the manifest destiny of the English race to occupy this whole continent and to display there that practical understanding in matters of government and colonization which no other race has given such proof of possessing since the Romans." Territorial expansion in the interest of America's republican mission was justifiable, expansion in the interest of slavery was not.[25]

The drama in the early 19th century, David Grimsted has written, served as "an unusually sensitive barometer" of the age's attitudes and concerns. Patronized by Americans of all social classes, it was highly dependent for its success on popular appeal. By the 1840s, "nationality" was an essential element in dramatic production. The theatre became part of the effort to develop an American national culture, as both audiences and playwrights insisted that the drama reflect the nation's uniqueness and bear the impress of its republican institutions. The stage became an arena for the promotion of patriotism and national pride. Native themes and settings did not matter so long as the principles of republican freedom emerged from the plots and dialogues. Popular movements against oppression and tyranny, whether in ancient Greece and Rome, medieval England or 16th-century Spain, became a staple in American theatrical productions. It was not even unusual for plays with classical or European settings to include eulogies to American greatness.[26]

America's own struggle for freedom became a persistent stage-theme during the heyday of spread-eagle nationalism in the 1840s, and other historic events—the War of 1812, the partisan rivalries of the Jackson years, the Texas revolution, the Oregon crisis—were brought to the stage, often in such hurried and exaggerated form that the quality left much to be desired. Yet in spite of shortcomings and brief runs (often written and performed only to celebrate national holidays), popular demand for such productions was high.

The Mexican War was dramatized in what were known as "national dramas" almost before the guns had cooled and the facts were known. Authenticity of detail was no problem for dramatists eager to capitalize on the popular interest in the war. The first war play, "The Bombardment of Matamoras and the Repulse of the Mexicans," was rushed to the stage within hours of the report (later proved false) that the Mexican town had been destroyed by Taylor's artillery. Billed as a "great national drama," it played for three performances before being replaced by a production that was more factually accurate.[27]

The new play, "Campaign on the Rio Grande, or Triumphs in Mexico," was written by Walter M. Leman, author of several "national dramas" on Revolutionary and Indian themes, with the country's new heroes, General Taylor, Captain May, and Captain Walker, heading the cast. It opened in Philadelphia at the end of May 1846 to a long run and was revived a year later when the anniversary of the battles was celebrated. A similarly titled play by A. W. Fenno opened at New York's Bowery Theatre shortly afterward. The Bowery, which became the principal house in New York for war productions, was renovated in the fall of 1847, when a new drop curtain depicting a battle scene in Mexico was installed.[28]

The first months of the war saw the production of comparable plays in other parts of the country as well as in the two centers of theatrical activity, Philadelphia and New York. In St. Louis, for example, "a new and original national drama" entitled "Palo Alto, or, The Hero of the Rio Grande" presented "the recent *brilliant incidents* of the Mexican campaign" to enthusiastic audiences. A double bill on July 4 at New York's Greenwich Theatre featured "The Rio Grande," and in September the same house paired "The Rio Grande Volunteer" with Edward Bulwer-Lytton's popular "The Lady of Lyons." In May 1847, the Bowery Theatre celebrated the first anniversary of the war as well as the two recent battles with a performance to an overflow crowd of "The Battle of Buena Vista and the Bombardment of Vera Cruz" and in St. Louis, Independence Day and the return of Doniphan's volunteers were honored with "the new patriotic drama" titled "Our Flag Is Nailed to the Mast," followed by a panorama illustrating the battles of Palo Alto, Resaca de la Palma, Monterey, Chihuahua, Vera Cruz, Buena Vista, and Cerro Gordo.

In January 1848 "The Battle of Mexico, or, The Capture of the Halls of the Montezumas," written and produced by Thomas Barry, celebrated the war's conclusion. With a cast of twenty, the play presented "a brave array of scenes, of Mexican palaces, landscapes and battlefields." The *Spirit of the Times* found it "a most wonderful military spectacle"; not only were the scenes deemed authentic but the "impersonation" of Generals Scott, Worth, Shields, Twiggs, and others was regarded as "most excellent." In November, following the Presidential campaign, Welch's Amphitheatre in Philadelphia honored Taylor's election with "The Triumphs of Rough and Ready; or, The Past, Present, and Future."[29]

Among the most ambitious Mexican War dramas was Joseph C. Foster's "The Siege of Monterey, or, The Triumph of Rough and Ready," which played to capacity audiences at the Bowery Theatre in October 1847, after a successful Philadelphia run a year earlier. It proved highly lucrative to the theatre's management. The house, wrote a reviewer, was "crowded to suffocation" and large numbers of people were turned away. "The national pride is gratified by the event celebrated in the drama, and the people have a glorious opportunity to exult in the triumph of American arms." A month after it opened, the play was still drawing large crowds; a number of short farces had been added to the bill as second features, and toward the end of its run the "Bedouin Arabs," an acrobatic group, thrilled the audiences with their "somersetting" and "flying-leaps."

Foster, who later wrote a musical melodrama entitled "The Knight of the Lion Heart, or Golden Days of Chivalry," allowed his romantic instincts full play. The cast, headed by the tragedian W. Marshall playing General Taylor, included eleven Mexican and eighteen American characters plus a large number of "auxiliaries." To add to audience interest, a Yankee peddler, a stock character that brought humor to the piece, was played by the well-known stage-Yankee Charles Burke; Mrs.

H. C. Jordan capped the performance with her patriotic portrayal of "The Genius of America." The scenery, executed by Isherwood, an actor who doubled as scene-painter, was acclaimed for its "correct representations" of the Mexican battlefields.

The curtain rose on Fort Brown in the moonlight. After inspecting the entrenchments, accompanied by a soldiers' chorus, General Taylor fell asleep and while sleeping beheld four visions that foretold the future of his campaign: the fall of Matamoros, the capture of Monterey, the bombardment of Vera Cruz, and the battle of Buena Vista. When the mist cleared at daybreak, Taylor awoke to the sounds of reveille. He then fought the battles of Palo Alto and Resaca de la Palma before moving on to Monterey. In the final climactic scene, "the entire area of the vast stage" was thrown open and the play ended with the three days' battle for Monterey. The fighting in the streets, with the "slaughter of our own troops and those of the Mexicans," was described as "beautifully illustrated."[30]

The *Spirit of the Times* suggested reasons for the popularity of Mexican War plays, aside from the high interest in "national drama" generally. The audiences were anxious for an opportunity "to revive feelings of patriotism" but beyond this the plays demonstrated their fondness for pageantry and military themes. Because of the war, "military spectacles at this moment have an almost irresistible fascination." The fascination also found expression in other forms of public entertainment. The circus, which was enjoying a rising popularity as acrobats, equestrians, and clowns were merged with wild animal menageries, found the war's pageantry well suited to its program. Battles were reenacted, in some instances circus managers going to great lengths to duplicate the battle scenes.[31]

Public interest in the war was further gratified by the moving panorama, a fairly new form of popular art that combined dramatic presentation with the curiosity of travel to strange and distant places. An early version of the travelogue, or, as John Francis McDermott has called it, "newsreel—old style," the moving panorama consisted of scenes painted on a canvas of extensive length (usually highly exaggerated in the advertising) and wound on an upright roller. The movement was achieved by unwinding the canvas from one roller and winding it on another. The scenes were explained in a detailed pamphlet or program distributed to each member of the audience, a commentator usually offered further explanation, while a piano provided background music. Many of the panorama painters were scene-painters on the stage; among their most popular subjects was the great valley of the Mississippi. At least five panoramas of the Mississippi were produced, the most successful of which was the work of John Banvard, whose 1846 panorama was shown throughout the country. Banvard boasted that his panorama, painted on three miles of canvas, was "the largest Picture ever executed by Man."

The Mexican War provided a popular and timely subject for moving panoramas. Capitalizing on the excitement following the first battles of the war, a panorama of the engagements was rushed to completion and exhibited at New York's Coliseum by the end of May 1846. Most of the war panoramas, however, were shown at the war's end, probably because of the time required to prepare them. Banvard's Panorama Hall in New York featured a "thrilling exhibition" of "The Bombardment of Vera Cruz" complete with a pyrotechnic display to add realism to the event. A veteran of the war, Corydon Donnavan, whose *Adventures in Mexico* was published in 1847, enlisted the aid of several painters to produce a panorama that would illustrate the scenes and episodes of his book (and, no doubt, increase its sales). Exhibited first in Cincinnati, it was later taken on tour to Boston and New York. In St. Louis the war was combined with Biblical and other illustrations in a kind of triple feature, "Sacred Panorama, Dissolving Scenes and the Bombardment of Vera Cruz." Panoramic views of the "sublime and beautiful scenery" of the Garden of Eden and the "awful destruction of the world" in the Great Deluge were followed by the Shipwreck of the Medusa, the Black Forest in Spain and a Midnight Mass in Rome, all building to the climax of the bombardment of Vera Cruz. The panorama with one of the longest runs was Sherman and Tousey's "Mammoth Panorama" of Taylor's campaign in Mexico, advertised as "the greatest Painting in the world, covering 19,000 square feet of canvas."[32]

The moving panorama was more often associated with the theatre than with art but its popularity also revealed a public interest in the pictorial representation of the war. Art, like the drama, reflected the popular taste for works that conveyed a sense of national identity, reinforced the public's faith in republican government and democracy, and depicted the heroism of America's national origins. Art's nationalistic purpose was conveyed through the development of an American school of historical painting, a portrayal of the nation's historic events designed to encourage patriotism (or, as Charles Lanman suggested, pamper national vanity). Aside from the romantic view that art was morally uplifting and that both beauty and truth could be found in commonplace subject-matter, art seemed also to fill a timely need in the 1840s not unlike that which some Americans attached to the Mexican War itself—to recall an America gripped by materialism and acquisitiveness back to national pride and duty. Art offered an antidote to the "selfish and corrupt passions" of the "money-lover," elevating and purifying the feelings of a people swayed by desire for gain.

Whether from feelings of national vanity or from a nobler patriotism, the Mexican War generated a flood of graphic art ranging from crude woodcuts to the refined and polished efforts of some of the nation's leading painters. The war, a reviewer believed, advanced not only America's military reputation but its artistic reputation as well. Like most wars, it proved a natural stimulus to artistic expression. The "brilliant fires of Monterey, Cerro Gordo, and Churubusco" illumined the world and the "radiance of American military glory will no longer be unseen."[33]

The same technology that brought the war to a mass reading public also carried pictures of the war to the people. The Mexican War was the first major event in American history to be so thoroughly illustrated. Americans could view their armies in action, could see the massed troops beneath the towering sierras at Buena Vista, the shells arching their way into Vera Cruz, the volunteers struggling up the steep slopes of Cerro Gordo. Daguerre had developed his photographic process a decade before the war, but only a handful of Mexican War daguerreotypes exist. Daguerreotypists accompanied the soldiers (at least one became a casualty to enemy action) and set up shop in the occupied towns, but their work has been lost. Examples that have survived depict scenes in and around Saltillo: the Virginia Regiment on parade, Mexican civilians grouped around an American officer, General Wool and his staff on horseback on a Saltillo street, a battery of artillery drawn up near Buena Vista. Photographic historian Robert Taft, who suggests that the pictures were probably made by a Mexican daguerreotypist, found these few scenes to be the "earliest photographic records of war now known."[34]

The close relationship of war and photography was still in the future. The Mexican War was rather seen in the woodcuts and engravings that appeared in books, periodicals, and newspapers and in the lithographic prints published for public sale. The popular historian John Frost was unequaled for his pictorial record of the war. His *Pictorial History of Mexico and the Mexican War* (1848) was only the most ambitious of his works on the war and its heroes. "Embellished" by 500 illustrations from designs by a number of artists (including the Philadelphia engraver William Croome), Frost's book combined a history of the ancient land in which Americans fought with the triumphs of the nation's armies. The illustrations reflected Frost's view of the war as a clash of civilizations that demonstrated American (or Anglo-Saxon) superiority over the Mexican people. Many of the portraits of the war's heroes were adapted from daguerreotypes which, Frost noted, provided an authenticity that was unknown "before the invention of this important art." Frost's success inspired others, as a spate of pictorial books soon appeared on a variety of historical and biographical subjects, including Benson Lossing's *Pictorial Field Book of the Revolution*.[35]

Popular magazines, like *Graham's*, the *Columbian Magazine*, and the *Union Magazine of Literature and Art*, provided their readers with portraits of war heroes and illustrations of dramatic battlefield moments. Magazine illustration (or "embellishment") by copper and steel engrav-

News from the War. From *Union Magazine of Literature and Art* (July 1847).

ings had developed in the 1830s; the increased circulation that followed more than compensated the publishers for their expense. Some
of the best war illustrations were executed by the New York painter
Tompkins H. Matteson, who probably produced more Mexican War
scenes than any other artist. His pictures were reproduced by the mezzotint process—a means for achieving a striking realism through light
and shadow—by one of the country's foremost engravers, the recent
English immigrant Henry S. Sadd. Matteson's portrayal of Ringgold's

death was lauded for its veracity, and his action picture of Lieutenant Schuyler Hamilton fighting off guerrillas, observed the *Literary World,* exceeded "in spirit and interest" anything yet seen. Caroline Kirkland, in whose *Union Magazine* the latter appeared, apologized for including a war scene in a magazine devoted to literature and the arts but praised its artistic quality. More in keeping with the magazine's character was Matteson's poignant "News from the War," depicting the tragic impact of the war on the wives and children of the soldiers who fell in battle. Matteson's illustrations of scenes from Cooper's novels and of America's early settlement were popular during the war, and his "Spirit of '76," reminding Americans of that earlier call to patriotism, was purchased by the American Art Union.[36]

Newspapers, led by the *New York Herald,* began illustrating their pages with woodcuts early in the 1840s but it was the Mexican War that gave pictorial journalism its first boost. The *Herald* declared its intention to illustrate "all the prominent places that have fallen, and may fall, into our hands" and urged subscribers to preserve the illustrations as an authentic record of the conflict. Some of the illustrations were cartoon commentaries on the war, not always favorable to the government. Others lampooned the public response to the war (for example, the crude illustration of "Some of the B'hoys Drilling for the Halls of the Montezumas") and denigrated the quality of the Mexican soldier ("Specimen of the Mexican Soldier . . . half Indian and half Negro"). Most were serious efforts to acquaint the public with the scenes and episodes of the war.

Special pictorial numbers were issued by *Brother Jonathan,* a "mammoth" paper founded in 1839 by Park Benjamin, including the paper's "Great Battle Sheet" issued in December 1847 to commemorate the "Triumphs of American Arms in Mexico." In the following year, a special *Pictorial Brother Jonathan* was published on the Fourth of July, featuring an immense engraving of Matteson's "Storming of the Castle of Chapultepec," the largest wood engraving "ever printed in the world," utilizing several hundred blocks of imported East Indian boxwood and measuring twenty-two by forty-four inches.[37]

The graphic depiction of the Mexican War benefitted from improvements in the art of lithography. The importance of lithography to news reporting had been demonstrated as early as the mid-1830s when America's most noted lithographer Nathaniel Currier entered the field. The following decade witnessed "an outburst of lithography," and by 1846 this art-form was preeminent in the field of popular illustration. The Mexican War, as with so many other aspects of popular communication, was the first major event to be recorded in lithography; the war was newsworthy, and, although the illustrations were often stylized in order to evoke sentiments of pride and patriotism, they also held journalistic importance.[38]

A large number of lithographers exploited the interest in the war to promote their work. Henry R. Robinson, a New York Whig caricaturist, was well known for his anti-Jackson political cartoons before his "flair for the news" caused him to turn to the war. His widely advertised print of the battle of Buena Vista, based on an eye-witness sketch, carried an authenticity that was lacking in other depictions of the battle. Robinson sent a copy of the print to Henry Clay and later used Clay's laudatory reply as a testimonial for his work. Napoleon Sarony, who had worked for both Robinson and Currier, formed his own lithographic establishment with Henry B. Major in 1846 and immediately began producing prints of the war. Regarded as "one of the most expert craftsmen, enterprising publishers, and vivid characters of the time," Sarony was best known for his prints of James Walker's dramatic painting of the storming of Chapultepec and Lieutenant Henry Walke's *Naval Portfolio,* but he produced many others besides. Acting quickly on the first news reports, he rushed his prints onto the market before accurate information was received. One of his early prints was of the "Repulsion of the Mexicans and the Bombardment of Matamoras," based on the same false report that inspired one of the first stage plays based on the war; his illustration of the battle of Palo Alto, part of a set on Taylor's victories on the Rio Grande, showed the battle being fought amid tropical luxuriance. Sarony's print of street-fighting in Monterey was undoubtedly influenced by Delacroix's scenes of the 1830 revolution in Paris.[39]

The most prolific and most popular lithographer of the Mexican War was Nathaniel Currier. Indeed, the lithography process itself owed much to Currier's pioneering efforts, for it was in Currier's establishment that many later lithographers first learned their art. Currier began specializing in the "journalistic print" early in his career. Exploiting the timeliness of the Mexican War, he produced more illustrations of the war than anyone else, covering the market with dramatic portrayals of the battles in inexpensive form. A recent checklist included more than eighty-five prints. The battle of Buena Vista topped the list with fifteen different depictions, followed by Vera Cruz with eleven, Monterey seven, Resaca de la Palma six (featuring Captain May's charge in four versions), Chapultepec four, and Cerro Gordo, Churubusco, and Palo Alto three each. The deaths of Ringgold, John J. Hardin, Henry Clay, Jr., and Pierce Butler were rendered in the heroic style common to all pictures of battlefield death.[40]

Most lithographers, Currier among them, were only interested in subjects that would sell and therefore were not overly concerned with accuracy. Their lithographs relied heavily on the imaginations of the artists. The soldiers were stiff, immaculate, and smartly dressed, always appearing to be going into battle as if they were on a review parade. Perspective was distorted for the printmakers tried to crowd too much into their pictures. The contending armies stood bunched together firing at each other at point-blank range. Finally, there was the obvious

Storming of the Castle of Chapultapec, by the American Army. From *Brother Jonathan*, July 4, 1848.

appeal to the romantic perceptions of the war. The Bishop's Palace at Monterey became a medieval fortress, and a formidable stone fortress was placed atop Cerro Gordo where none existed. War illustrations were in such demand that some printers and engravers resorted to "second-hand wood cuts," passing off views of the United States and of Europe as authentic Mexican scenes.[41]

Other printmakers, however, made considerable effort to base their illustrations on eye-witness accounts, or better yet on sketches made in the field by combatants. Ange Paldi, a Piedmontese musician and artist in the Fifth Infantry Regiment, sent his drawings of Palo Alto and Resaca de la Palma to a Cincinnati lithographer. Robinson's popular print of Buena Vista was based on a sketch made under fire by General Taylor's aide-de-camp. Navy Lieutenant Charles Crillon Barton's sketch of the Island of Lobos and his "spirited drawing" of the army's landing at Vera Cruz were produced by Peter S. Duval, a prominent Philadelphia lithographer, and Currier had the help of a young midshipman for his print of the "Attack of the Gun Boats upon the City and Castle" of Vera Cruz.

The two best-known combat artists were Daniel P. Whiting, a captain in the Seventh Infantry trained in topographical drawing, and Lieutenant Henry Walke, executive officer of the bomb-brig *Vesuvius*. Whiting's scenes of Taylor's army as it moved from Corpus Christi to Monterey were lithographed in color and published in New York as *Army Portfolio No. 1* (no further portfolios appeared). Walke took part in the bombardment of Vera Cruz (where he sketched the Naval Battery in action) and in the expeditions against Tuxpan and Tabasco. His illustrations, lithographed in color by Sarony and Major, were published as the *Naval Portfolio No. 1* (again, no other was published). *Godey's* praised the pictures as the "most beautiful specimens of colored lithographs we have ever seen."[42]

Two other artists who were eye-witnesses to some of the battle scenes they depicted, neither a member of the armed forces, were the German painter Carl Nebel and the English-born James Walker. Nebel's twelve illustrations of the war's major battles from Palo Alto to General Scott's entrance into Mexico City were clearly among the most handsome and authentic to be produced. Nebel had toured Mexico extensively between 1829 and 1834 sketching the architecture, the archaeological remains, and the people; in 1836, fifty of his illustrations were published in Paris with his account of the tour. Nebel apparently returned to Mexico some time during the war and arranged with New Orleans *Picayune* correspondent George Wilkins Kendall to produce a folio of battle prints. It is obvious that he was not present at all the engagements he illustrated; indeed, one authority believes that Nebel remained in Europe during the war, relying on his memory of Mexican terrain and on Kendall's notes to reproduce the engagements. There is evidence, however, that Nebel was in Mexico City shortly after its occupation, and Kendall himself insisted that the greater number of the prints had been drawn by Nebel on the spot. Nebel's work was lithographed in color in Paris and published, with Kendall's commentaries, in 1851 as *The War Between the United States and Mexico Illustrated*. No country, boasted Kendall, "can claim that its battles have been illustrated in a richer, more faithful, or more costly style of lithography." Nebel's battle scenes were clearly among the best illustrations of the war.[43]

James Walker, native of England and early immigrant to the United States, moved to Mexico in 1837, residing first in Tampico where he taught art at the military college and later in Mexico City. He was in the Mexican capital as Scott's army approached. Defying Santa Anna's order that all American residents leave the city, Walker went into hiding and later joined Scott's force at Puebla. He returned as an interpreter on General Worth's staff and witnessed the battles of Contreras, Churubusco, and Chapultepec. Soon after the occupation of Mexico City he began work on a painting of the "Storming of Chapultepec," relying on his own sketches as well as the observations of an engineering officer assigned by Scott to assist him. Walker produced fifteen known paintings of war scenes, all but one (the battle of Buena Vista) depicting episodes in the Valley of Mexico at which he was present. Based on drawings made on the spot, the paintings represented the actions in objective detail. Walker's work was later recognized when Congress commissioned him to paint the "Battle of Chapultepec" for the Capitol in Washington, where it was hung above the railing of the Senate staircase.[44]

It was inevitable that the Mexican War should influence the work of American artists. Mexican scenes and episodes from Mexico's history had been popular before the war and the presence of America's fighting men in Mexico added to their popularity. The continuing appeal of Prescott's history combined with the war to produce a number of paintings drawn from Mexico's past, among the more prominent of which were Emmanuel Leutze's "Storming of the Mexican Teocalli by Cortez," Peter Rothermel's portrait of Cortez following the Noche Triste (part of a series of Cortez paintings), and Edward Holyoke's "Death of Montezuma." More popular were subjects from the war itself, such as "Scott's Entry into Mexico City" painted by William Henry Powell, who was commissioned in 1847 to fill the last panel in the Capitol Rotunda with DeSoto's discovery of the Mississippi River.

One of the most acclaimed painters was Richard Caton Woodville who left America to study in Düsseldorf in 1845 and remained in Europe until his death eleven years later. Among the paintings Woodville sent for exhibition in New York were "Mexican News" and "Old 76 and Young 48," both of which were engraved for distribution to members of the Art-Union. Woodville's power for "seizing every day character and incident" and presenting them with vigor and spirit was revealed in "Mexican News," an illustration of the excitement in a Southern tavern as news of the war was received. "Old 76 and Young 48," showing a young soldier just returned from Mexico relating his adventures to his grandfather, a veteran of the Revolutionary War, was another effort to link the Mexican War with the Revolution, "a contrast," as one critic put it, "of the past and present age, the days of Washington and Taylor."[45]

The Mexican War was viewed by artists in the same romantic light that inspired writers, poets, dramatists, and songwriters. There was no Goya in America, one writer has recently observed, to record the horrors of warfare. Most of the art was strongly endowed with a patriotic purpose and most of the artists followed the "heroic representation" of war first popularized by Benjamin West and continued by John Trumbull. They were anxious to record America's moment in history, on the one hand to emphasize the republican nature of the conflict and on the other to remind Americans that the country could still produce heroism, courage, and sacrifice.[46]

When New Yorkers gathered in their great mass meeting on May 20, 1846, to celebrate Congress's passage of the war resolution, they opened their program with a new "national anthem" written by the "Song Writer of America," George Pope Morris. Morris's verses were a moving appeal to the patriotism of the people, a call for the defense of America's freedom, and a reminder of the nation's duty to God and its own proud revolutionary heritage:

> Freedom spreads her downy wings
> Over all created things;
> Glory to the King of Kings!
>   Bend low to Him the knee;
> Bring the heart before His throne—
> Bow to Him and Him alone;
> He's the only King we own,
>   And he has made us free!
>   Arm and on, ye brave and free!
>   Arm and strike for liberty!

Later in the program George Washington Dixon, an early popularizer of blackface singing, sang several less elevating verses to the minstrel tune of *Old Dan Tucker*, promising swift retribution to the Mexican "yellow skins" and their chiefs who had "slain our brethren in their camps."

> The Mexicans are on our soil,
> In war they wish us to embroil;
> They've tried their best and worst to vex us

By murdering our brave men in Texas.
 We're on our way to Rio Grande,
 On our way to Rio Grande,
 On our way to Rio Grande,
 And with arms they'll find us handy.

The God of War, the mighty Mars,
Has smiled upon our stripes and stars;
And spite of any ugly rumors
We'll vanquish all the Montezumas.
 We're on our way to Matamoras;
 On our way to Matamoras,
 On our way to Matamoras;
 And we'll conquer all before us!

The crowd responded with delight and tumultuous enthusiasm.[47]

Music played an important role in the public response to the war. It was a time when, in Carl Bode's phrase, "America burst into melody." Romanticism found expression in song, as hundreds of poets and composers sought to oblige a public that saw in music a reflection of itself, its values, aspirations, and national character. Indeed, it has been said that the history of early 19th-century America can be told in terms of its music. Sentimental ballads and intricate, often bombastic, compositions designed to evoke tears or terror teamed up with more earthy renditions of folk tunes and raucous entertainments to provide Americans with a varied musical fare that left an indelible stamp on the time. Furthermore, music, like the sister arts of drama and art, was expected to reflect America's unique nationality, "growing out of the life of the country" and "protected by the popular feeling." It was to be an *American* music. Patriotism was instilled through the keyboard, and great national events were celebrated musically.[48]

Every community boasted one or more musical societies and musical concerts were among the most popular forms of entertainment. Vocal and instrumental artists toured the country, as numerous as theatrical troupes, and European performers flocked to America to receive the plaudits of admiring and appreciative audiences. Brass bands were legion. The most popular music was that intended for the most romantic of instruments, the piano. The piano became a cultural symbol as well as a source of entertainment, and no household that aspired to aesthetic refinement was without one. The manufacture and sale of pianos in the United States rose sharply from 2500 in 1829 to more than 9000 in 1851. To meet the demand for piano music, publishers poured out an incessant stream of compositions. There was no dearth of composers, for "almost anyone . . . could gain publication in that era of a seller's market for parlor piano music." Music belonged to the people.[49]

Music historian Wiley Hitchcock has distinguished between two traditions that molded musical expression in the early 19th century: the cultivated and the vernacular. The musical response to the opening of the Mexican War at that first mass meeting in New York reflected this duality. George Pope Morris was one of those ubiquitous purveyors of popular culture which America's romantic era seemed so much to encourage. A journalist, poet, songwriter, playwright, and all-round defender of the popular arts, Morris founded the *New York Mirror* in 1823 and retained an editorial connection with the paper for over twenty years. His poems were widely printed in the press and later collected, while his songs enjoyed a continuing popularity, the most famous of which was probably *Woodman, Spare That Tree!*, set to music and sung by the English vocalist Henry Russell on his concert tours of America. Morris wrote a play based on events in the American Revolution and the libretto of an opera, *The Maid of Saxony*, that was performed in New York for two weeks in 1842. Believing that no other country could match the United States for its abundance of material for the development of a native culture, Morris quickly recognized the Mexican War as a theme for musical composition. His anthem, revealing the nationalistic exuberance with which Americans entered the war, was followed in 1848 by *The Soldier's Return. A Song for the People*, in which Winfield Scott's campaign against Mexico City and his triumphant return to New York were celebrated (published with an elegant color lithograph of the General "in all the glory of buckskin tights").

Morris was only the first of the songwriters and composers who celebrated the war in the "cultivated" tradition. Some of the nation's best-known musical talents helped to popularize the conflict. Stephen Foster's *Santa Anna's Retreat from Buena Vista*, full of "elegant pianistic effects," was an early example of Foster's determination to compose music that was more appropriate to the parlor than to the stage, music more genteel than the plantation songs that made him famous. John Hill Hewitt, now recognized as the "Father of the American Ballad," composed martial music after four years of rather desultory study at West Point. Itinerant music teacher, poet, playwright, and editor, as well as a successful composer, Hewitt was known for his sentimental ballads, more famous now for his Civil War songs (he supported the Confederacy) than for his Mexican War pieces. German-born Charles Grobe, teacher of music in a Delaware women's college, was said to have produced more compositions than any other American at the time, his Mexican War battle-pieces only part of a vast repertoire that included patriotic tunes, marches, dances, and variations on operatic and minstrel melodies. One of America's leading music publishers, William Cummings Peters, also composed music, including a number of war songs.[50]

Publishers of music, like their counterparts in the book trade, were quick to exploit the popular interest in the Mexican War, and the war's chronology could be told in the titles they issued. Published in piano arrangements in sheet-music form, the pieces were illustrated by highly stylized and romantic lithographs of the war's episodes. Although the illustrated title pages increased the costs of publication, they also increased the sales, usually at higher prices. Combining art with music, the song publications also had an important journalistic function, providing the public with both a visual and auditory awareness of the war.[51]

Marches and quicksteps appeared as soon as it was known that Taylor had moved to the Rio Grande, including *General Taylor's Encampment Quickstep, The Rio Grande Quick March,* and Peters's *Matamoras Grand March.* As the call for volunteers went out and news was received of the war's first victories, the publication of war songs increased dramatically. To such spirited compositions as *The Mexican Volunteer's Quickstep* was added the more plaintive appeal of Augusta Browne's *The Soldier's Departure,* wherein the volunteer responded to the bugle's call on his wedding day, and the patriotic strains of Hewitt's *Look Upon That Banner,* inspired by the mother's advice to her son to "Go to Mexico—revenge your brother's death and sustain your country's honor." The heroes of Palo Alto and Resaca de la Palma were honored musically as soon as the results of the battles were known. At least six compositions, including Hewitt's *On to the Charge!* and three funeral marches (one using a theme from Beethoven), lamented Ringgold's death. May's charge at Resaca de la Palma was recalled in two identically titled pieces, *Captain May's Quick Step,* Samuel Walker's adventures were treated in a quickstep by Charles Grobe, and General Worth was the subject of two adulatory compositions.[52]

The battles provided special challenges to wartime composers. So-called battle-pieces had been highly popular with concert audiences throughout the first half of the 19th century. Long, ambitious, elaborate, and full of bombast, the battle-piece carried listeners through a battle from start to finish, with musical flourishes illustrating each stage of the conflict and with cue cards to remind audiences of the battle's progress. One of the most popular battle-pieces, dating actually from the late 18th century, was Franz Kotzwara's *Battle of Prague.* Although written by a European, it was published in new arrangements by American musicians and remained a centerpiece in piano concerts before the Civil War. A Napoleonic battle-piece, Bernard Vignerie's *Battle of Maringo* [*sic*], was published in 1802 with instructions on how to simulate cannon shots. One of the earliest battle-pieces by an American was the *Battle of Trenton* (1797) by James Hewitt (father of John Hill Hewitt).

The Mexican War was a new field for the battle-piece. Grobe composed one combining Palo Alto and Resaca de la Palma; a second on Buena Vista was subtitled "a descriptive Fantasie for the Piano" and dedicated to Taylor, "The Hero who never lost a battle." Maurice Strakosch, the Galician impresario and (according to his press notices) pianist to the Emperor of Russia, composed and performed *The Storming of Monterey,* complete with the "thunders of cannon" and the "shouts of battle," and Francis Buck, after shorter pieces on Monterey and Vera Cruz, became best known for his battle-piece *The Fall of Vera Cruz and Surrender of the City & Castle of St. Juan D. Ulloa.*

Typical of the battle-piece was *The Battle of Resaca de la Palma,* composed by John Schell and published with an elaborately designed cover featuring military vignettes that bore little relation to the battle. After an introductory flourish, the sound of cannon was heard as "The Mexicans open on the American advance" with the "Mexican Lancers advancing to the charge." Trumpets blare (simulated on the piano) as "They are repulsed with great slaughter by Ridgley's Battery." General Taylor then summoned Captain May to silence the Mexican artillery, and May advanced "to the Charge." The battery was stormed, General de la Vega surrendered to Captain May and, again to the accompaniment of "Heavy cannon," the Mexicans fled in full retreat. A bugle call was followed by spirited trills as the Americans rejoiced over their victory but the enthusiasm quickly gave way to the somber "Cries of the wounded" and "Burial of the slain." The piece closed with a lively arrangement of *Yankee Doodle.*[53]

No battle inspired more music than did Buena Vista, an engagement that became fixed in the public mind as the war's most significant and dramatic encounter. There were Buena Vista polkas, quicksteps, and marches, including Stephen Foster's and one by Peters. William Ratel, who had written a Monterey march, also arranged *Santa Anna's March as Played by the Bands of the Mexican Army on the Field of Buena Vista, the night previous to the battle.* A note on the title page declared that "this beautiful air was brought on by some Kentucky Volunteers having heard it played by the Mexican Bands at Buena Vista while on sentry duty." Peters, not to be outdone, brought out his own *Santa Anna's March to which is added a Popular Melody composed on the Battle field of Buena Vista by an American Officer.* Incidents in the battle were also celebrated. William J. Lemon used Taylor's order to his artillery officer as a song title, *"A Little More Grape Captain Bragg,"* published with a spectacular color lithograph of the battle on the cover. The bravery of a sixteen-year-old volunteer in the Second Kentucky Regiment became the theme of *The Boy Defender of Kentucky's Honor.* F. Weiland's *Buena Vista Grand Triumphal March,* subtitled "General Taylor Never Surrenders," featured a lithograph of American soldiers storming the gate of what appeared to be a medieval fortress, an illustration more appropriate to Monterey (if even there) than to Buena Vista.

Music during the Mexican War, even if not focused on the war's events, was intended nonetheless to instill patriotism, reminding Americans of the glories of their past and their providential mission. One of the most celebrated composers in early 19th-century America was Anthony Philip Heinrich, a Bohemian immigrant whose sojourn in Kentucky had brought him the title "The Log-House Composer" (he preferred his own title, "The Beethoven of America"). Heinrich had

General Worth's Quick Step. Sheet music picturing the battle for Monterey. Courtesy University of Illinois Library, Urbana-Champaign.

achieved fame early for his *Dawning of Music in Kentucky* (1820), an attempt to create an American music that incorporated popular melodies and folk tunes. Heinrich's patriotic ardor for his adopted country knew no bounds. He continued to celebrate the national character in such compositions as *The Columbiad*, a "Grand American national chivalrous symphony," *The Jubilee*, a "grand national song of triumph" that embraced the "consummation of American liberty," and an oratorio *The Pilgrim Fathers.* The last was part of a larger design in which the composer expected "to render musically the greatest epochs in American history." Heinrich performed a section of *The Pilgrim Fathers* in a New York concert just a week before Congress recognized a state of war with Mexico, concluding with a "grand movement" that must have put his audience in a war mood, "descriptive [according to the program notes] of a battle, which winds up with the song of triumph, bearing the national melody in every part." It is not clear which "national melody" Heinrich employed, for he had a talent for weaving the strains of all three of the country's national airs through his compositions. His favorite was *Yankee Doodle.* A *Yankee Doodle Waltz* (as well as a *Hail Columbia! Minuet*) was included in his *Dawning of Music in Kentucky;* his *Wild Wood Spirits' Chant* was subtitled "Scintillations of Yankee Doodle"; and the second part of *The Jubilee* contained a "Grand heroic fantasia or Scintillations of Yankee Doodle for all the known orchestral instruments." He planned, but never completed, an elaborate composition to be called *Yankee Doodliad.*

Heinrich, like most composers of the time, recognized contemporary events in his compositions. He composed funeral marches for William Henry Harrison and Zachary Taylor, paid musical tribute to John Tyler's use of the veto, and joined the expansionist enthusiasm with *The Texas and Oregon March.* In the mid-1840s, he sought unsuccessfully to win Presidential endorsement for a work filled with "complicated harmony" and "wild and unearthly passages" that would illustrate the "greatness and glory of this republic, the splendor of its institutions and the indomitable bravery of its army and navy."[54]

The use of *Yankee Doodle* as a theme in serious piano compositions reflected that tune's immense popularity in early 19th-century America. It was ubiquitous, played so consistently on patriotic and ceremonial occasions that it was recognized as the unofficial anthem of the United States. It was the favorite of army bands in Mexico, played and sung more frequently than any other tune as a battle song to inspire soldiers as they engaged the enemy, as a concert piece in camp and as a triumphant hymn to the achievements of American arms. *Yankee Doodle* was a song for all times and occasions; with its verses altered to fit the contemporary circumstances it became a popular Mexican War song. At least two versions were brought out by music publishers: *Yankee Doodle in Mexico* and *Rough and Ready,* the latter a tribute to Taylor that was popularized by the Alleghanians, a singing group that toured the country during the war. Most of the versions were informal, crude affairs, often written by soldiers to demonstrate their determination to bring the Mexicans to heel; many were printed in the newspapers and in the songsters that were carried by the troops. One of the earliest versions appeared in the *New York Mirror* at the beginning of the war:

they attacked our men upon our land
and Crossed our river too Sir
now show them all with sword in hand
what yankee boys can do sir

Another, *We're the Boys for Mexico,* anticipated the "gold and silver images" the men would discover there, and Captain May's celebrated capture of General de la Vega provided the theme of still another. *Uncle Sam's Song to Miss Texas* warned of a broad conspiracy in support of Mexican defiance and threatened annexation to all who stood in America's way:

If Mexy, back'd by secret foes,
  Still talks of taken you, gal,
Why we can lick 'em all, you know,
  An' then annex 'em too, gal.[55]

The use of *Yankee Doodle* as a Mexican War song provided a bridge from the cultivated tradition of Heinrich, the sheet-music composers, and the concert artists on the one hand to what Hitchcock identified as the vernacular tradition on the other. When George Washington Dixon followed Morris's genteel, patriotic anthem at New York's mass meeting with a version of the popular minstrel tune *Old Dan Tucker* that called attention to Mexican perfidy and promised swift reprisal against "the Montezumas," he was exemplifying America's vernacular musical expression. It was, in Hitchcock's words, a music "more plebeian, native" in nature, "not approached selfconsciously" but understood and appreciated "simply for its utilitarian or entertainment value." In some of its forms it appealed to both class and mass.

The tunes were old and familiar, minstrel melodies, temperance songs, even English ballads. The words were new, often earthy, coarse, and humorous, less suited to the concert hall or the family parlor. Printed in the newspapers or published in the songsters, their authorship seldom identified, the songs revealed a response to the war on the most fundamental popular level. They in turn helped fuel the war spirit and keep excitement, both among soldiers and the folks at home, at a high pitch. Dixon himself represented the importance of vernacular music in popularizing the war. One of the first blackface singers, he achieved early success with his 1829 rendition of *Coal Black Rose,* the "first burnt-cork song of comic love." Aroused by the outbreak of the war, Dixon donned a military uniform, traveled to New Orleans, and announced his intention to go to Mexico as an irregular soldier, a plan he soon abandoned.[56]

Mexican War songs were collected and distributed in a number of song books, conveniently published in pocket-size. The first, appearing soon after the initial battles, was compiled by Philadelphian William M'Carty and dedicated to the men of the United States Army "who, on the 8th and on the 9th day of May, 1846, with matchless skill, and indomitable courage, sustained their own, and their country's honor, in the Battles of Palo Alto and Resaca de la Palma." Four years before, M'Carty had published his *Songs, Odes, and Other Poems, on National Subjects,* with a volume each for patriotic, naval, and military songs. His 1846 compilation supplemented that collection. No effort was apparently made to expand it as the war progressed. Eighty-nine songs and poems were printed, beginning with the rollicking *Taylor on the Rio Grande,* written to the tune of *The Barking Barber.* More solemn was *The American's Battle Prayer,* based on a theme from the opera *Norma,* which called upon George Washington to "Pour in our souls thy patriot fire, Against the foul conspiring foe." Paeans to the flag, to the volunteers of Seventy-Six and Forty-Six, and to the righteousness of America's cause were balanced by sneering allusions to murderous Mexican bandits and the tyranny of Mexico's leaders.

In the same year, the less extensive *General Taylor's Old Rough and Ready Songster* was published in New York and Philadelphia but the most popular and most widely copied was *The Rough and Ready Songster* which appeared in 1848, only several copies of which have survived. Collected by an officer who served in Taylor's army, *The Rough and Ready Songster* measured only three by four inches in size and was illustrated by a number of crudely drawn woodcuts.[57]

Music was an important part of the soldiers' lives. It relieved the tensions of the campaigns, revived spirits during periods of discomfort and fatigue, and eased fears at those moments when the men were most likely to doubt the wisdom of their presence in an enemy country. Virtually every regimental unit had its own band, and the musicians were ever ready to provide the therapy that only music could offer. After a hard day's march over desert mountains and plains, under Mexico's burning sun, the bands, as one soldier put it, served "to enliven us up." Men who had barely been able to keep up with the march during the day were fiddling and dancing at day's end, to the amazement of their officers. For one Indianan, such impromptu concerts "had a good effect upon our feelings . . . aroused the recollections of home . . . and told us that we had yet something to live for."[58]

In battle, music stiffened resolve and warded off fright, nowhere to greater effect than in the desperate contest for Monterey, where the soldiers moved into combat to the strains of America's national airs. At intervals during the struggle, when the firing subsided, the men relieved the tension by singing "popular negro melodies." As volunteers boarded the troop ships in preparation for their landing at Vera Cruz, they sang *We Are Bound for the Shores of Mexico* and their spirits were lifted. Music recognized no national distinctions. On the eve of Buena Vista, it was Santa Anna's band that prepared the soldiers for the ordeal that was to come. The notes of Mexico's "beautiful airs" were carried on the breeze to the American lines. When the music stopped, a

"most profound" silence fell over the two armies, the "craggy" mountains all around wrapped in "deep gloom and utter solitude." In Mexico's occupied cities, regimental bands performed daily concerts to
soften the resentments of the people and to show them that the *norte-
americanos* were not such barbarians after all. Men, women, and children gathered to listen and for a time the war seemed far away.[59]

Music in camp relieved the tedium, provided a bond that tied the
soldiers to one another, and linked them with the families and homes
they had left behind. Some volunteers carried their musical instruments with them when they enlisted; others picked up Mexican instruments on the battlefields or purchased them from vendors. Almost
immediately, informal instrumental groups and singing societies were
formed. (One group ran afoul of General Wool's effort to enforce an
obscure army regulation against playing musical instruments in camp
without authorization.) There were moments when the camp was given
over to a wide variety of musical entertainments. Wandering through
his encampment on the Rio Grande, a Tennessee volunteer reported

> some eight or ten, singing with full voice and spirit a number of good old
> camp-meeting songs, while near by another party are dancing to the music
> of a cracked violin; and jigs, hornpipes, cotillions, and "Old Virginny
> break downs," interspersed with extra specimens of the "pigeon wing,"
> "wiring," &c., are performed with an air of ease and nonchalance. . . .
> Yonder, too, a band of Ethiopian serenaders are entertaining a crowd with
> songs, glees, and melodies, and for an accompaniment they have called
> into requisition a half string fiddle, a tin pan, "bones," and Samson's fa-
> mous weapon.

The soldiers' songs were the same popular melodies that had entertained them back home—camp-meeting and temperance tunes, often
with new words to fit the circumstances of the war, and minstrel melodies. One such song which swept the army camps was Alexander
Meek's *The Rose of Alabama*. "Who is the 'Rose of Alabama'?" asked
correspondent George Wilkins Kendall. The soldiers "appear to think,
and especially to sing, about nothing else." Some of the older tunes
seemed to be cast aside. "Is D. Tucker Esq. dead," Kendall asked, "and
have the Misses Neal and Long been forgotten? Is a dandy from the
Carolinas whose first name was James, sunk into obscurity?" Kendall
assumed that *The Rose of Alabama* was "some new Ethiopian refrain
which has obtained a name and popularity at home."[60]

Even more popular was a song that has always held special meaning
to fighting men throughout the English-speaking world: Samuel
Lover's *The Girl I Left Behind Me*. Indeed, the tune became so popular
with the soldiers that the Mexicans themselves adopted it. Lover, an
Irish poet, songwriter, and novelist, toured the United States during
the war, presenting his "Irish Evenings" to audiences throughout the
country. The popularity of *The Girl I Left Behind Me* never waned; it
was sung by American soldiers throughout the 19th century and be-

yond. A parody of the song, "in compliment to Gen. Santa Anna," was circulated following the battle of Cerro Gordo, *The Leg I Left Behind Me.*

One night in camp after the men had retired following a long day's march, a Tennessee volunteer brought out his "clarionette" and began playing first *The Girl I Left Behind Me* and then *Home Sweet Home,* the notes floating "gently through the quiet air." Few songs struck the nostalgic chord among the soldiers in Mexico so well as John Howard Payne's 1823 composition. "I would at that time," wrote a convalescent Ohioan in a Vera Cruz hospital after having listened to *Home Sweet Home,* "rather have heard any other tune in the world than that." Thoughts of all the pleasures and comforts of his home and family poured in upon him. There is, he concluded, "no place like *Home.*" The song never failed to arouse feelings of melancholy sadness.

Music, like the popular arts generally, provided a barometer for gauging popular responses to the Mexican War and in doing so revealed much about the character of midcentury Americans. War songs, one recent study has suggested, reflect the basic emotions of the time, expressing in musical form what the populace already thinks and feels. The conflict with Mexico, the first American war in which music played an important patriotic and romantic role, clearly bears out this assertion.[61]

CHAPTER 9

The Historians' War

"Who is to write the history of the Mexican war?" asked the *Southern Quarterly Review* early in 1848. As the conflict drew to a close, the question gained in importance. That the war was a significant episode in the career of the American republic no one denied. Its significance seemed clear: the war strengthened republican government, not only in the Western Hemisphere but also in the world, a belief that appeared obvious as Europe became convulsed by revolution; the war also brought new respect and prestige to the United States, earning for it an acknowledged maturity in the world community of nations. Victory over Mexico revealed the power of a republic to mobilize its resources in time of crisis and, as a people's war, demonstrated the ability of a republic to fight a foreign war successfully without compromising its democratic institutions. In the context of the 1840s, neither had been conceded by those who questioned republicanism. Everything pointed to the Mexican War as the major event in American history since the Revolution, perhaps even as an event of great importance in world history.

Convinced of their uniqueness, Americans approached the past from an ethnocentric angle, seeking in history a legitimacy for their assumptions of mission and destiny. To examine the past was to find meaning for themselves and their institutions in the sweep of time; the study of history was an exercise in self-identity. With minds already set, it is not surprising that they found what they were looking for. That the "model republic" occupied a unique and unchallenged place in the progress of civilization was beyond doubt. Indeed, some midcentury historians saw the United States as the culmination of man's progress since prehistoric times.

Even so, there was a romantic ambivalence in the effort to discover an identity in world history. On the one hand, many believed that America had no past, that it represented something new and fresh and therefore unconfined by the bounds of history. America had, in Fred Somkin's phrase, triumphed over time. "Our national birth," announced the *Democratic Review* in 1839, "was the beginning of a new history . . . which separates us from the past and connects us with the future only." On the other hand there were those who felt that America's true identity and the real dimension of its providential mission could be defined only within the continuum of world history. Only then could the world significance of 1776 be properly recognized and appreciated. These attitudes were not as irreconcilable as might at first appear. It was in history, their own and the world's, that Americans sought clues to the destiny they were sure God meant them to have. "We are the children and heirs of the past," wrote George Bancroft at midcentury, "with which, as with the future, we are indissolubly linked together; and he that truly has sympathy with every thing belonging to man, will, with his toils for posterity, blend affection for the times that are gone by, and seek to live in the vast life of the ages."[1]

Interest in the past had never been more popular or seemed more relevant than in the mid-years of the nineteenth century. Romanticism's focus on organic development and on the continuity of history brought a new interest in origins. Popular notions of mission and destiny directed attention to the circumstances of the nation's revolutionary beginnings that gave those concepts meaning. Works on the American Revolution and the men who brought it to fruition filled the pages of periodicals and crowded the lists of publishers. The collection, and publication, of historical documents was a means for transmitting the revolutionary legacy to later generations. Every locality had its history, and the desire to place that history in the larger scheme of national and world history led to the establishment of state and local historical societies, themselves serving as media for the glorification of American uniqueness. Books of history were beneficiaries of the publication explosion, which technology and the expansion of educational opportunity made possible. "No province of literature," commented *Graham's Magazine,* "has been so modified by the vast increase of books as the writing of History." Books were being written "with a view to their being *read,*" and the scope of historical knowledge, once but a "small manor," had suddenly become a "kingdom." That there should be so strong a "spirit of historical research" in so "young and unhistorical a country" was nothing short of amazing to Europeans, who still regarded Americans as an unlettered and culturally backward people.[2]

For Americans at midcentury, history—the study of the past—was filled with instruction for the present. The survival of the republic, indeed of all republics, depended upon the wisdom and virtue of its people; it was from a knowledge of the past that these qualities drew their strength. "Wisdom cannot be acquired where the lessons of history are not pondered; virtue finds one of its strongest supporters and most eloquent defenders in the truthful records of the past." History not only taught how to avoid the errors of the past but also offered examples of "patriotic trial, of moral courage, of valor in the battle field" which by stimulating imitation would "keep alive national spirit and love of country." History, in short, had a great patriotic purpose.

George Bancroft, the age's greatest historian, believed that history, most notably American history, revealed God's design for mankind. The theme of human progress gave unity to the past and meaning to the present, and it was in the United States that progress—the steady advance of liberty and justice—had achieved its highest expression. "The measure of the progress of civilization," he wrote, "is the progress of the people." There was no doubt to him as well as to countless others that America stood at the pinnacle of this progression. America's mission to implement God's will for all people was, as Bancroft and other romantics would say, the "spirit of the age." History had much to teach, for it disclosed "the Herculean efforts" that had been made to expand and guarantee the rights of man, the struggles for freedom and justice, the long night of "ignorance, error, and oppression," and the faint glimmering of the new day that was dawning at last on the shores of the new world. All history, suggested the *American Review,* must be written and rewritten according to the "true American spirit"—that vision "made keen by a new experience, gazing through a new light, informed by new modes of thought and feeling." The birth of the American republic, with its providential mission of regeneration, had rendered obsolete all the history that had gone before.[3]

Historical study mirrored the commonly accepted notion of the "spirit of the age" and in doing so marked new pathways down which the historian was expected to march. The past, insisted the romantics of early 19th-century America, must speak to the "sensibility and imagination" as well as the understanding, the heart as well as the head. The events of the past must be made as "real to the mind" as any event which "experience has stamped on the memory." Infused with a transcendental quality, history, as Emerson declared, was the "Ultimate Reality." To the historian, it meant that the "romantic element" in history must be sought out in order to impart life into the "fleshless forms" of the past. History was real and full of drama, and the historian's mission was to convey this reality and dramatic effect, to bring the past alive and thus render it more meaningful, to extend the past into the present in order that its lessons might better be understood. The cold lifeless "*bas-reliefs*" of earlier historians were to be supplanted by the "glowing *pictures*" of the modern. Furthermore, history in this age of progress had a strong social responsibility; not only must it be brought to the people, it must be of and for the people as well. It must be, in short, the story of flesh-and-blood human beings, acting and reacting, living their lives from day to day as actors in a great moral drama. History, in speaking to the heart, must enable readers "to live with the people, fight by them in battle, sit with them at the table, make love, hate, fear and triumph with them."[4]

That American writers sought to define the Mexican War in historical terms, identifying its place in the sweep of the past and assessing its role in the nation's progress, was not surprising. Convinced of the significance of the war, they found in the conflict additional clues to national identity. No such war, wrote one historian, which exemplified the "boldest energies of man" and strengthened the reputation of the nation could be studied too often. The Mexican War revealed the "native germs of the American character and [was] full of instruction and encouragement for the future."[5] At the same time, problems and pitfalls were recognized, some inherent in the writing of history generally, others unique to the war. While some writers bolted out of the starting-gate almost before there was a war to write about, there were serious questions as to the appropriate moment for a meaningful history of the conflict.

"The present moment is not the time to attempt a compendious history of the war," warned the *Literary World* in July 1848. Much spade-work yet needed to be done. The records of the military units, the memoirs of the soldiers, the official records and documents of the government all had to be collected, scrutinized, and digested before work could begin. "There must be a great ferment before we can reach the full essence." Nor was that all. The facts of the war and, even more importantly, the spirit behind the facts must "simmer a good while in the brain of the historian" before their meaning could be ascertained. The perspective of time was essential. "It will be time enough for our Napier, a quarter of a century hence." The task would not be easy or simple nor would every aspiring historian be suited to undertake it. In the first place, the writer of "responsible history" must be a "*responsible man*—of a strong nerve—with an iron pen." Furthermore,

> he must plod months, perhaps years, through fields into which common men would not go, or which they would traverse with the greatest speed. There can be for him no railroads, or steam engines, or magnetic telegraphs. With his scrip[t] in one hand, and lantern in the other, he must creep warily and slowly, gathering a broken musket here, a scabbardless sword there; a dismantled cannon on one side, and an odd ball on the other; wading through trenches and climbing dilapidated ramparts, until not a rood is unexplored. Then, imbued with the spirit of the past, and with ability to put his finger on proofs of his statements, he may set about addressing the present and, perhaps, future ages.

To wait too long, however, only compounded the difficulty. "It is hard to write the history of an exciting event half a century after it has transpired," suggested the Whig party's *American Review,* for while the facts may be known, the spirit of the time may not be so easily recaptured. Facts clearly were not enough. The spirit cannot be recovered from cold statistical evidence, no matter how accurate, and without the spirit, history was a lifeless chronicle.[6]

"A thoroughly digested history of the Mexican war," suggested *Peterson's Magazine* early in 1848, "would be an addition to our literature, and we have no doubt that as soon as hostilities are over, if not before, such a book will be written by some able pen." But, the question was, by whose pen? Only the very ablest of historians, it was argued, should attempt the war's history, but who? However much Americans had disagreed over the necessity of the war or its justice, it was certain to go down to posterity "emblazoned with the reminiscent glory of conquest and territorial acquisition." The causes of the war would quickly be forgotten or submerged in its overarching significance, to be considered, if at all, by those who "delight to show their courage and ability in hacking men of straw." Only someone familiar with the events, versed in the "science of war," whose view of the "dignity" of history was worthy of the war's glory, could write its history. The "fame and character" of the United States depended on it. The subject was so full of drama and romance that only an individual of the stature of Prescott would satisfy.[7] Indeed, many asked, why not Prescott? Who better than the historian of the First Conquest of Mexico?

Few names were so closely associated with the Mexican War than that of America's great historian and chronicler of the Spanish conquest, the Bostonian William Hickling Prescott—an ironic association, for Prescott, a devout antislavery New England Whig, was strongly opposed to what he termed this "mad and unprincipled" war. The immense popularity of his *History of the Conquest of Mexico*, published just two and a half years before the war, had turned public attention toward Mexico, stimulated interest in that country, and familiarized countless Americans with the titanic struggle between Cortez and Montezuma. When relations between the United States and Mexico reached their nadir, the example of 16th-century Spain's conquest of Mexico, with all its romance and drama, was fresh in the American mind. Prescott deplored the "dare-devil war spirit" that seemed to overrun the country; what he did not realize was that his own work had much to do with stimulating that spirit. By describing "the *past* Conquest of Mexico" so eloquently, a friend pointed out, Prescott had in fact "foretold the *future* one."

The war in turn boosted the sales of the *History,* and Prescott's publisher, Harper and Brothers, exploited the new and flourishing market. Prescott watched with surprise as sales figures climbed. Loathe to attribute the book's success to the war, he pointed instead to the strong demand in America for works of history, proudly noting that "Brother Jonathan . . . reads something else besides newspapers and almanacs."[8]

Prescott's *History of the Conquest of Mexico* encouraged the enlistment of volunteers who hoped to find in Mexico some of the glory and romance they found in its pages. The historian had seen in the Spanish conquest "a beautiful epic," with "all the interest which daring, chivalrous enterprise, stupendous achievements, worthy of an age of knight-errantry, a magical country, the splendors of a rich barbaric court, and extraordinary personal qualities in the hero—can give." It was precisely the way many Americans viewed their own war with Mexico. John Blount Robertson, a young Tennessee lawyer, was one of the volunteers whose imagination had been fired by Prescott's work. The war, he wrote, gave him the chance to satisfy a "long cherished desire to visit . . . the scene of Cortes' conquests." Lew Wallace was so enthralled with the book's "adventure, exploration, combat, [and] heroisms" that he volunteered in part to relive some of its episodes. For the soldiers in Scott's army, following the track of Cortez, Prescott's history became a guidebook. A work of intense interest in any country at any time, wrote one soldier from Mexico City, "you may suppose how much it is enhanced here." Nor were the soldiers alone in their admiration for the book and its author. A Mexican edition, annotated by the eminent historian Lúcas Alamán, was widely advertised in the capital, and Prescott's name, the Americans were pleased to learn, was held "in sincere and hearty veneration." Some of the men who had read the book used the Mexican edition to help them learn the Spanish language.[9]

Among those who found Prescott's *History* relevant to his Mexican War experience was Caleb Cushing of Massachusetts, leading Democratic party politician and colonel of the state's volunteer regiment. Posted at San Angel, only a few miles from Mexico City, Cushing reread the *History*, as he wrote to Prescott, "among the scenes which it so graphically and beautifully describes." He assured Prescott, who had never visited Mexico, that his descriptions were accurate: "They could have received little additional force or truth from personal inspection." The "Second Conquest," Cushing added, afforded "many points of analogy with the First, which strike the observer on the spot." Although his occupation duties kept him busy, the colonel found time to ride around the countryside, visiting sites mentioned by Prescott. Furthermore, he informed Prescott, he was buying books and antiques. "An officer stationed in Mexico," he wrote, "could collect a great deal that is valuable in the way of MSS, the public archives and convents being in our hands, and of antiquities, for which proper researches by excavation have never been made." Large quantities of vases and figures had been turned up by soldiers erecting breastworks, and Cushing hoped that more organized and thorough excavations could soon be undertaken.

Cushing's comments aroused Prescott's interest. The "temporary possession" of the Mexican capital, he agreed, offered a rare opportunity "to disinter some of the Aztec monuments and MSS." The Spanish archives, both public and private, had been "hoarded up from the eyes of the scholar." With the American army in occupation, these manuscript treasures could be brought to light and made available to researchers. It would be an unexpected reward for the American victory. Prescott's concern was partially met when Charles Naylor, former Whig

Congressman and captain of a company of volunteers in the Second Pennsylvania Regiment, was appointed "librarian" and instructed to put the Mexican archives in order. Not only were the manuscripts "in a most confused condition," but many of them showed signs of "spoliation" and mutilation.

Prescott urged Cushing to contact Alamán, whom he described as "one of the most accomplished and clever men in Mexico." A former minister for foreign affairs and royalist in politics, the Mexican historian had supplied Prescott with information and documents on the Spanish conquest. Although anti-American in attitude, Alamán got along well with the occupation troops. Hearing that Cushing planned to write a book on Mexico, he sent the officer material and offered the use of his library. Some of the volunteers, aware of Alamán's reputation, called on him, and Alamán, who had custody of the Cortez family archives, repaid their visits by displaying 300-year-old manuscripts, including some bearing Cortez's signature.[10]

To Prescott, however, the war with Mexico remained a product of America's "mad ambition for conquest." With territory already too vast for the good of the republic (he had opposed the annexation of Texas and was lukewarm toward the acquisition of Oregon), the country hardly needed more. The war, he feared, would only weaken the republic and strengthen the power of slavery. An unshakable Whig, Prescott charged that the government, under Polk, was "in as bad hands" as it could possibly be.

At the same time, Prescott detected an inner strength in the American people that surmounted all obstacles. "We go ahead," he wrote, "like a great lusty brat that will work his way into the full size of a man, from the strength of his constitution, whatever quacks and old women may do to break it." There was a "renovating power" in the American character that carried the country through storms that would prostrate the "older and worn out countries of Europe." He found evidence of this "elastic vigour" in the war itself. The volunteers won his grudging admiration, for they were proof of America's "indomitable energy" and its capacity for "the highest and most difficult scenes of action." They were, he had written, the "pioneers of civilization."

By the spring of 1848, even Prescott was linking the American conquest with the Spanish conquest. Congratulating Cushing on the triumphant conclusion of the campaign against the Mexican capital, he judged the American victory to be "as brilliant as that of the great *conquistador* himself." He feared he might have exaggerated Spanish valor in his book, for the Mexicans "hardly maintained the reputation of their hardy ancestors." The Second Conquest, he asserted, should have been at least as difficult as the First, "considering the higher civilization & military science of the races who now occupy the country." But, he concluded, "it has not proved so."[11]

During the war, Prescott completed his sequel to the conquest of

Mexico, the history of Pizarro's conquest of Peru. "I have been carrying on the Conquest of Peru while the Government have been making the Conquest of Mexico," he wrote Lord Morpeth, "but mine is the best of the two, since it cost only the shedding of ink instead of blood." Harper's published the book in late June 1847. While it lacked the popularity of the earlier work, *The History of the Conquest of Peru* linked Prescott even more closely to the war, for reviewers often drew parallels between the conquest of Peru and the American invasion of Mexico.[12]

That Prescott should become the historian of the Second Conquest of Mexico appeared both logical and appropriate to many Americans, not the least of whom were General Winfield Scott and his Whig friends. In July 1848 Prescott received an invitation from Scott to write the history of the "second Mexican War" for which the General was ready to make available all his papers. The invitation was enclosed in a letter from Charles King, New York merchant and editor of the *Courier & Enquirer*, who had been pushing Scott's name for the Presidency since 1839. Received a few days after the Whig convention had passed over Scott in favor of Taylor, the invitation no doubt had a political motivation. Prescott was tempted. The subject was a brilliant one, a counterpart to Cortez's conquest of Mexico; furthermore, the popularity of the war and Scott's stature as one of its heroes meant that the "profits of authorship" would exceed those of anything he had yet written.

In the end, however, Prescott's reply was unequivocal. He was already at work on his biography of Philip the Second and was reluctant to interrupt it. He had determined, moreover, that contemporary events, personal feelings, and ambitions should play no part in shaping his literary life. The task would be "taking" but, he confided, he would "rather not meddle with heroes who have not been under ground—two centuries—at least." Prescott's decision was lauded by Bancroft. "The same motive which induced me long ago to give over writing reviews of living people's works," he wrote from his post in London, "is a good one for your decision about the new conquest of Mexico." To satisfy "the thousand and one heroes, each one of whom was in his own estimate at least the pivot of success," would mean scattering laurels "more abundantly than Alexander did gifts." If, on the other hand, Prescott could be content with the applause of his countrymen and indifferent to the complaints "of those whose deeds you record," Bancroft believed he would achieve a "brilliant success." The subject was a noble one, more picturesque even than that of Cortez's campaign. "The whole affair," Bancroft wrote, "was magical, and worthy of being told in your happiest manner."[13]

If America's foremost historian declined the opportunity to write the war's history, there were many other candidates for the honor. The solemn warnings of the difficulties that lay in the path of the historian did little to stanch the flow of books that began to flood the market. Writers were impatient, publishers were impatient, and, most important of all, the reading public was impatient. It was America's first foreign conflict, the first *real* war in a generation, and people were eager to learn as much as they could about it. There was a war spirit abroad in the land that demanded satisfaction. The result was a "Niagara of books" that showed no signs of abating.

Critics and reviewers found it difficult to keep up with the number of war books and complained that many of them were unworthy of notice. Mere "catch-penny affairs," they were the work of "stilted eulogists" whose pages "blaze ever with *red*." Books "foaming with excitement," written solely to quench the public's thirst for action, pushed aside those with more elevated themes. Passion and appetite replaced quiet enlightenment. "Our people are too Rough and Ready," one writer complained, "and because they are so, they must have books that will make them more so."[14]

The Mexican War also inspired a broader interest in war generally. "Military histories were never more . . . eagerly read." One of the leading suppliers was Joel Tyler Headley, ordained minister, editor, and traveler, whose books contained enough blood and carnage for him to secure a reputation as "the most popular of authors." Edgar Allan Poe called him the "Autocrat of all the Quacks," but in the minds of readers this reflected more on Poe than on Headley. He wrote what were termed "torpedo histories," works filled with battles and sieges and written with a "most vigorous flourish of all the wind-instruments of rhetoric." During the three war-years he published in quick succession books on Napoleon (dedicated to Winfield Scott), Washington, and Cromwell. Although he fostered a "war spirit" with his publications, Headley disclaimed all sympathy with warfare and insisted that work on his books had filled him with disgust and detestation. Critics were unconvinced and rightly so. There was something fascinating and mysterious in "gigantic slaughter," and Headley was only one of many who hastened to enter the market. The whole country was "fired with the spirit of Mars."[15]

For the history of the Mexican War, Americans turned to their military leaders. The *Southern Quarterly Review* insisted there could be but one qualified candidate to write the history of the war. "If we had to select the writer of the history of this war, we would point to the author of General Taylor's despatches as the man. Xenophon, Thucydides, Caesar and the Archduke Charles, wrote the history of their own wars." As one of the great captains of the world, Taylor had the required knowledge and experience, yet he remained a plain and simple man, able to see his achievements in perspective and to recognize the ability and skill of others. He was consistently praised for the brevity and simplicity of his writing style ("cool and concise, yet familiar"). "We have plenty of officers who can fight," James Fenimore Cooper wrote, "but, as yet, Rough and Ready carries off all the glories of the pen." He "really writes like a book." Who was better situated to record the military history of the Mexican War? Taylor, alas, was not interested. So far as is known, he never seriously entertained the suggestion that he become the war's historian. Yet, in a sense, he did play the role of historian, if not of the war at least of his own campaigns in northern Mexico, for his dispatches and reports were not only printed in the newspapers but also were at the heart of many of the war's histories. Few writers felt they could improve on Taylor's accounts, and it was through Taylor's words that many Americans formed their perceptions of the war.[16]

The feeling was strong that only the soldiers who had fought in Mexico could write authentic histories of the conflict. "Real actors in a battle describe it with more vividness than can possibly be done by the historian in his study." Early in 1849, the rumor that Major W. W. S. Bliss, Taylor's adjutant during the war, was preparing a history of Taylor's campaigns circulated, but no such history ever appeared. When Lieutenant Colonel Ethan Allen Hitchcock returned to the United States in the spring of 1848 he was "vigorously besieged" to write the history of the war. A man of broad interests and superior intelligence (he had already published a book comparing Spinoza and Swedenborg), Hitchcock commanded the Third Infantry Regiment in Taylor's army before being assigned to Winfield Scott's staff. Judged by some to be best qualified to write an "impartial" account, Hitchcock started on a history but quickly gave it up.[17]

While serving as editor of the *Southern Quarterly Review*, William Gilmore Simms encouraged Marcus Claudius Marcellus Hammond to write a series of ten articles on the war, which taken together constituted a fairly complete account of the military operations. A younger brother of the prominent South Carolina planter-politician, Hammond had served briefly in the army following his graduation from West Point, engaged in cotton planting, and for a short time during the Mexican War held the post of army paymaster. "Write on," Simms advised, "as if you were writing history." Simms also urged Hammond to write a history of South Carolina's Palmetto Regiment and to publish a translation of Henri Jomini's work on the art of war, but neither was ever undertaken.

Hammond intended simply "to make certain military points" rather than to offer a full history of the war. He complained that most writers on the war were "amateurs or book makers," ignorant of the science of arms and of the lessons of military history. Hammond revealed a profound acquaintance with military history from classical times through the Napoleonic wars and quoted frequently from the writings of Napoleon, Jomini, Thiers, and Napier. At the same time, his work was more than a close analysis of the military campaigns. He lauded Taylor, "a rare instance of sublime self-reliance" and "comparatively faultless," and Scott, who he felt would receive from later generations the acclaim that was withheld by his own. Furthermore, he hoped his articles would expose the difficulties involved in waging war in a foreign country and recall, for his countrymen, the "brilliant efforts of genius and heroism" that marked the war.

Like most of the war's historians, Hammond found responsibility for the conflict solely on the side of Mexico (although he believed the war might have been avoided had Polk sent a larger army to the Rio Grande). Aside from the immediate "pretext" of Texas's annexation, Mexico had nurtured a hatred for the United States that sprang from an "envy of our acknowledged superiority in every thing." The vast difference between the two republics—"the onward progress of the one, and the gradual, but certain decline of the other"—was not lost on Mexico. America's forbearance in the face of repeated insults merely increased Mexico's arrogance and magnified its conceit. While he thought the Mexicans had fought well, their defeat was foreordained. Hammond's explanation was simple: Mexico had encountered a "more advanced and more perfect race of men."[18]

The army was filled with would-be historians who did not require the urgings of their countrymen to put their pens to paper. Indeed, despairing critics were convinced that every soldier who marched off to Mexico fancied himself an historian. How many histories were begun but never finished (like that of Captain Daniel Ruggles of the Fifth Infantry Regiment) cannot be known, but in the long run they were hardly missed.

The distinction between a soldier's personal campaign narrative and a history was often blurred. Works like William Seaton Henry's description of Taylor's operations along the Rio Grande, James Henry Carleton's account of the Battle of Buena Vista, and Raphael Semmes's record of his experiences with the navy's Gulf Squadron and with Scott's army were all hailed as works of history. Semmes, who intended his book to be a "reliable *history*" of the war and an antidote to the "puerilities and puffings" with which the public had been bombarded, succeeded more than most. His *Service Afloat and Ashore During the Mexican War*, published in 1851, so captured the public's interest that the entire first edition was sold out in two weeks. "We have never read a history evidently so fairly written," wrote one critic. His accounts of shipwrecks and battles were "glowing and vehement," his descriptions of the Mexican landscape that of an artist. Semmes went beyond the sensational and romantic aspects of the conflict to include a political history of Mexico, an account of Mexican-American relations, and the "various complications" that led to the outbreak of war. Mexico, he believed, was in a state of decline, its people demoralized, its economy ruined, and its public men corrupt, conditions he attributed to Spain's long subjugation of the country and to the oppressive partnership of Church and military. With the Mexican War, time "brought another and a newer race, to sweep away the mouldered and mouldering institutions of a worn-out people, and replace them with a fresher and more vigorous civilization." It was the will of an all-wise Providence.[19]

Included in this legion of soldier-writers were volunteers who, like South Carolina's H. Judge Moore, combined patriotism and a desire for adventure with ambitions to play the historian. Moore believed he had the necessary equipment—an "impartial hand" and an "unbiassed head"—but his account of the Palmetto Regiment, even though fleshed out with material from a variety of historical and travel narratives, was too thin and flowery to serve as a reliable historical narrative. In 1853, Luther Giddings, a veteran of an Ohio regiment, published his "notes and memoirs" even though he conceded that a "strong and experienced corps of intelligent officers and literary camp-followers" had already taken the field with their pens. If the time was not yet right for the "impartial summing up by the historian," Giddings reasoned, at least his jottings might "serve the cause of History."[20]

More remarkable was the ambitious 600-page *The Twelve Months' Volunteer,* published in 1848 by George C. Furber, a Tennessee lawyer who had served in his state's volunteer cavalry regiment. Although Furber based his account on his personal journal, the book was more than a military reminiscence. Its scope was wide-ranging: the life of the soldier in camp, a description of Texas and Mexico "as seen on the march," the manners and customs of the Mexican people, and the operations of the volunteers, "including a complete history of the war with Mexico." Furber acknowledged the aid of fellow soldiers who had shared their notes and diaries with him but he consulted no other sources because, as he put it, he wished to avoid the "errors or carelessness of others."

Although the work fell short as a history of the war (it ended with the summer of 1847 when Furber and other twelve months' volunteers were sent home), it enjoyed a continuing popularity as one of the most successful campaign accounts by a participant in the conflict. Furber was later given the opportunity to complete his history when he was asked to finish the late Dr. Philip Young's *History of Mexico.* Young, whose work focused primarily on the story of Mexico's civil wars, died before he could carry the narrative beyond the American occupation of Vera Cruz. Furber continued the story to the end of the war and the ratification of the peace treaty. Encouraged by the favorable response to his work, he ventured into the realm of literature with the publication in 1849 of a collection of fictionalized episodes drawn from his experiences, *Camp Stories: or, Incidents in the Life of a Soldier.*[21]

Like most of those who published campaign accounts, Furber paid scant attention to the war's causes. Why the war happened was not as important as how the nation responded to it and how it was fought. Giddings skirted the question because of the controversy that hung over it and the "mists of passion and prejudice" that seemed to obscure the war's origins. The soldier-writers, however, generally agreed that

Mexico was responsible for the war and some of them (like Furber) took pains to demonstrate Mexico's bellicose attitude toward the United States. At the same time they were careful to separate the Mexican people from their rulers; by exposing the tyrannical designs of the Mexican leaders, the writers concluded, the American occupation helped the people to find their way toward a genuine republicanism.

The personal accounts of the soldiers, no matter how expanded by references to "authorities," proved unsatisfactory histories of the Mexican War. The dictum that the history of the war could best be written by a participant was not demonstrated by the results. Five years after the war ended, one publisher still contended that no "worthy" history had yet been written. The flood of books that had appeared were dismissed as the "dashing narratives" of "belligerent Hotspurs" or "eulogistic compilations" that made no contribution.[22]

It is ironic that the one history written by a soldier that stood out as an exception aroused so much controversy and was seen as so flawed with bias that its contribution to the historiography of the war was clouded from the beginning. Still, it occupied a position apart from all the other efforts and indeed won praise as the "only complete history yet written of the entire war" and as the only one "worthy of the library." The work was Roswell Sabine Ripley's two-volume *The War with Mexico,* published by Harper in 1849. A native of Ohio and an 1843 graduate of West Point, Ripley was a second lieutenant in the Second Artillery Regiment at the outbreak of the war. He took part in Taylor's battle for Monterey, was assigned to Scott's invasion force, and, promoted to first lieutenant, fought in every battle from the siege of Vera Cruz to the assault on Mexico City. During most of the period, he was aide-de-camp to the controversial Gideon J. Pillow, Polk's former law partner who was appointed brigadier general of volunteers in 1846. Following the evacuation of Mexico at the end of the war, Ripley was granted a year's leave of absence from the army to write his history.[23]

Ripley's intent was to render a "general and impartial account" of the war partly because it was of such "absorbing interest" and partly because its events would soon be regarded as the "most prominent of any which have occurred since the independence of the country." His emphasis was on the military operations, but unlike most of the early historians he did not ignore the political and diplomatic developments in both the United States and Mexico that lay behind those operations. His record as a soldier under both Taylor and Scott gave him an advantage in describing the land and its inhabitants and lent authenticity to his accounts of the battles. Ripley made heavy use of government documents, primarily those published by Congressional order, consulted Mexican and American newspapers, interviewed officers in both armies, and revealed a close familiarity with military tactics and strategy. He commented freely, and often critically, on the policies of the government and the army's commanders, offering his observations in carefully identified sections of the work. Many of his comments, he warned, would be "at variance" with those of his fellow officers. In a style "stripped of the show and ornament" that marked much of the war-writing, Ripley produced an authoritative, yet analytical, account of the war.[24]

Ripley was aware of the problems involved in writing a history of the war so soon after its conclusion. In the first place, there was the difficulty in keeping to the "strait and narrow path" at a time when national pride was at its peak, resisting the temptation to narrate only those events that reflected on the honor of the nation. Secondly, as after every great military achievement, there would be controversies over the relative merits of the commanders, their decisions, and the various units involved in the conflict. Rival claims to greatness would have to be dealt with in an impartial manner. Although Ripley supported the war policies of the Polk administration, his account was restrained and he was generally successful in avoiding an "undue gratification" of national pride. It was on the second problem that he foundered.

Ripley's close association with Pillow, a man known for his vanity, ambition, and reputation as an unscrupulous behind-the-scenes intriguer, rendered him suspect from the beginning. It was rumored that Pillow had collaborated with Ripley on the book and that much of it was written at Pillow's Tennessee residence. Some even said that Pillow had written it all, an allegation that was dismissed as giving the Tennessean credit for more talent than he possessed. The insinuations were serious, for they involved the character of Winfield Scott. It was widely known that Pillow in his reports had tried to discredit Scott while exaggerating his own role; furthermore, Pillow had succeeded in planting in the press anonymous letters, purportedly written by officers in Mexico, lauding his skill at the expense of Scott. Relations between the two men deteriorated into an open and angry confrontation. Scott placed Pillow under arrest, President Polk (who sided with Pillow) ordered a court of inquiry, and the two men were recalled from Mexico. Scott, a hero of the Mexican War, was forced to defend himself against Pillow's ill-advised and fraudulent charges, an ignominious sequel to the glory of victory. To add to the ignominy, Pillow was exonerated.[25]

Ripley's comments on Pillow and Scott in today's light hardly seem out of the ordinary, but in the heavily charged atmosphere of 1849 they were viewed as an attempt to inflate Pillow and destroy Scott. For example, Ripley attributed Pillow's costly and disastrous assault on the Mexican lines at Cerro Gordo to Scott's lack of reliable intelligence and his desire to satisfy the eagerness of the volunteers for battle. Pillow was portrayed as less trusting of Mexican promises, as disapproving Scott's ill-advised armistice after Churubusco, and as insisting that no negotiations be undertaken with the enemy until Mexico City was taken. Scott, Ripley implied, was motivated by political considerations and Presidential ambitions and jealousy of Zachary Taylor's popularity. To most reviewers, such statements could originate only in Pillow's connivance against his superior officer. When Pillow described Ripley's book as tearing Scott "all *to pieces*" the relationship seemed obvious. The second volume, according to M.C.M. Hammond, was so filled with Ripley's disparagement of Scott that the South Carolinian devoted eleven pages in the *Southern Quarterly Review* to a listing of Ripley's sins against historical truth. Not all who read the book, however, were so moved. It was left to the *Literary World* to offer the last word, if not chronologically then historically: "We do not hesitate to express the belief that the majority of readers will agree with Mr. Ripley long before the year 1900."[26]

Ripley's allegations were formally answered two years later when Isaac I. Stevens published his *Campaigns of the Rio Grande and of Mexico,* a small book with no pretension to being a history of the war. Stevens, an 1839 graduate of West Point, had served on Scott's staff as a first lieutenant of engineers and had been rewarded with brevets for his conduct at Contreras, Churubusco, and Chapultepec. His object in writing, he stated, was to vindicate "the truth of History" by correcting Ripley's "unjust criticisms" of the heroic officers and soldiers in Mexico. The book pleased General Scott's partisans but was too narrowly focused on Ripley's narrative to be of wide appeal, designed more for the military than for the civilian reader.[27]

The race to supply the public with accounts of the war began as soon as news of the first battles at Palo Alto and Resaca de la Palma was received. It was not surprising that the first publications appeared as biographies of Taylor, giving Old Rough and Ready the jump in the contest for heroic status. Containing only the barest outlines of Taylor's earlier career (of which most Americans were ignorant), they boasted a "complete" history of the Mexican War even though it did not extend beyond the battle of Resaca de la Palma in early May 1846. The war was, in any event, to be a very short one, or so people thought. The books' pages were padded with eulogies to the fallen soldiers, reports of newspaper correspondents, and official documents. As the war continued the books became more extensive, if not always more original. Published anonymously (no doubt simply compiled in the publishers' offices) were such titles as *Taylor and His Generals,* "Old Rough and Ready" or Taylor and His Battles, and *General Taylor and His Staff.* Some were little more than pamphlets. In thirty-six pages, the "one-legged Sergeant" presented not only a sketch of the life and character of Zachary Taylor but also a "concise" history of the war (concise, indeed!). The publisher of Fayette Robinson's history of the United States army, hastening to tap the market, issued the pages dealing with

Taylor separately as a biography, without the knowledge or the permission of the author. New York editor Henry Montgomery's life of Taylor was written and published in a record seven weeks; four years later it had reached its twentieth edition. Critics bemoaned the "hot haste" with which the books were produced and felt that Taylor—and the war—deserved better.[28]

Whether the war received better was uncertain at first. The public seemed satisfied with the anonymous, scissors-and-paste productions that appeared. When a Philadelphia publisher issued its *History of the War Between the United States and Mexico, From the Best Authorities,* one popular magazine pronounced it "just what is wanted at the present time," even though it contained little more than excerpts and quotations from documents, letters, and newspapers. More ambitious was *Halls of the Montezumas: or, Mexico, in Ancient and Modern Times.* "Ancient times" meant the conquest of Mexico by Cortez, summarized in a few pages, while "modern times" was the Mexican War; there was nothing in between. Presumably, the reader was encouraged to view the latter in terms of the former. The account of the war rested on the author's personal observations (which would suggest that it was written by a soldier) and on "all the standard authorities" on Mexican history. As for the Halls of the Montezumas, the author sought to correct the popular impression that they were "magnificent palaces, sparkling with gold and precious stones, and full of riches of every kind," that rivaled the "splendors of ancient Babylon." As the nation's soldiers have been "rioting" in those Halls, "it is time that they should be particularly described." The book had many of the characteristics of a guidebook, with information on a host of topics from the geography of Mexico, its manufactures, cities, and government to the habits, manners, and character of the people.[29]

Among those who raced to get into print following the war's first battles was Thomas Bangs Thorpe, the eastern-born Louisiana humorist whose pieces had been appearing in the *Spirit of the Times* since 1839. In that year, he published "Tom Owen, the Bee-Hunter," a name that soon became attached to Thorpe himself; his best-known story, "The Big Bear of Arkansas," appeared in 1841. Following the publication of his first book, *The Mysteries of the Backwoods* (1846), Thorpe purchased an interest in the New Orleans *Daily Tropic,* and when the Mexican War began he joined the army on the Rio Grande as a war correspondent.

Thorpe did not remain with the army for long, for by mid-June he had decided to write a history of the war. Like many others, he no doubt believed the war would soon be over and, sensing a demand for books on the conflict, he believed that time was of the essence. He hurriedly collected material, visited the battlefields, interviewed a number of officers, and examined official Mexican and American reports. "I believe I shall give you one of the most readable books of the season," he assured his publisher, "containing more stirring incidents, serious and comic, together with the war's particulars than is often in a volume." His would be the "only *descriptions of the battles* and subsequent scenes ever published." Thorpe spent the summer dashing off chapters and sending them to Philadelphia, while urging speed on his publisher. Other books were appearing on the market, causing Thorpe concern lest his be too late to reap the advantages of the public interest. It was not until October 1846, however, that Thorpe's *Our Army on the Rio Grande* made its appearance.

With his first book on the war completed, Thorpe proposed a volume on California but his friends urged him to continue his history instead. By the end of 1847 his second volume, *Our Army at Monterey*, had appeared. Originally intended to include Monterey and Buena Vista, Thorpe decided to put the latter in a separate volume to be titled *Our Army at Buena Vista*. The three volumes would then comprise a complete history of Taylor's campaigns. Still another volume was planned covering the operations of the army and navy at Vera Cruz, but neither this book nor the Buena Vista book ever appeared. Instead Thorpe turned his attention to Taylor's Presidential boom and in 1848 published *Anecdotes of General Taylor, and the Mexican War* (using the pseudonym, Tom Owen, The Bee-Hunter), a collection of more than 300 brief human-interest stories relating to the war, only some of which dealt with Taylor.[30]

"There are two kinds of history," Thorpe wrote in his preface to the anecdotes book, "one of which comprehends events of vast and extended importance, while the other treats of the individuals who have, in these events, acted a conspicuous part." The former, he believed, was of interest primarily to the "philosopher and moralist," the latter appealed to "all classes alike." It was to the broader audience that Thorpe addressed his work. He confessed that he was among those who had been "deeply excited" by the outbreak of the war and, being on the battlefields and among the heroes almost immediately after the events that "rendered them immortal," he was anxious to convey this feeling of excitement to his countrymen. In his three books, Thorpe contributed perhaps more than any other writer to the accumulation of a body of Mexican War soldier-lore.[31]

Thorpe was captivated by the romance of the march and the battlefield. His early training as an artist and his reputation as a landscape and portrait painter were evident in the care with which he portrayed the two armies in action. "A scene singularly thrilling and sublime, now presented itself—a scene such as was never before witnessed in warlike operations," he wrote of the battle of Palo Alto. "Two contending armies had met upon a battle field formed by an American prairie." The movements of the troops were a "moving panorama." Sharp lances, fluttering pennants, burnished muskets "glittering in the sun, and jets of light playing with terrible significance upon their bayonet points" evoked admiration and awe. Six thousand men stood on the richly carpeted prairie in battle array, their breasts heaving "with pent-up emotions and fierce passions." The regimental colors of the American army were unfurled "amidst deafening cheers," and the battle was begun. Thorpe's artist's eye presented a contrasting picture following the battle—the excitement gone, soldiers sunk in exhaustion, the groans of the wounded "as they breathed their last," the flickering torches of the medical staff and, with the gathering darkness, anxiety among the men for the morrow. The towns through which the army marched on its route to Monterey reminded Thorpe of the Crusades, or of the Alhambra, the countryside was an "earthly paradise." Again, at Monterey, the hearts of the volunteers "throbbed with emotion," ready to prove their courage and win their honor "at the cannon's mouth," knowing that the eyes of the civilized world were upon them.

Thorpe's view of the war was conventionally romantic. He felt it was the mission of the United States to uplift the Mexican people, to develop their resources, and to bring them into the 19th century. No progress would be made, however, until persons of a "higher order"—Americans—should be distributed through the country to provide a "new tone" to society and infuse a "new spirit" into the population.[32]

Thomas Bangs Thorpe did not achieve the acclaim as an historian that he expected. He blamed his lack of recognition partly on the slowness of his publisher in bringing out the two books on Taylor's operations, although some of the responsibility was certainly Thorpe's. The book market had become flooded with the campaign accounts of volunteers, histories, and sensational novelettes, and Thorpe felt the advantage his books would have was lost. He resented the intrusion of writers who had not been on the scene as he had and whose works lacked the authenticity he felt his bore. "I cannot understand how a history could be written," he complained to his publisher, "except it was done, from personal observation." Most of the efforts, he concluded, were put together from "shreds and patches," if they were not outright fiction.

It is perhaps strange that Thorpe was the only war correspondent to undertake a history of the war, but most of the others lacked Thorpe's experience as a writer and could not match his flair for telling a story. The best-known war correspondent was George Wilkins Kendall, of the New Orleans *Picayune*, whose literary fame was well established by the time of the Mexican War. His *Narrative of the Texan Santa Fe Expedition* (of which he had been a member) was published in 1844 and republished in new editions through the war years. When Kendall took to the field as a correspondent early in the war, it was expected that he would write the war's history as he had that of the Santa Fe expedition. "If no other advantage to the country is derived from his enlistment in this most just and holy war," commented the *New York Herald*, "literature will receive a valuable addition, and K. will write a book." Kendall,

however, did not, at least not the kind of book that had been anticipated. In 1851, he collaborated with the German artist Carl Nebel on
The War Between the United States and Mexico Illustrated published first in
Paris and later in New York. Kendall provided a general description of
each battle to accompany Nebel's paintings, but the work hardly constituted a history of the war.[33]

Sharing Thorpe's concern lest the heroism of the war be lost to
posterity were three of the most popular writers in midcentury America. Charles J. Peterson, John Frost, and Fayette Robinson were equally
at home with poetry, fiction, and history, and their prolific pens filled
the columns of books and magazines. They were arbiters of popular
culture, reflectors as well as molders of popular notions and tastes.
Each found in the Mexican War a subject for his talents. None of the
three had ever visited Mexico or the battle-scenes; only one, Robinson,
had been a soldier and thus was acquainted with military life.

Peterson, a member of Philadelphia's literary community during the
1840s, was associated with two leading literary magazines: *Graham's
Magazine* (where he shared editorial responsibilities briefly with Edgar
Allan Poe) and the *Ladies' National Magazine* (renamed *Peterson's Magazine* in 1848). Stories literally poured from his pen, ranging from the
most saccharine medieval romances to stirring tales of adventure in the
early years of the republic. His work included novels of the American
Revolution, tales of battles at sea during the War of 1812, and a series
on Revolutionary battlefields, but his most ambitious undertaking was
his trilogy on the heroes of the Revolution, the War of 1812, and the
Mexican War.

Like most of the popular writers of the day, Peterson looked to a
romantic past with nostalgic longing. He was captivated by tales of
"olden time" and by the European scene where "every hill-side has its
legend" and every "castle-crowned precipice its romance of feudal
times." America, he complained, lacked the legends that "fire the
imagination of the poet" and "guide the historian," a shortcoming he
was determined to overcome. He discovered America's "holy and venerated spots" on the battlefields of the Revolution and he found romance and chivalry in the heroes of the nation's wars.[34]

Peterson's history of the Mexican War was confined to the military
operations. "At least one generation, perhaps two," he stated, "must
elapse before an impartial estimate can be formed of this contest."
Because the judgment of history was always correct, he was willing to
leave to some future time the "examination of the justice and injustice,
the policy or impolicy of the Mexican war." Although he was mildly
critical of Polk and felt that the war might have been averted, his
narrative left no doubt that he viewed the American achievement with
romantic enthusiasm. Modern warfare, he claimed, furnished no parallel to Scott's successful invasion. "The enemy were confounded" by
Scott's daring and by the confidence of his troops as they "hurled the

gauntlet of defiance to all Mexico." Peterson had the romantic's eye for
nature and landscape. Mexico was a "land of enchantment" in which
the soldiers realized "their dreams of an earthly Paradise," their imaginations carried by the Saracenic architecture back to the "romantic days
of Old Spain."

Peterson also offered an extreme racial explanation for the American
victories. "There is more in race," he maintained, "than is generally
supposed." The Mexicans were but degenerate Spaniards, inheriting
few of the virtues and exaggerating the vices of their ancestry. The
"Caucasian stock," he insisted, was superior over all others but among
Caucasians, the "northern branches are better than the southern."
People have certain "constitutional tendencies" that are racially induced
and can never be changed, and the Mexican people (he called them
Creoles) were a case in point. They were weak, indolent, and wanting
in energy and enterprise; "subtlety and deceit" were national characteristics, marking alike the army general who breaks his oath and the
"lurking ranchero."[35]

In his strong racial bias Peterson may have been more outspoken
than other historians, but he was not unique. His popularity stemmed
precisely from the fact that his work reflected widely accepted views.
Within four years of its publication in 1848 *The Military Heroes of the
War with Mexico* had reached its tenth edition. In 1854 all three of
Peterson's "military heroes" books were issued in a single volume, *Peterson's American Wars*, which by 1860 had been reprinted three times.

Although Peterson was a more thoughtful and careful writer, John
Frost outpaced him in sheer production. It would be difficult to identify a writer who enjoyed more popularity in more fields or one who
both reflected and shaped popular perceptions more significantly. A
native of Maine and a graduate of Harvard College, Frost moved to
Philadelphia in the late 1820s, where he served as principal of a girl's
school and as professor of belles-lettres at the city's Central High
School. He retired from teaching in 1845 to devote his full time to
writing. Incredibly prolific, he employed a corps of researchers and
writers to assist him in turning out an estimated 300 works before his
death in 1859. While one recent writer has dismissed Frost as a "hack
of the first order" and another has charged him with feeding the "most
mindless kind of American patriotism," his reputation in the 1840s was
substantial. "Perhaps no one whose name appears in the list of the
literati of Philadelphia," suggested *Godey's*, "has done more to elevate
the literary character of the country." Although he produced principally books of history and biography, Frost, like Peterson, also published poetry and fictional romance. To one popular magazine he contributed a series on America's game birds that established his reputation as a bird-watcher.[36]

Frost's historical interests ranged over the entire globe. Books on
world history, classical Greece and Rome, England and Europe, Africa,

Asia, and South America carried his name on their spines. One of his most popular was the *Pictorial History of America, From the Earliest Times to the Close of the Mexican War*, a two-volume edition that sold over 50,000 copies. He wrote histories of the army, the navy, of border warfare, the heroism of women, and the American Revolution. His historical works were read throughout the country, "everywhere looked upon as authority, and everywhere deservedly popular." Disdaining the mere collection of narratives and documents, he made "no great parade of authorities" and engaged in no controversies. Rather, from "the capacious chambers of his mind" he told a "plain, straightforward story," and therein lay his great popularity. Frost was commended to the people, according to one critic, by the "*American* feeling" which permeated his writings, a patriotic spirit that not only fired the hearts of Americans but also (as in the war with Mexico) "nerve[d] their arms whenever a hostile hand" was raised against their country.[37]

"It is certainly a gratifying task to any patriotic American writer," Frost wrote, "to record the events of the recent war with the Mexican Republic." It was a task to which he devoted much of his time during the war years. " 'A round unvarnished tale' of the whole progress of the war," he insisted, was essential to the "historical library of every family." There was, moreover, a public "anxiety" to know something of the "whole antecedent history" of Mexico. In 1847 he published his *Life of Major General Zachary Taylor* and in the following year, *The Mexican War and Its Warriors* and *The Pictorial History of Mexico and the Mexican War*. In all three volumes, Frost focused on the heroism that the war had brought forth. Like many of his contemporaries, Frost saw in the war a reassuring antidote to the growing materialism of his time. The conflict allayed his fears and proved that "the heroic age, the age of American chivalry, has not yet quite passed away." Americans could still stand beside the heroes of the republic's early days. They were not the "mercenary, merchandizing people" their enemies charged; the long period of peace had not rendered extinct the "martial spirit of a free nation." The war indeed revealed qualities of valor and courage which "astonished the whole civilized world." The significance of the war to Frost lay in the strength it gave to the republican principle, reawakening in the people the spirit with which the nation had been founded. By laying the record of the Mexican War before the public, he hoped to "promote the cause of virtue."[38]

Less prolific than Peterson or Frost was Fayette Robinson, a Virginian who served in the First Dragoons for four years on the western frontier. Commissioned a second lieutenant in 1837 and promoted to first lieutenant two years later, he resigned from the army in 1841 for reasons of health. After recuperating on the Gulf coast, he moved to New York City where he died in 1859. Details of his life are sketchy; he seems not to have been a West Point graduate, as some maintained, nor is it likely that he ever resided in Mexico, as others have said. The

obscurity of his life contrasts markedly with the widespread popularity
his writings enjoyed and with the remarkable variety of his literary
achievements. Like his contemporaries, Robinson did not confine himself to a single genre. He wrote poetry, fiction, and at least one play.
His unusual linguistic abilities enabled him to translate the work of
Petrarch and other Italian poets, to publish a Spanish grammar, and to
earn fame as the American translator of George Sand's novels. He
published articles in *Graham's* on subjects ranging from Cincinnati to
Chateaubriand. In 1849, he published a guidebook to the gold fields of
California, which he certainly had never visited.

While he was recovering from his illness, Robinson began collecting
books and documents relating to the "history and antiquities of the
whole American Continent." The outbreak of the Mexican War, he
wrote, was fortuitous for it enabled him to "illustrate engrossing subjects which had acquired unforeseen interest." While chiding Americans for having neglected the history of their Latin-American neighbors, he proposed to meet their demand for information on the "self-
named" republic of Mexico with his *Mexico and Her Military Chieftains,
from the Revolution of Hidalgo to the Present Time,* published in 1847 (and
said to have sold 8000 copies in its first two weeks). It was the story of
Mexico's "sad descent," of a people superstitious, abject, and humili-
ated, prey to tyrannical power, cupidity, and avarice. Robinson speculated whether the "old creed" might not be correct, that "beautiful
countries were confided to degraded races until a firmer and worthier
stock were ready to occupy them." Suggesting that the country had
been in better hands under Montezuma, he believed the Spanish conquest retarded rather than promoted the progress of human enlightenment. Cursed by misgovernment, racked by repeated revolutions, Mexico's future seemed dim to Robinson, without hope unless the people
could learn, by a "series of calamities" if necessary, that freedom exacted sacrifice and required vigilance and virtue. In a free country the
"wishes of the individual must be sacrificed to the interests of a community" while under an absolute government the "interests of a community" are sacrificed to the "wishes of an individual."[39]

Robinson hinted that he might write a history of the Mexican War "at
some other day"; in the meantime, he was content simply to include a
brief comment on the war in his work on Mexico and to deal with the
war's heroes in his voluminous two-volume *Account of the Organization of
the Army of the United States* (1848) and several articles in *Graham's*.
Unlike Peterson and Frost, Robinson did not share the longing for a
chivalric age gone by. Instead, Robinson cautioned that "there was little
true poetry, and less feeling in the minds of the [old] heroes . . . than of
the veriest apostles of commerce of our own age." The Mexican War
simply marked the triumph of superior institutions over a people cor-
rupted and downtrodden by centuries of absolute rule.[40]

"During the progress of the war between the United States and Mexico . . . the public were favored with numerous histories of the events, as well as with biographies of the men who figured in its brilliant scenes and stirring events; but most of these accounts were hastily prepared, and necessarily incomplete and imperfect." So spoke Freeman Hunt's *Merchants' Magazine* in February 1849 in a review of John S. Jenkins's history of the war. Jenkins, the reviewer went on, had waited until the war ended thus enabling him to write a "complete and full" history. Not only was he able to consult all the documents pertaining to the conflict but he also had the advantage of those writers who had preceded him. "History is not history when it is not just," wrote historian Edward D. Mansfield; only time can do justice to the actors and events of the war, separating the evil from the good, the dross from the gold, the vain from the real. With the perspective of time, "men and events will take their proper place, and a righteous spirit direct the verdict of posterity."[41]

The notion that time must elapse before the full history of the Mexican War could be told was common. Many others had said it, but few had felt deterred by it, as the works of history rolled off the presses unabated. Nor was the situation any different with Jenkins or Mansfield. The latter published his history of the war in February 1848, before the treaty of peace was ratified; Jenkins waited until November 1848, hardly enough time in either case for history to assume its office of judgment. Two others brought out histories during the immediate postwar months, Brantz Mayer in 1848 and Nathan Covington Brooks in 1849. Of the four, only Mayer could claim strong credentials as an historian, and only he had already established a reputation as an authority on Mexico and Mexican-American relations.

Edward Deering Mansfield, Cincinnati editor, legal scholar, and former professor of constitutional law and history, was a West Point graduate who declined a commission in the army. His name was already well known as the author of a school text on constitutional government, *Political Grammar of the United States* (1834), and a treatise on the legal rights of women (1845). A loyal Whig, Mansfield supported Winfield Scott's Presidential ambitions with a biography first published in 1846 and brought up to date in subsequent editions.

Mansfield's history of the Mexican War reached its tenth edition just over a year after its initial publication early in 1848, an indicator of its popularity, and the book continued to be reprinted until 1860. Mansfield reflected the Whigs' ambivalence toward the war, an attitude reviewers were quick to detect. He "felt no pleasure," he wrote, in relating the causes of the war. The first American victories, he believed, tempted Americans to "indulge the rapacious lust for power," raising the question whether even the best of republics could resist "the universal tendency of man to build up Empires." But once having expressed his reservations, he put them aside and concentrated on the glory which the army's victories had brought to the United States.

The book is a paean of praise for the American soldier. The "brilliant results . . . against such immense superiority of force," the military skill of the officers, the heroism of the troops, were all sources of justifiable pride to the American people. The analogy between Scott and Cortez was deeply etched. Both conquerors had similar missions; both were carriers of civilization, impelled "by an invisible spirit" and carrying forward "the drama of Divine Providence on earth." There were racial overtones in Mansfield's argument. The descendants of that earlier conquering race, he stated, had perforce to give way before a "newer race" from the colder regions of the north, a race that had imbibed "other principles" and exhibited "stronger energies." Time had passed the Mexicans by, leaving them behind, unchanged in the image of their ancestors, indolent and fixed in their habits. The "Spanish Aztec" was still "the man of two thousand years ago," an anachronism in the 19th century. Not surprisingly, the *American Review* commended the work as a "judicious and impartial history"; the *Democratic Review* was more cautious in its judgment.[42]

By contrast, John Stilwell Jenkins was a fervent Democrat. Editor of an antislavery newspaper in western New York, he published a novelette in 1846 that opened a whole new career for him as a popular writer. In the next six years (he died in 1852 at the age of thirty-four), the words literally poured from his pen: an abridged version of Jabez Hammond's history of political parties in New York; condensations of the reports of several naval exploring expeditions; eulogistic biographies of Jackson, Calhoun, Silas Wright, and Polk; and biographical collections of the patriots and heroes "distinguished in the battles for American freedom," the generals of the War of 1812, the governors of New York, and the "heroines of history." Like his contemporaries, he also published poetry and short romances, including two set in Spain during the Inquisition. Perhaps his best known, because most useful, work was *The New Clerk's Assistant* (1846), a book of practical forms for the use of merchants, mechanics, and professional men in their business transactions. Its immense success may in fact have enabled him to devote his full time to his writing.

Jenkins's history of the Mexican War was written from a "patriotic view" (by which was meant a Democratic view that would have pleased Polk himself). Its partisanship, however, was overlaid by a sincere effort to write what the author hoped would be the first complete history of the war. A work of research, based on previously published soldiers' narratives, histories, government documents, and military reports, the book was highly factual (more facts, according to one critic, than had been brought together in any earlier publication).

Jenkins's interpretations did not always follow the well-worn pathways. Although he rejected the notion of Anglo-Saxon racial superiority, preferring rather to use the term "American," he obviously considered the Mexican people to be inferior, made so by centuries of inheritance and subjugation. Traces of the "more noble traits" of their Spanish ancestors might yet be found, he believed, but for the most part they were marked by the "baser passions and characteristics" of the various "races" with which they had mixed. Treacherous, cruel, indolent and selfish, they were a people unfit for the "rational enjoyment of free institutions." They need not always be so, Jenkins insisted, for the Mexican people were not beyond redemption. The war taught Mexico the advantages of firm, stable, and prudent government. If the lesson be heeded, then Mexico would find it easy "to redeem the past, and to accomplish a high destiny for the future." Perhaps in his rejection of innate racial differences, there were hints of his own antislavery stance.

As for the United States, Jenkins felt the conflict above all had demonstrated the nation's great capacity for war, no small achievement for a republic devoted to the arts of peace. He had words of warning for his compatriots, however, for he feared that their triumph might lead to an "overweening confidence" and "boastful arrogance." Should the American people abandon their high mission in order to seek glory in foreign conquests, they would not only provoke but also deserve the scorn of mankind. He denounced war as evil and inhuman, something not to be undertaken lightly. War and the fulfillment of the American mission were not, in the final analysis, compatible, and Jenkins hoped that the Mexican War would be the last war "in which our country shall be engaged."[43]

Mansfield the Whig and Jenkins the Democrat: although their views did not conform in all respects with the conventional assessments scholars have made of Whig and Democratic stands on the war, their histories of the war were regarded, in the aftermath of the conflict, as having sprung from partisan considerations. Nathan Covington Brooks, therefore, intended to offer a history of the war that would be "unaffected by any party preferences or prejudices whatever." Public opinion on the war, he wrote, was divided by the "political bias" of the two major parties, a fact that obscured the war's real meaning.[44]

Brooks was a Marylander, a graduate of St. John's College in Annapolis, and a teacher at the age of eighteen. In 1839 he assumed the post of principal of the Baltimore High School and nine years later was the founder and first president of the Baltimore Female College. Brooks was an unlikely individual to write a history of the war. A classical and Biblical scholar, he had published Latin and Greek grammars for use in the schools, a scriptural anthology, selections from the Greek Testament, a sixty-page poem on the history of the Church from the creation to the millennium, an edition of Caesar's *Commentaries,* and lectures on the utility of classical studies. At the same time, he became interested in military history, encouraged perhaps by his work on Caesar. He wrote several of the articles in *Graham's* series on the battlefields of America and in 1849 published *A Complete History of the Mexican War: Its Causes, Conduct, and Consequences.*

Brooks depended heavily upon the official reports of both American and Mexican commanders, which he often quoted at length. Almost no space was devoted to an analysis of Mexican character or to a description of Mexican society, and thus his book was strikingly free of racial insinuations. Written in a straightforward, restrained manner the work lacked the rhetorical fire and romantic flourish that marked most of the histories. Mexico's domestic turmoil clearly disturbed Brooks's law and order sentiments, and he castigated the country's disregard of international and civil law. The war might have been avoided, he believed, if time had been allowed to cool the prejudices and animosity of the Mexicans toward the United States. Polk, he felt, had overreacted when he ordered Taylor's army to the Rio Grande. Mexico's threats were mere bluster, and should have been recognized as such. Lest he be charged with a lack of patriotism, Brooks explained, "I love my country much, but the love of truth with a historian should be paramount to the love of country."

Mexico, Brooks argued, viewed America's progress, prosperity, and democratic vitality with "ill suppressed jealousy and distrust" and had longed for an opportunity to measure its strength with the United States. The United States, on its part, had "just grounds" for war against Mexico—its flag had been outraged, its citizens imprisoned and their property confiscated, and its treaties violated—but America's course should have continued to be one of "magnanimous forbearance," even though Mexico mistook this attitude for weakness. Still, he believed, Mexico was not to be trusted. When Winfield Scott, his "chivalric desire" awakened by the "forlorn situation of the Mexican people," granted Santa Anna an armistice after the battle of Churubusco, he was badly deceived, unable to imagine a people with so little sense of moral obligation.

Brooks had high praise for the accomplishments of America's citizen-soldiers. "The sons of the greatest statesmen of the republic" stood side by side with the "humblest tillers of the soil," a practical demonstration of American democracy. Each had fought from motives of "pure patriotism." The Mexican War, moreover, represented a new departure in warfare, for it was the first war in history to combine the "individual heroism of the old chivalric era" and the new military science of modern times.

The consequences of the war for the United States, Brooks contended, were immense and beneficial. Combining "youthful freshness of spirit" and "manly vigor," America had demonstrated the capacity of a republic to wage war without the expense of maintaining a large standing army. It had relieved the Mexican people of the oppression of despots and the exactions of the Church and brought them at last into an appreciation of "real liberty." The new respect which the United States earned in the world was a sure harbinger of prolonged world peace.[45]

Brooks's friend and fellow-Baltimorean Brantz Mayer was the only one of the four to bring experience in Mexico and a reputation as an historian to the history of the war. History, Mayer wrote, "should be carefully studied, not only in the account of the battles, the strategy, the conquests, the victories and successes and defeats of the nations engaged in wars, but also in the laws, the structure of government, its constitution, the distribution of power, the influence of climate, soil and mode of living, and especially the intellectual improvement and progress of the people." Historians, moreover, must become "men of the times and nations" they describe so that they might enter into the feelings and motives of the people.

Mayer's writings revealed the romantic's vision of history's long sweep. Each age, he insisted, was but a "step in the vast scheme of eternity," each following the one before in a steady progression upward. History contained the germ of the future sown in the soil of the past, a "solemn lesson of political, personal and national experience." Mayer rejected the notion that history must be little more than a "dry detail of facts," and called instead for an examination of the "principles" that lay behind the facts, for what he called internal as opposed to external history.[46]

Born in Baltimore in 1809, the son of a German immigrant, Mayer had traveled to China and southeast Asia before settling down to the study of law at the University of Maryland. In 1841 he was appointed secretary of the United States legation in Mexico City, where his fascination with Mexican history and antiquities began. He resigned his post two years later, returned to Baltimore, and in 1844 published *Mexico As It Was and As It Is*. A third, revised edition, "brought down to the present time," appeared serially in 1847. Turning from the law to the study of history, Mayer became a founder of the Maryland Historical Society and served as president of the Library Company of Baltimore. He published articles on Mexican society and on the origins of the Mexican War in the *Southern Quarterly Review*, to which he became a regular contributor, and in 1848 his *History of the War Between Mexico and the United States* appeared. Three years later he capped his interest in Mexico with the two-volume *Mexico, Aztec, Spanish and Republican*, a history of Mexico from the Spanish conquest to the present, in which he incorporated material from his earlier works.

Mayer has been described as the "most knowledgeable and certainly the most compassionate" American traveler in Mexico before 1846. As a resident for two years in the Mexican capital, he sought to avoid the superficial judgments of travelers by viewing Mexican society from within, but while he made an effort to be "just to Mexico" he found much there that disturbed him. The mixture of "antique barbaric show

and Indian rites" which he observed in the Catholic church was out of
keeping with the "spirit of the age" and Mexico's pretensions to republicanism. The growing power and wealth of the Church contrasted
sharply with the abject poverty and ignorance of the people. Matching
the power of the Church was that of the military, equally oppressive
and equally oblivious to the requirements of republican rule. Mexico,
indeed, was held under the "double dominion . . . of the drum and the
bell." The continuing turbulence of almost constant revolution was un-
progressive and pointless and made a mockery of republican forms.
The people, deprived of independence, docile, servile, and "ready to
pass from one chief to another," were the ultimate sufferers. "Nations,
habituated to be ruled for centuries," Mayer concluded, "cannot rule
themselves in a minute." Two years before the outbreak of the war,
Mayer regarded Mexico's future with apprehension. As one of the
Mexican travel books most widely read, *Mexico As It Was and As It Is*
shared honors with Prescott's history in preparing the public mind for
the war and in strengthening the popular perception of the enemy.[47]

The outbreak of hostilities enabled Mayer to take another look at
Mexico, but this time he found cause for optimism. "When the war
broke out between the United States and Mexico," he wrote, "we confess that we did not regard it with the horror that affected the nervous
sensibilities of some of our fellow-citizens." He strongly denied a belief
in the "manifest destiny of the Anglo-Saxon race," yet he hoped that
the Mexican War would "infuse the genius of our institutions among
the people, more readily than they can ever be taught by treatises on
abstract republicanism." With the help of the United States, he was
confident that the people of Mexico would soon enjoy the peace, education, and beneficent direction they so sorely needed to regenerate
their blighted country.[48]

Mayer's history of the war was clearly a fragment. It extended only to
the victories at Palo Alto and Resaca de la Palma and dealt primarily
(and in detail) with the origins of the war, a summary of which was
published in the *Southern Quarterly Review*. The war, he believed, was as
close to being inevitable as any war could be. While he gave some
attention to the claims issue and examined the Texas question in detail,
he maintained that these by themselves were not sufficient to provoke
war between the two countries. "No single act or cause can be truly
asserted to have originated it." Rather, the war was the "finale" of a
long train of events, the natural consequence of the actions, temper
and passions of both countries since the opening of their international
relations. But while he ascribed some responsibility for the situation to
a lack of statesmanship in the United States, he attached most of the
blame to Mexico. Indeed, he expressed considerable resentment
against Mexico for having forced the United States to fight its "first
and only offensive war."

Mayer ended on the same note of optimism he had expressed earlier.

The power of the Mexican army over the country's civilian population had been broken, he exclaimed, and its officers and men were forced to engage in "honest labor." The old political intriguers were in disgrace, and new men were emerging for whom the war had taught its "terrible but salutary lessons." A strong government, he thought wishfully, had appeared that would neither degenerate into despotism nor become corrupt, and the "true value of the representative system" was rapidly being accepted by the Mexican people. Mayer was persuaded that a "new era of civilization and progress" was dawning.[49]

What was it that drove so many Americans—army officers, volunteers, correspondents, writers of poetry and romance, teachers, editors, text writers, and even a Biblical scholar—to don the mantle of the historian? In the first place, there was little doubt in the American mind that the war was a grand event, possibly the greatest episode in American history, most surely the greatest in the lives of a generation that had yet to experience the Civil War. The war held an intrinsic interest and the demand to know its details tolerated no delay. While many writers conceded that the war's importance ought to be left to the judgment of time, there was little inclination to do so. Americans, it seemed, had already made up their minds.

It was necessary, moreover, not only to see the history of the war but also to see the war in the light of history, to be able to measure its significance in the totality of man's past. The war offered clues to national identity, gave meaning to the nation's existence, and helped raise a national consciousness. At a time when the values of the past seemed to be eroding, when sacrifice, courage, and heroism appeared to be withering under the hot sun of materialism, the war brought reassurance that the ideals of revolutionary republicanism had not totally disappeared. Americans could still act heroically in the service of the republic.

There was little doubt of how history would judge the Mexican War. Not for centuries, boasted one officer, had "so much been accomplished by so small a force, in so short a time, and at so little cost." The sentiment was echoed many times over. "What a picture will history present to a future generation, when the prominent points of the marches and combats shall stand out alone in bold relief!" wrote M.C.M. Hammond. "Where, in the records of mankind, can a parallel be found?" No one could yet know what "necessary link" the Mexican War would form in the chain of human events, observed Joel Tyler Headley, but one thing was certain: "That little army sleeping under the walls of Mexico, has at least turned over a new leaf in the book of history."[50]

CHAPTER 10

The War and the Republic

On May 25, 1846, the day news of Palo Alto and Resaca de la Palma reached Boston, the American Peace Society convened its eighteenth anniversary meeting in the city's Central Church. The war excitement, even in Boston, could hardly be ignored. Newsboys hawked accounts of the battles on the streets, and that night buildings were grandly illuminated in celebration of the victories. Members of the Society had worked hard to discourage war between the United States and Great Britain over the Oregon boundary question, only to witness, in the hour of their triumph, the outbreak of war in a less-expected quarter. Even on this day, when the reality of the Mexican War was suddenly brought home, the Society's resolutions were principally self-congratulatory that hostilities with the British had been averted. The mildness of the resolutions opposing the Mexican War belied the strong convictions of some of the members. After lamenting the outburst of a war spirit throughout the country and deploring its demoralizing effect on the mind of the nation, "especially the lower classes and the rising generation," the delegates went on to denounce wars in general. Amasa Walker, a vice-president of the Society, took the floor but warned he would have little to say about the Mexican War, for all wars were equally wrong. With the peaceful termination of the Oregon dispute, however, he declared that the "present year . . . marked an era in the Peace cause." It was difficult for the members to muster outrage against a war that had not been anticipated when the appalling prospect of war between two Anglo-Saxon countries had just been eliminated. The chances for a short conflict with Mexico appeared strong, and in any case Mexico was no Britain.

Although the meeting later adopted a less equivocal position in its report, charging the government with unprovoked aggression against a "poor, feeble, distracted country" and condemning those who would heap the "wrath of a bloody, vindictive, ferocious patriotism upon the

270

poor, despised Mexicans," the moderate stand angered the radical reform wing of the Society. Led by Elihu Burritt, several members withdrew from the Society, complaining that there was no reason why
Mexican and American soldiers, their bayonets dipped in blood, could
not under the present standards become members of the peace organization. One who withdrew, Boston merchant Joshua P. Blanchard,
condemned the war as one of "unprincipled depravity" and "unmitigated sin" and branded as shameful the public apathy toward the
conflict.[1]

George C. Beckwith, who continued to direct the affairs of the Society, published *The Peace Manual: or, War and Its Remedies* in 1847, but
the Mexican War was virtually ignored except as an occasional illustration of Beckwith's general condemnation of war. On the other hand,
the Society's journal, *The Advocate of Peace*, printed "horror" stories of
the mistreatment of volunteers, the incidence of immorality among the
soldiers, the cruelties of the battlefield, and the harsh impact of the war
on Mexico's civilian population. "The time has not yet come to write
the history of this war," wrote the editor, "but we think it well to
chronicle a few items as illustrations of its character." The stories were
"so many arguments for peace." Every possible argument against the
war was presented, and petitions were directed to the President to halt
the bloodshed. At its annual meeting in May 1847 members resolved
not to "dwell upon this war," since the time was not yet appropriate "to
write its mournful history," but they did repeat their earlier condemnation. They reported ruefully that over 200,000 men had responded to
the call for 50,000 volunteers and wondered "what will restrain men
from fighting in any war that their rulers may choose for any purpose
to declare." Ironically, they recognized that "eventual good to our
cause" would arise from the war, for it would teach the people lessons
they could not have learned "in any other school."[2]

To promote the cause of world peace by turning the war into a
warning "against resorts to the sword hereafter," the Peace Society
announced a contest for the best "*Review of the present War with
Mexico . . .* on the principles of Christianity, and an enlightened statesmanship." The prize was $500 and publication by the Society. Each
contestant was instructed to present a view that would commend itself
"to the good sense of fair-minded men in every party" once the hour of
"sober and candid reflection" shall have arrived, and because perspective was important the entrants were required to wait until the war was
over before making their submissions. A committee of judges headed
by Simon Greenleaf, Harvard University law professor, was selected.

Twelve manuscripts were submitted in the competition. The prize
was awarded to Abiel Abbot Livermore, a Unitarian minister from
Keene, New Hampshire, and his book, *The War with Mexico Reviewed*,
was published in 1850. In the meantime, one of the other submissions,
William Jay's *A Review of the Causes and Consequences of the Mexican War*,

was published at the author's expense, and a third entrant, the Rev. Philip Berry's *A Review of the Mexican War on Christian Principles,* submitted anonymously over the name "A Southern Democrat," was published in the *Southern Presbyterian Review,* later to be issued in book form by a South Carolina publisher. Jay was the most prominent of the authors, and his book the most popular of the three. By the end of 1849, it had appeared in four editions and in the following year was published in a Spanish translation in Mexico City. A New York judge and son of John Jay, he was active in the abolition movement as well as in the American Peace Society (of which he became president following the war). Berry, a graduate of Cambridge University in England, had been a deacon in the Episcopal Church in Jamaica before moving to the United States, where he served a parish in Maryland. Like Jay an active abolitionist, he represented the Peace Society at the 1849 World Peace Congress in Paris.[3]

The books received little notice in the periodical press (with the possible exception of some religious journals) and had little impact on popular perceptions of the war. Livermore's work was dismissed as a "one-sided attempt," although the author was credited with a lively style. "We opened his pages with a shrug," wrote one reviewer, "expecting to be bored with an old-fashioned peace essay in the well-known dialect of country preachers, but were agreeably disappointed by their spirit and vivacity." He had proved that war in the abstract was a calamity but, the reviewer went on, "no one denied that at the outset." His effort on the other hand to show the Mexican War to be "wicked in its inception and consummation" was deemed a failure. To Orestes Brownson the book contained a good deal of information with a "much greater amount of childish prattle and nonsense." No work published by the Peace Society, he insisted, was worth reading anyway. While Brownson expressed his dislike of war in general and of the Mexican War in particular, he could not accept the "nonsensical" arguments of the "namby-pamby peace men." Even the *Christian Examiner,* while praising both Jay and Livermore, suggested that most Americans had already made up their minds on the war and were not likely to be moved by any further reviews of its causes and consequences.[4]

Livermore argued that the basic cause of the Mexican War must be sought in the American character, particularly in the rise of military ambition in the United States. "The martial spirit is always a tiger, and we have given the tiger too much room and freedom." Literature promoted it and republicans used it to show that they were equal to any monarchists. "Pride of race" encouraged it by fostering the mistaken notion that America's destiny was one of conquest, thereby deflecting the "genuine Anglo-Saxon destiny" to raise up fallen races by extending peace, justice and "noble ideas." European immigration, he stated, exacerbated the martial spirit, as thousands of people "unbaptized into the spirit of liberty" brought to American shores the European penchant for violence and "bloody dramas"; and the American passion for land and land-ownership excited a lust for territory beyond the nation's borders. With this martial predisposition as its cause, Livermore found the principal motive for the war in an insatiable desire for new land over which to spread the blight of slavery. The claims issue and the Texas boundary question were mere pretexts, cloaking the real designs of the nation's leaders.

Jay's *Review* lacked the force of argument that characterized Livermore's book, which may be one reason why the latter won the Peace Society prize. Fully one-third of Jay's book was a tedious summary of the relations between the United States and Mexico up to Polk's election in 1844. The President was clearly his villain, carrying out the dictates of the slave-power by conquest after all other means for territorial aggrandizement had failed. But Taylor also bore a share of the blame, according to Jay, for prosecuting the war with such vigor following his arrival on the Rio Grande, without waiting for orders from Washington. Unlike Livermore, Jay stressed the inequity between the two countries—Mexico's feeble condition arising from the ignorance and superstition of its population and from years of instability and revolutionary turbulence—in language that was all too familiar to Americans in the 1840s.[5]

Both Jay and Livermore, like the Peace Society itself, professed to find some good in the war as a "new weapon" in the hands of peace. Teaching the folly and un-Christian character of war and the emptiness of military glory, the Mexican War was a "republican, an American lesson." The cause of peace, Livermore believed, assumed new strength because of the war and his confidence "in the ultimate triumph of the Gospel of peace" was not in the least shaken. Neither went so far in this belief as did Philip Berry. Indeed, there were moments when Berry's essay sounded like no tract for peace at all. He lauded the humane conduct of the American forces, the magnanimity of Taylor, and the chivalry of Scott, and suggested that they provided the world with as great examples of "unavenging and active humanity" as the annals of warfare have ever presented. Not only did Berry agree that the war brought the world closer to the day when universal peace would reign but he also felt the war hastened the time when Anglo-Saxon civilization would encircle the globe. The war had assumed a "*world-historical* character."[6]

The opposition of the American Peace Society to the Mexican War has been described as "mild and innocuous." It was ambiguous as well. There were some elements in the pacifist movement, like the New England Non-Resistance Society, that mixed pacifism with antislavery to denounce the war in more strident tones, but its membership was small and its influence virtually nonexistent. Viewing the war as having some potential for good, the Peace Society in effect came to terms with the martial spirit it so roundly censured.

A pacifist opposition to the war existed, of course, outside the sponsorship of the Peace Society. Charles T. Porter, a young upstate New York lawyer and graduate of Hamilton College, published his *Review of the Mexican War* in 1849, the title suggesting it may have been an entrant in the Peace Society contest. Porter, emphasizing the nonpartisan nature of his work, was insistent that slavery had no connection whatever with the war. "Conquest was the animating idea," he asserted. "The acquisition of the territory of another nation was the sole purpose for which this war was devised and carried on." That the war was unjustified and unnecessary was obvious, for the peaceful occupation of Mexican territory by "America's race of freemen" was inevitable. "The principle of democracy," he boasted, "is the prominent feature in the character of this race" and would have been planted on Pacific shores anyway. The war was a perversion of America's true mission to establish permanent peace among all the civilized nations of the world.[7]

There were some who felt that the Mexican War, far from setting back the cause of universal peace, actually furthered it by demonstrating that the United States possessed the strength and will to fight a successful foreign war. Peace advocates, it was argued, were among the beneficiaries of the new prestige won by the nation as a result of the war; their arguments would henceforth be treated with greater respect. Pacifists could no longer be taunted for supporting the outlawry of war because America was too weak to fight one.

No one exemplified this position better than Emma Hart Willard, pioneer in female education and founder of the Troy Female Seminary. Indeed, her attitude was not one of opposition to the war at all. On the contrary, she shared the enthusiasm for the war, blamed the conflict on Mexico and defended President Polk, showered praise on the American soldiers for their heroism, and extolled America's generosity toward its vanquished foe. Among the many productions of what one journal condescendingly called "Mrs. Willard's masculine mind" were texts in American history designed for the schools and, one might assume, for her school in particular. *Last Leaves of American History*, covering only the Mexican War and California, and the *Abridged History of the United States*, a new edition of a book published before the war, appeared in 1849. Willard viewed the war as a "providential occurrence" by which God "had so signally made the American armies the means of chastising the Spanish Mexicans, for national cruelties early begun and long continued." The American victory, moreover, was God's way of promoting the cause of world peace. With its newly won prestige, the United States must, she urged, move quickly to that leadership in the cause that rightfully belonged to those nations that exhibited "undoubted courage and ability in war." She proposed that the government dispatch one of its veteran generals, "while his laurels are yet fresh upon his brow," to Great Britain to negotiate the formation of a world-wide "Council of Peace" that would enforce the abolition of war.[8]

Willard's arguments left some of her readers in a quandary. Her battle descriptions hardly befitted the tenderness of her sex, her promised impartiality was less than successful. Disturbed at the liberality of her attitude toward the war, the *Christian Examiner* found compensation in her militant advocacy of a world council to enforce peace. Willard's views on the Mexican War, however, were consistent with those of most school-text writers. Unlike children's literature in general, which assumed a pacifist stance and criticized the war, the school-text writers blamed Mexico and found patriotism and heroism in the way Americans responded to the challenge. "I drew in patriotism from my mother's breast and on my father's knee," Willard wrote Thomas Hart Benton, and she had little patience with the "croakers" who always predicted some great calamity about to fall on the country.[9]

Willard's attitude revealed some of the difficulties under which opponents of the war labored. William Lloyd Garrison set the tone of the abolitionists' opposition just a few days after Polk sent his war message to Congress and before the news of the first victories on the Rio Grande had been received. The war was vigorously condemned as one "of aggression, of invasion, of conquest, and rapine—marked by ruffianism, perfidy, and every other feature of national depravity." The abolitionists had no doubt of its purpose. The war to them was waged solely to extend and perpetuate the institution of slavery. Two weeks later as volunteers rushed to sign up for service in Mexico, the Garrisonians pledged to withhold all aid and support for the government and "at every sacrifice to refuse enlistment, contribution, aid and countenance to the War." Unlike the pacifists, it was not always clear whether the abolitionists loathed war or slavery the more, for their opposition seemed to assume, mistakenly, that the Mexican War was but a stage in a slave-power plot to strengthen the hated institution.

Garrison's statements found echo in innumerable sermons, pamphlets, tracts, and addresses, as well as articles in the religious and antislavery press. But for all their efforts, the public remained largely indifferent to their arguments, if indeed people knew of them at all. The thrust of their opposition was also weakened by disagreement within their own ranks. The most notorious case was that of the Kentucky abolitionist Cassius M. Clay, who left his post as editor of an antislavery newspaper to join the volunteers. While he steadfastly insisted that the war had been "unjustly and wickedly begun," Clay believed that once it had started, he owed the government his support. Clay was taken prisoner early in 1847 just before the Battle of Buena Vista in one of the war's more celebrated incidents and spent eight months as a captive of the Mexican army. His decision to join the war was denounced by abolitionists, who prayed that he would be the "first to perish" on Mexican soil. A second antislavery spokesman became the target of abolitionist criticism when Gamaliel Bailey, editor of a Cincinnati antislavery paper and shortly to become editor-in-chief of the Washington *National Era,* announced that he would no longer print antiwar articles if they endangered the safety of American soldiers in Mexico.

No such scruples prevented some critics from publicly wishing for Mexican victories or from writing letters to Mexican leaders expressing support and sympathy. When Scott's army occupied Mexico City several such letters were found in the post office, a disclosure that brought outrage from individuals both outside and within the antislavery movement. Others openly expressed their wish that England would assist the Mexicans against the American army, a move that would surely have resulted in a war against Great Britain as well, the last thing New Englanders desired.

Even more upsetting was the bitter antiwar tirade delivered by Ohio's Whig Senator Thomas Corwin in February 1847 just before the victory at Buena Vista. Corwin condemned the war from moral (and political) rather than from antislavery grounds but he did so in language that even many in his own party thought ill-considered, injudicious, and extreme. Counseling the Mexicans to greet the volunteers "with bloody hands" and to welcome them "to hospitable graves," he characterized the war as organized thievery and castigated the nation's leaders as robber chiefs. Mexico, not displeased, made note of Corwin's harangue but so did the volunteers. Feeling betrayed, and convinced that the Senator's statements would lengthen the war and delay their homecoming, they unleashed their outrage. None was more furious than Alexander Doniphan, colonel of Missouri volunteers and like Corwin a Whig. After the volunteers' long trek through northern Mexico, he said, "during which nothing had been heard from the States, and while all hearts were yearning to hear from home, the *first* thing met with in American papers was the speech of *Corwin.*" Having marched hundreds of miles over Mexico's arid wastes and bested the enemy in several encounters, the men were now told that they were robbers and cutthroats. "It was a complete shower bath," Doniphan declared, and the men reacted with shock and outrage. In late April 1847 Ohio volunteers, choosing the field at Buena Vista for its symbolic value, burned Corwin in effigy for having rendered "aid and comfort" to the enemy.[10]

Such outbursts as Corwin's did much to weaken the credibility of the arguments against the war, but their impact was also blunted by a disturbing ambiguity among some of the war's opponents. Many antiwar critics qualified their belief that the war was wrong with an equally strong conviction that the government should be supported once the war had started. The official Whig organ revealed the ambivalence of the party when it chided the Peace Society for its attacks on those who were risking their lives in the service of their country. Whig reverence for the law and for the obligations of the citizenry to the state were not easily overcome, not even when individuals were convinced that the war was unjust and immorally begun. In any government "instituted with the consent of the governed," advised the *American Whig Review,* the citizens' first duty was obedience to the laws and, if necessary, the sacrifice of life itself for the "conservation of society in its integrity." Several months before the war, when conflict with Mexico appeared likely, the *Review* denounced all wars as "fraught with crime" and "dangerous to Liberty," yet added that if war should come it must be pushed to a prompt conclusion with all the strength the country could muster.

The journal's chief political contributor, former New York Congressman Daniel D. Barnard, defined the Whig position. The war, he contended, was the "great political and moral crime" of the age. Once the war had begun, however, the "part of patriotism" demanded a "respectful obedience" to the government. He commended Americans for the "singular unanimity" with which they had responded to the war but warned that the "sentiment of patriotism" could not erase the fact that the conflict had been perpetrated by Democratic blunders.[11]

Just as members of the peace movement looked for some good to come out of the conflict, so also did other antiwar critics anticipate a salutary result from the fighting. A vigorous prosecution of the war was seen as the only way to secure an "honorable peace" between the two countries that could provide a firm basis for amicable relations in the future. The exaggerated charges of the war's opponents (men like Corwin), it was believed, prolonged the war and postponed that result. Furthermore, the Mexican people, heretofore held in the tight grip of "ignorance, bigotry, vice and degradation," could not help but benefit from the introduction of "American liberal principles" into their land. While Whigs rejected the war as unjust and immoral, they also felt that it was unnecessary to achieve the ends for which the administration provoked the conflict. It was "as sure as the coming of time" that Mexico would fall before the advance of America's "superior" population, they predicted; Mexico's "weaker blood" would be exterminated and the civilization, laws, and religion of the Anglo-Saxon race would take root. The advance, however, must follow a regular and peaceful course, as befitted a great civilized and Christian nation, and ought not be undertaken with violence or in the spirit of conquest.[12]

The same concern over means and ends was voiced by Ralph Waldo Emerson, whose position on the Mexican War reflected the ambivalence of many of his fellow critics. Emerson had earlier expressed his belief that the Anglo-Saxon race would ultimately overrun the continent, impelled not by divine command but by what he called "race-drive." Although opposed to the annexation of Texas, he believed that Texas, Oregon, and even Mexico itself would fall to the United States, and "in the course of ages," he wrote, it would be "of small import by what particular occasions & methods it was done." When war came he predicted that Mexico would be conquered, but in winning he feared that the United States would be poisoned by an enemy that was degraded and corrupt. In an opening editorial statement in the short-lived *Massachusetts Quarterly Review,* Emerson declared, "We have a bad war, many victories—each of which converts the country into an immense chanticleer;—and a very insincere political opposition." Yet in the same address, he boasted confidently that "the American people are fast opening their own destiny." War, as a means for achieving America's destiny, was unacceptable to Emerson, but when it came he noted with a shrug that "most of the great results of history are brought about by discreditable means."[13]

Emerson's co-editor of the *Review,* the influential clergyman-abolitionist Theodore Parker, was more blunt in his opposition to the war. His arguments assumed a strong racial tone. The Mexicans, he declared, were poor, weak, and only half-civilized, quarreling among themselves ever since they won their independence and demonstrating their unfitness for republican government. They were powerless to stand before the Anglo-Saxon race, the "most formidable and powerful the world ever saw." Like Emerson, he looked to the day when the continent would fall under the sway of this "superior race, with superior ideas and a better civilization." Mankind would gain, he insisted, if the "idea of America" and all that it implied could be extended over Mexico. He was equally insistent, however, that war was not the means for accomplishing this end. "In the general issue between this race and that, we are in the right," he stated. "But in this special issue, and this particular war, . . . we are wholly in the wrong." In his first sermon against the war, preached less than a month after it began, Parker assumed a strong pacifist position and called on his countrymen to repudiate the government's war policy. His very boldness in advancing opinions "so contrary to the general voice of the people," suggested one editor, was bound to attract attention. Others, however, found Parker's stand to be unrelieved in its negativism and therefore of little constructive value. Denouncing Democrats as "knaves," Whigs as "time-serving cowards," and "libelling" the Mexicans, Parker seemed to offer little hope. Nevertheless, his influence among antiwar critics was great, extending even into the army camps in Mexico. Parker maintained a correspondence with Lieutenant Colonel Ethan Allen Hitchcock—commander of the Third Infantry and an aide to General Scott—who, like Parker, felt the war to be a mistake.[14]

Parker's sentiments found echo in the Congregationalist periodical *The New Englander.* Staunchly antislavery and opposed to expansion, the journal condemned the war as costly, demoralizing, and fraught with danger for the republic. While blaming the conflict on the administration's "reckless spirit" and on the designs of slavery expansionists editor E. Royall Tyler also saw the war as a contest between a "poor distracted country, cursed with a miserable government" on the one hand, and on the other a nation that sprang from the "noblest stock on earth's face." The war, he believed, would strengthen the cause of peace and result in "great good to the world—to this country—to Mexico herself." It was God's purpose to "bring out of this war a better condition of things."[15]

The ambivalence of the antiwar critics revealed the degree to which the war was accepted, even by its opponents. Implicit in their attitudes was a certain sense of relief that it was after all Mexico, and not Great Britain, that the United States was fighting. They did not hesitate to express their contempt for Mexico's past, its government, religion, and society and to give full vent to their feelings of racial difference and superiority. Their antiwar positions would assuredly have been different, less ambiguous, more consistent and forthright, had the enemy been Britain.

Peace advocates, Whigs, antislavery reformers, all tempered their stands against the war by seeking some ultimate good in the conflict. The popular support of the war itself seemed to offer encouragement to some. When Daniel Webster's son Fletcher justified the war in his 1846 Fourth of July oration in Boston's Tremont Temple, peace advocate Ezra Stiles Gannett viewed his comments as an unintended tribute to the strength of the peace movement. Orestes Brownson, condemning the war as impolitic and unjust, nevertheless expressed pride in the "earnest patriotism of the people which the war called forth" and in the "brilliant achievements of our brave troops in Mexico." The *New Englander* found the peace settlement with Mexico to be an "honorable" one. "We content ourselves with comparatively little, when we might have had much," and for what was taken Mexico was paid. If other nations should follow the American example, then "this Mexican war of ours will become quite an epoch in history." Who knows, asked the editor, but what there may ultimately be found a way of conducting wars of conquest and invasion "upon Christian principles?" One Indiana woman, finding the war repugnant and shocked by the carnage and bloodshed, summed it all up when she told a group of departing volunteers that the war was, after all, the only alternative left "consistent with National honor."[16]

One of the most pervasive arguments employed by critics of the Mexican War was that the war was inherently anti-republican, that it negated all that republics stood for and that if not stopped America's republican system would be placed in such peril that the very existence of republicanism as a form of government would be endangered. Americans proudly pointed to their role as the "model republic"; the idea had a firm hold on the popular mind as an expression of Amer-

ica's uniqueness, the basis of its mission and the defining characteristic
of its national identity. With the passing of the Revolutionary generation, responsibility for protecting and strengthening American republicanism became all the more important for a populace that had had no
direct involvement in the nation's birth. To some Americans, the war
with Mexico was a serious challenge to that responsibility.

From the beginning, the war was debated within the context of republicanism and the responsibilities republicanism imposed on the citizenry. Not all the arguments, however, were on one side. Recognizing
the dangers created by the war and sharing concern for the future of
the republic, other Americans argued that the Mexican War was necessary to the survival of republicanism in the world. Conceding that war
(not only the Mexican War but all war) was inimical to the purpose of
republics, they nevertheless insisted that the conflict with Mexico was
one war that had to be fought. Republicanism was a vague concept,
difficult to define and subject to differing interpretations and meanings; it was, moreover, argued on a simplistic and popular level which,
with its inconsistencies and changing uncertainties, only enhanced the
confusion. Nevertheless, its importance to the molding of attitudes toward the war is unquestioned; it both influenced and was influenced by
popular perceptions of the conflict.

Concern for the nature and meaning of republicanism was not new
to the latter 1840s. For decades, republicanism had been a subject of
inquiry on both the popular and the more sophisticated intellectual
levels as Americans sought to define and redefine it in terms of the
changes that swept over the maturing republic. The growth of industry, the new romantic democracy, the incredible technological developments that conquered both time and space, and the vision of an expanding nation, all placed traditional republicanism, the republicanism
of the Revolutionary fathers, under strain. Challenges were encountered that threatened to divert republicanism into unfamiliar
channels, even to rob it of its ideals and hence its force in the world.
Bothered by the contrast between their rapidly changing present and
the faith of their fathers, Americans in the first half of the 19th century
probed the meaning of the republic, seeking to adapt it to the new ways
while at the same time renewing their commitment to the model nurtured by the Revolution. That they could not have it both ways did not
appear obvious. As the "high noon of the nineteenth century" drew
closer, writers were moved to "take stock" of America's position half-
way through what all agreed was a truly remarkable century. The war
that had just ended, fresh in the national memory, played a large role
in the evaluations.

With the basic, abstract concept of republicanism there was little argument among mid-19th-century Americans. Indeed, the classical republicanism of the Revolution continued to command lip-service if not
a deep understanding. Revolutionary republicanism provided the in-

spiration for much of what Americans believed about themselves and their nation, and if there was a difference between republican theory and republican practice it was because they had not yet come to terms with the radical changes that engulfed them. Republics, as everyone knew, existed for the good of the people. Republican government rested on the sovereignty of the people, hence was no better or no worse than those who supported it. Success, indeed survival, depended upon the character and spirit of the people, upon what was termed the "public virtue." "A republican form of government," stated a writer in *DeBow's Review* early in 1846, can "never be established and maintained, except among a virtuous and intelligent people." It required the "sacrifice of private interest to the public good, the suppression and control of individual passions, . . . and above all, that high moral and mental culture which enables each citizen to sustain his part in the administration of the affairs of the nation of which he is a member." Several months after the outbreak of the Mexican War, a Philadelphia editor emphasized that "true republican virtue in the *citizens* consists in the prompt sacrifice of comforts, interests, and even life, for the nation." Service and sacrifice were the principal elements in the allegiance owed the republic by its citizens.

Where virtue was absent, republics could not exist, a point made over and over with respect to Mexico's republican pretensions. For some, virtue was at bottom a function of national character, even of race. "A weak and licentious people," argued one Whig writer, "may put on what fashion of government it fancies—may deck its disgraceful limbs with what robe of liberty it likes; it will still be the same." Without virtue in the people, institutions were meaningless. All governments, he declared, will fail "without permanent public virtue to direct and to guard them."[17]

If republics were the most democratic of governments, they were also the most fragile, for their survival depended upon the intelligence, good will, and sound judgment of the people. All the "most powerful sentiments of human nature," observed Charles J. Peterson, were invoked on behalf of the "permanency of the republic," but human nature, as many came to recognize, was not always steady and reliable. The real weakness of the republic, as Abraham Lincoln dramatically pointed out eight years before the war, was in the people, and he warned of the disaster that would befall the nation if and when the people lost their virtue. No external power threatened the freedom of the republic, the danger came only from within. Lincoln's warnings were not isolated but were echoed by countless individuals throughout the country during the ensuing decade. "When the people became corrupt," wrote Fanny Forrester (Mrs. Emily Chubbuck Judson) in the *Columbian Magazine*, "or so ignorant as to follow blindly in the wake of a reckless demogogue, then is ruin near." The strength of America's republican government, she added, was in the heart and the head of every person. When the people falter in their devotion to the greater good, the collapse of the republic would not be far behind.[18]

The first half of the 19th century was fraught with challenge to traditional, or Revolutionary republicanism. Indeed, since republicanism was "essentially a static ideal," the very fact of change was a threat to its survival. The rise of romantic democracy, with its expanded suffrage and mass politics, threatened to submerge the more restricted and stable pattern of republican behavior in a tyrannical public opinion that was as "sourceless as the wind, groundless as moonshine." The passion for freedom and impatience with restraint, the exaltation of the individual and the enthronement of the common man jeopardized the integrity of the republic, or so it seemed to some Americans. It was the transition from "classical republicanism to romantic democracy," according to a recent scholar, that constituted the "real American revolution." Lincoln found the greatest danger to the republic in the person of Andrew Jackson, yet Jackson too was concerned lest the loss of virtue among the people place the nation on the road to internal decay and death.[19]

Of greater concern to midcentury Americans were the dangers implicit in the nation's economic growth and especially in its potential impact on the American character. As the century's midpoint approached, the press was replete with woeful assessments of the debilitating effects of the commercial spirit on republican virtue. The precise role of commerce in the republic had been debated since the late 18th century and the uncertainties still lingered almost three-quarters of a century later. To some, commerce denoted corruption, and corruption was the antithesis of virtue. To others, commerce not only was compatible with republican virtue but also, as a civilizing force, presented the means for extending America's republican revolution. If disagreements over the abstract relationship between commerce and republicanism persisted, there was wide agreement that the traits of mind fostered by the commercial spirit—an excessive individualism, the love of gain and wealth, the fondness for luxury, the tendency to measure achievement by material standards—carried the power to undermine virtue and destroy the republic.[20]

Early in 1848 the Whig *American Review* joyfully announced that the United States had entered a "bank-note" age in which material interests would henceforth hold sway. Not everyone agreed that this was an unmixed blessing. A writer in the same journal had earlier cautioned that commerce, with its emphasis on the accumulation of wealth, might well prove fatal to the values of honor and freedom. Commerce softened the national character as it aroused man's selfish passions; the spirit of trade led ultimately to universal cupidity. Those civic virtues that formed the very soul of the nation's free institutions were in danger of failing before the pursuit of gain. In fact, as he viewed the new Democratic administration of James K. Polk, he was convinced that public virtue had already failed.

Others, primarily but not exclusively drawn from the conservative political and religious elements, joined in lamenting the acquisitiveness that had begun to mark the national character. Unitarian clergyman Andrew P. Peabody, soon to assume the editorship of the *North American Review*, bemoaned the domination of the values of the marketplace over those of the spirit; material prosperity, he noted, had become the supreme good in an age of "grovelling utilitarianism" and "self-gratulation." Edwin Percy Whipple, one of the country's most popular orators, found in the pursuit of wealth a key to the transformation of America itself. Liberty, he told a Fourth of July audience in 1850, no longer the "mountain nymph, with cheeks wet with morning dew and clear eyes that mirror the heavens" had become "an old dowager lady, fatly invested in commerce and manufactures, and peevishly fearful that enthusiasm will reduce her establishment, and panics cut off her dividends."[21]

Few were as outspoken or as critical of the times as the popular novelist Henry William Herbert. Two months after the Mexican War began, he denounced the "selfish greed" and "base love of gain" that he felt had come to characterize Americans. Chivalry, he complained, had become a "bye word and a mockery" and "the deathless love of liberty and country" had been all but quenched. America's "fat and lazy days of peace" had elevated utility, wealth, and trade to positions of power and dominance. Even war was welcome, Herbert declared, with all its horrors, as "the sole thing that can wipe away this loathsome and corrupting blight from the hearts of men." Only war could create "even a passing elevation in the minds of the multitude, which can lead them to suppose that men have higher capabilities than that of hoarding money . . . that there are such things, in a word, as truth and honor, as patriotism and glory."[22]

Not all those who recoiled in disgust at the pernicious effect of commerce on republican virtue were willing to embrace the Mexican War as the solution. On the contrary, the war was seen as a stimulus to a decline in public virtue. In what purported to be a fragment of an unpublished work entitled "The New Machiavel; or a Treatise on the Art of Destroying a Nation from Within," a writer in the *American Review* declared that a war of conquest was the most effective way to accomplish that end. With the institutions of the republic already erected, the only opportunity for the age's "ambitious spirits" to acquire distinction was "to pull down what their fathers created," and war (unnamed but obviously the Mexican War) offered the best chance of success. A war of conquest, the writer pointed out, destroyed property, sank productive capital in the maintenance of unproductive enterprises, increased the number of speculators and stock-jobbers, and augmented the public debt. The emphasis was economic, as befit the organ of the Whig party. Others found more idealistic arguments.

War was antithetical to all that republics stood for. It negated the dedication to the "arts of peace" that rendered republics unique and destroyed the moral basis upon which they rested. War, moreover, placed the goals of America's "legitimate destiny" in jeopardy. The people, it was feared, were being infected with "the vulgar robber passion of military adventure." The power of the government would be increased and centralized, replacing republican simplicity with splendor and extravagance and hastening the "progress of popular corruption." The American dream of "propagating over the earth those great ideas and principles by which the world is to be reformed" would be shattered. From the moment Americans chose war as the means for achieving their destiny, they repudiated republican doctrines and took a position alongside kings and tyrants.[23]

The transition of the United States from a peaceful to a military nation would be the death knell of republican government. Congress' authorization for an increase in the regular army was especially alarming. A large standing army, complained Greeley's *Tribune,* was a "relic of barbarism." The prospect of defending vast new territories from the plundering forays of warlike Indian tribes which "hover round our new empire like the Goths . . . upon aggressive Rome" was disheartening. A "thirst for conquest," encouraged by the successes of the war, would be a "consuming cancer," a fatal sign of corruption working within the republic. Every victorious general would be a popular idol and with the elevation of military men to public office, the subversion of the republic would be complete. "It is historically true," warned a southern writer, "that the entrance upon a career of conquest has ever marked the declining node of every republic which has ventured upon the hazardous and ruinous path." It remained to be seen whether virtue could yet preserve the republic or whether "the last hope of human freedom" would perish before the "blighting simoom of corruption, injustice, usurpation, selfishness and fanaticism."[24]

The republican argument against the war was brought to its ultimate expression by 87-year-old Albert Gallatin, who capped a long and distinguished career in public service with a ringing affirmation of the American mission. In his last years the aged diplomat and fiscal expert had turned to the promotion of historical study and to research on the native peoples of North America. Founder of the American Ethnological Society in 1842, he published his scholarly "Notes on the Semicivilized Nations of Mexico, Yucatan and Central America" three years later. His interest in the Mexican War was two-sided. He recognized that the war would certainly advance ethnological research; at the same time he feared for the impact of the war upon republican America. Gallatin sought information for his own studies of southwestern Indian culture from William H. Emory, an officer in General Kearny's Army of the West, and urged Winfield Scott to procure books and documents relating to Mexico's ancient civilization. Gallatin, however, also thought the war iniquitous and impolitic, confiding to Prescott his desire to write an essay on the Mexican War if his energy permitted it.[25]

The energy must have been forthcoming for Gallatin published not one but two pamphlets on the war: *War Expenses,* in which he drew upon his expertise in financial matters; and *Peace with Mexico,* in which he addressed the nation's moral responsibility to bring the conflict to a close. The latter, first printed in several newspapers late in 1847, was published as a pamphlet and distributed throughout the country in the hope that it would influence public opinion in favor of a just and moral peace with Mexico. Gallatin's purpose was twofold: to encourage the "numerous timid men" who were afraid to speak out lest they be charged with a lack of patriotism; and secondly, to awaken the "virtuous and intelligent part of the community" to the necessity of halting the war on the most elevated of principles.[26]

Gallatin conceded that the success of the American army in Mexico had surpassed all expectations. The Mexicans clearly had been no match for the "superior skill" of the American generals and the "unparalleled bravery" of the American soldiers. He lauded Scott for his "extraordinary success" and marveled that the general had been able to accomplish so much with so small a force. The most remarkable and unexpected development, he continued, was the devotion and courage of the volunteers who, although "undisciplined in every sense of the word," had proved superior to Mexico's "best regular forces." Gallatin's pride, however, was balanced by his conviction that the war was a grossly unequal contest. Mexico, heterogeneous in population and limited in resources, distracted by internal dissension and easy prey to military usurpers, occupied an inferior position among the nations of the world. There was little wonder that it was unable to contend against an "energetic, intelligent, enlightened and united nation . . . enjoying all the benefits of a regular, strong, and free government."[27]

In spite of its advantage, Gallatin insisted that America's success had been costly. Thousands of lives were sacrificed, more were disabled by disease. Capital expended on the war had been destroyed, applied as it was to unproductive objects, and would never be recovered. The disastrous impact of the war on the nation's fiscal position was not fully recognized only because it was obscured by the sudden increase in exports to Great Britain. The war's evils, he predicted, would soon be felt—rising interest rates as the government seeks new loans, the increased likelihood of new and burdensome taxes, the retardation of economic growth. Such consequences were perhaps tolerable in a defensive war, but in a war of invasion and conquest, Gallatin maintained, they were reprehensible. They placed the republic in serious jeopardy by centralizing power in the executive and by increasing the temptation to corruption.

Gallatin's concern was not only, or even largely, with the war's economic impact on the United States. He mustered all the arguments of his Jeffersonian faith to recall the American people to their republican responsibilities, reiterating the popular fear that the greatest danger to the republic came from within, from the people themselves. The people he declared, were blinded by the "romantic successes" of their armies, their minds captured by an "enthusastic and exclusive love of military glory." More importantly, they had forgotten their mission. The United States, he argued, had been placed by Providence in a position unlike that enjoyed by any other nation in the world; with this favored status went deep, even awesome, responsibilities. "Your mission is, to improve the state of the world, to be the 'Model Republic,' to show that men are capable of governing themselves, and that this simple and natural form of government is that also which confers most happiness on all, is productive of the greatest development of the intellectual faculties, above all, that which is attended with the highest standard of private and political virtue and morality." The eyes of the world were fixed on the republic; if it should falter, the "last hope of the friends of mankind" would be lost.

Instead of adhering to the highest principles of political morality and by example exerting a moral influence on mankind, the people, Gallatin charged, had allowed their worst passions to take control. Cupidity, unjust aggrandizement, the love of false glory had caused Americans to abandon the lofty position of their fathers in favor of the "heathen patriotism of the heroes and statesmen of antiquity." Patriotism, an essential virtue in a republic, had been carried to excess. Gallatin questioned the oft-repeated assertions that Americans enjoyed "an hereditary superiority of race" over the Mexicans and hence had a right to subjugate their country in order to uplift the people, improve their social state, and increase their happiness. Aside from the fact that hereditary anything was incompatible with democracy, the alleged superiority of the Anglo-Saxon race was not, he maintained, a license to infringe upon the rights of others. Blessed by superior institutions, Americans "may rightfully, and will, if they use the proper means, exercise a most beneficial moral influence over the Mexicans, and other less enlightened nations," but the use of force and the dismemberment of the nation were clearly not the "proper means."

The astonishing success of American arms, Gallatin concluded, placed the United States under the obligation of granting Mexico only the most generous peace terms. Surely the "most proud and vain" had been sufficiently satiated with glory and the "most reckless and bellicose" sufficiently glutted with "human gore." The moment was ripe for America to return to its republican mission. No more glorious end of the war could be conceived, he stated, than the voluntary abandonment of all the nation's conquests and the immediate withdrawal of the American forces from Mexico.

Gallatin's statement, in spite of its sincerity and uplifting tone, had little effect. Its publication coincided with the signing of the peace treaty and there seemed little point in further belaboring the question of peace terms. *Peace with Mexico* was Gallatin's last major pronouncement (he died in August 1849). As a clear exposition of America's republican mission, however, it not only reflected the concern felt by many Americans for the war's impact on the republic but it also transcended the immediate circumstances that inspired it.[28]

That the Mexican War posed a threat to the republic and its mission was, it goes without saying, a matter of dispute. Indeed, the number of Americans who reconciled the war with the duties and responsibilities of citizens in a republic and who believed that the war even strengthened republicanism outweighed those on the other side. The differences lay in differing perceptions of the meaning of republicanism and in the impact of events on the theoretical notions of what a republic should do and be.

On the conviction that war was basically evil there was little disagreement. One of the problems faced by the peace movement in mounting its crusade against the Mexican War was that Americans generally were, if not pacifists in the strict meaning of the word, at least strongly opposed to war in the abstract while accepting war with Mexico in the particular. Perhaps this explained the tendency of peace reformers to dilute their antiwar arguments by suggesting that the conflict might have some positive benefit. That war was unnatural and inimical to republics few would challenge. Some of the Mexican War's strongest supporters insisted that republics by their very nature were dedicated to the "arts of peace" and that war diverted them from their true purpose and mission. War and conquest, declared the stridently expansionist *Democratic Review,* were incompatible with the "genius of our institutions." "We declare our hearty detestation and horror of all wars," the *Review* continued, "and of this among the rest." If properly nourished and protected, republican doctrines must diminish warfare, not increase it.[29]

The republic, however, had been founded in violence and the military spirit was its "necessary legacy." While the progress of civilization had demonstrated the "wholesome truth" that war under all circumstances was evil, there were times when the evil must be overcome by the "stern compulsion of necessity." The qualification was significant. Although they agreed that war was incompatible with the nature and purpose of republics, Americans believed that there were some wars that even republics had to fight. Presumably the war with Mexico was such a conflict.[30]

The *Democratic Review* linked the Mexican War to what it called the "social duties of nations":

That we are at war with Mexico is, in some sort, our own fault, inasmuch that . . . we have too much neglected . . . the social duties of nations. Be-

longing, as we do, to the great family of the civilized nations, we have
duties to perform towards them similar to those which a good citizen owes
towards the other members of the community in which he lives. Hence,
when a nation keeps a "disorderly house," it is the duty of neighbors to
interfere.

The idea was drawn from the 18th-century Swiss philosopher Emmerich de Vattel whose work *The Law of Nations* had appeared in several
American editions by 1844. Mexico for a quarter-century had been just
such a "disorderly house," torn by internecine warfare and ruled by a
succession of military chieftains. Citing Vattel, the *Review* justified military intervention in Mexico. "It is an acknowledged law of nations,"
wrote the editor, "that when a country sinks into a state of anarchy,
unable to govern itself, and dangerous to its neighbors, it becomes the
duty of the most powerful of those neighbors to interfere and settle its
affairs." By appealing to a recognized authority on international law,
the *Review* sought to lend legitimacy to the popular attitude toward the
war, although its reading of Vattel was subject to question.

According to this view the war with Mexico assumed the force of a
moral imperative in keeping with the nation's role as the "model republic." Distasteful as the war might be and contrary to the true purposes
of the republic, it was nonetheless an instrument for the achievement
of higher moral results. War, it was said, was like a volcano, ever ready
to burst upon the world when "great moral causes stimulate its action,"
a means for purifying the moral atmosphere and improving the condition of nations. So it was with the Mexican War. Mexico had suffered
"debasement enough to drag down any nation," its people held in
ignorance by the selfishness of its rulers and the lust of a "bloated
Priesthood," its wealth squandered, "this blood-steeped land" required
drastic surgery. In assuming this responsibility, America was merely
responding to the "voice of the age." Whatever qualms some Americans might have had regarding the appropriateness of the war to the
republic were overriden by a sense of duty that was itself inherent in
republicanism.[31]

The Mexican War, therefore, was a necessary stage in human progress. "In the nineteenth century, the era of progress," wrote a Massachusetts citizen, "the civilized world will not permit a great country
like Mexico to relapse into enduring barbarism." The link between the
war and progress was crystal clear to Bostonian Nahum Capen, writer,
publisher, and educational reformer who would soon embark on an
ambitious history of democracy. In his book *The Republic of the United
States of America: Its Duties to Itself, and Its Responsible Relations to Other
Countries* (1848), Capen agreed that war was a calamity which every
true patriot must strive to avoid. Yet, he insisted, war was also an
instrument for advancing human freedom and for securing to the "citizen of every clime" a just and permanent government. Mexico had

become a reproach to republicanism, and Capen wondered that its "faithless and barbarous acts" had been tolerated for so long. "In what way," he asked, "could the evils of Mexico be reached, unless by the strong hand of war?" As the world's leading republic, the path of duty required that the United States rescue its benighted neighbor and see that justice be done its people. By so doing, he argued, America would be true to "the great cause of liberty, justice, and humanity . . . to republican principles . . . [and] to itself, wherein are centred the hopes, the strength of all republics throughout the world." The Mexican War taught the "great lesson" that "republics are not to be exempted from national calamities, if they permit national evils and national wrongs."[32]

Again, popular convictions found support from across the Atlantic, in this instance from the French philospher Victor Cousin whose *Introduction à l'histoire de la philosophie* was published in English translation in Boston in 1832 (his complete *Course of the History of Modern Philosophy* did not appear in America until the early 1850s). Cousin's writings had attracted particular notice in America; his thought, described by one reviewer as the "popular philosophy" of the day, was so well known that detailed analysis was not thought necessary. Cousin gave philosophical expression to the common romantic belief in a "spirit of the age." Each nation (or "people"), he wrote, represented an idea, and it was that nation whose idea was most in accord with the spirit of the time that would dominate. War was the means by which nations whose ideas had passed gave way before nations whose ideas had the "most future." Without war there could be no progress, the future would be retarded and civilization arrested. "Thus," Cousin concluded, "a nation is progressive only on the condition of war." Every nation "has an idea to realize; and when it has sufficiently realized it at home, it exports it in some way by war . . . every civilization which advances, advances by conquest." In Cousin was the perfect justification for the Mexican War as a war for progress. Americans chose to ignore Cousin's further conclusion that, once a nation had achieved its destiny, it fell into decay and was itself conquered; the applicability of this cyclical view to the United States, in any case, was considered moot, for the United States was unique and would always remain so.

When American soldiers retired to their "warrior's repose" on the night before their assault on the castle of Chapultepec, wrote M.C.M. Hammond, it was with the conviction that the next day would decide the fate of Mexico. "It was to decide," Hammond continued, "according to Victor Cousin whether a great question of human progress was involved in the American struggle, and by the issue, whether we or the Mexicans were to be, under a decree of Providence, dominant in principle for the world's benefit."[33]

Behind the belief that the Mexican War constituted a stage in world progress were the ever-present and much-touted beliefs in racial hegemony. The war came at a time when expressions of Anglo-Saxon superiority were at a peak; indeed, a recent scholar has pointed out that the principal catalyst in the appearance of overt Anglo-Saxon racialism was the encounter with the Mexicans. Racial arguments seemed to lend credence to Cousin's assertions, persuading doubters that no matter how injurious the war might be to the republic it served a higher destiny that could only in the end promote progress and strengthen republicanism.

Writing in *Knickerbocker*, R.W. Haskins sketched the racial argument in broad terms, emphasizing the importance of racial purity to America's leadership role in the world. It was the Spanish, he suggested, who had inflicted the "miserable Mexican" on the world. In contrast, "the proud and glorious experiment of our fathers" stood "in bold and imposing reality." The proof of America's racial superiority was in its achievement. In a half-century the United States had risen from a collection of dependent colonies to one of the first-rank powers of the world, and its career had only just begun. Nothing was more certain, he declared, than that America's preeminence resulted from the purity of the race and its preservation "from that commingling with others which has multiplied degenerate thousands upon the earth." The latter, the "hybrid fruits" of Spanish policy, were doomed and "so must finally pass away." Borrowing a term from George Perkins Marsh, Haskins predicted that the "Caucasian Goth" would sweep aside the inferior races until "he finally crowns his efforts in the universal possession and political dominion of the entire continent which he inhabits." Marsh, a New England Whig congressman, had argued that the Germanic ancestors of northwestern Europe, the Goths, were the "noblest branch" of the Caucasian race.[34]

Such statements were legion during the 1830s and 1840s. Individuals as diverse as the outspoken editor of the *Democratic Review* John L. O'Sullivan, James Fenimore Cooper, America's most popular writer of fiction, and Boston abolitionist-clergyman Theodore Parker joined in hailing the superiority of the Anglo-Saxon race. It was clear to all, the *American Review* insisted, that God had raised up, sustained, and qualified the Anglo-Saxon race "to perform a great work in reclaiming the world" and that He had entrusted "to them—to *us*—the destinies of the world." While many of those who espoused blatant doctrines of racial superiority also opposed the Mexican War, preferring that America achieve its racial destiny by peaceful rather than warlike means, there were others for whom it was but a short step to see the war as the inevitable consequence of an obvious racial superiority.[35]

The early contacts between Americans and Mexicans in Texas, the observations of an increasing number of travelers to Mexico, and finally the firsthand experiences of the soldiers (especially the volunteers) all seemed to substantiate the popular belief in American racial superiority. By portraying the Mexican people as inferior, they made it all the easier for Americans to justify the conflict in terms of conditions over which they had no control, thereby easing their consciences and preserving intact their moral antipathy toward war in general. Widespread racial arguments, moreover, doubtless contributed to a tacit acceptance of war with Mexico by many of its abolitionist and pacifist critics, when war with Great Britain, another Anglo-Saxon nation, would have been unthinkable.

When Thomas J. Farnham, whose travels had taken him into Mexico, rushed his descriptions of Mexican geography and society into print in 1846, he did so in order to inform Americans of the nature of their enemy. The Mexican people, he stated, were a race incapable of self-government, whose morals were debased and whose physical and mental powers declined with each generation. "Mexico," he maintained, "must eventually be peopled and governed by another race." Although American readers took exception to the observations of the British traveler George Frederick Ruxton concerning their conduct of the war, they readily accepted his judgment that the Mexican population was in a "state of utter debasement"—indolent, cunning, without energy, and cowards by instinct.

Soldiers in Mexico echoed the racial arguments as they observed Mexican life, strengthening the convictions of the folks back home in their letters and accounts. The popular Captain William Seaton Henry, after a rhapsodic description of the Rio Grande valley, concluded that "it certainly never was intended that this lovely land . . . should remain in the hands of an ignorant and degenerate race." The country could be saved, he believed, only if the "Anglo American race" should move in and govern it "with republican simplicity and justice." Indeed, the widely held views of Anglo-Saxon superiority dictated the "rescue" of the Mexican people from the oppression under which they had labored for centuries. Corydon Donnavan, a volunteer whose captivity by the Mexicans enabled him to observe the people more closely than most, hoped that the country's military despots would be overturned and the people aroused from the "Rip Van Winkle slumber of their ignorance." Through the American presence, he urged, they must be brought into the full enjoyment of liberty and security, their hearts imbued with republican principles, and a "tone of vigor" imparted to their efforts. To accomplish this would require something more radical than simply a change of rulers. "The best, perhaps the only remedy for the nation," wrote a volunteer, "is to Americanize it."[36]

Racial arguments, whether employed by those who urged the necessity of the Mexican War or by those who opposed it (in either case the basic assumptions were the same), were invariably linked with republicanism and all that that concept implied. Racial superiority was commonly measured in terms of achievement; because the United States appeared to be advancing further and more rapidly than any other nation—in popular liberty, democratic government, education and the dissemination of knowledge, economic and technological development—it was argued that Americans were a superior people with a monopoly on progress. That this superiority was racial, in the narrow sense in which that word was defined, seemed obvious; equally obvious was the assumption that it was granted by God. A fundamental element in the perception of racial superiority, indeed its *sine qua non*, was America's republican origin, character, and promise; the republic was the source from which, according to God's dictate, all blessings flowed. Whether the superiority be labeled Anglo-Saxon, Anglo-Norman, Anglo-American, Gothic, or just plain American, there was no doubt that humankind depended upon the United States.

While America's republicanism was the manifestation of its racial superiority, the evidence so to speak, the root of that superiority was not always clearly identified. Popular usage of the word "race" was as fuzzy in the mid-19th century as it has been since. To some, it suggested certain unmistakable and inherent biological characteristics. More commonly, however, it referred to a "people," a community of individuals united by a distinctive cultural configuration, implying descent from a common stock but also suggesting a peculiar amalgam of varied influences both inherited and acquired. In either case, a people always embodied a particular spirit or genius, an identifying characteristic that set it apart from other peoples. This was good romantic doctrine and for Americans provided a meaningful boost to their sense of uniqueness. They were convinced that because of the circumstances of their geographic location, social heterogeneity, and republican origin, no other people could possibly represent the spirit of the time as well as they. In common parlance, the words "people," "nation," and "race" often meant the same thing. When Americans in the 1840s argued their racial superiority, they were pointing to their superiority as a people or as a nation. Albert Gallatin made the distinction between race and people, between racial superiority and a superiority of institutions, but it was a distinction that was more often blurred than clarified.

The popular notion of American superiority was best articulated by the war's critics, perhaps because the critics, usually drawn from the country's intellectual leadership, were less content with mere slogans and phrases. While they shared the convictions of superiority espoused by the war's defenders, they rejected war as an instrument for progress. In July 1846 the *New Englander* addressed the war in terms of those elements that made America a superior nation:

> The United States . . . sprang from the noblest stock on earth's face, either of past or present times;—a stock the most intellectual, as well as moral, and a stock which in physical qualities had at the time the nation was founded, and yet has, no equal. The very best of the nation of this best

stock, founded the United States . . . From the earliest period of the country to this day, the noble stock that first came to these shores has been widening and strengthening in its principles, and though modified by the thousand other causes that must be at work in so large a people and one so situated, it is destined to perpetuate . . . its wisdom and worth to the latest generation. . . . the government of these United States, is believed by the far-judging of the whole world, to be the model government in the earth; and to be thought therefore worthy at least of being held up before other nations . . . as a sort of guide, by which they may direct their own steps in the cause of general progression of the human race.

That this superiority was *American*, rather than Anglo-Saxon or any other, was strikingly clear. "Anglo-Saxon superiority," for many people, had become too vague a concept.

Gamaliel Bailey, the Cincinnati abolitionist editor, insisted that Americans had only a "remote claim" to the achievements of the Anglo-Saxon race; Americans were, in fact, a "new, distinct people—a compound of different races." When Bailey insisted that America's destiny was to extend its sway over the entire continent (by peaceful example) he did so not only because he thought Americans represented a superior race but also because they had erected an "indestructible Civilization in a New World" upon the foundation of a "peculiarly favorable system of Government" that demonstrated the "Truth of the Democratic Principle."

It was too fine a distinction for some. "There is much superfluous eloquence wasted in what is said and written about the progress of the Anglo-Saxon race," commented a reviewer in the *Literary World,* but that the people of the United States were sustained by a "sense of power and constancy that alone belongs to destiny" was beyond doubt. However it might be explained, the badge of American superiority remained its dedication to the principles of republicanism. As one commentator reacted upon reading of Bailey's scheme to unite the continent under a single government: "Long live REPUBLICAN AMERICA!"[37]

America's destiny appeared all the more manifest when it was contrasted with that of Mexico. The Mexicans were benighted on more than one count: they were a "mongrelized" people, a mix of Spanish, Indian, and African and therefore patently inferior (while Americans took pride in their own mix, to amalgamate with nonwhite races was unthinkable); their culture rested on their static, even regressive, Hispanic heritage, a fact that was blamed for many of the country's problems; and they were the victims of centuries of absolute colonial rule, ground down by a political and religious tyranny that had left them incapable of governing themselves. But, withal, Mexico was still a "sister republic," following in the footsteps of the United States. How then could the Mexican War be justified? War, all agreed, was inimical to the true purpose of republics, although necessary under some conditions, but for one republic to war against another, no matter how strong the provocation, was to strike a blow against progress itself. So, at least, some Americans believed.

Among them was Joel R. Poinsett, the South Carolinian who had served as a special envoy to Mexico in 1822, as the first minister to Mexico following the recognition of Mexican independence, and later as secretary of war in Van Buren's cabinet. Poinsett's experiences and the publication in 1824 of his *Notes on Mexico* brought him early recognition as an authority on Mexican affairs. As minister, he spent four and a half years in the Mexican capital, instructed among other things to represent to the Mexicans "the practical operations and the very great advantages" of America's republican system. He carried out his instructions only too well. A confirmed champion of democratic government, he dedicated himself to the strengthening of Mexico's republican organization even to the point of aligning himself with the opposition to the aristocratic and monarchist elements that controlled the government. Poinsett's dedication to the encouragement of democracy in Mexico never wavered and later colored his attitude toward the Mexican War.

Confessing his "affectionate regard" for the Mexican people, Poinsett viewed the war with deep regret. He urged the invaders to treat the people with understanding and compassion, while they warred against the country's "tyrannical military despotism." It was unfair, he believed, to compare the United States and Mexico, for the advantages were all on the side of the former. "We, the descendants of the most energetic race the world has ever known, set upon our career as a nation, upon a footing of equality with the most civilized people of the age. The Mexicans, descended from the warlike, but indolent Spaniards, had been so entirely excluded from participation in the government and from all intercourse with foreigners, that their revolution found them two centuries behind the age." Americans should not forget the point from which the Mexican people began their progress toward self-government. They were "brother Republicans," more in need of encouragement and assistance than of invasion and conquest. Poinsett feared that the war might strengthen the prejudices against republicanism among upper-class Mexicans and play into the hands of the monarchical faction.

Poinsett was also alarmed at the prolongation of the war and the increasing demands for the acquisition of Mexican territory. Following the fall of Mexico City, he urged that the United States withdraw its forces immediately, lest their continued presence in Mexico seriously damage the country's movement toward democracy. "The people are republican," he declared, "so entirely republican" that if left to themselves they would in a few years "comprehend and practise a judicious civil polity." Poinsett remembered the day when America sympathized with Mexico's effort to create a government on the American model. "Why we are in the habit of abusing them now as a degraded race I do not understand."[38]

Poinsett's views were shared by critics of the war. The *New Englander* recalled Mexico's long struggle to free itself from Spain's "tyrannical harness," and the aid which Americans extended to their neighbors at that time. When independence was at last achieved, the United States "shouted to her in joy" and "bade her stand up as one of the republics of America." How could war against this very same republic now be sanctioned? Daniel Barnard admonished those (critics as well as defenders) who excused the war because it was "only" a war against Mexico, as if war with Mexico were a "small affair" and of "trivial importance." Mexico, he pointed out, was a respectable, civilized and Christian nation, entitled to respect. Especially should Mexico receive the support of those who, like the United States, "have had to conquer their own independence and freedom." The two countries were irrevocably tied by their common struggles against oppression and their dedication to republicanism. That the United States and Mexico, two republics, should be the first Christian nations of any note to disturb the peace in thirty years was a fact filled with ignominy.[39]

Obviously not all Americans saw the enemy in that light. When Robert H. Morris, onetime mayor of New York, addressed the great mass meeting in the city shortly after the war began, he voiced what was to become the popular viewpoint: "If it were not that this war was forced upon us, it would be one of the most unpleasant wars we could engage in, because we are warring against those who claim to be republicans, like ourselves." In reality, however, Mexico was "not the Mexico of free principles, that she professed" but was a country "trodden down by tyrants."

To the arguments of Poinsett and others like him, supporters of the war had a quick response. Mexico, they said, hardly deserved to be called a republic. The country presented the "singular spectacle" of a population ostensibly governed by a republican constitution, claiming all the "honors" of a republic, yet displaying to the world a military and religious oppression that left its people reduced to the "condition of slaves." Mexican republicanism, wrote Ripley, was no more than "a hot-house graft of freedom on the decayed trunk of despotism," delicate, fragile, and doomed to perish. Republics, reminded a writer in *De Bow's Review*, depended for their existence on the virtue and intelligence of their people, qualities which were not evident in Mexico. Historian Brantz Mayer, long a student of Mexican affairs, not only agreed that Mexico hardly qualified as a republic but he also doubted whether it was even a nation. In the "true sense of nationality," he contended, a nation was a great family, its people intimately united by bonds of interest, sympathy, and affection. In Mexico, these ties of kinship and the mystical quality they imparted to the community were noticeably absent.[40]

For a generation that looked with suspicion and ill-concealed hostility on Roman Catholicism, it was easy to identify a basic cause for Mexico's lack of "virtue and intelligence" in the power which the Church wielded over the people. Indeed, even opponents of the Mexican War paused in their criticism when they considered that Mexico was after all a Catholic country. Volunteers described scenes that seemed to come straight out of the 15th century. The Church, fostering "Ignorance, Superstition, Idolatry and Vice," held the people in a vise of "feudal degradation." Soldiers found incomprehensible the power of the priesthood over the everyday lives of the people and were astonished that reason, common sense, and instinct could be so subverted as to hold in veneration an institution that was "impious, tyrannous, and corrupt." The republican principle lost its vitality when its "sole sustenance" was derived from "ignorance and superstition," when mind and body were enslaved "under the pretext of the soul's emancipation." The people, wrote an Ohioan, were deprived of one of republicanism's essential requisites, religious liberty.[41]

Following a journey through northern Mexico, an Indiana volunteer pondered the "air of decay" that seemed everywhere to greet his view. The lives of the people, their agricultural practices, their primitive technology, all appeared to be at a "dead standstill." It was not only the violent and unstable character of the government that promoted "national indolence," he concluded, it was also (perhaps more significantly) the "social, political, religious & moral incubus" of the Church. No man could be free when his soul was in chains.

The conclusion that Mexico's republican government was a sham obviated the criticism that in warring against a sister republic the United States was committing an unnatural and unjust act. As the *Democratic Review* later contended, "No nation has a right . . . to blaspheme the holy name of Liberty." But while the absence of true republicanism in Mexico strengthened the conviction that the Mexican War was necessary in the larger scheme of things, it also placed upon American shoulders new burdens of responsibility. If the United States were to be true to its republican mission and to fulfill its providential destiny, it must then undertake the task of redeeming the Mexican people from the darkness of their oppression and bring them into a bright and beneficial republican light.[42]

On July 19, 1848, Jacob Oswandel, a young volunteer in Pennsylvania's First Regiment, boarded a steamer at Vera Cruz for his long-awaited voyage home. Several Mexicans boarded the vessel to say goodbye to the soldiers, including the wharf superintendent, who told Oswandel, "What a great change has taken place since the Yankees first landed on our shores!" Like so many other volunteers, Oswandel referred to the invasion and occupation in which he had taken part as "our mission to Mexico." He expressed the fondness he had developed for the country and the hopes he had for its future. The day, he felt, would not be far distant when Vera Cruz would be connected with Mexico City by a railroad, when manufacturing establishments would spring up all over the country, when "civilization, national reform, and morals" would be ordered and self-government be established. His hopes for Mexico's future did not obscure the difficulties in achieving these objectives. The power of the Church, he told his Mexican friends, would have to be broken, politics taken out of religion and religion out of politics. Life, liberty, and the pursuit of happiness must be guaranteed to every living being in Mexico. "Let the people rule."[43]

Through all the talk of American superiority, racial, institutional, or otherwise, and of America's providential destiny to expand by war or by peaceful means, there ran the theme of regeneration. While scholars have cast doubt on the sincerity of those who argued the reform nature of the Mexican War, the belief that it was America's duty to redeem the Mexican people was simply too widespread, too pervasive, to be dismissed as nothing more than an attempt to mask ulterior desires for power and gain. People from all walks of life, including the soldiers in Mexico, and from all parts of the country echoed the belief that America's mission was to bring Mexico into the 19th century. Critics like Gallatin and Prescott might scoff at the visionary rhetoric of the war's supporters but they too shared the view that America's role in Mexico must be a regenerative one. Pacifists, discouraged by the apparent popularity of the war, consoled themselves with the thought that the war's benefits for Mexico would be immense. Besides, asked Massachusetts lawyer and businessman E. Hasket Derby, "Has not heaven . . . confided to our nation, rather than the sovereigns of Europe, the renovation of this great country?" A new era would dawn upon Mexico, Derby was convinced, "and she would at length participate in the progress of the age."

To attempt Mexico's regeneration by conciliatory means, declared the *Scientific American,* by sending missionaries instead of soldiers to enlighten the people, was "utterly absurd" and useless under the existing state of Mexican society. "The present war is not against the *people,*" the journal's readers were reminded; on the contrary, the war was an "appeal" to the Mexican people, to show them their situation and to instruct them on how to improve it. The war had opened the way, as no other means could have, for "the operations of the engines of light, liberty and improvements." Furthermore, the journal implied, the matter was really out of America's hands: "This was not the design of our Government, but it was that of divine Providence."[44]

Reflecting the attitudes of the soldiers, a Missouri minister who was among the earliest volunteers to answer the call contended that the United States could not have gone to war against Mexico simply as a "momentary, enthusiastic past time." There had to be more important considerations involved. "Ever since the American Colonies were first

planted," he wrote, "we have been a progressive nation." There was a
larger design involved in the conflict that would, he felt, result in "an
entire change" in Mexico. The "moral shock" of their contacts with the
Americans, as Raphael Semmes put it, would give the Mexican people
the impetus they required for full participation in the "great race of
civilization." For America's fighting men, especially many of the volunteers for whom service in the war held a special meaning, the penetration of Mexico assumed the character of a crusade. Although some
feared that their "visitation" would be like a tempest on the prairie—
"for a moment we will agitate the grass that is in our track, but leave no
impression behind us"—their optimism was boundless. Mexico, they
felt, might even be grateful in years to come for America's effort to
offer the nation the "living waters" of liberty.[45]

The theme of regeneration received official sanction when General
Winfield Scott issued his first proclamation to the "Mexican nation" in
Jalapa on May 11, 1847, three weeks after Mexico's bloody defeat at
Cerro Gordo. In his statement, Scott mirrored attitudes that were being
expressed back home. Whatever may have been the origins of the war,
he declared, "we regard it as an evil." Governments, however, "have
sacred duties to perform, from which they cannot swerve," a sentiment
that paralleled the justification for the war some Americans drew from
Vattel (the "social duties of nations"). Mexican liberty and its republican system were threatened by a monarchical party supported by un-
friendly "foreign influences." He appealed to the Mexican people to
see through the deception practised by their leaders, to "cease to be the
sport of private ambition," and to conduct themselves like a "great
American nation." Most importantly, he admonished them to "abandon
at once those old colonial habits, and learn to be truly free—truly
republican."

Scott's appeal placed the United States in the role of the defender of
Mexican freedom and republicanism against the pressures, both internal and external, that would undermine them. He hoped to reach the
masses, but it is doubtful if many of them were made aware of the
statement. Indeed, some feared the proclamation would only exacer-
bate divisions within the ruling class and encourage the monarchical
faction. That the proclamation was written by a Mexican cleric (under
Scott's direction) seemed to reduce its effectiveness even further. Its
effect on the men in Scott's army, however, was quite different, for the
proclamation strengthened the convictions of those who already believed that they were fighting on behalf of republican government.
When the army later moved into the city of Puebla, one of the residents
noted that the men had "got by heart" Scott's appeal. "They talk of
nothing but fraternity between the two republics, and say they have
only come to save the democratic principle, threatened with a foreign
monarchy by the cabinets of Europe."[46]

Discussion of America's mission to salvage Mexican republicanism
was often tied to the question of Mexico's future relationship with the

United States. Some Americans believed that only through the annexation of all of Mexico—the annihilation, in other words, of Mexico's
nationality—could the mission of regeneration be properly accomplished. Indeed, such a proposal was made even before the war began.
A union of the two countries, it was suggested, would present to the
world a republic unequaled "even in the imaginations of visionaries."
Mexico would gain stability and the Mexican people "some promise of
that happiness which they never yet have had," while the United States
would acquire an extent of territory and resources undreamed of in
past times. The proposal was not very far from those of such war critics
as Gamaliel Bailey, who foresaw the eventual assimilation of all Mexico
by the peaceful operation of America's destiny, or of the editor of the
periodical *Nineteenth Century,* who denounced the war as immoral and
unjust but who felt that, once it had been won, the "most merciful
course" toward Mexico would be to take the whole. The all-of-Mexico
movement was largely restricted to the more strident politicians and
the expansionist press and never commanded a wide and serious following. The prospect of incorporating eight million Mexicans into the
United States overshadowed whatever benefit the acquisition might
have, for America or for Mexico. Racial antipathies were aroused, for
as William H. Prescott put it, "The Spanish blood will not mix well with
the Yankee."

Others argued that Mexico's regeneration could best be achieved
through an arrangement roughly similar to that employed by the ancient Romans. The Romans, commented the *Democratic Review,* ruled
their conquered territories not as "parts of the empire" but rather as
"appendages," leaving local administration in the hands of the vanquished people. Following this model, the United States could intro-
duce into Mexico the "gifts of the god of peace . . . the implements of
life   and   happiness"   and   school   the   Mexican   people   for
self-government.[47]

More common was the insistence, by most Americans including the
soldiers in Mexico, that the regeneration must be undertaken by the
Mexicans themselves under the benign tutelage of the occupation
army. The "poor degraded masses" must be liberated from their bondage, taught the responsibilities of self-government, and instilled with a
"love of country." The war was only the first step for, as New York *Sun*
correspondent Jane McManus Storms pointed out, the sword was not
an appropriate "implement of republicanism." She hoped that the
"rough attention" of the invading army would "electrify" the Mexican
people to a "better sense of republicanism." Once this was accomplished, education in the "arts of free government" must follow. The
process would require a long period of probation but it was one the
people, under a government of "native Mexicans to the exclusion of
the Spaniards," must do for themselves. Storms later reminded her
countrymen that it was America's particular mission to "cherish and
instruct, to protect, enrich, and liberate" Mexico's population.[48]

If free government was one side of the republican coin, free enterprise, or what was called the commercial spirit, was the other. Not all
Americans shared the gloomy predictions that the rise of commercialism
in the United States threatened to divert its citizens from their duties to
the republic. On the contrary, the commercial spirit was viewed as an
essential attribute of the mid-19th-century republic. "The curse of Mexico," stated the *Democratic Review,* lay precisely in its lack of the commercial principle, "that great conservator of peace and internal tranquility."

Freeman Hunt, the spokesman for America's business and commercial interests, agreed. Although a steadfast critic of the war (he had
denounced the conflict as anti-republican and anti-Christian), he was
also outspoken in his criticism of Mexico. The revolutionary violence
and military anarchy Mexico had experienced during its years of independence had closed the door to "those great conservative industrial
and commercial interests" without which stability was impossible. But,
Hunt wrote, no evil was so unmixed "that some good may not be
extracted from it." The war, as wrong as it was, provided the opportunity for Mexico's political regeneration. Commerce, he insisted, must
now be planted on her soil and a great commercial interest built up
that could stabilize the country, enforce the laws, and control the military. With the natural resources already at hand, Mexico needed only
"an industrious people" and an "efficient government" in order to take
its rightful place among the foremost commercial nations of the world.
The war, Hunt believed, could supply these missing elements. It was
America's mission, chimed in the *Democratic Review,* to "inoculate" Mexico with the commercial spirit and to do so by armed force if that was
the only way.[49]

A month after the war began, as volunteers were beginning to flock
to the recruiting offices, Boston's story-paper *Uncle Sam* printed the
words of a new patriotic song, "They Wait For Us."

> The Spanish maid, with eye of fire,
> At balmy evening turns her lyre
> And, looking to the Eastern sky,
> Awaits our Yankee chivalry
> Whose purer blood and valiant arms,
> Are fit to clasp her budding charms.
>
> • • •
>
> An army of *reformers,* we—
> March on to glorious victory;
> And on the highest peak of Ande,
> Unfurl our banners to the wind,
> Whose stars shall light the land anew,
> And shed rich blessings like the dew.

Nathan Covington Brooks, the classical grammarian turned historian,
was certain he knew how it would all turn out. Mexico, he wrote, "will

at length rise to an appreciation of real liberty, learn that her true policy is industry and peace, and . . . find her chief wealth and happiness in peaceful, health-inspiring toil. Relieved from the exorbitant exactions of her military and priesthood, her expenditures will be diminished, while increased attention to agriculture and manufactures will develop and augment her resources; and institutions of learning, after the manner of those of her northern sister, diffuse knowledge and virtue among her ignorant and half-civilized multitudes." Of such was mid-19th-century optimism made.[50]

It did not quite work out as Brooks hoped. Mexico's defeat left the nation's liberals, those who sought to restore republican government, in despair and wondering if indeed their country was really a nation or simply a collection of individuals lacking those bonds that constitute a nation. But with the despair, as Charles A. Hale has pointed out, went a new determination to address and remedy Mexico's problems. The years following the war witnessed "a strong reassertion of faith in Mexico's republican institutions" that found expression in demands for broad radical reforms, in the government and in the Church. The efforts, however, were frustrated by divisions within the liberal ranks and by the rising attacks of conservatives. While the war highlighted the need for reform to one group it also encouraged another to argue the desirability of monarchy. Leaders such as the historian Lucas Alamán identified republicanism with anarchy. Democracy, they said, was alien to the Mexican character, in which "the principles of monarchy, Catholicism, and respect for authority" were embedded. The war, instead of promoting the United States as a republican model for Mexico to follow, persuaded some Mexicans that imitation was out of the question, even impossible, considering the vast differences in the characters of the two peoples. Mexico was better advised to look to the monarchies of Europe.

The hopes which many Americans expressed for Mexico were not, then, immediately realized, although for the first time in Mexico's history a great debate over the validity of republican principles raged among the contending factions. But to people in the United States, nothing seemed to have changed. In an outburst reminiscent of the earlier years, the *Democratic Review* in 1858 declared that it must now be clear to everyone that "Mexico cannot govern herself." There was only one way to deal with the problem: "The time has come when it is as imperatively our duty—made so by Providence—to take control of Mexico, and wheel her into the train of the world's progress." By 1858, however, the words sounded faintly anachronistic.[51]

A New Epoch in American History

Early on the morning of March 18, 1848, the British Cunard steam packet *Cambria* docked in New York. Because of strong westerly gales her passage from Liverpool had taken twenty days. As she approached the harbor, the vessel was met by the *New York Herald*'s special express steamer, and the latest news from Europe was speeded to the newspaper offices. Within hours, the *Herald* was on the streets, its bold headlines announcing a revolution in France, the abdication of King Louis Philippe, and the proclamation of a French Republic "on the model of that of the United States."

The news sent waves of excitement throughout the country. Few Americans believed that revolutionary activity would be confined to France, and predictions that it would spread to other countries, to Prussia, Austria, Russia, perhaps even Great Britain, were offered. Impromptu concerts were held in city after city at which *La Marseillaise* was played and sung. Mass meetings were hastily summoned to hear speeches and pass resolutions lauding the French action. Within a week, New York's Bowery Theatre was advertising a "new national drama" entitled "The Insurrection of Paris," and in Boston a Millerite announced that the revolution was a sign that Jesus Christ would return to earth in 1848. French, Swiss, Italian, Irish, and Polish citizens gathered in their own meetings to offer sympathy and encouragement to European revolution.

Editors, orators, politicians sounded the death knell of monarchical absolutism. A new "age of revolutions" had opened, and the great and final contest between republicanism and monarchism was at hand. There was no doubt of the role of the United States. "This republic," commented the *Herald*, "is the model and exemplar of the revolution-

ists in France, and all of Europe. They copy our constitutions, imitate
our institutions, follow our political fashions, and adopt our principles
of public policy." The French uprising began on February 22, Washington's Birthday, a providential coincidence. With a victorious war just
ended, "We possess one of the highest characters in the world, at this
time."[1]

The news spread quickly through the camps of the occupation army
in Mexico. In Mexico City, American soldiers joined the celebration of
the city's French residents and paraded, sang patriotic songs, and invaded the bars and gambling houses. Some of the men really believed,
as one eloquent trooper put it, that the "millennium of republicanism
had arrived at last," and they rejoiced that the "refulgency of their
glorious stars" had penetrated the "noxious fogs of European despotism." To the soldiers, the French revolution carried an even more
immediate meaning—a quick acceptance by Mexico of the peace treaty
and an early return home.[2]

The explanation for the course of events in Europe seemed simple.
News of the French revolution reached the United States less than two
weeks after the Senate's ratification of the peace treaty, while Americans were still basking in the glow of their success. "Our destiny has
been more clearly developed within the past two years," boasted the
Herald, "than at any time before or since the Declaration of Independence." The military power and capacity demonstrated in the war had
won new strength and respect for republicanism, while the "great
credit and great honor" gained by the war propelled the nation into
leadership in the "history of civilization and the human race." The
French revolution was a clear consequence of the Mexican War.[3]

Americans had watched anxiously for European reactions to the war,
for they believed that republicanism itself was on trial and being tested
on Mexican battlefields. Indeed, they felt that the great contest between monarchism and republicanism had begun in Mexico, and the
future of republicanism, not only in Mexico but in the world as well,
depended upon the outcome of the war.

For years the American press had reported plans to place a European prince on a Mexican throne, and there was just enough credence
in the rumors to arouse concern. Europe's monarchs, it was charged,
had embarked on a course designed to thwart the natural growth of
the United States and frustrate its democratic mission.

The very existence of the United States was seen as an affront to the
European system. François Guizot, France's foreign minister, seemed
to reveal deeper monarchical intentions when he called for an "equilib-
rium of the great political forces in America." When it was learned that
Louis Philippe and Guizot were hatching a plot to place the former's
son, the duc de Montpensier, at the head of a Mexican monarchy,
European designs against America were confirmed. Spain provided
equally disquieting news. It was no secret that Spain regarded Mexico's

republican government as a farce, its independence only temporary. Plans had been made (with England's connivance, it was said) to establish a Mexican monarchy under a Spanish prince, presumably a young cousin of Queen Isabella II. European diplomats expressed their scorn for Mexico, the "sick man of North America." The only cure for the country's domestic turmoil and inability to honor its obligations was strong monarchical government.[4]

While not all the details of the European machinations were known to the American people, there were enough signs to cause anxiety. Support for a monarchy, they knew, existed among some of the powerful elements of the Mexican population. When General Paredes seized control of the government early in 1846, it was assumed that he did so in order to create a monarchy. Some sources reported that Paredes had opened negotiations with Louis Philippe, others that his seizure of power was part of a Spanish plot. Word came from Paris, moreover, that Santa Anna from his Cuban exile had contacted Spain, France, and England and offered to raise an army in order to plant monarchy in Mexico. At the time, it seemed to be the only way to stop an American invasion. The musings of the British press did not help matters. Plans to establish a monarchy in Mexico were rejected by one London paper in favor of Disraeli's proposal that a British protectorate be extended over Mexico, a scheme that was anathema to Anglophobic America.[5]

The success of the American army in Mexico reduced the fears of European intervention, although an occasional warning was still raised. In his message to Congress in December 1847, President Polk warned that a premature withdrawal of the troops from Mexico might cast that nation "into the arms of some European monarch." During the drawn-out peace negotiations, correspondents in Mexico thought they detected European influences behind Mexican intransigence, later suggesting that a "sort of American holy alliance" was forming among European powers in order to halt the "progress" of the United States. With characteristic bluster, one editor reminded Europe's crowned heads that they interfered in New World affairs at their own peril. The American army, he pointed out, offered a timely lesson to those who still itched to put their hands into North American affairs; it was inconceivable that the lesson would be ignored.[6]

Europeans in fact had followed the progress of the American army in Mexico with considerable interest. When John L. Stephens, explorer, author, and student of Central American antiquities, talked with Alexander von Humboldt at the Prussian royal palace in Potsdam in the summer of 1847 he found the aged scientist "full of our Mexican war." With the Prussian king and his advisers, Humboldt had followed Taylor's campaigns in northern Mexico, and each battle had become the subject for discussion. Prussia's generals were "struck with admiration" for the American army, and one Prussian staff officer was sent to join

Winfield Scott's army on its march to Mexico City. Stephens expressed
pride that the "leading military men of a military nation" should have
so much praise for America's volunteers. From Paris, American consul-
general Robert Walsh reported the "lively satisfaction" expressed by
members of France's Chamber of Deputies as they followed Taylor's
advance. Only Guizot and his friends appeared "chap-fallen."[7]

The reactions of no European country, however, meant so much to
Americans as did those of Great Britain. Feeling a natural affinity with
England, tied, by historical, cultural, and linguistic bonds, Americans
nonetheless played the role of rebellious children against an overbear-
ing parent, building their quest for national identity on a keen sense of
rivalry and competition with the onetime mother country. The bonds
of kinship between the two countries were balanced by a harsh (and
often irrational) enmity that exaggerated the rivalry, as Americans
seemed eager to demonstrate the wisdom of their separation by showing that they represented something newer and better in the world.
They were convinced that Britain, still viewing the United States as an
unruly upstart, regarded American growth as a threat to its own supremacy. America's Anglophobia was manifold, ranging from a stinging
sensitivity to the barbs of English critics against the nation's cultural
pretensions to an obsessive fear of British encirclement and strangula-
tion. Britain's contemptuous dismissal of America's self-styled mission
and the failure to recognize that Anglo-Saxon leadership had passed to
the "model republic" only exacerbated the attitude.

In the 1840s the belief that Britain was contemplating desperate
measures to contain the United States seemed borne out by events.
When both England and France took military action against Mexico in
1839 to force the latter to meet its debt obligations, rumors abounded
that England was demanding (and would receive) California as pay-
ment. The settlement of the Maine boundary in 1842 left many Americans dissatisfied. Britain's growing involvement in Central American
affairs, its efforts to dissuade Texas from accepting annexation, its
reported designs on Cuba, and finally its uncompromising stance on
the Oregon Question all seemed to point to a dangerous and threaten-
ing encirclement of the United States. War with Great Britain appeared
not only likely but to the more shrill expansionists downright desirable.

The peaceful settlement of the Oregon boundary in June 1846 (after
the Mexican War had begun) eased American apprehensions and it
soon became apparent that the fears of British intervention in Mexico
were groundless. The British government, to be sure, was aware of the
advantages a victory would bring the United States. A weakened Mexico meant a Mexico even less able to meet its obligations to British
bondholders. On the other hand, the annexation of all of Mexico by
the United States might mean the annexation of Mexico's debts as well.
Far from intervening, the British government went out of its way to
avoid a confrontation, respecting the American blockade of Mexico's

Gulf coast and approving the policies of the occupation forces, some of which were favorable to British trading interests.

From his post in London, America's minister George Bancroft reported that England had finally recognized that "America means to go on her own way, and that Europe . . . must give up the thought of swaying her destiny." The war, he felt, had compelled England's grudging respect. "You are the Lords of Mexico!" Lord Ashburton had declared, and Lord Grey asked unbelievingly, "How could you take the castle of Vera Cruz so soon?" For Lord Palmerston, the American victories had simply proved the "immense superiority" of the Anglo-Saxon race.[8]

The British press was not so easily reconciled. Before the war was barely under way, the papers printed taunting allusions to American weakness and ridiculed the rustic backwoods character of the American soldier. As a military nation the United States was "one of the weakest in the world," its army filled with "majors who serve out beer, and colonels who rub down the heels of one's horse, brigadiers driving stage-coaches, and generals with the pen behind their ear." President Polk was mockingly referred to as the "Napoleon of the backwoods." America's small and ill-trained army, it was expected, would be soundly drubbed by Mexico's more experienced professional force. The first victories at Palo Alto and Resaca de la Palma were dismissed as petty and insignificant engagements that had been exaggerated into "deeds of high chivalry." Zachary Taylor was an "unscrupulous highwayman" with all the "rapacity of a Cortes or a Raleigh."

When Scott planned his assault on Vera Cruz, British editors scoffed at his temerity, for the Mexican port, they declared, could never be taken. After the fall of Vera Cruz, they charged the General with folly as he marched his army into Mexico's interior. His advance was "as visionary as that of Napoleon upon Moscow." Even if Mexico City should be taken, the army would never make it back to Vera Cruz. All such comments were given publicity in the United States, raising American hackles and causing at least one journal to wonder if there was not some "special spite" that had suddenly deranged John Bull's newspapers.[9]

When it became clear that the American army had indeed triumphed, British papers were loathe to concede that the United States had demonstrated military superiority. Instead, they explained the successes in terms of Mexican weakness, incompetence, and cowardice and heaped scorn on Mexico's pretensions as a nation. "Greater impotency and cowardice were never displayed." Mexico, declared *The Times*, "bids fair to exhibit one of those tremendous catastrophes which stand out horribly distinct in the annals of human calamity." It hardly deserved to be a nation. To Americans, England's inability to credit their army with skill and bravery was irritating in the extreme.[10]

Some English critics received special treatment at the hands of

American editors. One was the Tory historian Sir Archibald Alison, whose "scholarly yet sonorous" history of Europe from the French Revolution to the fall of Napoleon appeared in an American edition in 1842. By 1846 it had been reissued six times. Its popularity in the United States can only be explained by the strong interest in history, and in military history in particular, for many of Alison's statements were received with outrage. Writing of the United States in the early 19th century in one of his frequent digressions, Alison scornfully dismissed America's military force as hardly equivalent to a single Roman legion, one-fifth the size of Bavaria's army, and out of all proportion to the "arrogant tone" adopted by Americans toward other countries. Its Lilliputian army and backwoods militia, he proclaimed, were incapable of carrying on a war, totally unfit and utterly unreliable as a military force.

Alison's slurs evoked an angry response. "Does he indulge the European notion that we are all demi-savages, and suppose that *all* the people of the United States are backwoodsmen?" asked the *Democratic Review*. A "ridiculous philosopher" and a "romancer," Alison was well known as an enemy of republicanism. The Mexican War had put the lie to Alison's statements, and one reviewer gleefully pointed out that America's army in Mexico clearly surpassed "all that is recorded of British valor, either on Indian or European fields."[11]

In August 1846, three months after the Mexican War began, the English adventurer George Frederick Ruxton landed in Vera Cruz to begin a long journey through central and northern Mexico, his desire to explore the wilds of North America having been whetted by the "adventures of Natty Bumppo." His attitude toward the United States was hardly charitable. He had earlier published a belligerent attack on the United States during the Oregon crisis and continued to believe that the Mexican War was simply a warm-up for a war against Great Britain. He scoffed at the army's success in Mexico and found the "intense glorifications" that followed the victories to be ludicrous. The war was popular with Americans, he stated, only because it flattered their national pride. Ruxton's strictures against the United States were exceeded only by his contempt for the Mexican people. The Mexican soldiers, he charged, were deficient in moral and intellectual capacity, treacherous and cunning, reflecting all the cowardice that was inherent in their race.

While readers in the United States found Ruxton's *Adventures in Mexico and the Rocky Mountains* (1848) entertaining, they were indignant over his attacks on the war and his failure to give their victories their proper due. Equally irritating were his condemnation of the Mexican people and his conviction that they could never be brought to a state of republican self-government, that only a monarchy could solve their problems. One volunteer concluded that Ruxton's criticism only proved that English writers found it impossible to do justice to American history, a condition, he felt, that had flawed English writing ever since Jackson humbled the British at New Orleans.[12]

Few criticisms cut so sharply as the charge of inhumanity that was cast against the American troops in Mexico. Writers reacted angrily against the accusations and reprinted long accounts of the British campaigns in the Peninsular War from the histories of Alison and Napier to show that Britain's own record was far from clean. Wellington's tactics had been more destructive and costly in military and civilian lives; there were no such scenes in Mexico as were witnessed at Badajoz and San Sebastian. When Douglas Jerrold, editor of *Punch*, charged that American misdeeds in Mexico were a reproach to the Anglo-Saxon race, he was reminded of the sufferings Ireland had endured since the days of Cromwell and of the "fire and desolation" that had been wreaked on "groaning India." Compared with the brutality of England's wars, the Mexican War was "humanity itself."

One American who shrugged off the attacks against "Yankeedoodledom" was the Brooklyn editor Walt Whitman. The English, Whitman observed, had always displayed a "most infamous and spiteful meanness toward this country." It was no matter. "Let the Old World wag on under its cumbrous load of form and conservatism," he wrote, "we are of a newer, fresher race and land."[13]

Traveling in America during the summer of 1848, the Englishman David Mitchell stopped at a roadside tavern in Virginia, where he was accosted by one of the customers. "I guess you English have been a little astonished at the way in which we carried everything before us in the Mexican war," commented the Yankee. "History don't record many such events as the taking of Chapultepec, the battle of Buena Vista, Monterey, and, in fact, the whole campaign." Following Mitchell's noncommittal reply, the man continued: "I guess we rather surprised the kings and aristocrats of Europe, winning battle after battle . . . our men, too, most of them volunteers." Pondering this exchange, Mitchell concluded that the war had contributed not a little "to inflate the national mind."

The Virginian, however, was correct. European observers of the Mexican War *had* expressed amazement at the apparent ease with which outnumbered and ill-trained soldiers had triumphed in battle. One English journal found it "so extraordinary, so perfectly unaccountable" that it concluded "there must be some mystery—some leading cause, imperfectly understood on our side of the Atlantic."[14]

That their country was "imperfectly understood" abroad most Americans would agree, but they disagreed that there was "some mystery" involved in their success in Mexico. When President Polk reviewed the results of the war, he pointed to the boost the war had given the country's national character abroad. The real meaning of the war, he believed, was in its demonstration that a democracy could successfully prosecute a foreign war "with all the vigor" normally associated with "more arbitrary forms of government." Critics, he said, had long charged republics with an inherent "want of that unity, concentration of purpose, and vigor of execution" that characterized more authoritarian governments. A popularly elected representative government with a volunteer army of citizen-soldiers had bested a military dictatorship. No more persuasive argument for the strength and superiority of the republican system could be advanced.[15]

Polk's view was widely shared. The United States was yet a young and fragile nation, its people acutely sensitive to the fact that in the eyes of the world they were still an unproven experiment in popular government. Europeans scoffed at America's national pretensions, its bluster and spread-eagle rhetoric, ridiculed its romantic faith in the popular voice, and magnified the weakness of its institutions. America's "forbearance and patience" toward Mexico, at a time when Great Britain and France were flexing their military muscles, was interpreted as a sign of torpor and a lack of determination. Incapable of mustering the strength of resources and purpose, the republic, it was thought, would surely collapse into disunity and paralysis at the very thought of waging offensive war. Americans responded with a defensiveness that bordered on paranoia. Viewing themselves as an island of republicanism surrounded by the tempestuous seas of monarchical oppression, they lashed out at their critics. To them, the Mexican War was a giant stride in their quest for national identity, testing American democracy as it had never been tested before. Not only had the test been passed but republicanism had also been strengthened in the only way Europeans could understand, by waging a successful war. Furthermore, America had triumphed without sacrificing its commitment to popular rule. The country had earned its distinction as the "model republic."

Although critical of the war at the beginning, Freeman Hunt maintained that Americans had shown the world that a people "devoted to the arts of peace" could vanquish a "military people, governed by military despots." The strength of popular government had been made clear to "doubting monarchists," wrote Nathan Brooks. Combining freshness of spirit with manly vigor, America had settled the question of a republic's capacity to engage in a foreign war. "Woe to the crowned head," warned a soldier in Mexico, "that interferes with rising, onward, onward America!"[16]

The Mexican War ended in a reaffirmation of the nation's mission and gave encouragement to those who saw the national role in terms of world-wide reform. "The age in which we live is one of Reform and Progress," declared one paper, and these words—Reform and Progress—found repeated assertion in relation to the war. The Victorian poet Martin Farquhar Tupper, as popular in the United States as in his native England, captured the spirit of the republic in his ode "To America":

> High to the stars thy tender leaflets shoot,
> > Deep dig thy fibres round the ribs of earth!
> From sea to sea, from south to icy north
> > It must ere long be thine, through good or ill,
> To stretch thy sinewy boughs: go—wondrous child!
> > The glories of thy destiny fulfill.

In 1845 South Carolina's Edwin DeLeon had given classic expression to "The Position and Duties of 'Young America,'" in which he pointed out that nations, like men, "have their seasons of infancy, manly vigor, and decrepitude." To many Americans, the Mexican War signaled the advance of the United States from youth into manhood. "The Young Giant of the West" now stood forth in the "full flush of exulting manhood." America, wrote James Fenimore Cooper, had passed "from the gristle into the bone."[17]

There was nothing to dim the prospect that lay ahead—or, almost nothing. Some saw danger signals in the renewed controversy over the extension of slavery, but for others the war's divisive legacy seemed insignificant when viewed in the perspective of national growth and destiny. There were clouds gathering in the bright morning skies of the republic, as one writer put it, but as long as the nation's leaders were guided by the precepts of the republic's founders there need be no fear for the Union. The security of the republic lay with the patriotism and virtue of her sons. The question of slavery's extension undoubtedly had its "mischiefs," declared the *American Quarterly Review*. It may disrupt "our social harmony" and disturb the political machinery, but in spite of the dire predictions "of the timid" it seemed "incapable of worse consequences than it has hitherto produced." With the new strength of victory over Mexico, the republic appeared indestructible. As well attempt the dissolution of the solar system as to sever the ties that "must forever bind together the American union." The American people, in 1848, put the question behind them.[18]

Six weeks after President Polk had declared the Mexican War officially at an end, a letter from a New York volunteer in California was printed in the *New York Herald*. Buried in the account of his adventures was the cryptic statement that a "gold mine" had recently been discovered on a branch of the Sacramento River. "Without allowing any golden hopes to puzzle my prophetic vision of the future," the soldier wrote, "I would predict for California, a Peruvian harvest of the precious metals." The item attracted little notice. Less than a month later, the information was dramatically confirmed when a young naval officer arrived in Washington after a record 47-day overland journey from California, carrying in his saddlebags a small vial of gold dust. When an army courier appeared in the capital in mid-November with a tea caddy full of dust and nuggets, all doubt was dispelled. Disbelief turned to awe and amazement. The long-sought El Dorado had been uncovered.

Reports of gold deposits and discoveries drifted eastward in increasing numbers, each more fantastic than the one before, challenging credulity and awakening the wildest dreams. "Never before, in the history of the world, had the actual so eclipsed the ideal—the fact outgrown the fiction." It was easy for an astonished populace to identify a larger national purpose in the event. The object of three centuries of desperate searching had been revealed, not to men lured by visions of instant wealth nor to adventurers motivated by a vulgar greed but to the "hardy emigrant," to the citizen of a republic! What had been denied the "indolent Spaniard" had been granted the energetic "Americo-Saxon." The ink on the peace treaty was scarcely dry before California disclosed its riches to its new owners. It was almost as if God had kept the gold hidden until the land came into the possession of the American republic.[19]

Coming on the heels of the Mexican War and the revolutions in Europe, the discovery of gold in California "awaked the last chord, and struck the last string, which was needed to immortalize the year 1848." The year surely stood as the "*annus mirabilis* in the eventful history of this eventful century." In December 1848 President Polk announced that "our beloved country presents a sublime moral spectacle to the world." There was little doubt in his mind that Americans were indeed the "most favored people on the face of the earth."[20]

The war with Mexico appeared to have prepared the bed from which both European revolution and the discovery of gold sprouted. A turning point in the nation's career had been reached. "Our country has entered on a new epoch in its history," insisted the *American Review*. "From this year we take a new start in national development; one that must, more than ever before, draw the world's history into the stream of ours." As he weighed the significance of the Mexican War to America's future, M.C.M. Hammond defined the challenge to which Americans must now respond. An entire continent lay at the nation's feet, "inviting the manners, laws, institutions, ideas, which have materially aided to propel her to early greatness."

Will she extend the beneficence to other peoples,—in other climes and other countries, live over her own days of glorious achievement and enjoyment, in stimulating and witnessing their development? Will she grasp what Providence apparently places within her reach, to redound to the ultimate benefit of the species? or, closing her hands in mock humility, and pursuing the avocations of avarice, will she remain supinely content amid the general yet tedious progress of the mass of mankind? Time will speak for her!

The Mexican War *did* bring America to a crossroads—but it was a crossroads of a different kind, unanticipated, baffling, and fraught with peril for the republic.[21]

Notes

Preface

1. *American Review,* VII (June 1848), 653.
2. *Graham's Magazine,* XXXIII (July 1848), 59; George Lippard, *Legends of Mexico: The Battles of Taylor* (Philadelphia, 1847), 27.
3. *American Review,* IX (April 1849), 334.
4. Emerson Davis, *The Half Century; or, A History of the Changes That Have Taken Place, and Events That Have Transpired, Chiefly in the United States, Between 1800 and 1850* (Boston, 1851), 100.

Prologue

1. Milo Milton Quaife, ed., *The Diary of James K. Polk During His Presidency, 1845 to 1849* (4 vols., Chicago, 1910), IV, 1–2; Frederick L. Harvey, *History of the Washington National Monument and Washington National Monument Society* (Washington, 1903), 26, 41–42; Washington *National Intelligencer,* June 6, 9, 10, 1848.
2. Washington *National Intelligencer,* June 26, July 6, 1848.
3. Harvey, *History of the Washington National Monument,* 111–12; Washington *National Intelligencer,* July 6, 7, 1848; *Niles' National Register,* LXXIV (July 12, 1848), 32.
4. Washington *National Intelligencer,* July 6, 1848; Robert C. Winthrop, "National Monument to Washington. An Oration Delivered at the Seat of Government, on the Occasion of Laying the Corner-Stone of the National Monument to Washington, July 4, 1848," in *Washington, Bowdoin, and Franklin as Portrayed in Occasional Addresses* (Boston, 1876), 9–28.
5. *Niles' National Register,* LXXIV (July 12, 1848), 32; Quaife, ed., *The Diary of James K. Polk,* IV, 2–3.
6. Washington *Union,* July 6, 1848; Quaife, ed., *The Diary of James K. Polk,* IV, 2–3; James D. Richardson, comp., *A Compilation of the Messages and Papers of the Presidents, 1789–1897* (10 vols., Washington, 1896–99), IV, 627.
7. Washington *National Intelligencer,* July 10, 1848; *Democratic Review,* XXIII (August 1848), 187; XXII (March 1848), 288.

Chapter 1: America's First Foreign War

1. Washington *National Intelligencer,* May 11, 13, 18, 1846; *Spirit of the Times,* XVI (May 23, 1846), 151, 156; *New York Herald,* May 13, 1846.

2. Washington *Union,* May 23, 18, 25, 1846; Washington *National Intelligencer,* May 18, 27, 29, 1846.

3. Melville to Gansevoort Melville, May 29, 1846, *The Letters of Herman Melville* (Merrell R. Davis and William H. Gilman, eds., New Haven, 1960), 29; Justin H. Smith, *The War with Mexico* (2 vols., New York, 1919), I, 193–94; *New York Herald,* June 4, 1846; John R. Kenly, *Memoirs of a Maryland Volunteer* (Philadelphia, 1873), 19.

4. Alexander Beaufort Meek, *Romantic Passages in Southwestern History* (2nd ed., Mobile, 1857), 201–2; [John Blount Robertson,] *Reminiscences of a Campaign in Mexico* (Nashville, 1849), 57; *New York Herald,* May 31, 1846. Meek was not the only one to employ the imagery of Scott's poem *The Lady of the Lake;* see also John Stilwell Jenkins, *History of the War Between the United States and Mexico* (Auburn, N.Y. 1849), 89.

5. *New York Herald,* May–June 1846, *passim.*

6. Washington *National Intelligencer,* May 14, 1846.

7. *Southern Quarterly Review,* XV (July 1849), 411, 412–13.

8. Russell F. Weigley, *History of the United States Army* (New York, 1967), 178–79, 182–83.

9. Erna Risch, *Quartermaster Support of the Army: A History of the Corps, 1775–1939* (Washington, 1962), 241–57; *House Ex. Doc. 8,* 30 Cong. 1 Sess., 548.

10. James A. Huston, *The Sinews of War: Army Logistics, 1775–1953* (Washington, 1966), 130–31; *Spirit of the Times,* XVII (June 19, 1847), 192; Roger Wolcott, ed., *The Correspondence of William Hickling Prescott, 1833–1847* (Cambridge, Mass., 1925), 601; *House Ex. Doc. 29,* 30 Cong., 1 Sess., 104–7; Roswell S. Ripley, *The War with Mexico* (2 vols., New York, 1849), II, 49–50.

11. *Southern Quarterly Review,* X (Oct. 1846), 435; *Niles' National Register,* LXXI (Sept. 19, Oct. 3, 1846), 38, 67–68.

12. *American Phrenological Journal,* IX (Nov. 1847), 339; *House Ex. Doc. 8,* 30 Cong., 1 Sess., 549; Henry W. Halleck, *Elements of Military Art and Science* (3rd ed., New York, 1862), 413.

13. Leonard D. White, *The Jacksonians: A Study in Administrative History, 1829–1861* (New York, 1956), 50–66; Weigley, *History of the United States Army,* 175–76.

14. Frank Luther Mott, *American Journalism: A History of Newspapers in the United States Through 250 Years, 1690 to 1940* (New York, 1941), 215, 228–52, 303–4, 314–15 (quotations, 215, 248–49).

15. Joseph J. Mathews, *Reporting the Wars* (Minneapolis, 1957), 56; B. H. Gilley, " 'Polk's War' and the Louisiana Press," *Louisiana History,* XX (Winter 1979), 5–23.

16. Fayette Copeland, *Kendall of the Picayune* (Norman, Okla., 1943), *passim* (quotation, 150); John S. Kendall, "George Wilkins Kendall and the Founding of the New Orleans 'Picayune,' " *Louisiana Historical Quarterly,* XI (April 1928), 261–85.

17. Copeland, *Kendall of the Picayune,* 141, 155, 158–59; Thomas J. Farnham, "Nicholas Trist & James Freaner and the Mission to Mexico," *Arizona and*

the West, XI (Autumn 1969), 247–60; Milton Rickels, *Thomas Bangs Thorpe: Humorist of the Old Southwest* (Baton Rouge, 1962), 117–21. For the press coverage of the Mexican War, see Thomas William Reilly, "American Reporters and the Mexican War, 1846–1848" (Ph.D. dissertation, University of Minnesota, 1975).

18. *New York Herald,* Sept. 29, 1846; Tom Reilly, "Jane McManus Storms: Letters from the Mexican War, 1846–1848," *Southwestern Historical Quarterly,* LXXXV (July 1981), 21–44; Copeland, *Kendall of the Picayune,* 180, 198–200; Mathews, *Reporting the Wars,* 55–56; Oliver Gramling, *AP: The Story of News* (New York, 1940), 13–21.

19. Lota M. Spell, "The Anglo-Saxon Press in Mexico, 1846–1848," *American Historical Review,* XXXVIII (Oct. 1932), 20–31; *Yankee Doodle,* II (April 17, 1847), 19; Tom Reilly, "Newspaper Suppression During the Mexican War, 1846–48," *Journalism Quarterly,* LIV (Summer 1977), 262–70, 349.

20. Ripley, *War with Mexico,* I, 145; *Niles' National Register,* LXXIII (Sept. 25, 1847), 53.

Chapter 2: A Dare-Devil War Spirit

1. Nathan Covington Brooks, *A Complete History of the Mexican War* (Philadelphia, 1849), 354; John Frost, *Pictorial History of Mexico and the Mexican War* (Richmond, 1848), 252; Raphael Semmes, *Service Afloat and Ashore During the Mexican War* (Cincinnati, 1851), 71; *New York Herald,* July 18, 1846; José Fernando Ramírez, *Mexico During the War with the United States* (ed. Walter V. Scholes, trans. Elliott B. Scherr, Columbia, Mo., 1950), 135.

2. *New York Herald,* May 30, 1846; George Frederick Ruxton, *Adventures in Mexico and the Rocky Mountains* (New York, 1848), 26; Thomas Bangs Thorpe, *Our Army at Monterey* (Philadelphia, 1848), 95; Thorpe, *Our Army on the Rio Grande* (Philadelphia, 1846), 152–53; *American Journal of Phrenology,* IX (May 1847), 155; *Spirit of the Times,* XVI (July 4, 1846), 222.

3. *New York Tribune,* July 15, 1848; *Niles' National Register,* LXXI (Sept. 26, 1846), 58; [John A. Scott,] *Encarnacion Prisoners* (Louisville, 1848), 49; George Wilkins Kendall, *The War Between the United States and Mexico Illustrated* (New York, 1851), 52; Brantz Mayer, *History of the War Between Mexico and the United States* (New York, 1848), 132–33.

4. *Baltimore Patriot,* quoted in Washington *National Intelligencer,* May 29, 1846; Philip Young, *History of Mexico . . . From the Period of the Spanish Conquest, 1520, to the Present Time, 1847* (Cincinnati, 1848), 357; J. W. Gibson, *Letter Descriptive of the Battle of Buena Vista, Written Upon the Ground* (Lawrenceburgh, Ind., 1847), 1.

5. *Niles' National Register,* LXXI (Sept. 12, 1846), 22; Washington *National Intelligencer,* May 28, 1846; *New York Herald,* May 29, 1846; Justin H. Smith, "La República de Río Grande," *American Historical Review,* XXV (July 1920), 662–65.

6. *Southern Quarterly Review,* XV (July 1849), 413–14.

7. *New York Herald,* May 28, 1846; *Rough and Ready Annual* (New York, 1848), 49–50; John S. Jenkins, *History of the War Between the United States and Mexico* (Auburn, N.Y., 1849), 17–18; Mayer, *History of the War Between Mexico and the United States,* 134.

8. *Democratic Review,* XX (June 1847), 483; [Nahum Capen,] *The Republic of the United States of America* (New York, 1848), 142–43.

9. Marcus Cunliffe, *Soldiers & Civilians: The Martial Spirit in America, 1775–1865* (2nd ed., New York, 1973), 17 (I am indebted to Cunliffe's insights at many points in the following pages); Alexander Mackay, *The Western World; or, Travels in the United States in 1846–47* (2 vols., Philadelphia, 1849), I, 148; Roger Wolcott, ed., *Correspondence of William Hickling Prescott, 1833–1847* (Cambridge, Mass., 1925), 597; Oran Perry, comp., *Indiana in the Mexican War* (Indianapolis, 1908), 18; *Brownson's Quarterly Review*, III (Oct. 1846), 507.

10. Abiel Abbot Livermore, *The War with Mexico Reviewed* (Boston, 1850), 227–29; *Harbinger*, VI (Feb. 12, 1848), 117.

11. *American Quarterly Register*, I (May 1848), 16; Perry, comp. *Indiana in the Mexican War*, 54, 107–8, 92; Lewis Leonidas Allen, *Pencillings of Scenes Upon the Rio Grande* (New York, 1848), 11; *New York Herald*, June 1, 1846; George C. Furber, *The Twelve Months' Volunteer* (Cincinnati, 1848), 43.

12. George Winston Smith and Charles Judah, eds., *Chronicles of the Gringos: The U.S. Army in the Mexican War, 1846–1848* (Albuquerque, 1968), 274; J. Jacob Oswandel, *Notes of the Mexican War* (Philadelphia, 1885), 16–17, 21–23.

13. Richard McSherry, *El Puchero; or a Mixed Dish from Mexico* (Philadelphia, 1850), 95; John R. Kenly, *Memoirs of a Maryland Volunteer* (Philadelphia, 1873), 77–78; S. Compton Smith, *Chile Con Carne; or, The Camp and the Field* (New York, 1857), 292–93; Cunliffe, *Soldiers & Civilians*, 172.

14. *New York Herald*, May 25, 1846; *Spirit of the Times*, XVII (May 15, 1847), 133; "Sketches of a Campaign in Coahuila," *American Whig Review*, XVI (Nov. 1852), 455.

15. J. M. Wynkoop, *Anecdotes and Incidents: Comprising Daring Exploits, Personal and Amusing Adventures . . . and Thrilling Incidents of the Mexican War* (Pittsburgh, 1848), 87–88, 84; Albert G. Brackett, *General Lane's Brigade in Central Mexico* (Cincinnati, 1854), 187, 231–33; Smith and Judah, eds., *Chronicles of the Gringos*, 34, 468; *Spirit of the Times*, XVII (June 5, 1847), 167.

16. Edward D. Mansfield, *The Mexican War: A History of Its Origin, and a Detailed Account of the Victories Which Terminated in the Surrender of the Capital* (New York, 1849), 75; Samuel E. Chamberlain, *My Confession* (New York, 1956), 7, 35; [John Blount Robertson,] *Reminiscences of a Campaign in Mexico* (Nashville, 1849), 58, 60; Francis Baylies, *Narrative of Major General Wool's Campaign in Mexico* (Albany, 1851), 5; Smith, *Chile Con Carne*, 3–4.

17. Oswandel, *Notes of the Mexican War*, 58; McSherry, *El Puchero*, 84; H. Judge Moore, *Scott's Campaign in Mexico* (Charleston, 1849), vi.

18. *American Review*, VII (March 1848), 313–14; Wolcott, ed., *Correspondence of William Hickling Prescott*, 648, 658; *Democratic Review*, XX (June 1847), 484.

19. Semmes, *Service Afloat and Ashore During the Mexican War*, 189; *Niles' National Register*, LXXI (Nov. 28, 1846), 197; LXXII (June 26, 1847), 266; Ramon Alcaraz et al., eds., *The Other Side: or, Notes for the History of the War Between Mexico and the United States* (New York, 1850), 417; [George Ballentine,] *Autobiography of an English Soldier in the United States Army* (New York, 1853), 138.

20. Moore, *Scott's Campaign in Mexico*, 96–98; *Littell's Living Age*, XIV (Aug. 21, 1847), 382–83.

21. *Literary World*, II (Aug. 28, 1847), 85; *Niles' National Register*, LXXII (May 22, 1847), 184; *Knickerbocker Magazine*, XXXI (Jan. 1848), 76–77; Emma

Willard, *Last Leaves of American History: Comprising Histories of the Mexican War and California* (New York, 1849), 97; Semmes, *Service Afloat and Ashore During the Mexican War,* 467–68.

22. *House Ex. Doc. 60,* 30 Cong., 1 Sess., 156–57, 166–67; Justin H. Smith, *The War with Mexico* (2 vols., New York, 1919), II, 220–21, 455–57; Henry O. Whiteside, "Winfield Scott and the Mexican Occupation: Policy and Practice," *Mid-America,* LII (April 1970), 102–18. See also, Thomas M. Davies, Jr., "Assessments During the Mexican War: An Exercise in Futility," *New Mexico Historical Review,* XLI (July 1966), 197–216.

23. *Niles' National Register,* LXXIV (Aug. 2, 1848), 68.

24. *Niles' National Register,* LXXI (Sept. 26, 1846), 57; George Frederick Ruxton, *Adventures in Mexico and the Rocky Mountains* (New York, 1848), 144; Smith and Judah, eds., *Chronicles of the Gringos,* 402.

25. [Ballentine,] *Autobiography of an English Soldier in the United States Army,* 268; Semmes, *Service Afloat and Ashore During the Mexican War,* 154; Smith and Judah, eds., *Chronicles of the Gringos,* 403.

26. *Niles' National Register,* LXXI (Sept. 26, 1846), 58; George Meade, *The Life and Letters of General George Gordon Meade* (2 vols., New York, 1913), I, 108–10; Smith and Judah, eds., *Chronicles of the Gringos,* 239–40.

27. Meade, *Life and Letters of General George Gordon Meade,* I, 109; Isaac Smith, *Reminiscences of a Campaign in Mexico* (Indianapolis, 1848), 31–34; Semmes, *Service Afloat and Ashore During the Mexican War,* 173.

28. *Niles' National Register,* LXXI (Nov. 14, 1846), 165; Frost, *Pictorial History of Mexico and the Mexican War,* 332–33; Scott quoted in Charles W. Elliott, *Winfield Scott, the Soldier and the Man* (New York, 1937), 448; Joel Tyler Headley, *The Lives of Winfield Scott and Andrew Jackson* (New York, 1852), 76.

29. Oswandel, *Notes of the Mexican War,* 345, 361; Brackett, *General Lane's Brigade in Central Mexico,* 132–33, 93; Smith and Judah, eds., *Chronicles of the Gringos,* 269–71.

30. Smith, *Chile Con Carne,* 194–95; [Ballentine,] *Autobiography of an English Soldier in the United States Army,* 272.

31. *House Ex. Doc. 60,* 30 Cong., 1 Sess., 1007; Smith, *Chile Con Carne,* 160–62; *Niles' National Register,* LXXII (May 22, 29, June 19, 1847), 184, 198, 252.

32. Chamberlain, *My Confession,* 89; Wynkoop, *Anecdotes and Incidents,* 91–92; *Niles' National Register,* LXXII (April 10, 1847), 89; Otto B. Engelmann, ed., "The Second Illinois in the Mexican War: Mexican War Letters of Adolph Engelmann, 1846–1847," *Journal of the Illinois State Historical Society,* XXVI (Jan. 1934), 439.

33. Walt Whitman, *Leaves of Grass* (Brooklyn, 1855; facs. ed, New York, 1966), 40; Chamberlain, *My Confession,* 39; Mark E. Nackman, "The Making of the Texan Citizen Soldier, 1835–1860," *Southwestern Historical Quarterly,* LXXVIII (Jan. 1975), 247–48, 243; Smith, *Chile Con Carne,* 294–95; Frank S. Edwards, *A Campaign in New Mexico with Colonel Doniphan* (Philadelphia, 1847), 155–56; Zachary Taylor, *Letters of Zachary Taylor, from the Battle-Fields of the Mexican War* (Rochester, 1908), 24.

34. Smith and Judah, eds., *Chronicles of the Gringos,* 38–39; McSherry, *El Puchero,* 95.

35. Young, *History of Mexico,* 445.

36. James D. Richardson, comp., *A Compilation of the Messages and Papers of the*

Presidents, 1789–1897 (10 vols., Washington, 1896–99), IV, 413, 508; Cunliffe, *Soldiers & Civilians,* 150.

37. Stephen E. Ambrose, *Duty, Honor, Country: A History of West Point* (Baltimore, 1966), 107–24: *North American Review,* LVII (Oct. 1843), 269–92; *American Review,* IV (Aug. 1846), 147, 149.

38. [Luther Giddings,] *Sketches of the Campaign in Northern Mexico* (New York, 1853), 280; John T. Hughes, *Doniphan's Expedition* (Cincinnati, 1848), 105; Brackett, *General Lane's Brigade in Central Mexico,* 34–35; Furber, *Twelve Months' Volunteer,* 433.

39. Smith and Judah, eds., *Chronicles of the Gringos,* 39–40; William Starr Myers, ed., *The Mexican War Diary of George B. McClellan* (Princeton, 1917), 16.

40. Ruxton, *Adventures in Mexico and the Rocky Mountains,* 178–79.

41. Henry W. Halleck, *Elements of Military Art and Science* (New York, 1846), 150; Smith and Judah, eds., *Chronicles of the Gringos,* 30; Myers, ed., *Mexican War Diary of George B. McClellan,* 18; Smith, *War with Mexico,* II, 318–19, 511–12.

42. Brackett, *General Lane's Brigade in Central Mexico,* 25; Mary Clinton Collins, ed., "Journal of Francis Collins, an Artillery Officer in the Mexican War," *Quarterly Publication of the Historical and Philosophical Society of Ohio,* X (April–July 1915), 72.

43. Taylor, *Letters of Zachary Taylor,* 51; *Niles' National Register,* LXXI (Dec. 26, 1846), 265, 266; Smith, *Reminiscences of a Campaign in Mexico,* 25.

44. Richard S. Fisher, *The Book of the World* (2 vols., New York, 1850–51), I, 105; *Addresses Delivered in the Chapel at West Point . . . by the Hon. Ashbel Smith, of Texas, and Col. A. W. Doniphan, of Missouri, June 16, 1848* (New York, 1848).

45. *Spirit of the Times,* XVI (June 13, 1846), 187; XVII (July 10, 1847), 228; *Literary World,* II (Dec. 11, 1847), 455; Edward D. Mansfield, *The Utility and Services of the United States Military Academy . . . An Address, Delivered June 18, 1847, at West Point* (New York, 1847), 27–28; *Southern Literary Messenger,* IV (Jan. 1849), 39.

Chapter 3: The True Spirit of Patriot Virtue

1. Baltimore *Patriot,* quoted in Washington *National Intelligencer,* May 29, 1846; Lucien B. Chase, *History of the Polk Administration* (New York, 1850), 467.

2. Merle Curti, *The Roots of American Loyalty* (New York, 1946), viii; Noah Webster, *An American Dictionary of the English Language* (New York, 1845), 595.

3. Curti, *Roots of American Loyalty,* 148, 155; *Southern Literary Messenger,* XIV (Dec. 1848), 727; *American Review,* II (Sept. 1845), 229.

4. Charles R. Hinds, ed., "Mexican War Journal of Leander M. Cox," *Register of the Kentucky Historical Society,* LV (Jan. 1957), 37; *New York Herald,* July 18, 1846; W. A. Crofutt, ed., *Fifty Years in Camp and Field: Diary of Major-General Ethan Allen Hitchcock* (New York, 1909), 217–18.

5. *Southern Literary Messenger,* XIV, 727; George W. Bethune, "Truth the Strength of Freedom. A Discourse on the Duty of a Patriot . . . July 6, 1845," in *Orations and Occasional Discourses* (New York, 1850), 321; Bethune, *The Claims of Our Country on Its Literary Men: An Oration Before the Phi*

Beta Kappa Society of Harvard University, July 19, 1849 (Cambridge, 1849), 10–11, 13, 14.

6. George Perkins Marsh, "Address [1844]," in Cephas Brainerd and Eveline Warner Brainerd, eds., *The New England Society Orations* (2 vols., New York, 1901), I, 412–13; Charles B. Haddock, *The Patriot Scholar: An Oration Pronounced Before the . . . Phi Beta Kappa at Yale College, August 16, 1848* (New Haven, 1848), 6, 17–19; *Brownson's Quarterly Review*, III (April 1849), 176–77.

7. Marsh, "Address," in Brainerd and Brainerd, eds., *New England Society Orations*, I, 411; George William Curtis, "Patriotism. An Oration Delivered Before the Graduating Class at Union College . . . July 20, 1857," in Charles Eliot Norton, ed., *Orations and Addresses of George William Curtis* (3 vols., New York, 1894), I, 45, 52; Thomas Starr King, "Patriotism: Delivered Before the Ancient and Honorable Artillery Company, Boston . . . June 2, 1851," in *Patriotism and Other Papers* (Boston, 1864), 36, 37, 40.

8. Edwin H. Chapin, *True Patriotism. A Discourse Delivered on Fast Day . . .* (Boston, 1847); *American Literary Magazine*, I (July 1847), 50; Haddock, *The Patriot Citizen. An Address, Delivered at Lebanon, N.H. . . . the Fourth of July, 1842* (Hanover, 1842), 14; *New York Herald*, June 30, 1846.

9. Edwin P. Whipple, "How Ought the American Mind Be Cultivated?" *Harper's Magazine*, XV (June 1857), 121; Whipple, "The American Mind," *ibid.*, XV (Oct. 1857), 695; Whipple, "Providence in American History," *ibid.*, XVII (Oct. 1858), 695; Robert P. Hay, "Providence and the American Past," *Indiana Magazine of History*, LXV (June 1969), 80.

10. [Thomas Bangs Thorpe,] *Anecdotes of General Taylor, and the Mexican War* (New York, 1848), 27–29.

11. Walt Whitman, *The Gathering of the Forces* (eds. Cleveland Rodgers and John Black, 2 vols., New York, 1920), I, 82–85.

12. J. Jacob Oswandel, *Notes of the Mexican War, 1846–47–48* (Philadelphia, 1885), 636–37; *Spirit of the Times*, XVI (Aug. 1, 1846), 272–73; XVII (April 3, 1847), 61; George Lippard, *Legends of Mexico: The Battles of Taylor* (Philadelphia, 1847), 11, 12.

13. [John Blount Robertson,] *Reminiscences of a Campaign in Mexico* (Nashville, 1849), 58; John T. Hughes, *Doniphan's Expedition* (Cincinnati, 1848), 131; Francis Baylies, *A Narrative of Major General Wool's Campaign in Mexico* (Albany, 1851), 60; [Benjamin Franklin Scribner,] *Camp Life of a Volunteer* (Philadelphia, 1847), 32–33.

14. Ralph Henry Gabriel, *The Course of American Democratic Thought* (New York, 1940), 88–100 (quotation, 100); *Spirit of the Times*, XVI (April 25, 1846), 97; *The War with Mexico . . . By an Officer in the Army* (Rochester, 1847), 7.

15. Milo Milton Quaife, *The Flag of the United States* (New York, 1942), 141; Curti, *Roots of American Loyalty*, 132; *New York Herald*, May 31, 1846; *Niles' National Register*, LXXI (Nov. 7, 1846), 156; Baylies, *Narrative of Major General Wool's Campaign in Mexico*, 60; William Seaton Henry, *Campaign Sketches of the War with Mexico* (New York, 1847), 215.

16. H. Judge Moore, *Scott's Campaign in Mexico* (Charleston, 1849), 21–22, 138; Charles J. Peterson, *The Military Heroes of the War with Mexico; with a Narrative of the War* (10th ed., Philadelphia, 1858), 127; George W. Hartman, *A Private's Own Journal: Giving an Account of the Battles in Mexico* (Greencastle, Penna., 1849), 20.

17. George C. Furber, *The Twelve Months' Volunteer* (Cincinnati, 1848), 414;

Oswandel, *Notes of the Mexican War,* 64–65; [George Ballentine,] *Autobiography of an English Soldier in the United States Army* (New York, 1853), 147.

18. *Spirit of the Times,* XVII (April 10, 1847), 75; XVI (June 13, 1846), 187; William B. McGroarty, ed., "William H. Richardson's Journal of Doniphan's Expedition," *Missouri Historical Review,* XXII (July 1928), 515; Thomas Bangs Thorpe, *Our Army at Monterey* (Philadelphia, 1847), 91–92; J. M. Wynkoop, *Anecdotes and Incidents: Comprising Daring Exploits, Personal and Amusing Adventures . . . and Thrilling Incidents of the Mexican War* (Pittsburgh, 1848), 19–20.

19. Frank S. Edwards, *A Campaign in New Mexico with Colonel Doniphan* (Philadelphia, 1847), 111–12; Hughes, *Doniphan's Expedition,* 302, 37.

20. Fred Somkin, *Unquiet Eagle: Memory and Desire in the Idea of American Freedom, 1815–1860* (Ithaca, N.Y., 1967), 68–69.

21. Charles J. Ingersoll, *Historical Sketch of the Second War Between the United States of America, and Great Britain* (2 vols., Philadelphia, 1845–49); Charles J. Peterson, *The Military Heroes of the War of 1812: With a Narrative of the War* (10th ed., Philadelphia, 1858), 5.

22. John William Ward, *Andrew Jackson: Symbol for an Age* (New York, 1955), 136–37; George M. Dallas, "Eulogy . . . June 26, 1845," and George Bancroft, "Eulogy . . . June 27, 1845," in B. M. Dusenberry, comp., *Monument to the Memory of General Andrew Jackson: Containing Twenty-Five Eulogies and Sermons Delivered on the Occasion of His Death* (Troy, N.Y., 1846), 56, 51; Joel Tyler Headley, *The Lives of Winfield Scott and Andrew Jackson* (New York, 1852).

23. Edward Everett, "On the March to the Mexican War," *Transactions Illinois State Historical Society,* 1905, 197; Alfred J. Henderson, ed., "A Morgan County Volunteer in the Mexican War," *Journal of the Illinois State Historical Society,* XLI (Dec. 1948), 388; Oran Perry, comp., *Indiana in the Mexican War* (Indianapolis, 1908), 81; Graham A. Barringer, ed., "The Mexican War Journal of Henry S. Lane," *Indiana Magazine of History,* LIII (Dec. 1957), 388; Oswandel, *Notes of the Mexican War,* 36–37; Albert G. Brackett, *General Lane's Brigade in Central Mexico* (Cincinnati, 1854), 226–30.

24. S. Compton Smith, *Chile Con Carne; or, The Camp and the Field* (New York, 1857), 4; Perry, comp., *Indiana in the Mexican War,* 99; Benson J. Lossing, *Seventeen Hundred and Seventy-Six, or the War of Independence* (New York, 1847), v; Michael Kammen, *A Season of Youth: The American Revolution and the Historical Imagination* (New York, 1978), 51.

25. *Godey's Magazine,* XXXVII (July 1848), 58; Donald A. Ringe, "The American Revolution in American Romance," *American Literature,* XLIX (Nov. 1977), 352; *Holden's Dollar Magazine,* I (Feb. 1848), 109; R. A. Yoder, "The First Romantics and the Last Revolution," *Studies in Romanticism,* XV (Fall 1976), 493–529.

26. Lossing, *Seventeen Hundred and Seventy-Six,* 18; Kammen, *Season of Youth,* 51–52.

27. Washington *National Intelligencer,* May 16, 1846; *Southern Quarterly Review,* XIV (July 1848), 197; *Spirit of the Times,* XVII (Oct. 2, 1847), 373; Lewis Leonidas Allen, *Pencillings of Scenes Upon the Rio Grande* (New York, 1848), 14.

28. Hartman, *A Private's Own Journal,* 14; Oswandel, *Notes of the Mexican War,* 201; Thorpe, *Our Army at Monterey,* 13; *Niles' National Register,* LXXII (Aug. 7, 1847), 361–62.

29. James Dixon, *Personal Narrative of a Tour Through a Part of the United States and Canada* (New York, 1849), 68–69; Peterson, *Military Heroes of the Revolution*, 205; John F. Berens, *Providence & Patriotism in Early America, 1640–1815* (Charlottesville, 1978), 92–93, 117–20.

30. Milton Jamieson, *Journal and Notes of a Campaign in Mexico* (Cincinnati, 1849), 72; *Brother Jonathan*, July 4, 1847; *Literary World*, III (Oct. 28, 1848), 774.

31. John Frost, *Pictorial Life of George Washington* (Philadelphia, 1848), 14; George Lippard, *Washington and His Generals: or, Legends of the Revolution* (Philadelphia, 1847), 522; *Washington and the Generals of the American Revolution* (2 vols., Philadelphia, 1847), I, 1–2. Lippard's Washington volume was a companion piece to his *Legends of Mexico*.

32. William Alfred Bryan, *George Washington in American Literature, 1775–1865* (New York, 1952), 16; *American Literary Magazine*, II (June 1848), 387; *Democratic Review*, XXI (Dec. 1847), 566; *Littell's Living Age*, XIII (May 29, 1847), 432.

33. Lippard, *Washington and His Generals*, 522–25; Lippard, *Legends of Mexico: The Battles of Taylor*, 12, 17, 53.

34. James Henry Carleton, *The Battle of Buena Vista* (New York, 1848), 29–30, 35–36; *Niles' National Register*, LXXII (April 10, 1847), 84; Smith, *Chile Con Carne*, 209–10, 206–7; Baylies, *Narrative of Major General Wool's Campaign in Mexico*, 29.

35. William W. Carpenter, *Travels and Adventures in Mexico* (New York, 1851), 79; John Frost, *The Mexican War and Its Warriors* (New Haven and Philadelphia, 1848), 204.

36. Somkin, *Unquiet Eagle*, 110–11; Edgar Allan Poe, "Marginalia," *Graham's Magazine*, XXIX (Dec. 1846), 312. Poe preferred the "music" of "Appalachia" to the guttural "Alleghania."

37. *Democratic Review*, VI (Nov. 1839), 427.

38. Robert H. White, " 'The Volunteer State,' " *Tennessee Historical Quarterly*, XV (March 1956), 53–56; Claude M. Fuess, *The Life of Caleb Cushing* (2 vols., New York, 1923), II, 37.

39. Henry Washington Benham, "Recollections of Mexico and Buena Vista," *Old and New*, IV (July 1871), 47; Justin H. Smith, *The War with Mexico* (2 vols., New York, 1919), I, 559; [Thorpe,] *Anecdotes of General Taylor, and the Mexican War*, 96; Daniel J. Ryan, "Ohio in the Mexican War," *Ohio Archaeological and Historical Society Publications*, XXI (1912), 282.

40. Barringer, ed., "Mexican War Journal of Henry S. Lane," *Indiana Magazine of History*, LIII, 413; Isaac Smith, *Reminiscences of a Campaign in Mexico* (Indianapolis, 1848), 8–9; Perry, comp., *Indiana in the Mexican War*, 126.

41. *Niles' National Register*, LXXII (March 13, 1847), 21.

42. R. Carlyle Buley, "Indiana in the Mexican War," *Indiana Magazine of History*, XVI (March 1920), 46–68; Herman J. Viola, "Zachary Taylor and the Indiana Volunteers," *Southwestern Historical Quarterly*, LXXII (Jan. 1969), 335–46.

43. James D. Richardson, comp., *A Compilation of the Messages and Papers of the Presidents, 1789–1897* (10 vols., Washington, 1896–99), IV, 631; Marcus Cunliffe, *Soldiers & Civilians: The Martial Spirit in America, 1775–1865* (2nd ed., New York, 1973), 294–95; St. George L. Sioussat, ed., "Mexican War Letters of Col. William Bowen Campbell, of Tennessee, Written to Gover-

nor David Campbell, of Virginia, 1846–1847," *Tennessee Historical Magazine,* I (June 1915), 136.

44. Sioussat, ed., "Mexican War Letters of Col. William Bowen Campbell," *Tennessee Historical Magazine,* I, 148, 151; Roy F. Nichols, ed., "The Mystery of the Dallas Papers," *Pennsylvania Magazine of History and Biography,* LXXIII (July 1949), 66.
45. *Literary World,* III (July 22, 1848), 484.

Chapter 4: Visions of Romance and Chivalry

 1. Nathaniel Hawthorne, *Life of Franklin Pierce* (Boston, 1852), 67, 105–6.
 2. That America lacked the essential requisites for romance and a genuine national literature was a common theme in the early 19th century. For a summary of the arguments, with a convincing refutation, see [W. H. Gardiner,] "The Spy, a Tale of the Neutral Ground," *North American Review,* XV (July 1822), 250–82 (quotations, 252–53); Johan Huizinga, *Homo Ludens: A Study of the Play Element in Culture* (London, 1970), 117; *Literary World,* II (Nov. 27, 1847), 400.
 3. Alice P. Kenney and Leslie J. Workman, "Ruins, Romance, and Reality: Medievalism in Anglo-American Imagination and Taste, 1750–1840," *Winterthur Portfolio 10* (ed. Ian M. G. Quimby, Charlottesville, 1975), 163; G. Harrison Orians, "The Romance Ferment After *Waverley,*" *American Literature,* III (Jan. 1932), 409; *Literary World,* II (Dec. 25, 1847), 518; III (April 22, 1848), 223.
 4. Alice Chandler, "Chivalry and Romance: Scott's Medieval Novels," *Studies in Romanticism,* XIV (Spring 1975), 187; Brian Stock, "The Middle Ages as Subject and Object: Romantic Attitudes and Academic Medievalism," *New Literary History,* V (Spring 1974), 537, 538, 540.
 5. D. H. Barlow, "Chivalry of the Nineteenth Century," *Graham's Magazine,* XXVI (April 1845), 157; *American Review,* VII (Feb. 1848), 170; I (March 1845), 275–79. Burke's quotation, in slightly different form, may be found in his *Reflections on the Revolution in France* (ed. Conor Cruise O'Brien; Harmondsworth, Eng., 1969), 170.
 6. Charles Mills, *The History of Chivalry or Knighthood and Its Times* (London, 1825), vii; Barlow, "Chivalry of the Nineteenth Century," *Graham's Magazine,* XXVI, 157, 159; G.P.R. James, *The History of Chivalry* (New York, 1839), 30–31; Sir Walter Scott, *Quentin Durward* (New York, 1906), 3.
 7. Malcolm Vale, *War and Chivalry* (Athens, Ga., 1981), 1 and *passim;* Scott, "Essay on Chivalry," *Essays on Chivalry, Romance, and the Drama* (*The Miscellaneous Prose Works . . . ,* VI, Edinburgh, 1834), 10, 20–21, 43.
 8. *Literary World,* II (Aug. 28, 1847), 85–86; George Lippard, *Legends of Mexico: The Battles of Taylor* (Philadelphia, 1847), 11; *Rough and Ready Annual; or Military Souvenir* (New York, 1848), 140; *Southern Quarterly Review,* XIII (Jan. 1848), 52; *Knickerbocker Magazine,* XXXI (Jan. 1848), 74.
 9. Charles Sumner, *The True Grandeur of Nations* (Boston, 1845), 7–8, 35, 40; Philip Berry, *A Review of the Mexican War on Christian Principles* (Columbia, S.C., 1849), 82–83.
10. Richard Coulter, "The Westmoreland Guards in the War with Mexico, 1846–1848," *Western Pennsylvania Historical Magazine,* XXIV (June 1941),

102–3; Marcus Cunliffe, *Soldiers & Civilians: The Martial Spirit in America, 1775–1865* (2nd ed., New York, 1973), 420.

11. Sumner, *The True Grandeur of Nations*, 39; Simms to James H. Hammond, June 4, 1847, *The Letters of William Gilmore Simms* (ed. Mary C. Simms Oliphant and T. C. Duncan Eaves, 5 vols., Columbia, S.C., 1953), II, 322; Simms, *The Life of the Chevalier Bayard* (New York, 1847), 2, 3–4, 341, 396.

12. John Frost, *The Mexican War and Its Warriors* (New Haven and Philadelphia, 1848), 149; *Spirit of the Times*, XVI (May 30, 1846), 162; XVII (May 15, 1847), 132; *Southern Quarterly Review*, XX (July 1851), 15; *Graham's Magazine*, XXXVI (May 1850), 319.

13. Cunliffe, *Soldiers & Civilians*, 402, 392–93, 397.

14. *Southern Quarterly Review*, XIV (July 1848), 242; *Literary World*, II (Oct. 23, 1847), 283; *Holden's Dollar Magazine*, I (March 1848), 188.

15. John Keegan, *The Face of Battle* (New York 1976), 118; W. F. P. Napier, *History of the War in the Peninsula, and in the South of France; From the Year 1807 to the Year 1814* (New York, 1847), iii–v; *Literary World*, III (Aug. 12, 1848), 552; *Littell's Living Age*, XIV (July 10, 1847), 90.

16. James W. Pohl, "The Influence of Antoine Henri de Jomini on Winfield Scott's Campaign in the Mexican War," *Southwestern Historical Quarterly*, LXXVII (July 1973), 88–89, 92–93, 109; Napier, *History of the War in the Peninsula*, iv; Joel Tyler Headley, *Napoleon and His Marshals* (2 vols., New York, 1846), II, 2, 10; *New York Herald*, June 29, 1846; Raphael Semmes, *Afloat and Ashore During the Mexican War* (Cincinnati, 1851), 283; J. M. Wynkoop, *Anecdotes and Incidents: Comprising Daring Exploits, Personal and Amusing Adventures . . . and Thrilling Incidents of the Mexican War* (Pittsburgh, 1848), 22–23.

17. Harold Bloom, "Napoleon and Prometheus: The Romantic Myth of Organic Energy," *Yale French Studies* (1960–61), 79–82; Howard Mumford Jones, *Revolution & Romanticism* (Cambridge, Mass., 1974), 248, 251, 293–95; *Southern Literary Messenger*, XIV (Jan. 1848), 39; Ralph Waldo Emerson, *Representative Men: Seven Lectures* (Boston, 1891), 180, 182, 200, 192.

18. *Literary World*, I (March 27, 1847), 173.

19. Headley, *Napoleon and His Marshals*, I, ix–x, xi, 18–20.

20. [Hunt's] *Merchants' Magazine*, XVII (Oct. 1847), 444; *Anglo-American*, IX (May 29, 1847), 139; *Methodist Quarterly Review*, XXX (Jan. 1848), 84; *Knickerbocker Magazine*, XXVIII (July 1846), 73.

21. [Hunt's] *Merchants' Magazine*, XVII (Dec. 1847), 640; Headley, *Napoleon and His Marshals*, I, xii–xiv; *Literary World*, II (Jan. 29, 1848), 628–29.

22. Mary Clinton Collins, ed., "Journal of Francis Collins, an Artillery Officer in the Mexican War," *Quarterly Publication of the Historical and Philosophical Society of Ohio*, X (April–July 1915), 46.

23. Francis Baylies, *A Narrative of Major General Wool's Campaign in Mexico* (Albany, 1851), 8; *Niles' National Register*, LXXI (Sept. 26, 1846), 56.

24. Isaac Smith, *Reminiscences of a Campaign in Mexico* (Indianapolis, 1848), 93–95; George Winston Smith and Charles Judah, eds., *Chronicles of the Gringos: The U.S. Army in the Mexican War, 1846–1848* (Albuquerque, 1968), 284; Graham A. Barringer, ed., "The Mexican War Journal of Henry S. Lane," *Indiana Magazine of History*, LIII (Dec. 1957), 395–96; J. Jacob Oswandel, *Notes of the Mexican War* (Philadelphia, 1885), 167–68.

25. *Southern Literary Messenger*, XXI (July 1855), 433; Emma Jerome Black-wood, ed., *To Mexico with Scott: Letters of Captain E. Kirby Smith to His Wife* (Cambridge, Mass., 1917), 66–67; John R. Kenly, *Memoirs of a Maryland Volunteer* (Philadelphia, 1873), 224; Thomas Bangs Thorpe, *Our Army at Monterey* (Philadelphia, 1847), 43, 33–34.

26. William Matthews and Dixon Wecter, *Our Soldiers Speak, 1775–1918* (Boston, 1943), 131; Smith, *Reminiscences of a Campaign in Mexico*, 64; *Niles' National Register*, LXXI (Oct. 17, 1846), 103; Thorpe, *Our Army at Monterey*, 45–46; Henry Kirby Benner, "Ballads of the Campaign in Mexico," *Graham's Magazine*, XXXV (April 1850), 237.

27. Blackwood, ed., *To Mexico with Scott*, 70, 73; *Spirit of the Times*, XVI (Nov. 21, 1846), 463. For the medieval influence on depictions of the battle, see the illustrations in *Halls of the Montezumas; or, Mexico, in Ancient and Modern Times* (New York, 1848); and Ronnie C. Tyler, *The Mexican War: A Lithographic Record* (Austin, 1973), 26, 28. Whiting's drawing is in Tyler, p. 25.

28. Thorpe, *Our Army at Monterey*, 104; "Taylor's Battles in Mexico," *Harper's Magazine*, XI (July 1855), 181.

29. *Littell's Living Age*, XIII (April 17, 1847), 124; Blackwood, ed., *To Mexico with Scott*, 140, 142; Collins, ed., "Journal of Francis Collins," *Quar. Publ. Hist. and Phil. Soc. of Ohio*, X, 93–94; Samuel E. Chamberlain, *My Confession* (New York, 1956), 182. James, a prolific English writer of historical romances, opened so many of his novels with "a solitary horseman" or "a party of cavaliers" riding through the countryside as day passed into evening that they became the object of satirical comment.

30. *New York Herald*, May 31, 1846; George A. McCall, *Letters from the Frontiers: Written During a Period of Thirty Years' Service in the Army of the United States* (Philadelphia, 1868), 453–54.

31. Cunliffe, *Soldiers & Civilians*, 402–3; Smith and Judah, eds., *Chronicles of the Gringos*, 263.

32. Smith, *Reminiscences of a Campaign in Mexico*, 80; Oswandel, *Notes of the Mexican War*, 445; [Benjamin F. Scribner,] *Camp Life of a Volunteer* (Philadelphia, 1847), 63.

33. [G. N. Allen,] *Mexican Treacheries and Cruelties. Incidents and Sufferings in the Mexican War* (Boston and New York, 1848), unnumbered page; Richard McSherry, *El Puchero; or a Mixed Dish from Mexico* (Philadelphia, 1850), 105; *Niles' National Register*, LXXI (Oct. 17, 1846), 101; LXXII (July 10, 1847), 303.

34. Blackwood, ed., *To Mexico with Scott*, 65; *Niles' National Register*, LXXI (Nov. 7, 1846), 156; *Spirit of the Times*, XVI (Nov. 7, 1846), 434; XVII (May 15, 1847), 131.

35. *Niles' National Register*, LXXII (July 10, 1847), 303; LXXI (Oct. 24, 1846), 116; [George Ballentine,] *Autobiography of an English Soldier in the United States Army* (New York, 1853), 194–95; H. Judge Moore, *Scott's Campaign in Mexico* (Charleston, 1849), 61–62; Barringer, ed., "The Mexican War Journal of Henry S. Lane," *Indiana Magazine of History*, LIII, 411–12.

36. Captain of Volunteers, *Conquest of Santa Fe and Subjugation of New Mexico* (Philadelphia, 1847), 40; Oran Perry, comp., *Indiana in the Mexican War* (Indianapolis, 1908), 128; Ernest M. Lander, Jr., *Reluctant Imperialists: Calhoun, the South Carolinians, and the Mexican War* (Baton Rouge, 1980), 137.

37. Lewis Leonidas Allen, *Pencillings of Scenes Upon the Rio Grande* (New York, 1848), 21; [Scribner,] *Camp Life of a Volunteer*, 13, 22.

38. John Russell Bartlett, *Dictionary of Americanisms* (New York, 1848), 290. For a classic mid-19th-century definition of "seeing the elephant," see George Wilkins Kendall, *Narrative of the Texan Santa Fe Expedition* (2 vols., New York, 1844), I, 110.

39. Oswandel, *Notes of the Mexican War,* 431; *Littell's Living Age,* XIV (July 31, 1847), 204; George Walcott Ames, Jr., "A Doctor Comes to California: The Diary of John S. Griffin, Assistant Surgeon with Kearny's Dragoons, 1846–47," *California Historical Society Quarterly,* XXI (Sept. 1942), 217; *Godey's Magazine,* XXXVI (April 1848), 248; *The Elephant,* I (Jan. 22, 1848), 2.

40. *Niles' National Register,* LXXI (Sept. 26, 1846), 55, 56.

41. "Sketches of a Campaign in Coahuila," *American Review,* XVI (Nov. 1852), 456; *Niles' National Register,* LXXI (Sept. 12, 1846), 23; Kenly, *Memoirs of a Maryland Volunteer,* 211; Walter B. Hendrickson, ed., "The Happy Soldier: The Mexican War Letters of John Nevin King," *Journal of the Illinois State Historical Society,* XLVI (Summer 1953), 153.

42. Collins, ed., "Journal of Francis Collins," *Quar. Publ. Hist. and Phil. Soc. of Ohio,* X, 57; Albert G. Brackett, *General Lane's Brigade in Central Mexico* (Cincinnati, 1854), 82; *Spirit of the Times,* XVII (April 10, 1847), 75; Kenly, *Memoirs of a Maryland Volunteer,* 177.

43. William B. McGroarty, ed., "William H. Richardson's Journal of Doniphan's Expedition," *Missouri Historical Review,* XXII (April 1928), 334, 336–37.

44. Although figures vary, most sources agree that about 1,500 soldiers died in battle or of battle-sustained wounds while almost 10,800 died of disease, making the Mexican War statistically the costliest war in American history; Thomas R. Irey, "Soldiering, Suffering, and Dying in the Mexican War," *Journal of the West,* XI (April 1972), 285–98; Roger G. Miller, "Yellow Jack at Vera Cruz," *Prologue,* X (Spring 1978), 43–53.

45. *Niles' National Register,* LXXI (Oct. 24, 1846), 119; Smith and Judah, comps., *Chronicles of the Gringos,* 285; Charles F. Hinds, ed., "Mexican War Journal of Leander M. Cox," *Register of the Kentucky Historical Society,* LV (July 1957), 217; Brackett, *General Lane's Brigade in Central Mexico,* 78.

46. Barringer, ed., "Mexican War Journal of Henry S. Lane," *Indiana Magazine of History,* LIII, 414, 429; *Niles' National Register,* LXXII (July 10, 1847), 303; *Spirit of the Times,* XVI (Sept. 26, 1846), 367.

47. *Southern Quarterly Review,* XXII (Oct. 1852), 311–13.

48. *Niles' National Register,* LXXII (March 27, 1847), 59–61, 64.

49. [Scribner,] *Camp Life of a Volunteer,* 58; Smith and Judah, eds., *Chronicles of the Gringos,* 302; C. P. Kingsbury, "Battle of Buena Vista," *American Review,* VIII (Nov. 1848), 448.

50. *Niles' National Register,* LXXII (April 17, 1847), 100, (April 10, 1847), 84; *Spirit of the Times,* XVII (April 24, 1847), 100–01; Chamberlain, *My Confession,* 118–19; Kingsbury, "Battle of Buena Vista," *American Review,* VIII, 449.

51. S. Compton Smith, *Chile Con Carne; or, The Camp and the Field* (New York, 1857), 224–25, 238–39; [Henry Washington Benham,] "Recollections of Mexico and Buena Vista," *Old and New,* IV (July 1871), 50.

52. *Niles' National Register,* LXXI (Nov. 14, 1846), 168; Moore, *Scott's Campaign in Mexico,* 19; George C. Furber, *The Twelve Months' Volunteer* (Cincinnati, 1848), 100.

53. James Henry Carleton, *Battle of Buena Vista* (New York, 1848), 95–97; [Scribner,] *Camp Life of a Volunteer*, 60–65; Smith, *Chile Con Carne*, 236–38; J. W. Gibson, *Letter Descriptive of the Battle of Buena Vista* (Lawrenceburgh, Ind., 1847), 5; Smith, *Reminiscences of a Campaign in Mexico*, 52.

54. Carleton, *Battle of Buena Vista*, 129–30, 212; [Scribner,] *Camp Life of a Volunteer*, 66–69; Maurice Garland Fulton, ed., *Diary & Letters of Josiah Gregg* (2 vols., Norman, Okla., 1941–44), II, 55–56.

55. *Southern Quarterly Review*, XIX (Jan. 1851), 180; *Literary World*, III (Feb. 5, 1848), 12–13.

56. Walt Whitman, *The Gathering of the Forces* (eds. Cleveland Rodgers and John Black, 2 vols., New York, 1920), I, 81; *The War with Mexico* (Rochester, 1847), 25; John Frost, *The Life of Major-General Zachary Taylor* (New York, 1847), 335.

57. "The Capture of Vera Cruz," *Knickerbocker Magazine*, XXX (July 1847), 2; Moore, *Scott's Campaign in Mexico*, 5–6; [John Blount Robertson,] *Reminiscences of a Campaign in Mexico* (Nashville, 1849), 218–19; Fitch W. Taylor, *The Broad Pennant; or, A Cruise in the United States Flag Ship of the Gulf Squadron, During the Mexican Difficulties* (New York, 1848), 136; Collins, ed., "Journal of Francis Collins," *Quar. Publ. Hist. and Phil. Soc. of Ohio*, X, 48–49.

58. [Ballentine,] *Autobiography of an English Soldier*, 147; *Southern Quarterly Review*, XX (July 1851), 37; Semmes, *Service Afloat and Ashore During the Mexican War*, 126.

59. *Memoirs of Lieut.-General Scott, Written by Himself* (2 vols., New York, 1864), II, 423–24; E. Parker Scammon, "A Chapter of the Mexican War," *Magazine of American History*, XIV (July–Dec. 1885), 568; K. Jack Bauer, *Surfboats and Horse Marines: U.S. Naval Operations in the Mexican War, 1846–48* (Annapolis, 1969), 83–92.

60. *Knickerbocker Magazine*, XXX (July 1847), 3–4; Moore, *Scott's Campaign in Mexico*, 11.

61. Moore, *Scott's Campaign in Mexico*, 15–16; *Niles' National Register*, LXXII (April 14, 1847), 122; [Jacob K. Neff,] *Thrilling Incidents of the Wars of the United States* (New York, 1851), 579–80.

62. Oswandel, *Notes of the Mexican War*, 98–99; *Niles' National Register*, LXXII (May 1, 1847), 136; Furber, *Twelve Months' Volunteer*, 555–61; *Knickerbocker Magazine*, XXX (July 1847), 6–8. The verses were from Longfellow's peace poem "The Arsenal at Springfield," published in *Graham's Magazine*, XXIV (April 1844), 225.

63. George Frederick Ruxton, *Adventures in Mexico and the Rocky Mountains* (New York, 1848), 25–26; *Memoirs of Lieut.-General Scott*, II, 424–25.

64. Joel Tyler Headley, *The Lives of Winfield Scott and Andrew Jackson* (New York, 1852), 83; Semmes, *Service Afloat and Ashore During the Mexican War*, 143; Ramon Alcaraz *et al.*, *The Other Side: or Notes for the History of the War Between Mexico and the United States, Written in Mexico* (ed. and trans. Albert C. Ramsey, New York, 1850), 198.

65. *New York Herald*, March 25, 30, 31, April 1, 3, 11, 1847.

66. Lander, *Reluctant Imperialists*, 99–101; *New York Herald*, May 7, 1847; *New York Tribune*, May 8, 1847; Washington *National Intelligencer*, May 8, 10, 1847; *Niles' National Register*, LXXII (May 15, 1847), 162; Allan

Nevins, ed., *Polk: The Diary of a President, 1845–1849* (New York, 1929), 229.

Chapter 5: A New Stock of Heroes

1. *Holden's Dollar Magazine,* III (Feb. 1849), 89.
2. Roy P. Basler *et al.,* eds., *The Collected Works of Abraham Lincoln* (9 vols., New Brunswick, N.J., 1953–55), I, 115; *Southern Quarterly Review,* XIV (Oct. 1848), 512.
3. Walter E. Houghton, *The Victorian Frame of Mind, 1830–1870* (New Haven, 1957), 305, 306, 310; Peter L. Thorslev, Jr., *The Byronic Hero: Types and Prototypes* (Minneapolis, 1962), 15–16.
4. Thomas Carlyle, *On Heroes, Hero-Worship, and the Heroic in History* (Everyman's Library, New York, 1908), 239, 249, 252.
5. *Southern Quarterly Review,* XIV (July 1848), 77–78, 88; Henry D. Thoreau, "Thomas Carlyle and His Works," *Graham's Magazine,* XXX (March 1847), 145–52, 238–45; Walt Whitman, *The Gathering of the Forces* (eds. Cleveland Rodgers and John Black, 2 vols., New York, 1920), II, 290.
6. Emerson, "Heroism," in *The Complete Essays and Other Writings of Ralph Waldo Emerson* (ed. Brooks Atkinson, New York, 1940), 252–56; Theodore L. Gross, *The Heroic Ideal in American Literature* (New York, 1971), 7–9.
7. John M. Vlach, "Fenimore Cooper's Leatherstocking as Folk Hero," *New York Folklore Quarterly,* XXVII (Dec. 1971), 323–38; Francis Parkman, "James Fenimore Cooper," *North American Review,* LXXIV (Jan. 1852), 148, 151; *Holden's Dollar Magazine,* III (Feb. 1849), 90; Kenneth Kurtz, "Emerson and Cooper: American Versions of the Heroic," *Emerson Society Quarterly,* No. 42 (I Quarter 1966), 2–4; Henry Giles, *Lectures and Essays* (2 vols., Boston, 1850), 181.
8. Edward G. Parker, *The Golden Age of American Oratory* (Boston, 1857), 2, 4; Lorenzo Sabine, "The Past and Present of the American People," *North American Review,* LXVI (April 1848), 426–27, 433, 435; Henry T. Tuckerman, "The Modern Hero," in *Poems* (Boston, 1851), 69–73.
9. Gerald W. Johnson, *American Heroes and Hero-Worship* (New York, 1943), 11; *Literary World,* III (April 8, 1848), 189; [Hunt's] *Merchants' Magazine,* XVII (Nov. 1847), 544; Edwin P. Whipple, "Heroism," *Harper's Magazine,* XV (Aug. 1857), 407.
10. Emerson, *Representative Men: Seven Lectures* (Boston, 1891), 30; *Democratic Review,* XXI (Oct. 1847), 372; *Literary World,* II (Nov. 13, 1847), 360; *Spirit of the Times,* XVI (June 20, 1846), 197.
11. *Spirit of the Times,* XVI (Sept. 5, 1846), 326.
12. John Frost, *Life of Major-General Zachary Taylor* (New York, 1847), 13; [Thomas Bangs Thorpe,] *Anecdotes of General Taylor, and the Mexican War* (New York, 1848), 5.
13. John Frost, *The Mexican War and Its Warriors* (New Haven, 1848), 19.
14. *Taylor and His Generals* (Philadelphia, 1847), iii–iv; *Spirit of the Times,* XVI (Aug. 1, 1846), 274; *National Police Gazette,* I (Aug. 15, 1846), 413; *Southern Quarterly Review,* XI (April 1847), 508; *Yankee Doodle,* II (June 26, 1847), 111; *Literary World,* II (Aug. 7, 1847), 18.

15. *Pictorial Life of General Taylor* (Philadelphia, 1847), v; *Literary World,* I (July 24, 1847), 582; Whitman, *Gathering of the Forces,* II, 188–89.

16. J. Reese Fry and Robert T. Conrad, *A Life of Gen. Zachary Taylor* (Philadelphia, 1847), 13; *Holden's Dollar Magazine,* III (March 1849), 181; Frost, *Life of Major-General Zachary Taylor,* 15; "General Zachary Taylor," *Graham's Magazine,* XXXI (July 1847), 26–32; Washington *National Intelligencer,* May 29, 1846. See also John Q. Anderson, "Soldier Lore of the War with Mexico," *Western Humanities Review,* XI (Autumn 1957), 327–29.

17. William Seaton Henry, *Campaign Sketches of the War with Mexico* (New York, 1847), 276; [Luther Giddings,] *Sketches of the Campaign in Northern Mexico* (New York, 1853), 71–72; Thomas Bangs Thorpe, *Our Army on the Rio Grande* (Philadelphia, 1846), 160–62; Frost, *Life of Major-General Zachary Taylor,* 265.

18. J. M. Wynkoop, *Anecdotes and Incidents: Comprising Daring Exploits, Personal and Amusing Adventures . . . and Thrilling Incidents of the Mexican War* (Pittsburgh, 1848), 97; Henry Montgomery, *The Life of Major General Zachary Taylor* (Auburn, 1847), 274; J. W. Gibson, *Letter Descriptive of the Battle of Buena Vista* (Lawrenceburgh, Ind., 1847), 2; W. A. Crofutt, ed., *Fifty Years in Camp and Field: Diary of Major-General Ethan Allen Hitchcock* (New York, 1909), 349; *Spirit of the Times,* XVII (June 19, 1847), 197.

19. *Niles' National Register,* LXXIII (Dec. 25, 1847), 257.

20. *Scientific American,* II (Oct. 31, 1846), 45; *Knickerbocker Magazine,* XXX (Dec. 1847), 554; *Godey's Magazine,* XXXVII (Aug. 1848), 119.

21. *General Taylor and His Staff* (Philadelphia, 1848), iii; Charles J. Peterson, *The Military Heroes of the War with Mexico* (Philadelphia, 1848), 137; St. George L. Sioussat, ed., "Mexican War Letters of Col. William Bowen Campbell, of Tennessee," *Tennessee Historical Magazine,* I (June 1915), 166.

22. Charles Winslow Elliott, *Winfield Scott: The Soldier and the Man* (New York, 1937), 426–30, 489; Crofutt, ed., *Fifty Years in Camp and Field,* 366–67.

23. Peterson, *Military Heroes of the War with Mexico,* 211–12; *Spirit of the Times,* XVII (Nov. 20, 1847), 456; *Graham's Magazine,* XXXII (April 1848), 235; *The War with Mexico . . . By an Officer of the Army* (Rochester, N.Y., 1847), 30.

24. *Memoirs of Lieut.-General Scott,* II, 535, 539; Edward D. Mansfield, *Life and Services of General Winfield Scott* (New York, 1852), 370; "Scott's Battles in Mexico," *Harper's Magazine,* XI (Aug. 1855), 324.

25. Elliott, *Winfield Scott,* 565–90; Mansfield, *Life and Services of General Winfield Scott,* 503–4; Daniel D. Barnard, "The Administration: Its Treatment of General Scott," *American Review,* VII (June 1848), 553–72.

26. Crofutt, ed., *Fifty Years in Camp and Field,* 329; C. Frank Powell, *Life of Major-General Zachary Taylor* (New York, 1846), 56.

27. Peterson, *Military Heroes of the War with Mexico,* 169–76, 189–94; Francis P. Blair, "Biographical Sketch of General William O. Butler," *Graham's Magazine,* XXXII (Jan. 1848), 49–56; Maurice Garland Fulton, ed., *Diary & Letters of Josiah Gregg* (2 vols., Norman, Okla., 1941–44), I, 218; *Littell's Living Age,* XX (March 10, 1849), 474.

28. Fayette Robinson, "Major-General Worth," *Graham's Magazine,* XXXII (May 1848), 275–76; Peterson, *Military Heroes of the War with Mexico,* 177.

29. Peterson, *Military Heroes of the War with Mexico, passim; American Whig Review,* XVI (Nov. 1852), 393.

30. Isaac Smith, *Reminiscences of a Campaign in Mexico* (Indianapolis, 1848), 57;

Brantz Mayer, *Mexico, Aztec, Spanish and Republican* (2 vols. in 1, Hartford, 1853), I, 353; Peterson, *Military Heroes of the War with Mexico*, 204, 208.

31. J. Thomas Scharf, *The Chronicles of Baltimore* (Baltimore, 1874), 516; *New York Herald*, May 25, 27, 1846; Thorpe, *Our Army on the Rio Grande*, 191–92.

32. Peterson, *Military Heroes of the War with Mexico*, 161–64; *General Taylor and His Staff*, 174–76.

33. Powell, *Life of Major-General Zachary Taylor*, 54–55; Basler *et al.*, eds., *Collected Works of Abraham Lincoln*, II, 85.

34. William M'Carty, *National Songs, Ballads, and Other Patriotic Poetry, Chiefly Relating to the War of 1846* (Philadelphia, 1846), 131, 83–87; Washington *National Intelligencer*, May 27, 1846; *Columbian Magazine*, VII (May 1847), 239–40; Marcus Cunliffe, *Soldiers & Civilians: The Martial Spirit in America, 1775–1865* (2nd ed., New York, 1973), 406 (Baillie); *An Album of American Battle Art* (Washington, 1947), 130, 148 (Nagel); *Columbian Magazine*, VI (July 1846), 48 (Matteson).

35. *New York Herald*, May 19, July 15, July 12, 1846; *Spirit of the Times*, XVI (Sept. 26, 1846), 361; Francis S. Gruber, *William Ranney: Painter of the Early West* (New York, 1962), 26, 27.

36. Thorpe, *Our Army on the Rio Grande*, 96–97; *New York Herald*, June 7, 1846.

37. *The War with Mexico . . . By an Officer of the Army*, 15; *New York Herald*, June 7, 1846; William H. C. Hosmer, "Captain May," *Poetical Works of William H. C. Hosmer* (2 vols., New York, 1854), II, 135–36; Samuel E. Chamberlain, *My Confession* (New York, 1956), 111; *Columbian Magazine*, VI (Sept. 1846), 143.

38. *Columbian Magazine*, VI (Sept. 1846), frontispiece; *Spirit of the Times*, XVII (Aug. 14, 1847), 296; *Rough and Ready Annual* (New York, 1848), 67–69; Washington *National Intelligencer*, June 19, 1848.

39. M'Carty, *National Songs, Ballads, and Other Patriotic Poetry*, 72–73; Sarah Anna Lewis, *Child of the Sea, and Other Poems* (New York, 1848), 168–72; *Spirit of the Times*, XVI (Aug. 1, 1846), 269; *New York Herald*, July 17, 1846; *Scientific American*, II (Jan. 2, 1847), 114.

40. Justin H. Smith, *The War with Mexico* (2 vols., New York, 1919), I, 467.

41. *Anglo-American*, IX (May 29, 1847), 139.

42. *Anglo-American*, IX (Sept. 25, 1847), 537; *Literary World*, II (Nov. 13, 1847), 360; *Southern Literary Messenger*, XXI (Jan. 1855), 11.

43. [Thorpe,] *Anecdotes of General Taylor, and the Mexican War*, 60; *Southern Literary Messenger*, XV (Dec. 1849), 759; *Union Magazine*, II (Jan. 1848), 21.

44. *Rough and Ready Annual*, 85; *Niles' National Register*, LXXII (April 10, 1847), 86.

45. [Thorpe,] *Anecdotes of General Taylor, and the Mexican War*, 13; [G. N. Allen,] *Mexican Treacheries and Cruelties* (Boston, 1848), unnumbered page; Arthur Hobson Quinn, *A History of the American Drama: From the Beginning to the Civil War* (New York, 1946), 430.

46. *Niles' National Register*, LXXII (April 10, 1847), 84, 86; *Union Magazine*, I (July 1847), 44; *Spirit of the Times*, XVII (May 1, 1847), 113.

47. *Anglo-American*, IX (Aug. 14, 1847), 402–4; *Spirit of the Times*, XVII (Oct. 16, 1847), 395; *Literary World*, II (Nov. 13, 1847), 360.

48. Henry William Herbert, "Long Jakes, the Prairie Man," *New York Illustrated Magazine*, II (July 1846), 169.

49. Texas independence was won in 1836 following a brief struggle in which

the most enduring episode was the desperate and unsuccessful defense of the Alamo against Mexican attack. In 1841, the Texas government attempted to sieze Santa Fe but, after suffering severe hardships on the march, the survivors of the expedition were taken prisoner and held in the Mexican fortress of Perote. In the following year, a demonstration against Mexican troops on the Rio Grande ended in disaster for the Texans at the small northern Mexico town of Mier. The survivors were imprisoned at Perote; a number of them, drawing black beans from a pitcher of white beans, were executed in the famous "lottery of death."

50. [John A. Scott,] *Encarnacion Prisoners* (Louisville, 1848), 18; *Southern Literary Messenger*, XI (Nov. 1845), 684; William Gilmore Simms, *Areytos; or, Songs of the South* (Charleston, 1846), 21–22.

51. Frost, *Mexican War and Its Warriors*, 294, 295; *American Review*, I (March 1845), 283; Thomas Bangs Thorpe, *Our Army at Monterey* (Philadelphia, 1847), 76; Samuel C. Reid, Jr., *The Scouting Expeditions of McCulloch's Texas Rangers* (Philadelphia, 1848), 23, 192.

52. [Scott,] *Encarnacion Prisoners*, 33–37; *Spirit of the Times*, XVII (March 20, 1847), 44–45; Charles Wilkins Webber, "Captain Dan Henrie; His Adventure with the Wolves," *Democratic Review*, XXIV (Jan. 1849), 33; Joseph Leach, *The Typical Texan: Biography of an American Myth* (Dallas, 1952), 46.

53. Fayette Robinson, "Captain Samuel Walker," *Graham's Magazine*, XXXII (June 1848), 301–2; Lota M. Spell, *Pioneer Printer: Samuel Bangs in Mexico and Texas* (Austin, 1963), 132.

54. J. Jacob Oswandel, *Notes of the Mexican War* (Philadelphia, 1885), 198; *Democratic Review*, XXVII (Nov. 1850), 418; [Thorpe,] *Anecdotes of General Taylor, and the Mexican War*, 43–44, 53; M'Carty, *National Songs, Ballads, and Other Patriotic Poetry*, 127–28; Henry Kirby Benner, "Ballads of the Campaign in Mexico," *Graham's Magazine*, XXXVI (Feb. 1850), 134.

55. Eliza Allen Billings, *The Female Volunteer, or The Life and Wonderful Adventures of Miss Eliza Allen, a Young Lady of Eastport, Maine* (n. p., 1851); Miller J. Stewart, "Army Laundresses: Ladies of the 'Soap Suds Row,'" *Nebraska History*, LXI (Winter 1980), 421–36.

56. *Littell's Living Age*, XIII (June 19, 1847), 544; H. Judge Moore, *Scott's Campaign in Mexico* (Charleston, 1849), 195; [Thorpe,] *Anecdotes of General Taylor, and the Mexican War*, 62; *Spirit of the Times*, XVI (Nov. 28, 1846, Jan. 2, 1847), 475, 534.

57. *Niles' National Register*, LXXI (Dec. 19, 1846), 242; Ramon Alcaraz et al., eds., *The Other Side: or Notes for the History of the War Between Mexico and the United States* (Albert C. Ramsey, trans., New York, 1850), 76–77; Rev. James Gilborne Lyons, "The Heroine Martyr of Monterey," *American Quarterly Register*, II (June 1849), 483–84.

58. *Godey's Magazine*, XXXIV (March 1847), 173; Washington *National Intelligencer*, June 29, 1846.

59. Dixon Wecter, *The Hero in America: A Chronicle of Hero-Worship* (New York, 1941), 477; *Rough and Ready*, Jan. 23, 1847.

60. Lewis Leonidas Allen, *Pencillings of Scenes Upon the Rio Grande* (New York, 1848), 22–24; *New York Herald*, July 21, June 29, 1846; [Thorpe,] *Anecdotes of General Taylor, and the Mexican War*, 96–98; [G. N. Allen,] *Mexican Treacheries and Cruelties*, unnumbered page; Edward S. Wallace, "The Great Western," *New York Posse Brand Book*, V (1958), 58–59, 61–62, 65–66.

61. Isaac George, *Heroes and Incidents of the Mexican War, Containing Doniphan's Expedition* (Greensburg, Penna., 1903), 141–44; St. Louis *Reveille,* July 1, 3, 1847; *General Scott and His Staff* (Philadelphia, 1848), 181–87 (Benton's address); George Frederick Ruxton, *Adventures in Mexico and the Rocky Mountains* (New York, 1848), 303–4.

62. *New York Herald,* April 16, 1848; *Niles' National Register,* LXXII (July 10, 1847), 302–3; Alexander Beaufort Meek, *Romantic Passages in Southwestern History* (Mobile, 1857), 194.

63. Brackett, *General Lane's Brigade in Central Mexico,* 314; Oswandel, *Notes of the Mexican War,* 591–617.

64. *New York Tribune,* July 28, 1848; Thomas L. Nichols, *Forty Years of American Life* (2 vols., London, 1864), I, 290–91; *Literary World,* III (Nov. 11, 1848), 811–12.

65. *New York Tribune,* July 28, 1848; *Peterson's Magazine,* XIV (Sept. 1848) 77; *Godey's Magazine,* XXXIV (March 1847), 173; Washington *National Intelligencer,* May 29, 1846; *Southern Quarterly Review,* XXII (July 1852), 79.

Chapter 6: Travelers in a Foreign Land

1. Washington *National Intelligencer,* July 3, 1846; Walter Millis, *Arms and Men: A Study of American Military History* (New York, 1956), 94; James Fenimore Cooper, "American and European Scenery Compared," in *The Home Book of the Picturesque* (New York, 1852), 51.

2. *Southern Literary Messenger,* XII (July 1846), 456; *Niles' National Register,* LXXI (Nov. 21, 1846), 179–80; "Martial Men and Martial Books," *New Englander,* VI (Oct. 1848), 483–84.

3. *Holden's Dollar Magazine,* IV (Dec. 1849), 761.

4. S. Compton Smith, *Chile Con Carne; or, The Camp and the Field* (New York, 1857), 2–3; *Rough and Ready Annual* (New York, 1848), 86; [Luther Giddings,] *Sketches of the Campaign in Northern Mexico* (New York, 1853), 26–27; [William Watts Hart Davis,] "Notes on Mexico," *American Quarterly Register,* III (Sept. 1849), 156–57.

5. *Literary World,* II (Nov. 27, 1847), 400; Brantz Mayer, *Mexico, Aztec, Spanish and Republican* (2 vols. in 1, Hartford, 1853), I, 1–2.

6. *Graham's Magazine,* XXX (Feb. 1847), 111.

7. *Holden's Dollar Magazine,* II (Aug. 1848), 497; James Fenimore Cooper, *The Heidenmauer; or, The Benedictines* (London, 1836), 101; *Southern Literary Messenger,* XVII (April 1851), 256; A. M. Metwalli, "Americans Abroad: The Popular Art of Travel Writing in the Nineteenth Century," *Exploration: Journal of the MLA Seminar on the Literature of Exploration and Travel,* IV (1976), 15–24.

8. [Davis,] "Notes on Mexico," *American Quarterly Register,* III, 157. See also Drewey Wayne Gunn, *American and British Writers in Mexico, 1556–1973* (Austin, 1974); Raymund A. Paredes, "The Mexican Image in American Travel Literature, 1831–1869," *New Mexico Historical Review,* LII (Jan. 1977), 5–30; and John T. Flanagan and Raymond L. Grismer, "Mexico in American Fiction Prior to 1850," *Hispania,* XXIII (Dec. 1940), 307–18.

9. John Frost, *The Mexican War and Its Warriors* (New Haven, 1848), 120; *Niles' National Register,* LXXII (May 8, 1847), 155; *Yankee Doodle,* I (Dec. 5, 1846), 100.

10. *Niles' National Register,* LXXII (May 8, 1847), 155; *Spirit of the Times,* XVI (Jan. 9, 1847), 546; *New York Herald,* July 15, 1846.

11. Smith, *Chile Con Carne,* 292–93; [Giddings,] *Sketches of the Campaign in Northern Mexico,* 96; Lew Wallace, *An Autobiography* (2 vols., New York, 1906), I, 105.

12. *Spirit of the Times,* XVII (June 19, 1847), 193; George Winston Smith and Charles Judah, eds., *Chronicles of the Gringos* (Albuquerque, 1968), 295, 494.

13. Graham A. Barringer, ed., "The Mexican War Journal of Henry S. Lane," *Indiana Magazine of History,* LIII (Dec. 1957), 422; W. A. Crofutt, ed., *Fifty Years in Camp and Field: Diary of Major-General Ethan Allen Hitchcock* (New York, 1909), 207; Roger Wolcott, ed., *The Correspondence of William Hickling Prescott, 1833–1847* (Cambridge, Mass., 1925), 590.

14. Robert A. Law, ed., "A Letter from Vera Cruz in 1847," *Southwestern Historical Quarterly,* XVIII (Oct. 1914), 215; Dayton W. Canaday, "Voice of the Volunteer of 1847," *Journal of the Illinois State Historical Society,* XLIV (Autumn 1951), 205.

15. William B. McGroarty, ed., "William H. Richardson's Journal of Doniphan's Expedition," *Missouri Historical Review,* XXII (Jan. 1928), 209, (April 1928), 352–53.

16. Walter T. Durham, "Mexican War Letters to Wynnewood," *Tennessee Historical Quarterly,* XXXIII (Winter 1974), 392; *Niles' National Register,* LXXI (Sept. 26, 1846), 57; *The War with Mexico . . . By an Officer in the Army* (Rochester, 1847), 3; *Spirit of the Times,* XVI (Nov. 21, 1846), 463; George A. McCall, *Letters from the Frontiers* (Philadelphia, 1868), 456.

17. *Yankee Doodle,* I (Dec. 12, 1846), 114; *Niles' National Register,* LXXII (April 10, 1847), 86; *Spirit of the Times,* XVI (April 25, 1846), 97.

18. Smith and Judah, eds., *Chronicles of the Gringos,* 14; *Holden's Dollar Magazine,* I (April 1848), 255; *Niles' National Register,* LXXII (April 10, 1847), 88; Raphael Semmes, *Service Afloat and Ashore During the Mexican War* (Cincinnati, 1851), v–vi.

19. "American Adventure," *Blackwood's Edinburgh Magazine,* LXVII (Jan. 1850), 34; *Harbinger,* VI (Nov. 13, 1847), 15; *Spirit of the Times,* XVII (Nov. 6, 1847), 429.

20. John T. Hughes, *Doniphan's Expedition* (Cincinnati, 1848), 407; *Literary World,* III (Feb. 19, 1848), 60; *Godey's Magazine,* XXXVI (Feb. 1848), 131.

21. Henry T. Tuckerman, "William Beckford and the Literature of Travel," *Southern Literary Messenger,* XVI (Jan. 1850), 9–12.

22. Washington *National Intelligencer,* May 25, 1846; Christopher Mulvey, *Anglo-American Landscapes: A Study of Nineteenth-Century Anglo-American Travel Literature* (Cambridge, Mass., 1983), 18.

23. Philip St. George Cooke, *The Conquest of New Mexico and California* (repr. ed., Albuquerque, 1964), 25.

24. D. E. Livingston-Little, ed., *The Mexican War Diary of Thomas D. Tennery* (Norman, Okla., 1970), 76; T. Harry Williams, ed., *With Beauregard in Mexico: The Mexican War Reminiscences of P. G. T. Beauregard* (Baton Rouge, 1956), 101; Emma Jerome Blackwood, ed., *To Mexico with Scott: Letters of Captain E. Kirby Smith to His Wife* (Cambridge, Mass., 1917), 138; *Littell's Living Age,* XIII (June 19, 1847), 549; John William Larner, Jr., ed., "A Westmoreland Guard in Mexico, 1847–1848: The Journal of William Jos-

eph McWilliams," *Western Pennsylvania Historical Magazine,* LII (July 1969), 235.

25. *Rough and Ready Annual,* 61–62.

26. Charles S. Hamilton, "Memoirs of the Mexican War," *Wisconsin Magazine of History,* XIV (Sept. 1930), 85–87.

27. Albert G. Brackett, *General Lane's Brigade in Central Mexico* (Cincinnati, 1854), 159; Milton Jamieson, *Journal and Notes of a Campaign in Mexico* (Cincinnati, 1849), 77–78; *Democratic Review,* XXVI (June 1850), 546–47; *Niles' National Register,* LXXIII (Oct. 2, 1847), 77; J. Jacob Oswandel, *Notes of the Mexican War* (Philadelphia, 1885), 231; H. Judge Moore, *Scott's Campaign in Mexico* (Charleston, 1849), 116; Semmes, *Service Afloat and Ashore During the Mexican War,* 297; *Autobiography of the Late Col. Geo. T. M. Davis* (New York, 1891), 186.

28. *New York Tribune,* July 10, 1848; *Scientific American,* III (June 3, 1848), 290; *Literary World,* II (Jan. 1, 1848), 541; *Niles' National Register,* LXXIV (Oct. 25, 1848), 272.

29. John R. Kenly, *Memoirs of a Maryland Volunteer* (Philadelphia, 1873), 415–17, 411; Oswandel, *Notes of the Mexican War,* 424; Larner, ed., "A Westmoreland Guard in Mexico," *Western Pennsylvania Historical Magazine,* LII, 388; Robert Anderson, *An Artillery Officer in the Mexican War, 1846–7* (New York, 1911), 324.

30. William H. Goetzmann, *Army Exploration in the American West, 1803–1863* (New Haven, 1959), 127–38; *Graham's Magazine,* XXXIV (Jan. 1849), 84.

31. Hughes, *Doniphan's Expedition,* 74–75; Frank S. Edwards, *A Campaign in New Mexico with Colonel Doniphan* (Philadelphia, 1847), 43–44; *Niles' National Register,* LXXI (Oct. 10, Nov. 7, 1846), 91–92, 158.

32. Hughes, *Doniphan's Expedition,* 75, 194–95; William H. Emory, *Notes of a Military Reconnoissance, from Fort Leavenworth, in Missouri, to San Diego, in California* (Washington, 1848), 64, 457, 472, 492; *Spirit of the Times,* XVII (July 17, 1847), 239.

33. Emory, *Notes of a Military Reconnoissance,* 68, 81–82, 596–99; Dwight L. Clarke, ed., *The Original Journals of Henry Smith Turner: With Stephen Watts Kearny to New Mexico and California, 1846–1847* (Norman, Okla., 1966), 107–8; *Niles' National Register,* LXXV (Feb. 28, 1849), 142.

34. *Southern Quarterly Review,* XV (July 1849), 532–33; *Literary World,* III (Oct. 14, 1848), 728; IV (June 2, 1849), 477; *American Review,* VIII (Nov. 1848), 504; *American Journal of Science and Arts,* VII (March 1849), 153–57; B. M. Norman, *Rambles in the Yucatan* (7th ed., Philadelphia, 1849), quoted in *Literary World,* V (Aug. 18, 1849), 125.

35. James Fenimore Cooper, "American and European Scenery Compared," *The Home Book of the Picturesque,* 61, 69; Blake Nevius, *Cooper's Landscapes: An Essay on the Picturesque Vision* (Berkeley, 1976), 32–33. See also Mary E. Woolley, "The Development of the Love of Romantic Scenery in America," *American Historical Review,* III (Oct. 1897), 56–66.

36. *Niles' National Register,* LXXIII (Oct. 23, 1847), 113; [Thomas Bangs Thorpe,] *Anecdotes of General Taylor, and the Mexican War* (New York, 1848), 92; *Spirit of the Times,* XVI (Oct. 24, 1846), 411; Rhoda Van Bibber Tanner Doubleday, ed., *Journals of the Late Brevet Major Philip Norbourne Barbour* (New York, 1936), 104; Kenly, *Memoirs of a Maryland Volunteer,* 91.

37. *Niles' National Register,* LXXII (Aug. 21, 1847), 398; Smith and Judah, eds.,

Chronicles of the Gringos, 422; *Spirit of the Times,* XVI (Sept. 12, 1846), 344; XVII (June 26, 1847), 203.

38. *Southern Literary Messenger,* XXI (Aug. 1855), 491; [Benjamin F. Scribner,] *Camp Life of a Volunteer* (Philadelphia, 1847), 51; McCall, *Letters from the Frontiers,* 468–70; Croffut, ed., *Fifty Years in Camp and Field,* 287.

39. Brackett, *General Lane's Brigade in Central Mexico,* 68; St. George L. Sioussat, ed., "Mexican War Letters of Col. William Bowen Campbell," *Tennessee Historical Magazine,* I (June 1915), 141; *The Plough, the Loom, and the Anvil,* I (Oct. 1848), 253; Fulton, ed., *Diary and Letters of Josiah Gregg,* I, 371–74.

40. Livingston-Little, ed., *The Mexican War Diary of Thomas D. Tennery,* 63; [Giddings,] *Sketches of the Campaign in Northern Mexico,* 256; *Spirit of the Times,* XVI (Feb. 28, March 7, May 30, 1846), 1, 18, 162; George A. McCall, *American Journal of Science and Arts,* IV (Nov. 1847), 421; VII (Jan. 1849), 114–15; Oswandel, *Notes of the Mexican War,* 512. The contributions of Mexican War soldiers to scientific and technological knowledge deserve further study.

41. *Spirit of the Times,* XVI (Oct. 10, 1846), 386; *New York Illustrated Magazine,* I (1845), 351; E. L. Magoon, "Scenery and Mind," *The Home Book of the Picturesque,* 25–26. See also Walther Kirchner, "Mind, Mountain, and History," *Journal of the History of Ideas,* XI (Oct. 1950), 412–47.

42. [John A. Scott,] *Encarnacion Prisoners* (Louisville, 1848), 55; Blackwood, ed., *To Mexico with Scott,* 140.

43. Richard McSherry, *El Puchero; or, A Mixed Dish from Mexico* (Philadelphia, 1850), 24; Brackett, *General Lane's Brigade in Central Mexico,* 39; *Littell's Living Age,* XVII (June 24, 1848), 610; Mayer, *Mexico, Aztec, Spanish and Republican,* II, 188–93.

44. Semmes, *Service Afloat and Ashore During the Mexican War,* 172, 186; Collins, ed., "Journal of Francis Collins," *Quar. Publ. Hist. and Phil. Soc. of Ohio,* X, 69–70; *Autobiography of the Late Col. George T. M. Davis,* 192; McSherry, *El Puchero,* 61; Oswandel, *Notes of the Mexican War,* 453–56.

45. McSherry, *El Puchero,* 150; "A Visit to Popocatepetl," *Putnam's Monthly Magazine,* I (April 1853), 408–16.

46. Blackwood, ed., *To Mexico with Scott,* 68–69; "A Letter from Mexico," *Tennessee Historical Magazine,* IX (Jan. 1926), 280; Cecil Robinson, *With the Ears of Strangers: The Mexican in American Literature* (Tucson, 1963), 18.

47. [Scott,] *Encarnacion Prisoners,* 21; Oran Perry, comp., *Indiana in the Mexican War* (Indianapolis, 1908), 129; *Spirit of the Times,* XVI (June 13, 1846), 187; *The War with Mexico . . . By an Officer in the Army,* 17.

48. [George Ballentine,] *Autobiography of an English Soldier in the United States Army* (New York, 1853), 230; Collins, ed., "Journal of Francis Collins," *Quar. Publ. Hist. and Phil. Soc. of Ohio,* X, 64; Oswandel, *Notes of the Mexican War,* 145; Walter B. Hendrickson, ed., "The Happy Soldier: The Mexican War Letters of John Nevin King," *Journal of the Illinois State Historical Society,* XLVI (Summer 1953), 163; Ludwell H. Johnson, ed., "William Booth Taliaferro's Letters from Mexico, 1847–1848," *Virginia Magazine of History and Biography,* LXXIII (Oct. 1965), 459; George C. Furber, *The Twelve Months' Volunteer* (Cincinnati, 1848), 604.

49. Robinson, *With the Ears of Strangers,* 100; *Halls of the Montezumas; or, Mexico, in Ancient and Modern Times* (New York, 1848), 20; *Scientific American,* II

(May 22, 1847), 276; Samuel E. Chamberlain, *My Confession* (New York, 1956), 129.

50. *Rough and Ready Annual*, 94; Blackwood, ed., *To Mexico with Scott*, 78–79; Smith and Judah, eds., *Chronicles of the Gringos*, 411.

51. Semmes, *Service Afloat and Ashore During the Mexican War*, 37; *New York Herald*, June 15, 1846; [Giddings,] *Sketches of the Campaign in Northern Mexico*, 52; Frank S. Edwards, *A Campaign in New Mexico with Colonel Doniphan* (Philadelphia, 1847), 132; Blackwood, ed., *To Mexico with Scott*, 154.

52. *Southern Literary Messenger*, XXI (Aug. 1855), 351; W. W. Bishop, *A Journal of the Twelve Months Campaign of Gen. Shields' Brigade, in Mexico, in the Years 1846–7* (St. Louis, 1847), 25; Smith and Judah, eds., *Chronicles of the Gringos*, xvii.

53. Moore, *Scott's Campaign in Mexico*, 106.

54. Blackwood, ed., *To Mexico with Scott*, 34; *New York Herald*, August 8, 1846; Bishop, *Journal of the Twelve Months Campaign*, 7; *Spirit of the Times*, XVI (May 16, 1846), 138; [Scribner,] *Camp Life of a Volunteer*, 29; Moore, *Scott's Campaign in Mexico*, 68; Brackett, *General Lane's Brigade in Central Mexico*, 138.

55. *Littell's Living Age*, XIII (May 15, 1847), 330; Semmes, *Service Afloat and Ashore During the Mexican War*, 193; *Spirit of the Times*, XVII (Sept. 11, 1847), 337; Thomas Bangs Thorpe, *Our Army at Monterey* (Philadelphia, 1847), 123.

56. Jamieson, *Journal and Notes of a Campaign in Mexico*, 49; Semmes, *Service Afloat and Ashore During the Mexican War*, 269.

57. Cooke, *The Conquest of New Mexico and California*, 69–70; Charles J. Peterson, *Military Heroes of the War with Mexico* (10th ed., Philadelphia, 1858), 78, 204; *Southern Quarterly Review*, XI (Jan. 1847), 266. See also Donald C. Biggs, *Conquer and Colonize: Stevenson's Regiment and California* (San Rafael, 1977).

58. Wolcott, ed., *Correspondence of William Hickling Prescott*, 648; *Democratic Review*, XX (June 1847), 484; XXI (October 1847), 291.

59. *Saint Louis Reveille*, Sept. 28, 1846; *Spirit of the Times*, XVI (Dec. 19, 1846), 508.

60. *Littell's Living Age*, XIII (April 17, 1847), 122; *Democratic Review*, XXVII (Nov. 1850), 420; *Southern Literary Messenger*, XXI (Aug. 1855), 489.

61. *New York Herald*, July 15, 25, 1846; *Littell's Living Age*, X (Aug. 22, 1846), 387.

62. Kenly, *Memoirs of a Maryland Volunteer*, 160; Semmes, *Service Afloat and Ashore During the Mexican War*, 149; *Niles' National Register*, LXXII (May 22, 1847), 185; McSherry, *El Puchero*, 132; *Littell's Living Age*, XV (Nov. 13, 1847), 333; Ramon Alcaraz et al., eds., *The Other Side: or, Notes for the History of the War Between Mexico and the United States* (Albert C. Ramsey, trans., New York, 1850), 417; Henry A. Wise, *Los Gringos; or, An Inside View of Mexico and California* (New York, 1849), 256.

63. *New York Herald*, Aug. 6, 1846; Moore, *Scott's Campaign in Mexico*, 123; *Autobiography of Joseph Jefferson* (ed. Alan S. Downer, Cambridge, Mass., 1964), 54–62; George L. Chindahl, *A History of the Circus in America* (Caldwell, Idaho, 1959), 70. References to circus and theatrical performances are scattered throughout the soldiers' accounts.

64. *Lippincott's Magazine*, VI (Oct. 1870), 414; Lady Emmeline Stuart Wortley,

Travels in the United States, etc., During 1849 and 1850 (New York, 1851), 181–82; Oswandel, *Notes of the Mexican War,* 462; Henry T. Tuckerman, *America and Her Commentators, With a Critical Sketch of Travel in the United States* (New York, 1864), 434, 435.

Chapter 7: A War-Literature

1. Grace Greenwood, *Greenwood Leaves: A Collection of Sketches and Letters. Second Series* (Boston, 1854), 252.
2. Greenwood, *Greenwood Leaves: A Collection of Sketches and Letters* (Boston, 1850), 317; Greenwood, "The Volunteer," *Greenwood Leaves, Second Series,* 100–21; Greenwood, *Poems* (Boston, 1851), 102–4.
3. Alexander Mackay, *The Western World, or, Travels in the United States in 1846–47* (3 vols., London, 1849), III, 238; John Tebbel, *A History of Book Publishing in the United States, Vol. I: The Creation of an Industry, 1630–1865* (New York, 1972), 240–45, 257–62; *Southern Literary Messenger,* XIV (Jan. 1848), 58.
4. Henry T. Tuckerman, "The Profession of Literature," *Graham's Magazine,* XXVI (May 1845), 220–21; *Literary World,* V (Dec. 22, 1849), 546; *Southern Literary Messenger,* XI (March 1845), 172; XIII (May 1847), 292.
5. *Graham's Magazine,* XXVII (Sept. 1845), 101; *Holden's Dollar Magazine,* IV (July 1849), 399; F. D. H[untington]., "Cheap Literature and the Newspaper Press," *Christian Examiner,* XXXVIII (May 1845), 388; *New-York Mirror,* III (Jan. 17, 1846), 240.
6. [Huntington,] "Cheap Literature and the Newspaper Press," *Christian Examiner,* XXXVIII, 386; *Graham's Magazine,* XXVII, 100; *The Parthenon,* I (July 1847), 142.
7. *American Review,* X (Nov. 1849), 498; *North American Review,* LXX (April 1850), 265.
8. *Literary World,* I (March 27, 1847), 173–74. See also Charles G. Leland, "The Romantic in Literature and Art," *Sartain's Magazine,* V (Nov. 1849), 297–303.
9. James Smith Allen, *Popular French Romanticism: Authors, Readers, and Books in the 19th Century* (Syracuse, 1981) 7–8, 21 and *passim; American Review,* X, 500–502.
10. [Harry Franco,] "The Mission of Novellettes," *Holden's Dollar Magazine,* I (April 1848), 217–19; *Democratic Review,* XXIX (Sept. 1851), 211; XIX (July 1846), 79.
11. John T. Flanagan and Raymond L. Grismer, "Mexico in American Fiction Prior to 1850," *Hispania,* XXIII (Dec. 1940), 307.
12. Timothy Flint, *Francis Berrian, or The Mexican Patriot* (2 vols., Boston, 1826), I, 12–13; William Gilmore Simms, *The Yemassee: A Romance of Carolina* (2 vols., New York, 1835), I, vi. Simms distinguished between the romance and the novel but most midcentury writers used the words interchangeably. For a modern treatment see Richard Chase, *The American Novel and Its Tradition* (Garden City, N.Y., 1957), 12–28.
13. Benjamin Keen, *The Aztec Image in Western Thought* (New Brunswick, N.J., 1971), 310; *Southern Literary Messenger,* I (July 1835), 648.
14. William Gilmore Simms, *The Vision of Cortes, Cain, and Other Poems* (Charleston, 1829), 148, 28; *Southern Literary Messenger,* I (Feb. 1835), 315.

15. Curtis Dahl, *Robert Montgomery Bird* (New York, 1963), 50, 74–75; Clement E. Foust, *The Life and Dramatic Works of Robert Montgomery Bird* (New York, 1919), 80; Robert Montgomery Bird, "Preface to the New Edition," *Calavar; or, The Knight of the Conquest: A Romance of Mexico* (Philadelphia, 1847), iii; William Hickling Prescott, *History of the Conquest of Mexico* (3 vols., New York, 1845), II, 336.

16. Bird, *Calavar; or, The Knight of the Conquest: A Romance of Mexico* (Philadelphia, 1834), xxviii, iii; Bird, *Calavar* (1847 ed.), iii–iv; *Godey's Magazine,* XXXVI (Jan. 1848), 69.

17. [Bird,] *A Brief Review of the Career, Character & Campaigns of Zachary Taylor* (Washington, 1848), 7–14.

18. *New-York Mirror,* III (Nov. 15, 1845), 90; *Democratic Review,* XVIII (Jan. 1846), 76; Edward Maturin, *Montezuma: The Last of the Aztecs* (2 vols., New York, 1845), I, iii–iv, 9–10, 45; *New York Illustrated Magazine,* II (Oct. 1846), 368.

19. *Knickerbocker Magazine,* XXX (Dec. 1847), 556; *The Letters of Henry Wadsworth Longfellow* (ed. Andrew Hilen, 5 vols., Cambridge, Mass., 1966), II, 108; Samuel Longfellow, ed., *Life of Henry Wadsworth Longfellow, With Extracts from His Journals and Correspondence* (3 vols., Boston, 1893), II, 35; Joseph Holt Ingraham, *Montezuma the Serf; or, The Revolt of the Mexitili. A Tale of the Last Days of the Aztec Dynasty* (2 vols., Boston, 1845), I, 82.

20. William T. Coggeshall, *The Poets and Poetry of the West* (Columbus, 1860), 471; William W. Fosdick, *Malmiztic the Toltec; and the Cavaliers of the Cross* (Cincinnati, 1851), v, vi, 60, 135; *Literary World,* IX (Sept. 27, 1851), 245.

21. *Blackwood's Edinburgh Magazine,* LXVII (Jan. 1850), 34; Charles Winterfield [Charles Wilkins Webber], "Adventures on the Frontiers of Texas and Mexico," *American Review,* II (Oct. 1845), 365.

22. Albert Pike, *Prose Sketches and Poems Written in the Western Country* (ed. David J. Weber, Albuquerque, 1967), ix-xxii, 38, 247; Susan B. Riley, "Albert Pike as an American Don Juan," *Arkansas Historical Quarterly,* XIX (Autumn 1960), 207–24.

23. Edwin W. Gaston, Jr., *The Early Novel of the Southwest* (Albuquerque, 1961), 35, 51, 217–18; A. T. Myrthe [Anthony Ganilh], *Ambrosio de Letinez, or The First Texian Novel* (2 vols., New York, 1842), I, iii, v, vii, 53; II, 31; Flanagan and Grismer, "Mexico in American Fiction Prior to 1850," *Hispania,* XXIII, 314.

24. Joseph Leach, *The Typical Texan: Biography of an American Myth* (Dallas, 1952), 118–19, 120–21; *Holden's Dollar Magazine,* III (May 1849), 315; *Knickerbocker Magazine,* XXIV (Aug. 1844), 185; *Blackwood's Edinburgh Magazine,* LXVII (Jan. 1850), 35. Other fictional treatments of the Texas Revolution appearing on the eve of the war were James Wilmer Dallam, *The Lone Star: A Tale of Texas* (1845), and Alice Cleveland, *Lucy Morley; or, The Young Officer* (1846).

25. James M. Day, *Black Beans & Goose Quills: Literature of the Texan Mier Expedition* (Waco, 1970), 69–81; William Preston Stapp, *The Prisoners of Perote* (Philadelphia, 1845, repr. Austin, 1977), 2.

26. "My First Day With the Rangers. By a Kentuckian," *American Review,* I (March 1845), 280; Charles Winterfield [Charles Wilkins Webber], "Adventures on the Frontiers of Texas and Mexico," *American Review,* III (Jan. 1846), 25; Webber, "Hawthorne," *American Review,* IV (Sept. 1846), 302,

303, 308. Following the war, Webber published his most important works, *Old Hicks the Guide; or, Adventure in the Camanche Country in Search of a Gold Mine* (1848); and *The Gold Mines of the Gila* (1849).

27. Merle Curti, "Dime Novels and the American Tradition," *Yale Review*, XXVI (Summer 1937), 761; *Western Literary Messenger*, VIII (May 22, 1847), quoted in Albert Johannsen, *The House of Beadle and Adams and Its Dime and Nickel Novels: The Story of a Vanished Literature* (3 vols., Norman, Okla., 1950) I, 3.

28. Abiel Abbot Livermore, *The War with Mexico Reviewed* (Boston, 1850), 227, 229.

29. *Godey's Magazine*, XXXVI (June 1848), 367; *Spirit of the Times*, XVI (Oct. 24, 1846), 420; *New York Tribune*, March 25, 1848.

30. Johannsen, *The House of Beadle and Adams*, II, 75, 167–74; Jay Monaghan, *The Great Rascal: The Life and Adventures of Ned Buntline* (Boston, 1952), 125–28.

31. Longfellow, ed., *Life of Henry Wadsworth Longfellow*, II, 35; Monaghan, *Great Rascal*, 283.

32. Norman D. Smith, "Mexican Stereotypes on Fictional Battlefields: or Dime Novel Romances of the Mexican War," *Journal of Popular Culture*, XIII (Spring 1980), 537. A pioneering assessment of Mexican War novelettes, Smith's study is nonetheless flawed by oversimplification and the same stereotypical treatment that he finds objectionable in the novelists.

33. Ned Buntline [Edward Zane Carroll Judson], *The Volunteer; or, The Maid of Monterey. A Tale of the Mexican War* (Boston, 1847); Newton Mallory Curtis, *The Vidette; or, The Girl of the Robber's Pass. A Tale of the Mexican War* (New York, 1848).

34. Elizabeth Reid, *Mayne Reid: A Memoir of His Life* (London, 1890), 7 and *passim;* Joan Steele, "Mayne Reid, A Revised Bibliography," *Bulletin of Bibliography*, XXIX (July-Sept. 1972), 95–100; J. Jacob Oswandel, *Notes of the Mexican War* (Philadelphia, 1885), 426–27.

35. *Spirit of the Times*, XVII (May 1, 1847), 109–11, (Dec. 11, 1847), 489, (Dec. 18, 1847), 507–9 (quotation, 110); *Graham's Magazine*, XXXIII (Sept. 1848), 172–73; (Oct. 1848), 211–13; XXXIV (Jan. 1849), 50–52; *Harper's Magazine*, III (Sept. 1851), 481–84.

36. *Graham's Magazine*, XXXIII, 211–13, 172–73; XXXIV, 50–52; Mayne Reid, *The Rifle Rangers; or, Adventures of an Officer in Southern Mexico* (2 vols., London 1850), II, 297, 326; Reid, *The War Trail; or, The Hunt of the Wild Horse* (London, 1857), 3.

37. Roy W. Meyer, "The Western Fiction of Mayne Reid," *Western American Literature*, III (Summer 1968), 115–32; *Southern Quarterly Review*, XXII (July 1852), 252; XXI (Jan. 1852), 252; *Literary World*, IX (Oct. 11, 1851), 286; Mayne Reid, *The Scalp Hunters; or, Romantic Adventures in Northern Mexico* (3 vols., London, 1851), I, vii.

38. Robert Addison Bain, "John McConnel and Pre-Civil War Fiction of the Middle West" (Ph.D. dissertation, University of Illinois, 1964), 64, 18–19 and *passim;* [McConnel,] *Talbot and Vernon: A Novel* (New York, 1850), 80, 107–8, 270–303, 340–44. McConnel also published two shorter tales of the Mexican War under the title "Campaigning Stories" in *Graham's Magazine*, XXXVIII (May 1851), 367–80; XXXIX (Sept. 1851), 159–65, (Oct. 1851), 205–12; XL (March 1852), 241–52.

39. Daniel Aaron, *The Unwritten War: American Writers and the Civil War* (New York, 1973), xiii; Lionel Stevenson, *Dr. Quicksilver: The Life of Charles Lever* (London, 1939), 76.

40. Aaron, *Unwritten War*, xv–xix; [John Weiss,] "War and Literature," *Atlantic Monthly*, IX (June 1862), 676, 677, 681. I am indebted to Aaron's book for calling my attention to Weiss's article.

41. [William Alfred Jones,] "Nationality in Literature," *Democratic Review*, XX (March 1847), 267. For the efforts to define a national literature in the 1840s see John Stafford, *The Literary Criticism of "Young America": A Study in the Relationship of Politics and Literature, 1837–1850* (Berkeley, 1952) and Benjamin T. Spencer, *The Quest for Nationality: An American Literary Campaign* (Syracuse, 1957).

42. Melville to Gansevoort Melville, May 29, 1846, *The Letters of Herman Melville* (eds. Merrell R. Davis and William H. Gilman, New Haven, 1960), 29; Luther Stearns Mansfield, "Melville's Comic Articles on Zachary Taylor," *American Literature*, IX (Jan. 1938), 411–18; Fred Somkin, *Unquiet Eagle: Memory and Desire in the Idea of American Freedom, 1815–1860* (Ithaca, 1967), 56; *Holden's Dollar Magazine*, III (June 1849), 370 (Charles F. Briggs); *Southern Literary Messenger*, XV (May 1849), 309 (Park Benjamin). Melville's articles on Taylor are in *Yankee Doodle*, II (July 24, 31, Aug. 7, 14, 21, 28, Sept. 11, 1847), 152, 167, 172, 188, 199, 202, 229.

43. Nathaniel Hawthorne, *Life of Franklin Pierce* (Boston, 1852); Lee H. Warner, "Nathaniel Hawthorne and the Making of the President—1852," *Historical New Hampshire*, XXVIII (Spring 1973), 21–36; Warner, "With Pierce, and Hawthorne, in Mexico," *Essex Institute Historical Collections*, CXI (July 1975), 213–20.

44. William Southworth Hunt, *Frank Forester [Henry William Herbert]: A Tragedy in Exile* (Newark, N.J., 1933), *passim; Harper's Magazine*, V (Aug. 1852), 422–23; *Southern Quarterly Review*, XXII (July 1852), 271; Herbert, *Pierre, the Partisan: A Tale of the Mexican Marches* (New York, 1848), 12, 9, 38, 73, 99, 33. For a bibliography of Herbert's work, see William Mitchell Van Winkle, comp., *Henry William Herbert [Frank Forester]: A Bibliography of His Writings, 1832–1858* (New York, 1971).

45. Herbert, "Long Jakes, The Prairie Man," *New York Illustrated Magazine*, II (July 1846), 169–74.

46. Herbert, *Pierre, the Partisan*, 66, 67, 73, 80, 84; Hunt, *Frank Forester*, 106.

47. Larzer Ziff, *Literary Democracy: The Declaration of Cultural Independence in America* (New York, 1981), 94; Emilio De Grazia, "The Life and Works of George Lippard" (Ph.D. dissertation, Ohio State University, 1969), abstract; John T. Frederick, "Hawthorne's 'Scribbling Women,'" *New England Quarterly*, XLVIII (June 1975), 239. See also David S. Reynolds, *George Lippard* (Boston, 1982).

48. Heyward Ehrlich, "The 'Mysteries' of Philadelphia: Lippard's Quaker City and 'Urban' Gothic," *ESQ* (1st Quarter 1972), 50–65; J. V. Ridgely, "George Lippard's *The Quaker City:* The World of the American Porno-Gothic," *Studies in the Literary Imagination*, VII (Spring 1974), 77–94.

49. *Holden's Dollar Magazine*, II (July 1848), 423; *New York Tribune*, Feb. 26, 1848; *Massachusetts Quarterly Review*, I (Dec. 1847), 125.

50. Lippard, *Blanche of Brandywine; or, September the Eleventh, 1777* (Philadelphia, 1846), iv–v; Lippard, *The Battle-Day of Germantown: Original Revolu-*

tionary Chronicle (Philadelphia, 1843), 1; Lippard, *Washington and His Generals: or, Legends of the Revolution* (Philadelphia, 1847), iii, iv, 526.

51. Lippard, *Legends of Mexico: The Battles of Taylor* (Philadelphia, 1847), 136, 26–27, 19, 22–23; De Grazia, "Life and Works of George Lippard," 241–42; *Brother Jonathan,* Nov. 15, 1847.

52. Philadelphia *Citizen Soldier,* Oct. 11, 1843, quoted in De Grazia, "Life and Works of George Lippard," 99–100; Lippard, *Legends of Mexico,* 11, 15, 16, 53, 102–3.

53. Lippard, *'Bel of Prairie Eden. A Romance of Mexico* (Boston, 1848), 36–37.

54. *Christian Examiner,* XLII (Jan. 1847), 106; James Franklin Beard, ed., *The Letters and Journals of James Fenimore Cooper* (6 vols., Cambridge, Mass., 1960–68), V, 140.

55. *Democratic Review,* X (June 1842), 539; Beard, ed., *Letters and Journals of James Fenimore Cooper,* V, 52, 119, 143, 149, 186–87, 195, 253.

56. Cooper, *Jack Tier; or, The Florida Reef* (Mohawk ed., New York, 1896), iv; Beard, ed., *Letters and Journals of James Fenimore Cooper,* V, 367; Cooper, *The Spy: A Tale of the Neutral Ground* (Mohawk ed., New York, 1896), vii–viii.

57. Beard, ed., *Letters and Journals of James Fenimore Cooper,* VI, 87, 124, 206; *Anglo-American,* IX (June 5, 1847), 162; *Niles' National Register,* LXXII (June 26, July 3, 1847), 258, 274.

58. Albert H. Smyth, *The Philadelphia Magazines and Their Contributors, 1741–1850* (Philadelphia, 1892), 221; Thomas Philbrick, *James Fenimore Cooper and the Development of American Sea Fiction* (Cambridge, Mass., 1961), 203–9; Cooper, *Jack Tier,* 144, 153, 305–6.

59. *Literary World,* III (April 8, 1848), 189.

Chapter 8: Poetry and the Popular Arts

1. *Merchants' Magazine,* XVII (Nov. 1847), 541.

2. *Literary World,* II (Nov. 13, 1847), 361.

3. Fayette Robinson, "History of the Costume of Men," *Graham's Magazine,* XXXIV (April 1849), 264; *Godey's Magazine,* XXXIV (June 1847), plates; [Luther Giddings,] *Sketches of the Campaign in Northern Mexico* (New York, 1853), 66.

4. John Russell Bartlett, *Dictionary of Americanisms* (New York, 1848), 270.

5. Bartlett, *Dictionary of Americanisms,* xxi–xxii; (2d ed., Boston, 1859), xxiv.

6. *New York Herald,* June 11, 1846.

7. Washington *National Intelligencer,* June 15, 1848.

8. *New York Herald,* June 17, 1846; *Spirit of the Times,* XVII (May 22, 1847), 141; *Holden's Dollar Magazine,* II (Aug. 1848), 500; *Literary World,* II (Sept. 11, 1847), 130.

9. *Knickerbocker Magazine,* XXIV (Dec. 1849), 558; [Sheppard M. Ashe,] *Monterey Conquered: A Fragment from La Gran Quivera; or, Rome Unmasked* (New York, 1852), v, 24; [William F. Smith,] *Guadaloupe: A Tale of Love and War* (Philadelphia, 1860), 8–10, 61.

10. Robert Cantwell, "Introduction," William C. Falkner, *The White Rose of Memphis* (New York, 1953), ix–xv, xxi–xxiii; Hilton Anderson, "Colonel Falkner's Preface to the *Siege of Monterey,*" *Notes on Mississippi Writers,* III (Spring 1970), 36–40.

11. *Spirit of the Times*, XVI (Sept. 5, 1846), 332; XVII (May 1, 1847), 109; George Washington Cutter, *Buena Vista: And Other Poems* (Cincinnati, 1848), 8, 23; *Literary World*, XIII (July 16, 1853), 565; *Knickerbocker Magazine*, XXIX (March 1847), 199.

12. William M'Carty, *National Songs, Ballads, and Other Patriotic Poetry, Chiefly Relating to the War of 1846* (Philadelphia, 1846), 56; J. Jacob Oswandel, *Notes of the Mexican War* (Philadelphia, 1885), 83; H. Judge Moore, *Scott's Campaign in Mexico* (Charleston, 1849), 59; *Spirit of the Times*, XVI (Sept. 5, 19, 1846), 332, 350; *Graham's Magazine*, XXXVI (Feb. 1850), 133–34, (March 1850), 182–83, (April 1850), 237–38, (May 1850), 318–19, (June 1850), 402–3; XXXVIII (March 1851), 137–38.

13. *Rough and Ready Annual* (New York, 1848), 238; *Literary World*, II (Nov. 6, 1847), 332; M'Carty, *National Songs, Ballads, and Other Patriotic Poetry*, 65, 27, 61, 70.

14. *Woodville* (Miss.) *Republican*, March 6, 1847; M'Carty, *National Songs, Ballads, and Other Patriotic Poetry*, 49–50; *Elephant*, I (Jan. 29, 1848), 14; Springfield *Illinois State Register*, May 14, 1847.

15. *Knickerbocker Magazine*, XXVIII (Sept. 1846), 275; *Literary World*, II (Dec. 25, 1847), 515; *The Poems of Alfred B. Street* (2 vols., New York, 1867), II, 143–60; *New York Illustrated Magazine*, III (Jan. 1847), 15; *The Poetical Works of William H. C. Hosmer* (2 vols., New York, 1854), II, 135–36. Aaron Kramer, *The Prophetic Tradition in American Poetry, 1835–1900* (Rutherford, N. J. 1968), 43–92 *passim*, argues wrongly that the Mexican War poetry that dwelt on the war's horrors was, *ipso facto*, antiwar poetry.

16. *Ladies' National Magazine*, XII (Oct. 1847), 138; *Knickerbocker Magazine*, XXX (July 1847), 9; *Southern Literary Messenger*, XIV (Nov. 1848), 657; *Godey's Magazine*, XXXV (Nov. 1847), 263; Oran Perry, comp., *Indiana in the Mexican War* (Indianapolis, 1908), 209–10.

17. *The Letters of William Gilmore Simms* (eds. Mary C. Simms Oliphant, Alfred Taylor Odell, and T. C. Duncan Eaves, 5 vols., Columbia, S. C., 1952–56), II, 132, 372, 430; *Godey's Magazine*, XXXII (June 1846), 285; Simms, *Lays of the Palmetto: A Tribute to the South Carolina Regiment, In the War with Mexico* (Charleston, 1848), *passim*.

18. Evert A. and George L. Duyckinck, *Cyclopaedia of American Literature* (2 vols., New York, 1855), II, 477; Edgar Allan Poe, *The Literati: Some Honest Opinions About Autorial Merits and Demerits* (New York, 1850), 112–15; *Spirit of the Times*, XVI (Nov. 21, 1846), 460; *Literary World*, II (Sept. 25, 1847), 185; Homer F. Barnes, *Charles Fenno Hoffman* (New York, 1930), 166; *Holden's Dollar Magazine*, II (Aug. 1848), 469.

19. *Columbian Magazine*, VI (July 1846), 48; *Literary World*, II (Sept. 25, Dec. 25, 1847), 184–85, 515. A third poem by Jose de Saltillo, "a popular Mexican poet at Vera Cruz," in which the poet condemned America and American slavery while arousing Mexican patriotism, appeared in the *Liberator*, XVI (July 10, 1846), 112; it was in fact written by John Greenleaf Whittier.

20. Kramer, *The Prophetic Tradition in American Poetry*, 56; *Graham's Magazine*, XXXVI (May 1850), 318–19; Grace Greenwood, *Greenwood Leaves: A Collection of Sketches and Letters* (Boston 1850), 318.

21. For these and other examples of the *Liberator*'s antiwar poetry, see the

following: XVII (Feb. 12, 1847), 27, 28; XVI (May 29, 1846), 88, (June 5, 1846), 92, (July 17, 1846), 116; XVII (Jan. 8, 1847), 8, (Jan. 22, 1847), 14, (March 5, 1847), 40.

22. *The Letters of John Greenleaf Whittier* (ed. John B. Pickard, 3 vols., Cambridge, Mass., 1975), II, 19, 20; *Liberator*, XVI (July 10, 1846), 112. On the use of Hoffman's hoax, see Thomas Franklin Currier, *A Bibliography of John Greenleaf Whittier* (Cambridge, Mass., 1937), 318–20.

23. Washington *National Era*, April 15, May 20, 1847.

24. *The Writings of James Russell Lowell* (10 vols., Boston, 1890), VIII, 155–56; Charles Eliot Norton, ed., *Letters of James Russell Lowell* (2 vols., New York, 1894), I, 115; Thomas Wortham, *James Russell Lowell's The Biglow Papers: A Critical Edition* (DeKalb, Ill., 1977), 50, 51, 52, 59, 61, 123, xiv.

25. Norton, ed., *Letters of James Russell Lowell*, I, 296.

26. David Grimsted, *Melodrama Unveiled: American Theater and Culture, 1800–1850* (Chicago, 1968), ix, 137–70.

27. *New York Herald*, July 15, 1846. Unless otherwise noted, information on Mexican War plays has been derived from Arthur Herman Wilson, *A History of the Philadelphia Theatre, 1835–1855* (Philadelphia, 1935) and George C. D. Odell, *Annals of the New York Stage* (7 vols., New York, 1970), V (1843–50).

28. *New York Herald*, June 9, 1846; *Spirit of the Times*, XVII (Sept. 25, 1847), 368.

29. *Saint Louis Reveille*, Aug. 23, 1846, July 4, 1847; *New York Herald*, July 4, Sept. 2, 1846, May 7, 1847; *Spirit of the Times*, XVII (Jan. 22, 1848), 572.

30. *Spirit of the Times*, XVII (Oct. 2, 9, 16, 23, 1847), 380, 392, 404, 416; Meade Minnigerode, *The Fabulous Forties, 1840–1850* (New York, 1924), 167–68.

31. *Spirit of the Times*, XVII (Feb. 5, 1848), 596; *Scientific American*, III (March 11, 1848), 198; *New York Herald*, April 1, 1848.

32. Richard McLanathan, *The American Tradition in the Arts* (New York, 1968), 306–9; John Francis McDermott, *The Lost Panoramas of the Mississippi* (Chicago, 1958), 7, 14–15; Odell, *Annals of the New York Stage*, V, 310, 499; *New York Herald*, Feb. 1, 1849; *New York Tribune*, Aug. 28, 1848.

33. Miss Ludlow, *A General View of the Fine Arts, Critical and Historical* (intro. Daniel Huntington, New York, 1851), 11–12; Lillian B. Miller, *Patrons and Patriotism: The Encouragement of the Fine Arts in the United States, 1790–1860* (Chicago, 1966), 214; Charles Lanman, "On the Requisites for the Formation of a National School of Historical Painting," *Southern Literary Messenger*, XIV (Dec. 1848), 727–28; *Democratic Review*, XXI (Dec. 1847), 567.

34. Robert Taft, *Photography and the American Scene: A Social History, 1839–1889* (New York, 1938), 223–24, 484–85.

35. John Frost, *Pictorial History of Mexico and the Mexican War* (Richmond, 1848), iii.

36. *Columbian Magazine*, VI (July 1846), 92; *Literary World*, II (Dec. 18, 1847), 487; *Union Magazine*, II (Jan. 1848), 21; I (July 1847), 48.

37. *New York Herald*, July 30, 1846; *Brother Jonathan*, Nov. 15, 1847; *Pictorial Brother Jonathan*, July 4, 1848.

38. Ronnie C. Tyler, *The Mexican War: A Lithographic Record* (Austin, 1973), 6; Harry T. Peters, *America on Stone: The Other Printmakers to the American People* (Garden City, N.Y., 1931), 23.

39. Peter C. Welsh, "Henry R. Robinson: Printmaker to the Whig Party," *New*

York History, LIII (Jan. 1972), 25–53; *An Album of American Battle Art, 1755–1918* (Washington, 1947), 131, 140–41; Tyler, *Mexican War,* 26–27, 8, 24; Peters, *America on Stone,* 351, 353–54.

40. *Album of American Battle Art,* 144; Frederic A. Conningham (Updated by Colin Simkin), *Currier & Ives Prints: An Illustrated Check List* (New York, 1970), *passim.*

41. [Albert Lombard,] *The "High Private," With a Full and Exciting History of the New York Volunteers* (New York, 1848), 1; *Spirit of the Times,* XVII (March 20, 1847), 48.

42. Marcus Cunliffe, *Soldiers & Civilians: The Martial Spirit in America, 1775–1865* (New York, 1973), 115; *Album of American Battle Art,* 128, 131, 137–38; *Godey's Magazine,* XXXV (Sept. 1847), 155–56; XXXVII (Dec. 1848), 392; *Knickerbocker Magazine,* XXX (Nov. 1847), 464.

43. Tyler, *Mexican War,* 18–20; [John James Peck,] *The Sign of the Eagle: A View of Mexico—1830 to 1855* (ed. Richard F. Pourade, San Diego, 1970), 165; George Wilkins Kendall, *The War Between the United States and Mexico Illustrated* (New York, 1851), iii–iv.

44. Marian R. McNaughton, "James Walker—Combat Artist of Two American Wars," *Military Collector & Historian,* IX (Summer 1957), 31–35; *Autobiography of the Late Col. Geo. T. M. Davis* (New York, 1891), 263–65; Kent Ahrens, "Nineteenth Century History Painting and the United States Capitol," *Records of the Columbia Historical Society,* L (1980), 207–8.

45. *American Whig Review,* XVI (Aug. 1852), 143; *Literary World,* II (Nov. 6, 1847), 330; IX (Dec. 13, 1851), 471; *Bulletin of the American Art Union,* II (May 1849), 9; *Graham's Magazine,* XXXVII (Oct. 1850), 260.

46. Tyler, *Mexican War,* 6; *Literary World,* IX (Dec. 13, 1851), 471–72; *Bulletin of the American Art Union,* II (April 1849), 25; Charles Mitchell, "Benjamin West's 'Death of General Wolfe' and the Popular History Piece," *Journal of the Warburg and Courtauld Institutes,* VII (1944), 20, 32.

47. *New York Herald,* May 21, 1846; Washington *National Intelligencer,* June 8, 1846. Morris's anthem was later published in his *Poems* (New York, 1860).

48. Carl Bode, *The Anatomy of American Popular Culture, 1840–1861* (Berkeley, 1959), 19; Gilbert Chase, *America's Music: From the Pilgrims to the Present* (New York, 1966), 165–66; Christopher Hatch, "Music for America: A Critical Controversy of the 1850s," *American Quarterly,* XIV (Winter 1962), 578–86.

49. H. Wiley Hitchcock, *Music in the United States: A Historical Introduction* (Englewood Cliffs, N.J., 1969), 73–75.

50. Hitchcock, *Music in the United States,* 51, 75–76; *Holden's Dollar Magazine,* IV (Dec. 1849), 737–45; *Literary World,* III (May 20, 1848), 312; Chase, *America's Music,* 176–77, 291.

51. Lester S. Levy, *Picture the Songs: Lithographs from the Sheet Music of Nineteenth-Century America* (Baltimore, 1976), 1–3.

52. *Spirit of the Times,* XVI (May 23, 1846), 156; *Union Magazine,* I (Oct. 1847), 188–89. For these and other Mexican War songs, see Elize K. Kirk, "Sheet Music Related to the United States War with Mexico (1846–1848) in the Jenkins Garrett Library, University of Texas at Arlington," *Notes,* XXXVII (Sept. 1980), 14–30. A quickstep was a popular military cadence, measuring 108 steps per minute.

53. Hitchcock, *Music in the United States,* 46–47; *New York Tribune,* July 11, Aug.

2, 1848; John Schell, *The Battle of Resaca de la Palma, Composed for the Piano Forte* (Baltimore, 1848).

54. William Treat Upton, *Anthony Philip Heinrich: A Nineteenth-Century Composer in America* (New York, 1939), 171, 173, 184–87, 280–81; John Hill Hewitt, *Shadows on the Wall or Glimpses of the Past* (Baltimore, 1877), 82–85.

55. Harry Dichter and Elliott Shapiro, *Handbook of Early American Sheet Music, 1768–1889* (New York, 1977), 20; Washington *National Intelligencer,* June 8, 1846; M'Carty, *National Songs, Ballads, and Other Patriotic Poetry,* 72–73, 100–01.

56. Hitchcock, *Music in the United States,* 51; Chase, *America's Music,* 261; *New York Herald,* Sept. 6, 1846; Hughson Mooney, "The Past as Prelude: American Popular Music, 1840–1895," *Connecticut Review,* IX (May 1976), 51, 52.

57. M'Carty, comp., *National Songs, Ballads, and Other Patriotic Poetry, passim;* Edward Arthur Dolph, *"Sound Off!" Soldier Songs from the Revolution to World War II* (New York, 1942), 396; *The Rough and Ready Songster . . . By an American Officer* (New York, 1848). The *Old Zack Songster* was published in the summer of 1848 to provide songs to Taylor's campaign for the Presidency.

58. Albert G. Brackett, *General Lane's Brigade in Central Mexico* (Cincinnati, 1854), 29–30, 132.

59. *Niles' National Register,* LXXI (Nov. 14, 1846), 168; J. Jacob Oswandel, *Notes of the Mexican War* (Philadelphia, 1885), 63, 211; S. Compton Smith, *Chile Con Carne; or, The Camp and the Field* (New York, 1857), 214.

60. J. M. Wynkoop, *Anecdotes and Incidents: Comprising Daring Exploits, Personal and Amusing Adventures . . . and Thrilling Incidents of the Mexican War* (Pittsburgh, 1848), 44; [John Blount Robertson,] *Reminiscences of a Campaign in Mexico* (Nashville, 1849), 96; *Spirit of the Times,* XVI (Sept. 5, 1846), 329, (Jan. 9, 1847), 552.

61. Oswandel, *Notes of the Mexican War,* 223; *New York Herald,* Sept. 29, 1846; George C. Furber, *The Twelve Months' Volunteer* (Cincinnati, 1848), 120; Milton Jamieson, *Journal and Notes of a Campaign in Mexico* (Cincinnati, 1849), 31; Willard A. and Porter W. Heaps, *The Singing Sixties: The Spirit of Civil War Days Drawn from the Music of the Times* (Norman, Okla., 1960), 7.

Chapter 9: The Historians' War

1. *Southern Quarterly Review,* XIII (Jan. 1848), 53; Fred Somkin, *Unquiet Eagle: Memory and Desire in the Idea of American Freedom, 1815–1860* (Ithaca, 1967), 55–90; *Democratic Review,* VI (Nov. 1839), 426; George Bancroft, *History of the United States, From the Discovery of the American Continent* (10 vols., Boston, 1834–75), IV (1852), 9.

2. *Graham's Magazine,* XXXII (June 1848), 354; *Eclectic Magazine,* XXV (March 1852), 303.

3. *Literary World,* II (Sept. 4, 1847), 101; III (April 1, 1848), 164; Russel B. Nye, *George Bancroft* (New York, 1964), 149, 154; *American Review,* III (May 1846), 540.

4. *Graham's Magazine,* XXXIII (July 1848), 59; XXXII (June 1848), 354; George Lippard, *Legends of Mexico: The Battles of Taylor* (Philadelphia, 1847), 27.

5. *Southern Quarterly Review,* XXIV (July 1853), 95–96.

6. *Literary World,* III (July 22, June 10, 1848), 483, 363; II (Oct. 30, Dec. 4, 1847), 310, 440; *American Review,* VII (June 1848), 653. The *Southern Literary Messenger,* XVI (Aug. 1850), 520, felt that "it must be reserved for another generation to do impartial justice to the actions of our own."

7. *Peterson's Magazine,* XIII (March 1848), 126; *Literary World,* VI (Jan. 26, 1850), 78; IV (Feb. 3, 1849), 111.

8. Roger Wolcott, ed., *The Correspondence of William Hickling Prescott, 1833–1847* (Cambridge, Mass., 1925), 648, 614–15, 597, 645. Emma Willard was among those who suggested that Prescott's popularity promoted the country's war spirit, *Last Leaves of American History: Comprising Histories of the Mexican War and California* (New York, 1849), 43.

9. C. Harvey Gardiner, ed., *The Literary Memoranda of William Hickling Prescott* (2 vols., Norman, Okla., 1961), II, 29; [John Blount Robertson,] *Reminiscences of a Campaign in Mexico* (Nashville, 1849), 60; Lewis Wallace, *Lew Wallace, An Autobiography* (2 vols., New York, 1906), II, 88–89; Richard McSherry, *El Puchero; or a Mixed Dish from Mexico* (Philadelphia, 1850), 167–69.

10. Claude M. Fuess, *The Life of Caleb Cushing* (2 vols., New York, 1923), II, 60–63; George Winston Smith and Charles Judah, eds., *Chronicles of the Gringos: The U.S. Army in the Mexican War, 1846–1848* (Albuquerque, 1968), 407, 408; *Autobiography of the Late Col. Geo. T. M. Davis* (New York, 1891), 266; McSherry, *El Puchero,* 177.

11. Wolcott, ed., *Correspondence of William Hickling Prescott,* 656, 629, 657–58, 648; Smith and Judah, eds., *Chronicles of the Gringos,* 406–7.

12. Wolcott, ed., *Correspondence of William Hickling Prescott,* 634; *North American Review,* LXV (Oct. 1847), 366–400 (esp. 382–83); *Methodist Quarterly Review,* XXX (Jan.–April 1848), 5–28, 268–82 (esp. 282).

13. Gardiner, ed., *Literary Memoranda of William Hickling Prescott,* II, 181; George Ticknor, *Life of William Hickling Prescott* (Boston, 1864), 272; M. A. DeWolfe Howe, *The Life and Letters of George Bancroft* (2 vols., New York, 1908), II, 36. For others who urged Prescott to write the history of the Mexican War, see C. Harvey Gardiner, ed., *The Papers of William Hickling Prescott* (Urbana, 1964), 268–69.

14. *Literary World,* II (Sept. 4, 1847), 115; *Southern Literary Messenger,* XXI (Jan. 1855), 1; *Methodist Quarterly Review,* XXX (Jan. 1848), 84–85; *American Review,* VI (Dec. 1847), 654–55.

15. *Southern Quarterly Review,* XIV (July 1848), 242; *Holden's Dollar Magazine,* IV (July 1849), 438; *Southern Literary Messenger,* XVI (Oct. 1850), 610; *Democratic Review,* XXVI (Jan. 1850), 28; *Union Magazine,* I (Aug. 1847), 95; *American Literary Magazine,* IV (May 1849), 687.

16. *Southern Quarterly Review,* XIII (Jan. 1848), 53; *Literary World,* IV (Feb. 24, 1849), 184; James Franklin Beard, ed., *The Letters and Journals of James Fenimore Cooper* (6 vols., Cambridge, Mass., 1960–68), V, 205, 210.

17. [Jacob K. Neff,] *Thrilling Incidents of the Wars of the United States* (New York, 1851), 548; *Literary World,* IV (Feb. 3, 1849), 111; W. A. Crofutt, ed., *Fifty Years in Camp and Field: Diary of Major-General Ethan Allen Hitchcock* (New York, 1909), 331–33.

18. *The Letters of William Gilmore Simms* (eds. Mary C. Simms Oliphant, Alfred Taylor Odell, and T. C. Duncan Eaves, 5 vols., Columbia, S. C., 1952–56), III, 149, 83. Hammond's articles appeared in the *Southern Quarterly Review*

between 1850 and 1853; quotations from XX (July 1851), 1; XXI (Jan. 1852), 136; XIX (Jan. 1851), 188, 189; XXI (April 1852), 385–86; XVIII (Nov. 1850), 428, 429, 463.

19. *Literary World,* IX (Sept. 13, July 19, 1851), 214, 45; *Harper's Magazine,* III (Oct. 1851), 711; *Southern Quarterly Review,* XXI (Jan. 1852), 124–27; Semmes, *Service Afloat and Ashore During the Mexican War* (Cincinnati, 1851), vi, 126, 43.

20. H. Judge Moore, *Scott's Campaign in Mexico* (Charleston, 1849), iii–iv; [Luther Giddings,] *Sketches of the Campaign in Northern Mexico* (New York, 1853), v.

21. George C. Furber, *The Twelve Months' Volunteer* (Cincinnati, 1848), v–vi (the subtitle, not heretofore cited, is *Journal of a Private, in the Tennessee Regiment of Cavalry, in the Campaign, in Mexico, 1846–7*); Philip Young, *History of Mexico: Her Civil Wars, and Colonial and Revolutionary Annals . . . Continued to the Treaty of Peace, 1848, by George C. Furber* (Cincinnati, 1848). Furber's *Camp Stories* was republished in 1852 under the title *Ike McCandless, and Other Stories; or, Incidents in the Life of a Soldier.*

22. [Giddings,] *Sketches of the Campaign in Northern Mexico,* vi; [George Ballentine,] *Autobiography of an English Soldier in the United States Army* (New York, 1853), v–vi (Publisher's Preface).

23. *Southern Quarterly Review,* XIX (Jan. 1851), 149; *Southern Literary Messenger,* XVI (Jan. 1850), 63.

24. Roswell S. Ripley, *The War with Mexico* (2 vols., New York, 1849), I, xv, xvii.

25. Ripley, *War with Mexico,* I, xiv, xvi, II, 286; *Southern Quarterly Review,* XIX (Jan. 1851), 150; XXI (Jan. 1852), 145; Crofutt, ed., *Fifty Years in Camp and Field,* 365.

26. Ripley, *War with Mexico,* II, 82–83, 149–50, 321; Justin H. Smith, *The War with Mexico* (2 vols., New York, 1919), I, 405; *Southern Quarterly Review,* XIX (Jan. 1851), 149–61; *Literary World,* V (Dec. 15, 1849), 512.

27. Isaac I. Stevens, *Campaigns of the Rio Grande and of Mexico* (New York, 1851), 5, 7.

28. *A Sketch of the Life and Character of Gen. Taylor . . . Together with a Concise History of the Mexican War. By the One-legged Sergeant* (New York, 1847); *John-Donkey,* II (July 8, 1848), 19; Henry Montgomery, *Life of Major General Zachary Taylor* (20th ed., Auburn, N.Y., 1850), vi; *Southern Quarterly Review,* XI (April 1847), 509.

29. *Godey's Magazine,* XXXVI (Feb. 1848), 131; *Halls of the Montezumas: or Mexico, in Ancient and Modern Times* (New York, 1848), 11.

30. Milton Rickels, *Thomas Bangs Thorpe: Humorist of the Old Southwest* (Baton Rouge, 1962), 119–28, 148–55; Eugene Current-Garcia, "Thomas Bangs Thorpe and the Literature of the Ante-Bellum Southwestern Frontier," *Louisiana Historical Quarterly,* XXXIX (April 1956), 209–17.

31. [Thomas Bangs Thorpe,] *Anecdotes of General Taylor, and the Mexican War* (New York, 1848), Preface; Thorpe, *Our Army on the Rio Grande* (Philadelphia, 1846), Preface.

32. Thorpe, *Our Army on the Rio Grande,* 74, 83, 157; Thorpe, *Our Army at Monterey* (Philadelphia, 1847), 33, 48, 10.

33. Current-Garcia, "Thomas Bangs Thorpe and the Literature of the Ante-Bellum Southwestern Frontier," *Louisiana Historical Quarterly,* XXXIX, 211; *New York Herald,* July 25, 1846.

34. Albert H. Smyth, *The Philadelphia Magazines and Their Contributors, 1741–1850* (Philadelphia, 1892), 225–29; *Peterson's Magazine*, XVI (Dec. 1849), 223; *Graham's Magazine*, XXIV (May 1844), 228.

35. Peterson, *The Military Heroes of the War with Mexico; With a Narrative of the War* (Philadelphia, 1848), v–vi, 133, 107, 92, 46, 16–18, 22–23.

36. *An Album of American Battle Art, 1775–1918* (Washington, 1947), 135; Clive Bush, *The Dream of Reason: American Consciousness and Cultural Achievement from Independence to the Civil War* (London, 1977), 152; *Godey's Magazine*, XXXIII (Aug. 1846), 53; *Graham's Magazine*, XXXII–XXXV (1848–49), *passim*.

37. *Godey's Magazine*, XXXIII, 53–54.

38. Frost, *Pictorial History of Mexico and the Mexican War* (Richmond, 1848), iv, iii; Frost, *The Mexican War and Its Warriors* (New Haven and Philadelphia, 1848), 5; Frost, *Life of Major General Zachary Taylor* (New York and Philadelphia, 1847), 3–4.

39. Robinson, *California and Its Gold Regions* (New York, 1849, repr. 1973), Preface; Robinson, *Mexico and Her Military Chieftains* (Philadelphia, 1847), v–vi, 149–50, 152, 14–15.

40. Robinson, *Mexico and Her Military Chieftains*, 283, 149; *Graham's Magazine*, XXXIV (Jan. 1849), 71; Robinson, *California and Its Gold Regions*, 121.

41. [Hunt's] *Merchants' Magazine*, XX (Feb. 1849), 239; Edward D. Mansfield, *Life and Services of General Winfield Scott* (New York, 1852), 257, 513.

42. Mansfield, *The Mexican War: A History of Its Origin, and a Detailed Account of the Victories Which Terminated in the Surrender of the Capital* (New York, 1849), iii–iv, 43, 165, 173, 206; *American Review*, VII (June 1848), 653; *Democratic Review*, XXII (March 1848), 287.

43. *Literary World*, III (Dec. 2, 1848), 873–74; Jenkins, *History of the War Between the United States and Mexico* (Auburn, N.Y. 1849), vi, 16–17, 19, 499–500, 504–6.

44. Nathan Covington Brooks, *A Complete History of the Mexican War: Its Causes, Conduct, and Consequences* (Philadelphia and Baltimore, 1849), v.

45. *Ibid.*, 62–63, 103, 348, 102, 395, 441, 341.

46. [Brantz Mayer,] "The Study of History," *Southern Quarterly Review*, X (July 1846), 129, 135, 139–40; Mayer, *Commerce, Literature and Art* (Baltimore, 1848), 24; Bernard C. Steiner, "Brantz Mayer," *Maryland Historical Magazine*, V (March 1910), 1–22.

47. Raymund A. Paredes, "The Mexican Image in American Travel Literature, 1831–1869," *New Mexico Historical Review*, LII (Jan. 1977), 16; Mayer, *Mexico As It Was And As It Is* (New York, 1844), v–vi, 347–48, 354.

48. B[rantz]. M[ayer]., "Mexico—Her People and Revolutions; With a View of Spanish Misrule in America as the Cause of Present Spanish American Decadence," *Southern Quarterly Review*, XII (Oct. 1847), 372–73; Mayer, *History of the War Between Mexico and the United States* (New York, 1848), 23–24.

49. B[rantz]. M[ayer]., "Origin of the War with Mexico," *Southern Quarterly Review*, XV (April 1849), 84, 101; Mayer, *History of the War Between Mexico and the United States*, 101, 114; Mayer, *Mexico, Aztec, Spanish and Republican: A Historical, Geographical, Political, Statistical and Social Account* (2 vols. in 1, Hartford, 1853), I, 1–2, 431; "Brantz Mayer's Mexico," *Southern Quarterly Review*, XXII (July 1852), 117–41.

50. *New York Tribune,* Jan. 11, 1848; *Southern Quarterly Review,* XXIII (Jan. 1852), 52; Joel Tyler Headley, *The Lives of Winfield Scott and Andrew Jackson* (New York, 1852), 127–28.

Chapter 10: The War and the Republic

1. *Advocate of Peace, and Universal Brotherhood,* n. s. I (June 1846), 129–31, 139–40, (July 1846), 168, (Nov. 1846), 255, (Dec. 1846), 275–76; Peter Brock, *Pacificism in the United States: From the Colonial Era to the First World War* (Princeton, 1968), 644–48.
2. George C. Beckwith, *The Peace Manual: or, War and Its Remedies* (Boston, 1847), *passim; Advocate of Peace,* n. s. II (Jan. 1847), 6, (Oct. 1847), 115, (July 1847), 75, 84.
3. *Advocate of Peace,* n. s. II (June 1847), 71.
4. *Literary World,* VI (Jan. 26, 1850), 78; *Brownson's Quarterly Review,* n. s. IV (April 1850), 271–72; *Christian Examiner,* XLVII (Sept. 1849), 306; XLVIII (March 1850), 323–24.
5. Abiel Abbot Livermore, *The War with Mexico Reviewed* (Boston, 1850), 6–13, 209, 31–32, 50; William Jay, *A Review of the Causes and Consequences of the Mexican War* (Boston, 1849), 119, 143, 223.
6. Livermore, *War with Mexico Reviewed,* 283, 285; Philip Berry, *A Review of the Mexican War on Christian Principles* (Columbia, S.C., 1849), 34–35, 50–51.
7. John H. Schroeder, *Mr. Polk's War: American Opposition and Dissent, 1846–1848* (Madison, 1973), 94; Charles T. Porter, *Review of the Mexican War* (Auburn, N.Y., 1849), vi, 114, 133–34.
8. [Hunt's] *Merchants' Magazine,* XV (July 1846), 124; Emma Willard, *Last Leaves of American History: Comprising Histories of the Mexican War and California* (New York, 1849), 38, 92, 97–98, 103–5.
9. *American Literary Magazine,* IV (April 1849), 627; *Christian Examiner,* XLVII (Sept. 1849), 307; John Lord, *The Life of Emma Willard* (New York, 1873), 230.
10. *Liberator,* XVI (May 22, June 5, 1846), 83, 91; Schroeder, *Mr. Polk's War,* 101, 105, 80–81; Roswell S. Ripley, *War with Mexico* (2 vols., New York, 1849), I, 73; *Saint Louis Reveille,* July 3, 1847; Isaac Smith, *Reminiscences of a Campaign in Mexico* (Indianapolis, 1848), 82. For a sympathetic treatment of Corwin's speech, see Hal W. Bochin, "Tom Corwin's Speech Against the Mexican War: Courageous but Misunderstood," *Ohio History,* XC (Winter 1981), 32–54.
11. *American Whig Review,* XII (Sept. 1850), 287; *American Review,* II (Sept. 1845), 221, 229; V (April 1847), 325; III (June 1846), 578; IV (July 1846), 1–2.
12. *Scientific American,* II (Jan. 2, 1847), 117; *American Review,* V (March 1847), 239.
13. *Journals of Ralph Waldo Emerson* (eds. William H. Gilman *et al.,* 14 vols., Cambridge, Mass., 1960–78), IX, 74, 430–31; *Massachusetts Quarterly Review,* I (Dec. 1847), 4–5, 1; Emerson, *The Conduct of Life* (Boston, 1904), 256; Emerson, "War," *Aesthetic Papers* (ed. Elizabeth P. Peabody, Boston, 1849), 36–50; John Q. Anderson, "Emerson on Texas and the Mexican War," *Western Humanities Review,* XIII (Spring 1959), 191–99.
14. *Massachusetts Quarterly Review,* I (Dec. 1847), 11; *Collected Works of Theodore*

Parker (London, 1863), IV, 23–24; *New York Herald,* June 10, 1846; *Literary World,* II (Dec. 18, 1847), 483.

15. *New Englander,* IV (July 1846), 382, 428–29; V (Jan. 1847), 140–42, (July 1847), 388–401.

16. *Christian Examiner,* XLI (Sept. 1846), 175; *Brownson's Quarterly Review,* n. s. I (July 1847), 363; *New Englander,* VI (April 1848), 294–95; Oran Perry, comp., *Indiana in the Mexican War* (Indianapolis, 1908), 54.

17. *Christian Examiner,* XLVIII (May 1850), 373; Gordon S. Wood, ed., *The Rising Glory of America, 1760–1820* (New York, 1971), 5–6; *DeBow's Review,* I (Feb. 1846), 132; *Spirit of the Times,* XVI (Sept. 5, 1846), 326; *American Review,* II (July 1845), 97–98.

18. Charles J. Peterson, *Military Heroes of the Revolution* (Philadelphia, 1848), 21; *Columbian Magazine,* VI (Sept. 1846), 142.

19. J. G. A. Pocock, "Virtue and Commerce in the Eighteenth Century," *Journal of Interdisciplinary History,* III (Summer 1972), 121; Andrew P. Peabody, "The Intellectual Aspect of the Age," *North American Review,* LXIV (April 1847), 279; Wood, ed., *The Rising Glory of America,* 9; Richard B. Latner, "The Nullification Crisis and Republican Subversion," *Journal of Southern History,* XLIII (Feb. 1977), 28–29.

20. Pocock, "Virtue and Commerce in the Eighteenth Century," *Journal of Interdisciplinary History,* III, *passim;* Drew R. McCoy, *The Elusive Republic: Political Economy in Jeffersonian America* (Chapel Hill, 1980), chap. 3.

21. *American Review,* VII (Feb. 1848), 170; II (July 1845), 90–99; *North American Review,* LXIV (April 1847), 273–92 (Peabody); Edwin Percy Whipple, *Character and Characteristic Men* (Boston, 1870), 322–23.

22. Henry William Herbert, "Long Jakes, the Prairie Man," *New York Illustrated Magazine,* II (July 1846), 169.

23. *American Review,* VII (Feb. 1848), 207–9; *New Englander,* V (Oct. 1847), 604–13; IV (July 1846), 371.

24. *New York Tribune,* April 29, July 18, 1848; *Southern Quarterly Review,* XIV (July 1848), 159, 154–55, 165.

25. William H. Emory, *Notes of a Military Reconnoissance* (Washington, 1848), 127–30; Henry Adams, ed., *The Writings of Albert Gallatin* (3 vols., Philadelphia, 1879), II, 650–52; Roger Wolcott, ed., *Correspondence of William Hickling Prescott, 1833–1847* (Cambridge, Mass., 1925), 655.

26. Adams, ed., *Writings of Gallatin,* II, 656–58.

27. Gallatin, *Peace with Mexico* (New York, 1848), 3; Adams, ed., *Writings of Gallatin,* II, 650.

28. Gallatin, *War Expenses* (New York, 1848), 3, 13, 16–17, 18–19; Gallatin, *Peace with Mexico,* 24, 25–26, 27, 28–29, 30.

29. *Democratic Review,* XXI (Nov. 1847), 388; XXII (May 1848), 472.

30. *Pictorial Life of General Taylor, the Hero of Okee Chobee, Palo Alto, Resaca de la Palma, Monterey, and Buena Vista* (Philadelphia, 1847), 15–17.

31. *Democratic Review,* XX (May 1847), 455, (Feb. 1847), 101; *Literary World,* II (Dec. 11, 1847), 455, (Aug. 28, 1847), 82. The *Review's* reading of Vattel was probably based on Book II, nos. 53, 70, 78, and Book III, nos. 28, 41; Emmerich de Vattel, *The Law of Nations; or Principles of the Law of Nature, Applied to the Conduct and Affairs of Nations and Sovereigns* (Sixth American Edition, from a New Edition by Joseph Chitty, Philadelphia, 1844), 154, 160, 163, 302–3, 306–7.

32. [Hunt's] *Merchants' Magazine*, XVIII (Feb. 1848), 142; [Nahum Capen,] *The Republic of the United States of America* (New York, 1848), 38, 52–53, 152, 159, 162–63.
33. *North American Review*, LIII (July 1841), 1, 6; Victor Cousin, *Course of the History of Modern Philosophy* (2 vols., New York, 1866), I, 183, 191; *Southern Quarterly Review*, XXIII (Jan. 1853), 20–21.
34. Reginald Horsman, *Race and Manifest Destiny: The Origins of American Racial Anglo-Saxonism* (Cambridge, Mass., 1981), 208, 181; *Knickerbocker Magazine*, XXX (Nov. 1847), 406, 399.
35. *American Review*, VII (Jan. 1848), 43; Horsman, *Race and Manifest Destiny*, chaps. 9–12.
36. Thomas J. Farnham, *Mexico: Its Geography—Its People—and Its Institutions* (New York, 1846), 3; *Literary World*, III (Feb. 19, 1848), 43; *Spirit of the Times*, XVI (Aug. 1, 1846), 271; Corydon Donnavan, *Adventures in Mexico* (Cincinnati, 1847), 111–12; "Rambles About Monclova," *Southern Literary Messenger*, XXI (June 1855), 350.
37. *New Englander*, IV (July 1846), 429; Gamaliel Bailey, Jr., *American Progress: A Lecture Delivered Before the Young Men's Mercantile Library Association of Cincinnati, December 8, 1846* (Cincinnati, 1846), 8, 21; *Literary World*, I (Feb. 27, 1847), 81; *Knickerbocker Magazine*, XXIX (Feb. 1847), 173.
38. J. Fred Rippy, *Joel R. Poinsett, Versatile American* (Durham, 1935), 106, 109; [Poinsett,] "The Mexican War," *De Bow's Review*, II (July 1846), 21–24; [Poinsett,] "Mexico and the Mexicans," *ibid.*, II (Sept. 1846), 165; Washington *National Intelligencer*, Jan. 20, Feb. 2, 18, 1848.
39. *New Englander*, IV (July 1846), 429; *American Review*, III (June 1846), 571–72.
40. *New York Herald*, May 21, 1846; *Rough and Ready Annual* (New York, 1848), 192; Roswell S. Ripley, *The War with Mexico* (2 vols., New York, 1849), I, 27; *De Bow's Review*, I (Feb. 1846), 117, 131–32; Brantz Mayer, *Mexico, Aztec, Spanish and Republican* (2 vols. in 1, Hartford, 1853), II, 160.
41. *Sketches of the War in Northern Mexico*, 58; *Democratic Review*, XXI (Dec. 1847), 514; Mary Clinton Collins, ed., "Journal of Francis Collins," *Quarterly Publication of the Historical and Philosophical Society of Ohio*, X (April–July 1915), 88; "Rambles About Monclova," *Southern Literary Messenger*, XXI (Aug. 1855), 347; Milton Jamieson, *Journal and Notes of a Campaign in Mexico* (Cincinnati, 1849), 50.
42. Graham A. Barringer, ed., "The Mexican War Journal of Henry S. Lane," *Indiana Magazine of History*, LIII (Dec. 1957), 410–11, 425–26; *Democratic Review*, XLI (May 1858), 345.
43. J. Jacob Oswandel, *Notes of the Mexican War* (Philadelphia, 1885), 584–85.
44. [Hunt's] *Merchants' Magazine*, XVIII (Feb. 1848), 140, 142; *Scientific American*, II (May 29, 1847), 285.
45. Lewis Leonidas Allen, *Pencillings of Scenes Upon the Rio Grande* (New York, 1848), 18; Raphael Semmes, *Service Afloat and Ashore During the Mexican War* (Cincinnati, 1851), 475, 479; *Niles' National Register*, LXXI (Sept. 26, 1846), 58.
46. *House Executive Document 60*, 30 Congress, 1 Session, 971–74; *Southern Quarterly Review*, XXI (April 1852), 394–95; *Littell's Living Age*, XIV (Aug. 21, 1847), 383.

47. *Littell's Living Age,* VIII (Jan. 3, 1846), 56; *Nineteenth Century,* I (1848), 397–98; Wolcott, ed., *Correspondence of William Hickling Prescott,* 643; *Democratic Review,* XXII (May 1848), 396–97.

48. *Southern Quarterly Review,* XIII (Jan. 1848), 211–12; Tom Reilly, "Jane McManus Storms: Letters from the Mexican War, 1846–1848," *Southwestern Historical Quarterly,* LXXXV (July 1981), 35–36, 38; *Nineteenth Century,* I (1848), 683.

49. *Democratic Review,* XXI (Nov. 1847), 381, 389–90; [Hunt's] *Merchants' Magazine,* XVII (Dec. 1847), 615; XVI (May 1847), 455–58.

50. William M'Carty, comp., *National Songs, Ballads, and Other Patriotic Poetry, Chiefly Relating to the War of 1846* (Philadelphia, 1846), 45–46; Nathan Covington Brooks, *Complete History of the Mexican War* (Philadelphia, 1849), 540.

51. Charles A. Hale, "The War with the United States and the Crisis in Mexican Thought," *Americas,* XIV (Oct. 1957), 153–73; *Democratic Review,* XLI (May 1858), 341, 343.

Epilogue

1. *New York Herald,* March 19, 20, 21, 30, 1848.

2. John R. Kenly, *Memoirs of a Maryland Volunteer* (Philadelphia, 1873), 407–8; [George Ballentine,] *Autobiography of an English Soldier in the United States Army* (New York, 1853), 283–84; Milton Jamieson, *Journal and Notes of a Campaign in Mexico* (Cincinnati, 1849), 81.

3. *New York Herald,* March 19, 25, April 11, 1848.

4. Frederick Merk, *The Monroe Doctrine and American Expansionism, 1843–1849* (New York, 1966), 50–56, 87–88; Henry Blumenthal, *A Reappraisal of Franco-American Relations, 1830–1871* (Chapel Hill, 1959), 35–36; Nancy N. Barker, "Monarchy in Mexico: Harebrained Scheme or Well-Considered Prospect?" *Journal of Modern History,* XLVIII (March 1976), 51–68.

5. New Orleans *Picayune,* Feb. 12, 1848; David M. Pletcher, *The Diplomacy of Annexation: Texas, Oregon, and the Mexican War* (Columbia, Mo., 1973), 357–59; *Littell's Living Age,* X (July 4, 1846), 55; XI (Oct. 17, Nov. 21, 1846), 119–20, 391. The assumptions that Paredes sought, with Spanish help, to establish a monarchy in early 1846 were correct; see Miguel Enrique Soto Estrada, "The Monarchist Conspiracy in Mexico, 1845–1846" (Ph.D. dissertation, University of Texas, 1983).

6. James D. Richardson, comp., *A Compilation of the Messages and Papers of the Presidents, 1789–1897* (10 vols., Washington, 1896–99), IV, 545–46; *New York Herald,* Feb. 26, 1848.

7. *Literary World,* II (Oct. 2, 1847), 197; *Southern Quarterly Review,* XXII (Oct. 1852), 285; *Littell's Living Age,* X (Aug. 15, 1846), 338.

8. Justin H. Smith, "Great Britain and Our War of 1846–1848," *Massachusetts Historical Society Proceedings,* XLVII (June 1914), 451–62; Wilbur Devereux Jones, *The American Problem in British Diplomacy, 1841–1861* (Athens, Ga., 1974), 60–61; M. A. DeWolfe Howe, *The Life and Letters of George Bancroft* (2 vols., New York, 1908), II, 5, 17.

9. Smith, "Great Britain and Our War of 1846–1848," *Mass. Hist. Soc. Proc.,* XLVII, 455–56; William H. Mullins, "The British Press and the Mexican

War: Justin Smith Revised," *New Mexico Historical Review,* LII (July 1977), 212–20; *Fraser's Magazine,* XXXVII (Jan. 1848), 122; *Littell's Living Age,* XIII (April 10, 1847), 94.

10. *Eclectic Magazine,* IX (Sept. 1846), 57; *Littell's Living Age,* XIV (July 3, 1847), 39–43; *Anglo-American,* IX (July 10, 1847), 280.

11. *Literary World,* IX (July 12, 1851), 27; Archibald Alison, *History of Europe from the Commencement of the French Revolution . . . to the Restoration of the Bourbons* (7th ed., 20 vols., Edinburgh and London, 1848), XIX, 39–40; *Democratic Review,* XXIII (Sept. 1848), 227–28; *American Review,* I (April 1845), 341.

12. George Frederick Ruxton, *Adventures in Mexico and the Rocky Mountains* (New York, 1848), 304–6, 115–16; [Ruxton,] "Sketches of the Mexican War, II: The Battle of Buena Vista," *Fraser's Magazine,* XXXVIII (July 1848), 102; *Literary World,* III (Feb. 19, 1848), 42; H. Judge Moore, *Scott's Campaign in Mexico* (Charleston, 1849), 39, 43.

13. *Literary World,* I (June 19, 1847), 466–67; Walt Whitman, *The Gathering of the Forces* (eds. Cleveland Rodgers and John Black, 2 vols., New York, 1920), I, 46–47, 32–33.

14. D. W. Mitchell, *Ten Years in the United States: Being an Englishman's Views of Men and Things in the North and South* (London, 1862), 53–54; *Fraser's Magazine,* XXXVIII (Oct. 1848), 434.

15. Richardson, comp., *Messages and Papers of the Presidents,* IV, 587–88, 631–32.

16. [Hunt's] *Merchants' Magazine,* XVIII (April 1848), 463; Nathan Covington Brooks, *A Complete History of the Mexican War* (Philadelphia, 1849), 539; William Seaton Henry, *Campaign Sketches of the War with Mexico* (New York, 1847), 116.

17. *New York Tribune,* Feb. 11, 1848; Martin Farquhar Tupper, *Tupper's Complete Poetical Works* (Boston, 1850), 324; Edwin DeLeon, *The Position and Duties of "Young America." An Address Delivered Before the Two Literary Societies of the South Carolina College, December, 1845* (Columbia, S. C., 1845), 25; James Fenimore Cooper, "Introduction," *The Spy: A Tale of the Neutral Ground* (New York, 1848), vii–viii.

18. *Columbian Magazine,* IX (May 1848), 218–19; *American Quarterly Register,* I (Sept. 1848), 319; *Bankers' Magazine,* II (Feb. 1848), 461.

19. *New York Herald,* August 19, 1848; *Virginia Historical Register,* II (Jan. 1849), 41–44; [Hunt's] *Merchants' Magazine,* XX (Jan. 1849), 61; *Democratic Review,* XXIV (Jan. 1849), 3, 5.

20. Richard S. Fisher, *The Book of the World* (2 vols., New York, 1850), I, 328; *Methodist Quarterly Review,* XXX (Oct. 1848), 535; Richardson, comp., *Messages and Papers of the Presidents,* IV, 629.

21. *American Review,* IX (April 1849), 334; *Southern Quarterly Review,* XXIII (Jan. 1853), 52.

Index

Aaron, Daniel, 194, 195
Abert, James W. (regular officer), 158
Abolitionists: opposition to Mexican
War, 214–18, 275–76
Acoma, 158
Adams, John, 108
Adams, John Quincy, 108, 215
Alabama, volunteers, 78
Alamán, Lúcas (Mexican historian),
246, 247, 301
Albany Arsenal, 14
Alison, Sir Archibald (British
historian), 74, 307, 308
Alleghanians (singing group), 12, 236
Allen, James Smith, 177
American Art Union, 225, 229
American Bible Society, 149
American Ethnological Society, 159,
284
American Peace Society: opposition to
Mexican War, 270–74, 276
American Revolution: Mexican War
compared with, 57–62
Anglo-Saxon press, see Press
Anton Lizardo, 53, 91
Arista, Mariano (Mexican general), 8,
116, 166
Arkansas, volunteers: atrocity, 37; Bu-
ena Vista, 37, 97; captured by Mexi-
cans, 64–65. See also Pike, Albert;
Yell, Archibald
Armstrong, Arthur (writer), 188
Army, Mexico: characterized, 21–25
Army, United States: mobilization, 10–
15; discipline, 33–39; food, 88–89;

disease, 89–90; as travelers, 152–70,
173, 204; as pioneers, 170–71, 173;
casualties, 325
Army, United States: regulars, 34–35,
39–44
Army, United States: volunteers, 10–
11, 24–43, 63–67, 97, 141–43, 148–
52. See also state names
Art: nationalistic purpose, 222. See also
Mexican War: art
Ashburton, Alexander Baring, Lord,
306
Ashe, Sheppard M. (poet), 207–8
Associated Press, 19
Audubon, John James, 162
Austen, Jane, 194
Averill, Charles (writer), 188
Aztecs, 155–57, 158–59, 166, 179–83

Badajoz (Peninsular War), 308
Bailey, Gamaliel (abolitionist), 276,
293, 299
Baillie, James S. (lithographer), 125
Ballentine, George (regular soldier), 100
Baltimore, volunteers, 53. See also Wat-
son, William H.
Bancroft, George (historian), 56, 58,
242, 243, 248, 306
Banvard, John (panorama artist), 221
Barbour, Philip N. (regular officer), 85
Barnard, Daniel D. (Whig writer), 277,
295
Barnum, Phineas T., 106
Barry, Thomas (playwright), 220

353

Hill, Daniel Harvey (regular officer), 35, 84, 161, 168
History: meaning, 55, 241–44; romanticism, 69–70; military, 74, 249; and Mexican War, 241, 244–69
Hitchcock, Ethan Allen (regular officer), 250, 278
Hitchcock, Wiley, 231, 237
Hoffman, Charles Fenno (poet), 60, 213–14, 215
Holmes, George Frederick (writer), 176
Holyoke, Edward (artist), 229
Hosmer, William H. C. (poet), 211, 212
Houghton, Walter E., 108
Houston, Sam, 124
Huamantla, 36, 136
Hughes, John T. (volunteer), 51, 55, 153
Huizinga, Johan, 68
Humboldt, Alexander von, 147, 156, 304
Hunt, Edward (professor), 40
Hunt, Freeman (editor), 77, 112, 263, 300, 309
Huntington, F. D. (writer), 200

Illinois, volunteers, 37, 64, 88; enlistment, 11, 63; character, 28–29; Buena Vista, 97. *See also,* Hardin, John J.; Kunze, Alexander
Indiana, volunteers, 27, 40, 56, 84, 86, 89; Huamantla, 36; on Rio Grande, 43, 64, 79, 87, 90; Buena Vista, 65, 85, 92, 95, 97. *See also* Bowles, William A.; Lane, Henry S.; Lane, Joseph; Scribner, Benjamin Franklin
Ingersoll, Charles Jared (Congressman, writer), 56
Ingraham, Joseph Holt (writer), 182, 188
Isabella II, Queen (Spain): monarchy in Mexico, 303–4
Isherwood (scenery designer), 221
Iturbide, 62
Ixtaccihuatl, Mt., 184

Jackson, Andrew, 56, 108, 282
Jalapa, 19, 33, 46, 166, 193
James, G. P. R. (British writer), 70, 71, 83, 324
Jay, William (peace advocate), 271–72, 273

Jefferson, Joseph (actor), 173
Jefferson, Thomas, 108
Jenkins, John Stillwell (historian), 263, 264–65
Jerrold, Douglas (British editor), 308
Jesup, Thomas S. (Quartermaster General), 15
Johnson, Gerald, 111
Johnson, Reverdy, 124
Johnston, Joseph E. (regular officer), 101
Jomini, Henri de (French military strategist), 75, 250
Jones, Justin (Harry Hazel; writer and publisher), 187–88
Jones, William Alfred (literary critic), 195
Jones Publishing Office, 187, 189
Jordan, H. C., Mrs. (actress), 220–21
Judson, Edward Zane Carroll (Ned Buntline; writer), 188–90
Judson, Emily Chubbuck (Fanny Forrester; writer), 281–82

Kammen, Michael, 57, 58
Kearny, Stephen Watts (Brigadier General), 87, 157, 158, 170, 202
Kendall, George Wilkins (war correspondent), 17, 18, 23, 228–29, 239, 258
Kentucky, volunteers: state pride, 64; captured, 64–65; sickness, 90; Buena Vista, 97. *See also,* Clay, Henry, Jr.; McKee, William R.
King, Charles (editor), 248
King, Thomas Starr (clergyman), 48, 49
Kinglake, A. W. (British traveler), 145, 147
Kingsbury, Charles (regular officer), 92
Kirkland, Caroline (editor, writer), 132, 177, 225
Kotzwara, Franz (composer), 233
Kunze, Alexander (volunteer), 28–29

Lamartine, Alphonse de (French writer), 175
Lane, Henry S. (volunteer), 90
Lane, Joseph (volunteer), 36, 65, 89, 95, 123
Lanman, Charles (writer, artist), 46, 47, 222

La Vega, Romulo Díaz de (Mexican
general), 127, 128, 129, 234, 237
Leatherstocking, 111, 115, 133, 136
Lee, Arthur T. (army poet), 210
Leman, Walter M. (playwright), 219
Lemon, William J. (composer), 234
Leutze, Emmanuel (artist), 229
Lever, Charles (British writer), 89, 149
Lewis, Sarah Anna (poet), 128
Lincoln, Abraham, 16, 108, 125, 281,
282
Lincoln, George (regular officer), 73,
97, 130, 131
Lippard, George (writer), 60–61, 72,
196, 198–200
Literature: Mexican War, 175, 186–
202; Spanish Conquest, 179–83;
Southwest, 183–85
Lithography, Mexican War, 225–26,
228–29
Livermore, Abiel Abbot (clergyman,
peace advocate), 271, 272–73
Lobos, Island of, 78, 91, 212, 228
Longfellow, Henry Wadsworth, 14,
103, 150, 182
Lossing, Benson J. (writer), 58, 223
Louis Philippe, King (France), 302;
monarchy in Mexico, 303–4
Louisiana, volunteers, 17, 29, 50
Lovell, John E. (writer), 46
Lover, Samuel (songwriter), 239
Lowell, James Russell (poet), 215,
217–18
Luff, Lorry (writer), 188
Lumsden, Francis A. (war correspon-
dent), 17

M'Carty, William (compiler of songs),
237–38
McClellan, George B. (regular officer),
41, 42
McClung, Alexander (volunteer), 130
McConnel, John Ludlum (writer), 194
McCulloch, Ben (Texas Ranger), 134
McDermott, John Francis, 221
McKee, William R. (volunteer), 97, 130
McSherry, Richard (army surgeon), 85
Mackay, Alexander (British traveler),
175
Madison, Dolley, 4
Madison, James, 15
Magoon, E. L. (clergyman), 162–63
Major, Henry B. (lithographer), 226,
228

Mansfield, Edward Deering (historian),
43, 263–64, 265
Marcy, William L. (Secretary of War),
10, 36, 119
Marryat, Frederick (British writer),
185, 187
Marsh, George Perkins (writer), 47, 49,
290
Marshall, John, 27, 60
Marshall, W. (actor), 220
Maryland, volunteers, 79, 87
Massachusetts, volunteers, 29, 59, 62,
64, 92. *See also* Cushing, Caleb
Matamoros, 22, 51; occupation, 8, 34–
35, 54, 115, 172; false report of
bombardment, 11, 126; in drama,
11, 126, 221; Anglo-Saxon press, 19;
sermon at, 49–50; Fourth of July,
59; description, 79, 87, 165–66
Mathews, Cornelius (writer, editor), 87
Matteson, Tompkins H. (artist), 126,
224–25
Maturin, Charles Robert (British
writer), 182
Maturin, Edward (writer), 182
May, Charles A. (regular officer), 4,
75; Resaca de la Palma, 127–28,
129, 131; art, 128, 226; music, 128,
233, 234, 237; poetry, 211; drama,
219
Mayer, Brantz (historian), 212; Mexican army, 23; republicanism, 25; description of Mexico, 146, 148, 150;
history of the war, 263, 267–69;
Mexican republicanism, 268–69, 295
Meade, George G. (regular officer), 35
Meek, Alexander Beaufort (writer),
142, 239
Melville, Herman, 10, 147, 196
Mexican War: art, 125–26, 128, 222–
30; drama, 11, 126, 132, 135–36,
219–22; history, 241–69; literature,
175, 186–202; music, 12, 118, 125,
128, 230–40, 237–38; news gathering, 16–20; opposition to, 214–18,
270–79; poetry, 125, 127, 128, 136,
138, 206–18; republicanism, 279–
301
Mexico: towns and cities, 79, 87, 164–
67, 172–73; food, 89, 168–69;
people, 164–72; Church, 167–68,
266–67, 268, 295–96; republicanism, 168, 293–301; women, 169–70;
in American literature, 179–83;
privateers, 202; influence on Ameri-